LANGUAGE,
METAPHYSICS,
AND DEATH

LANGUAGE, METAPHYSICS, AND DEATH

Edited by
JOHN DONNELLY

New York
FORDHAM UNIVERSITY PRESS
1978

CONTENTS

EDITOR'S PREFACE

DESPITE EPICURUS' ADMONITION in his *Letter to Menoeceus* that we "become accustomed to the belief that death is nothing to us," most of us rightly disregard his sophistry and even a few of us, in his words, "crave for immortality." We are often at one with Plato who reminds us in the *Phaedo* that true philosophers are always occupied in the practice of dying. Construed as a descriptive statement about the philosophical life, the Platonic view is no doubt false, yet interpreted as a regulative prescription it would appear profoundly insightful.

However, there has been surprisingly little public philosophical preoccupation with death until very recently. Only a decade ago, Robert Olson in his article "Death" in *The Encyclopedia of Philosophy* (II 307) could write (rather accurately) that "we are likely to discover more about the topic [of death] in the writings of men of letters than in those of technical philosophers." Yet in coming to terms with the reality of death, philosophers are coming to grips also with the meaning of life. Spinoza's dark saying in the *Ethics* seems on the mark: "A free man thinks of nothing less than of death, and his wisdom is not a meditation upon death but upon life" (Prop. LXVII).

This collection of essays attempts to analyze certain basic issues inherent in a philosophy of death. The themes dealt with are fundamental to a philosophical analysis of thanatology, involving as they do the meaning of death, the nature of the soul, and the prospects for immortality.

Introduction

JOHN DONNELLY
University of San Diego

> The syllogism he had learnt from Kiesewetter's logic: "Caius is a man, men are mortal, therefore Caius is mortal," had always seemed to him correct as applied to Caius, but certainly not as applied to himself. That Caius—man in the abstract—was mortal, was perfectly correct, but he was not Caius, not an abstract man, but a creature quite, quite separate from all others.[1]

THE FIRST EIGHT ESSAYS of *Language, Metaphysics, and Death* focus on the meaning of death. It is often pointed out by philosophers that persons are contingent entities who are generable and corruptible. Roderick Chisholm, however, in his essay "Coming Into Being and Passing Away: Can the Metaphysician Help?" suggests that such an Aristotelian description of the person is not to be properly interpreted in purely physiological terms. For example, if by "corruptible" we mean "capable of passing away" or "able to cease to be," then to say that a person is *corruptible* is not the same as saying that his body is corruptible.

> It is logically possible that, when the person's body dies, then the person does *not* cease to be. And it is also *logically* possible that the person ceases to be *before* his body dies.[2]

For Chisholm, persons are what the medievals termed *entia per se*, real entities and not convenient logical constructions, so that their coming into being and passing away is not a case of simple alteration as gradualistic theories would have it. A consequence of Chisholm's metaphysical investigation is that we cannot know just when it is that a person came into being or when it is that a person passes away, with the result that the various proposed biological theories of death are inadequate.

> When my body dies, then it is altered in a certain way. And if it happens to be the case that I then cease to be, as it well may be, then my ceasing to be is *not* just the fact that my body has been altered in a certain way. And when I came into being, this may well have been at the time of a certain alteration of the fetus, or of a certain alteration of matter that was going to become a part of the fetus. But whatever alteration that may have been, that alteration was not the same event as my coming into being.

Chisholm is maintaining, then, that a *person's* coming into being and passing away is not a gradual process, *although* a person's entrance into and exit from the class of *human beings* may involve such a gradual process.

It has been pointed out by many linguistic philosophers that we have no awareness of death in any specifically metaphysical way, where death is viewed as the complete cessation of experience, with the result that death as a phenomenal state apparently characterizes absolutely nothing. Does it then make sense to talk of death? James Van Evra in "On Death as a Limit" suggests an *affirmative* answer to such a question, inasmuch as the concept of death serves as a limit which acts as an ordering function to guide our conceptual inquiries.

Utilizing a number of scientific analogues, Van Evra tries to show how death-talk (assuming the truth of scientific materialism) is meaningful. For instance, we know from the third law of thermodynamics that no body can have a temperature of absolute zero, *yet* the concept of such a temperature is employable even though there are no bodies existing at such a temperature. Likewise, Van Evra suggests, it is permissible to use the concept of death while maintaining that there are no experienceless selves (i.e., just as we can speak of the limit of the visual field as unseeable, so too we can speak of death as unexperienceable). "The significance of the limit is not as something independently real, but as an operational device."

Of course, even to raise a question about the linguistic appropriateness of death-talk would strike an existentialist as but another example of linguistic philosophy's naïveté. Needless to say, the literature of existentialism is permeated with philosophical discussions of death.

However, Paul Edwards in "Existentialism and Death: A Survey of Some Confusions and Absurdities" suggests that there are a considerable number of muddles in existentialist writings on death. For example, death is often compared with deep sleep, an identification Edwards finds as ludicrous as the suggestion that an empty soda bottle is saturated with ethereal liquid. Existentialists, in response, claim that they are approaching the study of death on an ontological level. That is, they are asking: What is death like to the dead? Accordingly, Edwards turns to a conceptual analysis of some ontological accounts of death, specifically those of Paul Tillich, José Ferrater Mora, and John Macquarrie.

The ontological view of death regards death as a state which is either unknowable (Tillich) or partially knowable (Mora and Macquarrie). But such a quest for a phenomenological insight into death is absurd, Edwards believes, for these existentialists are really asking "what kind of experiences does a person have who no longer has any experiences?"! We might here note that ontological, thanatological inquiries are distinct from the more metaphysical questions "Is there life after death?" or "Why does death occur?" Edwards writes:

> . . . while feeling the coolness of the night, reaching the last stop of a journey, arriving in a strange country from which one will never return, sleep, and rest, sustaining losses . . . undergoing pain and torture, feeling isolated and all alone and even finding oneself surrounded by impenetrable darkness are states or experiences of living human beings, death is not a state.

Edwards contends that it is philosophically worthwhile to raise various *psychological* questions about death (e.g., "How should I prepare myself for death?" or "How can I relieve my suffering over my wife's demise?"), but not worthwhile (and indeed nonsensical) to continue to seek some phenomenological insight as to what death is like from the inside.[3] Edwards proceeds to point out other alleged muddles in existentialist writings on thanatology, such as the facile equation of death with dying, and constructively points out how many existential claims interpreted as statements properly about dying *and not death* are meaningful and possibly true (e.g., a person could find himself in dying but not in death). Edwards also suggests that the doctrine of the privacy of death (that no one can understand any other person's death or dying but his own) is either trivial or, if significant, false.[4]

Thomas Nagel in "Death" raises the question as to why death is regarded as an evil. His point seems to be that death is so regarded because it involves the loss of life, the deprivation of all human possibilities (the reader might here note that Van Evra, Edwards, and Nagel all beileve that death marks the irreversible end of life, so that there is no form of post-mortem survival), so that no matter how inevitable death is, it remains the grand evil for it removes all possibilities of continued life.

But there are several philosophical objections to the view that death is an evil. First of all, are there any evils such as death which solely consist in the selfless unexperienced deprivation of good? Secondly, there seems to be a difficulty attached to picking out a subject of misfortune, for if S exists, S has not yet died, and if S has died, S no longer exists, so how is death qua the grand misfortune ascribed to S? Finally, there is an apparent asymmetry between our attitudes to posthumous nonexistence which is characteristically negative, and our attitude to prenatal nonexistence which is value neutral.

Nagel attempts to answer the above objections and to show that death remains rightly classified as an evil. However, he does confess to some hesitation with regard to his counter of the last objection (see his discussion of Nozick's spore-case). The reason why he feels that the first two objections are misplaced is primarily based on Nagel's belief that it is arbitrary to restrict goods and evils to non-relational properties ascribable to persons at various times. Instead, Nagel argues, a person's history and possibilities count more than a person's momentary categorical state.

> There are goods and evils which are irreducibly relational; they are features of the relations between a person, with spatial and temporal boundaries of the usual sort, and circumstances which may not coincide with him either in space or in time. . . . If death is an evil it must be accounted for in these terms, and the impossibility of locating it within life should not trouble us.

However, Nagel is not entirely satisfied with his dismissal of the various objections. For one, he realizes that "we still have to set some limits on how possible a possibility must be for its nonrealization to be a misfortune." Also, one might ask, can death be an evil if it is inevitable, that is, normal to the species?

Michael Slote in "Existentialism and the Fear of Dying" criticizes various strategies which seek to prevent a person from authentically contemplating his impending mortality. For instance, some philosophers stoically claim no fear of death, because living world historically they expect to overcome death by attaining immortality through their works. Slote sees this stoic dodge as a paradigm of self-deception, for such philosophers reveal "an unconscious defense mechanism of the ego that protects [them] from conscious fear about death by repressing that fear and counter-balancing it in such a way that it for the most part remains unconscious." Slote also finds the view self-defeating inasmuch as it somewhat inconsistently posits the person as both living and not-living.

Slote is herein doing existential psychoanalysis. He wishes to take seriously the existentialist's claim that the quality of a human's life is intimately associated with his attitudes on his own impending mortality. To be sure, by getting involved in what Kierkegaard calls "busyness," or getting absorbed in what Heidegger terms the "they," or even a Sartrean form of "bad faith," we may allay somewhat our own fear of dying. But such dodges only serve to mask our real anxiety and add confirmatory weight to the view that anxiety concerning death is a fundamental characteristic of the human condition. Indeed such self-trickery, assuming that it is true that the quality of a person's life is causally connected with his attitudes on his own death, might well explain the psychic ills of our or any age.

In my paper "Suicide and Rationality" I consider the problem Camus has labeled the "one truly serious philosophical problem." Despite a rather prevalent philosophical sentiment which regards suicide as a legitimate philosophical and thereby presumably rational option (e.g., Hume, Nietzsche, Holland, Williams, Brandt), I attempt to argue that suicide is not rational on an epistemological level, and, as a possible consequence, non-moral on an ethical level. In the language of epistemic logic, my thesis is that the claim "Suicide is not philosophically justified" is at worst *presumable* and at best *evident*, but in any case its negation is *unreasonable*.

Of course, if by "suicide" we meant simply "self-annihilation," the deliberate taking of one's own life, then I would agree that suicide in at least some cases is rational (e.g., cases of euthanasia, heroic self-sacrifice). It is the task of philosophy to analyze basic concepts of fundamental importance to human experience, however, and such a definition of suicide as self-annihilation is far too nebulous and open-textured.

Instead, I propose that we refer to a specific action as suicide whenever the following conditions are satisfied: S performs an act of suicide X provided S directly and deliberately wills, either through his own causal efficacy or that of others, that his life be totally or partially preternaturally extinguished for reasons of an egoistic and/or altruistic sort *except* in cases where: (1) S can preserve his life only by performing a morally dishonorable act where such an act is adjudged dishonorable by anyone who is willing to take the moral point of view, and/or cases in which (2) S is in a state of terminal illness such that without extraordinary (artificial) medical apparatus S would die in a rather brief period of time.

I attempt to clarify the equivocation surrounding the terms "death" and "suicide" and consider four possible types of cases involving attempted justifications of suicide and argue that none of them succeeds, despite a person's particular conceptual framework (i.e., dualistic interactionism or scientific materialism).

For many philosophers, the brute fact of death seems to cast considerable doubt on the meaningfulness of life. Thomas Nagel in "The Absurd" attempts to analyze the meaning of absurdity. Absurdity results from a clash between pretension and reality. We take our lives very seriously and yet reflecting on our contingency it is possible to regard it all as arbitrary, since we are all eventually going to die. Human beings have the capacity for self-transcendence, however, and this poses our basic human problem. Nagel suggests that we face this existential crisis, not with scorn or romantic self-pity, but rather with irony.

> If *sub specie aeternitatis* there is no reason to believe that anything matters, then that does not matter either, and we can approach our absurd lives with irony instead of heroism or despair.

In "Death and Ivan Ilych," I consider the philosophical implications of Leo Tolstoy's novel *The Death of Ivan Ilych*. Ilych, as Tolstoy narrates the story, supposedly found his authentic self in dying, and consequently had dominion over death.

Tolstoy seems to be suggesting not just that a man is dead when he suffers irreversible loss of cerebral activity, but, most importantly, that a person is dead when stripped of his autonomy. Tolstoy emphasizes the point that questions about whether a man has a soul or not, or whether a man is dead or not, are not simply empirical in scope, but rather questions about the kind of life a man is living. Through the moral reappraisal of his life and despite the imminence of biological death, Ilych could still say: " 'Where is it? What death?' There was no fear because there was no death. In place of death there was light."[5]

Death then is viewed as alienation from virtue. A man is dead for Tolstoy, given such a normative definition of death, either when he chooses to renounce his integrity and the complex set of moral practices and beliefs associated with and constitutive of that integrity, or when he has his integrity violated against his wishes.

I contend that a careful analysis of the deontic maxim that "ought implies can," and the discovery of what I term the "can of expectability," will dissipate somewhat this Tolstoyan optimism such that it would be unrealistic for most persons (except the fated, famous, and/or fortunate) to expect to attain or regain moral integrity and consequently have dominion over death, as Ivan Ilych did.

I also explore the logic of violence as violation of personal autonomy which has the effect of making our present violent age at best a period of lethargic amorality. Given such a moral climate, the conduct required by morality, for most people, becomes a matter of supererogation.

The next three essays of *Language, Metaphysics, and Death* deal with the nature of the soul and the soul's relation to death. Richard Taylor in a delightfully sardonic essay "De Anima" relates the fable of Walter's Amoebiary, wherein is described the various futile attempts of Walter the keeper of the amoebiary to determine the lineage of his amoebae so that he might more effectively influence the breeding of future amoebae.

As is well known, amoebae reproduce by splitting into two. Naturally, the inevitable metaphysical question arises, who is the parent and who the offspring? Attempts to formulate an answer to this query by various criteria of markings, size, behavioral traits, etc., all seem to fail.

The result is that Walter soon realizes that his problem was a pseudo-problem, for he had overlooked the essential metaphysical aspects of the problem. What Walter had failed to realize and now does realize is that amoebae lacked souls and souls are what uniquely characterize entities as distinct individuals. Of course, Taylor is here being facetious, his point being that it is an erroneous metaphysical supposition to think that (by analogy) souls uniquely characterize us as separate and distinct human beings.

In contrast to Taylor's negative views on the existence of souls (minds, transcendental selves), Roderick Chisholm in "On the Observability of the Self" tries to show how philosophers have been mistaken in reaching such negative views vis-à-vis the apprehension of the self (or soul).

Hume's classic bundle-theory, of course, claimed that the self is not observable, and that there is no such mental substance as a soul or self. Chisholm points out that Hume's view is inconsistent with his stated findings, namely, "I never can catch *myself* at any time without a perception, and never can observe anything but the perception." Moreover, to restate the theory to avoid the self-defeating findings of Hume to read "Nothing but perceptions are found" (by whom?) is too rash empirically. Chisholm writes:

> The fact that a man finds a certain proposition p to be true does warrant a subjectless report to the effect that p is true. . . . But the fact that he fails to find a certain proposition q to be true does not similarly warrant any subjectless report about q. For one's failure to find that q is true entails nothing about the truth of q. The fact that a man fails to find that q is true entitles him to say only that *he*, at least, does not find that q is true. And this would not be a subjectless report.

Chisholm goes on to suggest that the self or soul is transparent. To know that I perceive myself to be thinking is not necessarily to realize that I perceive a proper part of myself. For instance, in the locution "I feel depressed" (and *not* "I have a depressed feeling"), "being depressed" is not a predicate of the feeling but rather "feeling depressed" is a predicate of the man. In short, Chisholm argues that in being aware of ourselves as experiencing, we are *ipso facto* aware of the self or person as being affected in a certain way: ". . . the items within the bundle are nothing but states of the person. . . . what ties these items together is the fact that that same self or person apprehends them all."

John Hick in "Biology and the Soul" takes up the religious (more specifically Christian) view of man which holds that God creates an individual soul for each person either at birth or at conception. Such a view suggests that there are certain characteristics of the soul which are not inherited or explained solely in terms of various biological factors.

What qualities does the soul possess? Is the soul merely an unknown metaphysical substratum? What does it mean to speak of the soul as the animating principle of the body? If (as Taylor seems to suggest) the body can be construed as the principle of individuation, what need have we for the soul? In short, Hick asks, is there a content and function for the soul? Are there any innate personal characteristics of the soul not traceable to heredity or environment but only to divine infusion?

To claim that there is a content and function for the soul as traditional conceptions allow, Hick claims, is to speak of the soul as a cluster of psychic factors, the repository of all basic dispositional characteristics of a moral and spiritual sort. Hick rejects such a metaphysical view, arguing that the soul cannot be literally viewed as a metaphysical entity, divinely infused by God. Rather, Hick claims, soul-talk is basically metaphorical. We speak of "saving our souls" or "selling our souls," but here "soul" serves as an indicator of value. Hence, soul-talk is evaluative, not descriptive!

> To speak of man as a soul is, then, to speak mythologically, but in a way which is bound up with important practical attitudes and practices. The myth of the soul expresses a faith in the intrinsic value of the human individual as an end in himself.

The final six essays of *Language, Metaphysics, and Death* deal with the topic of immortality. Is death merely an event in life so that there is some form of post-mortem experience, or is death the end of life? Roland Puccetti in "The Conquest of Death" answers that death is the end of life, yet that man is mortal strikes Puccetti as but a well-founded empirical generalization. Puccetti also takes issue with recent arguments such as that of Bernard Williams to the effect that natural death is a welcomed friend. Opting for a definition of a person's death as the irreversible cessation of neocortical activity, Puccetti writes: "if someone suggested to me that my body might survive death of the neocortex for several months or years, provided it were fed and cleaned properly, etc., that would have no greater appeal to me than preservation of my appendix in a bottle of formaldehyde."

One innovative technological means to conquer death is the so-called "Freeze Dead" school of thought. For a large sum of money, one can have his corpse cryogenically interred in a liquid-nitrogen environment to await the neurosurgeons of the future who will reconstruct the damaged brain. Puccetti is not sanguine about the prospects of this procedure, however, given the need to restore thousands of millions of destroyed and lost neurons. A second theory —the so-called "Freeze Alive" school—posits genetic engineering's advancing to a point where suspended animation may be attained without attendant biological risk. Here also Puccetti remains the pessimist, inasmuch as genetic engineering is not likely to change the genotype itself.

Instead Puccetti favors the technological creation of cyborg man. If distinctly human life is rooted in neocortical activity, it would seem that such a technological discovery would allow for the indefinite prolongation of life and at least the temporary conquest of death. Puccetti suggests that

. . . we could someday build prosthetic bodies housing portable, miniaturised heart-and-lung machines that keep the brain—comfortably installed in the head cavity—well-nourished with blood and glucose, etc. Descending neural pathways from the brain would end at, say, the medulla oblongata, where the electrical charges they emit could activate a miniaturised digital computer to perform limb-movements. Conversely, receptors in the prosthetic body would send messages up to the computer, which could in turn fire the proper sequence of ascending nerve fibres that transform these into proprioceptive, kinesthetic, somesthetic, and tactile sensations in the brain. . . . Even vision and hearing could be achieved . . . by having mechanical sensors fire the appropriate neurons in the visual and auditory cortices directly. . . .

But what if, *pace* Puccetti, a person is not identical to his brain, and death is not the end of life but rather an event in life? Could one clarify or outline the contents of such a post-mortem mode of existence? H. H. Price in "Survival and the Idea of 'Another World' " is concerned with just these questions, that is, with the issue of the *meaningfulness* of the survival hypothesis rather than the factual support for such a theory.

Given his Cartesian sympathies, Price views the next world as a world of desire (cf. the Hindu notion of Kama Loka), that is, a world of mental images which are *imagy* and not imaginary. Price views the next world as one in which *imaging* replaces sense-perception, and he posits the epistemic possibility that memories, desires, images, etc. could exist upon the dissolution of our bodily parts: ". . . the 'stuff' or 'material' of such a world would come in the end from one's memories, and the 'form' of it from one's desires. To use another analogy, memory would provide the pigments, and desire would paint the picture." Such a next world, Price contends, need not prove a solipsistic nightmare for an individual discarnate personality, because the next world would presumably have causal laws of a psychological sort (probably Freudian), and could be spoken of as spatial and public, via telepathic apparitions.

With regard to the location-difficulty, Price claims that the next world could provide its own *where*. That is, mental images are in a space of their own, having spatial relations to each other, but not to our own physical space. Hence, passage to the next world is not a movement in space so much as a change of consciousness for a discarnate personality, which unlike the relation of waking consciousness to dreaming is irreversible. Price also believes that there could be many next worlds, each consisting of like-minded personalities. Indeed, as (a) wish fulfillment world(s), it seems fair to think that our ante-mortem repressed desires would come to fruition so that we could have the philosophical correlates of hell, heaven, and purgatory.

The reader may be impressed with the creative and vivid depiction of Price's outline of a next world, but doubtless still be left wondering how sensation talk can be ontologically rooted to that which has no physical counterpart. How, for instance, can there be sight without an optic nerve? How can there be rational capabilities without an occipital cortex? Is not spatio-temporal bodily continuity a necessary condition of personal identity? If a person is an indissoluble psycho-physical unity, then how can I be identical to Price's discarnate personality?

Stewart Sutherland in "Immortality and Resurrection" raises these and other interesting questions concerning various proposed survival hypotheses. In addition, Sutherland questions the alleged religious value of such accounts of survival. Recall the words of the Psalmist: "I am poured out like water, and all my bones are out of joint; my heart is like wax, it is melted within my breast . . . and my tongue cleaves to my jaws; thou dost lay me in the dust of death." Irish wakes and the euphemisms of the funeral business notwithstanding, the Judaeo-Christian view of death is insistent that death is terrible and terrifying. Is it then not religiously unorthodox to entertain such Pricean projects and in so doing treat death as somehow less than death? Also, is the post-mortem realm, if conceivable as Price suggests, to be equated with endless duration or eternal life? How do accounts of bodily resurrection (cf. Geach) avoid the criticism of offering only reduplication and exact similarity but not strict (numerical) identity?

In short, are accounts of either disembodied survival or resurrected bodies adequate to the Judaeo-Christian conception of life after death? Sutherland writes:

> Much is communicated which is not stated, and I think here of the novel and play rather than the nod and wink. Perhaps the denial that death is irreversible annihilation must be communicated otherwise than by unequivocal statement.

Peter Geach (somewhat disregarding Sutherland's counsel) in "Immortality" offers a contemporary restatement of the traditional Thomistic view of interactionism and its ramifications for a thesis of immortality. Geach dismisses extreme dualistic-talk of ethereal bodies, as contemporary scientific canons give us no account of their mysterious causal relations. Like Wittgenstein, Geach disavows the privacy theory of meaning (found in Price's theory), and quotes Wittgenstein to the effect that we do not get the concept of pain by having a pain any more than we get the concept of a minus quantity by running up an overdraft.

Geach is careful to insist that he is not a behaviorist. "But it is not a question of whether seeing is (sometimes) a private experience, but whether one can attach meaning to the verb 'to see' by a private uncheckable performance; and this is what I maintain one cannot do to any word at all." Nonetheless, Geach ultimately seems to sympathize with Aquinas' attribution of thoughts and volitional states to mental remnants, although one cannot ascribe sensations and feeling states to such discarnate personalities. In short, Geach opts for the Thomistic doctrine that "my soul is not I" and the belief in the theistic hypothesis of resurrection without which there can be no immortality of the person. For Geach, unlike Price, assurances of personal immortality rest in theology, not parapsychology.

John Clarke in "Mysticism and the Paradox of Survival" feels that the survival hypothesis offers a promissory note of the soul's transformation to a better mode of existence, but that most accounts of immortality offer only partial or complete continuation of our ante-mortem mode of life. Hence the paradox: either we survive in a resurrection world in embodied form (possibly having astral bodies), but a world that is replete with pre-mortem difficulties; or we survive in disembodied form with the subsequent dissolution of our unified personhood (*anima mea non est ego*).

> In neither case is the problem for which survival has been offered as a solution —the problem of providing a meaningful and happy apotheosis to a supposedly miserable and senseless existence—solved. The first solution merely restates, in a large measure, the problem; the second dissolves, in varying degrees, the being for whom it is supposedly a solution. Is there any *tertium quid*? Can we offer an account of survival which takes care of both prerequisites, which allows for *persons*, not shadows or memories, to survive, and which makes such survival worthwhile?

Clarke outlines mystical schemata to allow for both personal survival and a rational apotheosis. Such a mystical experience involves the removal of a sense of alienation from our environment, the development of a sense of total harmony and tranquillity, loss of multiplicity in space and time, and loss of desires and regrets. The reader might compare the prospects for such a mystical theory of the after-life with Price's Cartesian outline of the same.

Finally, Bernard Williams in "The Makropulos Case: Reflections on the Tedium of Immortality" argues that, *pace* Price and Clarke, the survival hypothesis is *meaningless* in the sense of "without significance": ". . . from facts about human desire and happiness and what a human life is, it follows both that immortality would be, where conceivable at all, intolerable, and that (other things being equal) death is reasonably regarded as an evil."[6] One is here reminded of Achilles' advice to Odysseus that it is better to be a poor laborer on earth than king among the dead. Williams bases his view on a consideration of the (fictitious) case of Elina Makropulos who, having taken an elixir, is now 342, having been 42 for 300 years. Despite the panacea, she finds her endless life a bore (her categorical desires have ceased) and suicide the only tolerable way out. Williams contends that it is not just a contingent fact about a person that his categorical desires are finite in number.

Williams' article would provide an even stronger caveat to the bio-technical use of cryonic storage or the development of Puccetti's cyborg man than the legendary case of Tithonus who according to Greek myth was granted immortality by Aurora, but who soon longed for death, since he was not given eternal youthfulness by Aurora. Williams would warn every youthful neo-Tithonian that boredom may be a greater evil than death, and that one may be *felix opportunitate mortis*.

NOTES

1. Leo Tolstoy, *The Death of Ivan Ilych* (New York: New American Library, 1960), pp. 131–32.

2. Cf. Lawrence C. Becker, "Human Being: The Boundaries of the Concept," *Philosophy and Public Affairs*, 4 (1975), 334–59.

3. Edwards elsewhere writes: "I can start sleeping in a (suitably ventilated) coffin and I can simulate death, but none of this will be a 'preenactment' of death

analogous to the 'reenactment' of past events. If 'existential preenactment of death' is not to be a senseless expression, it can mean no more than realizing that one is going to die and that death is total annihilation and not a low-grade form of consciousness." "Heidegger and Death as 'Possibility'," *Mind*, 84 (1975), 562.

4. In *ibid.*, Edwards draws some important distinctions between the terms "deadness," "the death-moment," "death-producing events," and "dying." *Deadness* involves the total, irreversible annihilation of all life processes (perhaps Heidegger's "measureless impossibility of existence") which takes place at a certain time on a certain date—*the death-moment*. *Death-producing events* are those states of affairs which causally bring about a person's *deadness*, the beginning and end of which is the phase of life called *dying*. Existentialists who speak of death as the "crown and culmination of human life" are, given Edwards' lexicon, not speaking intelligibly if speaking of *deadness* or *the death-moment*, although their claims are intelligible (albeit usually false) if referring to a person's *dying* or *death-producing events*.

5. Tolstoy, *op. cit.*, pp. 155–56.

6. Williams' thesis might be attacked by arguing that he fails to consider adequately the logic of eternity—namely, that eternity can be spoken of only in terms of such categories as transcendence and timelessness. Consequently, whereas categorical desires diminish over time, this may not be so in a timeless eternity.

1

Coming into Being and Passing Away: Can the Metaphysician Help?

RODERICK M. CHISHOLM

Brown University

WHAT WE HAVE A RIGHT TO BELIEVE ABOUT OURSELVES

I ASSUME THAT, in our theoretical thinking, we should be guided by those propositions we presuppose in our ordinary activity. They are propositions we have a right to believe. Or, somewhat more exactly, they are propositions which should be regarded as innocent, epistemically, until there is positive reason for thinking them guilty.

A list of such propositions would be very much like the list of propositions with which G. E. Moore began his celebrated essay, "In Defence of Common Sense."[1] The list I might make for myself may be suggested by the following: "(1) I am now thinking such and such things and have such and such beliefs, feelings, and desires. I now see people, for example, and I do not see any unicorns. And I have thought such and such other things in the past and then had such and such other beliefs, feelings, and desires. (2) I now have a body of such and such a sort and I had a body of such and such a different sort in the past. And (3) I am now acting with the intention of bringing about such and such things—and I could instead have acted with the intention of bringing about such and such other things. In the past I have acted with the intention of bringing about such and such other things, and I could then have acted with the intention of bringing about such and such other things instead."

There is such a list that each of us might make. The items on the list are obvious and, one might think, so trivial as not to be worth mentioning at all. Yet some of those who now say that these things are trivially true may say, at the end, that strictly speaking they are false. But one cannot have it both ways.

A skeptic may ask: "Might it not be that I'm mistaken in suggesting there

Reprinted by permission from *Philosophy and Medicine* Vol. III, edd. H. Tristram Engelhardt, Jr., and Stuart Spicker (Dordrecht: Reidel, 1977).

are these things we know about ourselves? Isn't it possible that I'm deluded about these things?" Of course, it is *possible* that I am deluded about these things. It is *possible* that I will wake up in a few minutes and find myself in a hospital. But from the fact that it is thus theoretically possible that I am deluded it hardly follows that it is now reasonable for me to think that I am in fact deluded. Until you give me some very good positive reason to think the contrary, it is now reasonable for me to assume that I am in a room with other people and not suffering from hallucination or delusion.

These are some obvious truths about myself, then, which it is now reasonable for me to accept. But these truths, if we take them at their face value, imply that I am an *ens per se*, that is to say, they imply that, in the strictest sense of the word "is," there *is* a certain thing which is I.

Now, some philosophers have held that the word "I" is a logical construction, a mere *façon de parler*, like the expressions "—5" and "the average plumber." One can *show* that "—5" and "the average plumber" are logical constructions. For one can take sentences in which these ostensible terms occur ("—5 is 2 less 7" and "the average plumber has 2.6 children") and translate them into other sentences no longer containing terms ostensibly referring to —5 and the average plumber. If I, too, am simply a logical construction, or *façon de parler*, then the various truths on the list that I have made could be reformulated without reference to me. They could be re-expressed in new sentences which contain no terms, such as the word "I," which ostensibly designate me. The new sentences might contain terms designating what I now call my sensations, as Ernst Mach and Bertrand Russell once thought, or they might contain terms designating my body or certain parts of my body, as other philosophers have thought. But these various philosophers do not *know* that the word "I" is thus a logical construction, a mere *façon de parler*. No one can take the sentences I have cited—the truisms about myself—and translate *them* without loss of meaning into sentences referring only to things other than me. If you think that I am mistaken about this, just consider the truth which I can now express by saying, "I do not see any unicorns," and try to put exactly what *that* says in sentences which do not refer to me.

Perhaps you will say on reflection: "Well, I can't do it now, but maybe some day somebody will do it." This would be like the skeptic we just considered. It is possible that you can show I am a mere *façon de parler*. And it is possible that I am now lying in a hospital bed somewhere. But what have these mere possibilities to do with what is going on in fact? They certainly do not mean that I *am* deluded with respect to the truisms that I began. No one has been able to show that these truths can be paraphrased as truths about some entity or entities other than myself. And therefore no one has been able to show that I am not an *ens per se*.

I say, then, that we have a right to assume that persons are *entia per se*, that there *are* persons, in the strict and philosophical sense of the expression "there are." You and I, in short, are real things and the terms which designate us are not linguistic fictions. But if there *are* persons, in the strictest sense of the expression "there are," then persons are such that either (i) they exist forever or (ii) they come into being but will not pass away or (iii) they will pass away but never come into being or (iv) each is such that it came into being and will pass away. I assume that the last of these four possibilities is the one that is most likely. You and I exist now but there was a time before which we did not exist and there will be a time after which we will no longer exist.

We should be clear, at the outset, about one very simple point. The concepts of *coming into being* and *passing away* are not merely physiological concepts. Consider the relation, for example, between the concepts of *passing away* and *dying* and assume (what, of course, is doubtful) that the latter concept is pretty clearly fixed. If by "passing away," we mean, as I do, *ceasing to be*, then if we say that the body dies we cannot say that it passes away—for the body continues to exist but in such a way that it is no longer alive. It may well be that, when the body dies, then the person whose body it is passes away—that the person ceases to be. But the two concepts are different. It is *logically* possible that, when the person's body dies, then the person does *not* cease to be. And it is also *logically* possible that the person ceases to be *before* his body dies. To admit this distinction is not to say that there is any likelihood that these possibilities are actual. The point is only that it is one thing to say that a person's body has died and it is another thing to say that the person has ceased to be, even if in fact the two events coincide.

And, similarly, the concept of *coming into being* is not the same as any physiological concept. Conceivably there is some physiological event which coincides uniformly with the coming into being of a person, but to say that this physiological event occurs is not the same as saying that a person comes into being.

The points I have just made are typically philosophical. I know they will bring forth two quite different reactions. One reaction will be: "But why insist upon what is trivial and obvious?" And the other reaction will be: "What you say is obviously false." As long as there are people who react in the second way, and I know that there are such people, it is worthwhile to insist upon what is obvious, even if it is trivial. For, as Aristotle said, if you *deny* what is trivial, then there is no hope for your investigation.

Of course there may be philosophers or there may be people practicing medicine who do not think there are any persons. And this means, if they are consistent, that they do not believe with respect to themselves that they ever came into being or that they will ever pass away. For people who do really believe that, I have no message—except to urge them to think again.

ALTERATION

One of the ways in which a metaphysician can help a nonmetaphysician is to protect him from bad metaphysics.

People are sometimes led to think that nothing persists through any period of time and hence that all things are constantly ceasing to be and new things are constantly coming into being to replace them. This was the view of Heraclitus who said "You cannot step into the same river twice." (One of Heraclitus' followers, according to Aristotle, held that things are in such constant flux that you cannot even step into the same river once.) If this view is true, then it would be incorrect to say that you and I have existed for any period of time. The things which bore our names at any given moment yesterday have since then ceased to be and you and I are no more the same people as those people of yesterday than we are identical with each other. This view is a disastrous beginning, if our aim is to understand coming into being and passing away.

Why would anyone think that such a thing is true? Respectable philosophers, I regret to say, have accepted this view. When philosophers do not simply pick their theories out of the air, they arrive at them in attempting to deal with philosophical puzzles. The kind of puzzle which has led philosophers to think that everything is in flux, in the sense in question, may be illustrated as follows.

You say to me: "I see you have a new fence in your back yard." I say: "No, it's the same fence I've always had." You say: "But your fence is red; the fence you used to have was white." I say: "No, it's the *same* fence; I painted it, that's all." And you say: "But it *couldn't* be the same fence. If something A is identical with something B, then whatever is true of A is true of B. But if today's fence is identical with yesterday's, how can it be that the old one is red and the other is white?"

Very great philosophers, I am afraid, have tripped up over that one. (Some have been led to conclude, not that everything is in flux, but that things can be identical with each other even though they do not have all their properties in common.) What went wrong in the dialogue we have just imagined?

Consider the sentence: "Today's fence is red and yesterday's fence was white." One trouble with it is that the dates are in the wrong place. For what we know is not merely that there was something which was *yesterday's fence* and which was white. It is rather that there *is* something which is a fence and which was *white yesterday*. And it is not merely that there is a thing which is *today's fence* and is red. It is rather that there is a fence which is *red today*. The fence I have now and the fence I had yesterday have *all* their properties in common. I have had just one fence—one which is red today and which was white yesterday.

If you do not see the error which was involved in using the expressions "today's fence" and "yesterday's fence," perhaps this analogy will help. Consider someone who reasons as follows: "Mr. Jones, the husband, is very meek and submissive. Yet Mr. Jones, the father, is extremely authoritative and overbearing. But one and the same thing can't be meek and submissive and *also* authoritative and overbearing. Therefore there are two Mr. Jones—Mr. Jones, the husband, and Mr. Jones, the father."

Saying what went wrong in this case is like explaining a joke. But perhaps we should risk it. It is not that Mr. Jones the husband has properties that are different from those that Mr. Jones the father has. It is rather that Mr. Jones is such that he is meek and submissive toward his wife and overbearing and authoritative toward his children!

All this is to spell out, once again, what ought to be obvious. But let us keep the moral in mind: The fact that a thing has *altered* in a certain way does not imply that the thing has ceased to be and that some new thing has come into being.

COMING INTO BEING AND PASSING AWAY *Secundum Quid*

We are assuming, then, that persons—you and I—are real things, *entia realia*. And we are also assuming that they come into being and pass away. But this means that the coming into being and the passing away of persons is also the real thing. That is to say, it is not a pseudo kind of coming into being and passing away; it is not that kind of merely apparent coming into being and passing away which some of the scholastics called coming into being and passing away *secundum quid*. Let us consider for a moment this pseudo kind of coming into being and passing away.

In his book *Generation and Corruption*, Aristotle considers a man who had a talent for music and who then lost this talent but continued to exist for some time thereafter. Aristotle described this fact by saying: "The musical man passed away and an unmusical man came to be, but the man persists as identically the same" (I.4.319B). One is inclined to ask: "Why on earth did Aristotle express himself *that* way? After all he was just talking about a certain alteration. Why did he not say that a man *ceased to be musical*, instead of saying that a musical man *ceased to be*?"

It should be noted that we, too, sometimes talk that way. That is to say, we sometimes use such expressions as "coming into being" and "passing away" to describe what is in fact the mere alteration of a persisting subject. Thus you may ask me: "How is our old friend Jones?" And I may reply by saying: "The Jones you knew doesn't exist any more. He's just dull and bitter now." A reporter once wrote, after visiting one of our great comedians in a nursing home in California: "Alas, the great comedian is no more." But the man—the man who had been a comedian—persisted for some time after that.

It was a result of Aristotle's way of talking ("the musical man ceased to be") that medieval philosophers—St. Thomas, for example—came to distinguish between (1) coming into being and passing away *per se* and (2) coming into being and passing away *per accidens* or *secundum quid*.

We have coming into being *per accidens*, or *secundum quid*, when a thing alters in some way or other—when there is something which so changes that it first has a certain property and subsequently has a certain other property instead. This is what happens if a musical man is said to cease to be and an unmusical man to come into being when in fact one and the same man persists through the change.

Let us consider some other examples.

SOME ADDITIONAL EXAMPLES

It is sometimes said that, when one becomes aware of a feeling or of a sensation, then the feeling or sensation is something that comes into being *ex nihilo*. When British and American philosophers, in the first third of the present century, were concerned about the status of what they called appearances or sense-data, they took very seriously the possibility that these are things that come into being, *ex nihilo*, when the appropriate physiological and psychological conditions obtain.[2] But is not the fact of the matter that, when a feeling or sensation is thus said to "come into being," what actually happens is that the person or subject is simply altered in a certain way? In making me feel sad, for example, what you do is, not to cause a feeling of sadness to come into being *ex nihilo*, but to cause me to have a certain property—that of feeling in a certain way. And analogously for making me aware of an "appearance" or "sense-datum." What you do is simply to cause me to sense in a certain way. But if this is true, then the so-called coming into being and passing away of feelings and sensations is simply coming into being and passing away *per accidens* or *secundum quid*—and not coming into being and passing away *per se*.

Let us consider another type of case. One might say: "If I turn the light on over our heads, I will make a *shadow* come into being out of nothing. And if I then turn the light out again, I will cause the shadow to go out of existence—without leaving any traces behind. And so isn't this genuine coming into being and passing away, coming into being and passing away *per se*?"

I think the answer is no. But it is instructive to consider the case somewhat further. What we conveniently describe as a shadow coming into being and passing away can also be described, somewhat less conveniently, as an alteration in what we might call the shadowed object, or the shadowed objects. When I create a shadow on the floor, what I do is merely cause a certain part of the floor to be darker, to reflect less illumination than it had before. And when I make the shadow cease to be—to disappear without remainder—all that I do is to cause the relevant parts of the shadowed object to reflect light once again. So we do not have a coming into being and passing away *per se* of shadows. All we have is a coming into being and passing away *per accidens* or *secundum quid*—a mere alteration in the shadowed object.

Let us note that a shadow is a paradigm case of what some medieval philosophers called an *ens per alios*—and what we might call an "ontological parasite." *Entia per alios* were thought of as things which got all their being, so to speak, from *other* things. Thus a shadow has no being of its own. Anything we seem to be able to say about it is something that really is a truth just about some shadowed object or other. The shadow is entirely parasitical upon its object. And this is really to say that there are not such things as shadows.

Whatever thus comes into being or passes away *secundum quid* is not a real thing: it is an ontological parasite, at best a mere *façon de parler*.

THINGS THAT BECOME OTHER THINGS

Sometimes we say that a certain thing x *became* a certain other thing y. And we take our statement to imply that the first thing x then ceased to be and the second thing y then came into being. In such a case, we are speaking of coming into being and passing away *secundum quid*; x and y are ontological parasites and not *entia per se*. This may be seen as follows.

If the first thing became the second thing, then we may say:

(1) There exists a z such that z once was x and z now is y.

Suppose now we add

(2) x has now ceased to be and y had not yet come into being when z was x.

If we take "coming into being" and "passing away" literally and thus mean coming into being and passing away *per se*, then our two statements will imply

(3) There exists a z such that (i) z was once identical with x, (ii) z is now identical with y, and (iii) x but not y no longer exists.

But (3) is absurd. Therefore, if (1) and (2) are true, they must be taken to refer to coming into being and passing away *secundum quid*. The fact of the matter was simply that z was altered in a certain way.

If, at a certain time, a thing literally *becomes identical* with something it had not been identical with before, then the thing came into being at that time and it was not identical with anything before.[3]

ELANGUESCENCE

Reflection upon the coming into being and passing away of sensations, feelings, and shadows may bring to mind a monstrous hypothesis proposed by Kant in the *Critique of Pure Reason*. Different things, he said, may have different *degrees of reality*. It is possible, he thought, for the degree of reality of a thing to increase or to decrease in a continuous manner. And so, he said, a thing "may be changed into nothing, not indeed by dissolution, but by gradual loss [*remissio*] of its powers, and so, if I may be permitted the use of the term, by elanguescence."[4]

Kant is to be taken literally here. He was clear that existence is not a predicate. Yet he thought that some things could have *more* existence than others. It is as though he thought that there is a path between being and nonbeing, so that one day you may set out from nonbeing and head in the direction toward being with the result that the farther you go in that direction the more being you will have. But surely there is *no* mean between being and nonbeing. If something *is* on a certain path, then that something *is*. Or if it *is not* yet, then it cannot be on the path between being and nonbeing.[5]

Of course, things may be more or less endowed. But things cannot be more or less endowed with respect to being. What is poorly endowed *is* poorly endowed and therefore *is*.

One might object: "Consider an intense pain that becomes less and less intense and finally fades away. Doesn't it become less and less real and thus gradually cease to be?" The objection would ignore the point we have just made about ceasing to be *secundum quid*. When we say that the pain gradually faded away, we are talking about the alteration of a person; we are speaking about the way in which a person felt or the way he experienced something. Thus one might say, similarly, that the feeling of sadness faded away and finally ceased to be altogether. But the fact of the matter is only this: a person felt less and less sad until he finally reached the point where he did not feel sad at all. And we should remind ourselves, moreover, that even if we do reify pains and feelings of sadness, we have no ground whatever for saying that the feeling which is less intense is *less real* than the feeling which is more intense.

"But if one thing has more properties than another isn't it more real than the other?" *No* thing has any more or any less properties than does any other thing. Every property and every thing is such that either the thing has that property or the thing has the negation of that property. If you can play the viola and I cannot, you do not have *more properties* thereby than I do. To be sure, you have the property of being someone who can play the viola and I do not have *that* property. But I have the property of being someone who cannot play the viola and *you* do not have that property.

THE COMING INTO BEING AND PASSING AWAY OF PERSONS

If persons are real things or *entia per se*, then the coming into being and passing away of persons is *not* a matter merely of something or other being *altered* in a certain way. When my body dies, then it is altered in a certain way. And if it happens to be the case that I then cease to be, as it well may be, then my ceasing to be is *not* just the fact that my body has been altered in a certain way. And when I came into being, this may well have been at the time of a certain alteration of the fetus, or of a certain alteration of matter that was going to become a part of the fetus. But whatever alteration that may have been, that alteration was not the same event as my coming into being. For our assumptions imply that persons are *entia per se* and not *entia per alios*—not ontological parasites like shadows.

What does all this have to do with the facts of biology and physiology, with the questions about when human life begins and ends? Not very much, I am afraid. What I have said so far will not help anyone in dealing with *those* questions. But if you begin at the point at which I have begun, you will want to put the question first the other way around. What do the facts of biology and physiology, the things we know about the beginning and ending of human life, tell us about the coming into being and passing away of persons? Here, too, I am afraid, the answer is, not very much—or, not very much as far as anyone can possibly know. But there may be some relevant points which the metaphysician can make.

The United States Supreme Court decreed, in the case of *Roe v. Wade*, in 1973, that the fetus prior to a certain stage of development is not a "person in the whole sense." Possibly the ruling presupposes Kant's absurd hypothesis about degrees of reality. Then it would be telling us that, in its fetal stage, the person is somewhere between being and not being ("On the one hand, he doesn't really exist, and on the other hand, he doesn't really not exist"). But it would be more charitable not to assume that the court was presupposing bad metaphysics. And it is more likely that the court meant only that becoming a human being is a gradual process: the fetus is on the way to becoming a human being but, at its early stages at any rate, has not gotten there yet. One could take a similar view about the process of ceasing to be a human being. The one who is moribund is gradually ceasing to be a human being; in the early stages of his illness he is still a human being, but in the later stages not.

This view has recently been set forth by Lawrence C. Becker.[6] It may be summarized in the two theses, "Entry into the class of human beings is a process" and "Exit from the class of human beings is a process."[7] The expression "human being" is certainly a proper term of biology and physiology; one cannot quarrel with these theses on terminological grounds. But I am not at all convinced that this gradualistic theory, even if it is true, will help us very much in dealing with the philosophical and ethical questions which are involved in the coming into being and passing away of those things which may thus gradually become or cease to be human.

To see that these theses may not help very much, let us consider the consequence of assuming that they are true. We may do this by relating them to what we have already said.

Consider just the process of becoming a human being. (As Professor Becker makes clear, much of what we can say about the process of becoming a human being can also be said, *mutatis mutandis*, about the process of ceasing to be a human being.) Let us consider this thesis, that entrance into the class of human beings is a gradual process, and take it together with what we have already assumed. Thus we have:

(1) I am one of the members of the class of human beings
(2) There was a time at which I did not exist
(3) Entrance into the class of human beings is a gradual process.

Let us now consider our three premisses together. I am as certain as I am of anything that the first of these premisses is true. And I do not think that there are many of us who would challenge the second. The third premiss is the statement of the biological hypothesis we are now considering.

Our premisses, quite clearly, have these two consequences:

(4) There was a time at which I was not one of the members of the class of human beings
(5) My entrance into the class of human beings was a gradual process.

The second of these consequences—"My entrance into the class of human beings was a gradual process"—may suggest the process of entering a room. If we consider a man who is entering a room, we may say that his entrance is gradual in this sense: it begins with the entrance of the front part of one of his feet and this is followed by the entrance of more and more parts of his body. And then, when he gets them all in, he has entered the room. But perhaps a more accurate figure would be that of a sober man who becomes drunk: his entry into the class of the people who are drunk might be thought to be gradual.

But now consider this further consequence:

(6) There was a time at which I existed but had not yet entered the class of human beings.

If I went through the process of *becoming* a human being as (5) tells us, then I was not *already* a human being when I started to go through this process. What (6) tells us can be rephrased this way:

(7) My coming into being antedated my entry into the class of human beings.

Consider Aristotle's conception of the musical man once again. Aristotle might have said: "A musical man came into being but the man himself had existed long before." And then he could have said that the man's coming into being antedated his entrance into the class of musicians. For the man can become more and more musical without thereby coming into being, just as a man can become more and more drunk without thereby coming into being. And, analogously, one could say that I came to be more and more human but without thereby coming into being. In each case, the thing which went through the process of gradual entrance is assumed to have antedated that process.

This is a consequence, then, if we take what is obvious and combine it with the thesis that "entrance into the class of human beings is a process."

If entrance into the class of human beings is a process, then my coming into being antedated my entrance into the class of human beings. This means that that event which is my coming into being is not the *same* as that event which is my entrance into the class of human beings. There was a time, before I entered the class of human beings, when I existed. And so, if someone at that time could have caused me to cease to be, my ceasing to be as well as my coming into being would have antedated my entrance into the class of human beings.

And if in the future someone causes me gradually to leave the class of human beings, then, while he is doing this, while I *am* gradually leaving the class of human beings, I will be there to make the exit, and the man will not yet have caused me to cease to be. When I am half way out of the room, *I am* somewhere, partly in the room, partly outside, and partly in the doorway. Perhaps, once you have gotten me all the way out of the class of human beings, then you will have caused me to cease to be. But I suppose no one knows.

Would it help if we replaced the concept of *entrance* by the pair of concepts, *full* and *partial* entrance? Then we could distinguish between *full* and *partial* entrance into the class of human beings. And we could also do this in the case of entering a room. As soon as I get a part of my body in the room, then, however small the part may be, I have partially entered the room. And it is not until I have all the parts of my body in the room that I can say that I have fully entered the room. But I do not think this will help. For if we replace "entrance" by the two concepts "full entrance" and "partial entrance," then we have to give up the process theory. One has only to reflect just a little to see that both partial and full entrance can only be instantaneous.[8]

I am certain, then, that this much is true: if I am a real thing and not just a *façon de parler*, then neither my coming into being nor my passing away is a gradual process, however gradual may be my entrance into and my exit from the class of human beings.

If now we give the biologist and physiologist the term "human," perhaps we have a right to use the term "person" for the sort of thing which you and I are. Suppose now we define *a person* in terms of what it *could* become. We might say, for example, that a person is a thing which is such that it is physically possible (it is not contrary to the laws of nature) that there is a time at which that thing consciously thinks.[9]

If we thus define a person—as that which is such that it is physically possible that there is a time at which it consciously thinks—then we cannot say that anything gradually becomes a person or gradually ceases to be a person. For, if a thing has the property of being such that it is not contrary to the laws of nature that there is a time at which it consciously thinks, then it has that property from the moment it comes into being until the moment it passes away.[10] And so the questions we thought we escaped with our gradualistic concept of being a human may arise once again with the concept of a person.

THE MORAL OF THE STORY

If all of this is right, as it seems to me to be, then no one could have known just when it was that I came into being. And no one will know just when it is that I will pass away. Or perhaps the latter point should be put more cautiously: the present state of our knowledge is such that, if I have the misfortune to be one of those people who, as Lucretius put it, "leave the light dying piecemeal," then no one will know just when it is that I will pass away.

Hence it *may* be, for all anyone knows, that by terminating my mother's pregnancy at a certain very early stage, one could have caused *me* then to cease to be. (But it may also be that I did not come into being until after that stage.) And it *may* be, for all anyone knows, that, by disconnecting a life-sustaining device at a very late stage in my gradual exit from the class of human beings, you will *then* cause me to cease to be. (But it may also be that I already ceased to be, sometime before that.)

Analogous things may be said about you and about everyone else.

And so where does this leave us with respect to the moral problems which are involved in causing someone to cease to be? Surely it is right, sometimes, to terminate a pregnancy or to disconnect a life-sustaining device. Doubtless such acts always call for an excuse.[11] But let us not pretend that, when we perform them, probably we are not causing anyone to cease to be. Let us have the courage to face the moral facts of the matter: occasionally it *is* right for one person to annihilate another.

NOTES

1. G. E. Moore, *Philosophical Papers* (London: Allen & Unwin, 1959), pp. 32–59.

2. See, e.g., the discussion of "Causation and Creation" in C. D. Broad, *Scientific Thought* (London: Kegan Paul, Trench, Trübner, 1923), pp. 535ff.

3. Aristotle attempts to circumvent this conclusion with his doctrine of prime matter and substantial change. I cannot believe that Aristotle was successful. But I think it is clear that, if one does wish to circumvent this conclusion, then one must appeal to a concept which is very much like that of prime matter.

4. See the "Refutation of Mendelssohn's Proof of the Permanence of the Soul" in I. Kant, *The Critique of Pure Reason*, trans. Norman Kemp Smith (London: Macmillan, 1933), B414 (p. 373). Compare also Kant's discussion of the "degrees of reality" in the "Anticipation of Perception," B207ff.

5. Compare the criticism of Kant's doctrine in Franz Brentano, *Kategorienlehre* (Hamburg: Meiner, 1968), pp. 92–97.

6. Lawrence C. Becker, "Human Being: The Boundaries of the Concept," *Philosophy and Public Affairs*, 4 (1975), 334–59.

7. *Ibid.*, 335, 336.

8. We can, of course, retain proposition (6) above—i.e., "There was a time at which I existed but had not yet entered the class of human beings"—if we replace "entered" by "fully entered." What if we replace it by "partially entered"? For all we know, the result might be a proposition that is false. It may be that, from the time I *did* come into being, whenever that was, I already had one foot in the door, so to speak, and was *part way* into the class of human beings.

9. The moral philosopher might insist upon defining a person as a thing having *rights* of a certain sort. If now we should give *him* the term "person," then we might appropriate the term "self" and consider our definition as a definition of *a self*.

10. And so we are saying more than that persons are things that are "potentially thinkers." For if we take "potential" in its ordinary sense, then we may say that our potentialities are variable and dependent on our circumstances at any particular time. But our potentialities, in this sense of the term, are a function of what it is physically possible for us to be—a function of what the laws of nature do not preclude us from being. And physical possibilities, in this latter sense, are invariable. I have attempted to distinguish these various senses of possibility in more detail in Chapter 2 of my *Person and Object: A Metaphysical Study* (LaSalle, Ill.: Open Court; London: Allen & Unwin, 1976).

11. Can part of the excuse be that the persons involved are not then humans in the complete sense? This moral question falls outside the scope of the present paper.

2

On Death as a Limit

JAMES VAN EVRA

University of Waterloo

PHENOMENALLY SPEAKING, dying is simply a matter of ceasing to think and experience, and death presumably is the state of such experiencelessness. But while it seems perfectly reasonable to describe death in this way, to do so invites some potentially troublesome questions. For instance, it might be asked whether there need be anything which (phenomenal) death as a state characterizes. In describing death as a state, that is, are we tacitly committed to accepting the personal survival of death, in the sense that we need *something* of which we can say that it once thought and experienced, but, while still existing, does no longer? On the other hand, if we do not recognize the existence of experienceless selves, can sense be made of talking about phenomenal death as a state at all?

In this paper, I shall develop a view in which death is seen to be a state which characterizes absolutely nothing, and hence requires no commitment to the belief in selves which survive death. At the same time, the concept of death will be shown to retain all of its "ordinary" significance.

The heart of the view to be presented is an elaboration of Wittgenstein's view that death is like a limit, in the sense that we can approach it, but cannot reach it. The elaboration consists in pointing out that, like states which serve as hypothetical limiting constructs in science, death gains what significance it has, not by serving as a state characterizing things, but as a *function* which orders members of the series limited. In this way, the significance of the concept of (phenomenal) death can be retained, while the need to recognize the existence of things characterized by death can be rejected.

The paper is divided into three parts: first, Wittgenstein's basic analogy will be considered. This is followed by a discussion of the extension of the analogy, just outlined. Finally, the significance of the expanded view for more traditional views of death will briefly be considered.

I

In a terse comment entirely typical of the *Tractatus*, Wittgenstein says that "Our life has no end in just the way in which our visual field has no limit"

Reprinted by permission from *Analysis*, 31 (1971), 170–76.

(6.4311). The analogy contained in Wittgenstein's remark should be understood as follows: Our visual field has no limit in the sense that there is no seeable bound to the visual field. Try as I may, I cannot see the limit, for to see something is to place it in the visual field, which would necessarily place it within the limits of the field. It could not, therefore, be the limit itself.

Of course, saying that, from the point of view of sight *simpliciter*, the visual field has no limit is not to say that the visual field is not limited in *any* sense. I infer, quite consistently with the fact that I cannot see the limit of the visual field, that my visual field is limited in a different sense (hereinafter called "limited*") by, for instance, making inferences from the *manner* in which things appear in my visual field, as well as from evidence obtained from the other senses. That is, as things pop into and out of my visual field with some measure of consistency and coherence, it becomes useful to account for such intermittence by holding that, somehow, these things persist outside of my immediate field of vision. And because I can add to this evidence of the existence of such things from the other senses, the firm conclusion that my visual field is limited* is easily drawn.

Pressing the analogy then: if my life has no end in *just the way* that my visual field has no limit, then it must be in the sense that I can have no experience of death, conceived as the complete cessation of experience and thought. That is, if life is considered to be a series of experiences and thoughts, then it is impossible for me to experience death, for to experience something is to be alive, and hence to be inside the bound formed by death.

Holding that my life has no end in this sense is perfectly consistent with the belief *that* I will die, in the same way that holding that my visual field has no (seeable) limit is perfectly consistent with the belief *that* my visual field is limited*. For just as I have grounds other than sight for believing that my visual field is limited*, I have grounds other than thought and experience as such for the belief that I will permanently cease to think and experience. I might, for instance, arrive at such a belief by realizing that I experience, from time to time, bodies which have ceased to function physiologically. From this I infer, on the basis of the analogy which I draw to my own (physiological) self, that I too will cease to function physiologically. Then on the basis of the belief that certain physiological functions are necessary for the occurrence of thought and experience, I infer that I will cease to think and experience, i.e. that I will die in this particular sense.

In sum, then, Wittgenstein is saying that within the phenomenal frame of reference, death is unexperienceable as the limit of the visual field is unseeable.

II

The elaboration of the analogy can be arrived at by first considering the following question: does the fact that I make use of the concept of the limit of the visual field depend on the existence of the limit? Need there be, that is, a field which is identical with my visual field in every respect except that it is inherently impervious to vision? To deny the reality of such a limit is, of course, not to deny that things or states of affairs exist unseen, for, as previously noted, in-dependent grounds can be found for admitting their existence. Rather, to deny the reality of the limit is just to deny that there is a non-visual "field" which is complementary to my visual field but necessarily resists sight. Furthermore, were the limit, i.e. the complementary field, proved to exist (in some sense not involving vision) or if it were shown not to exist, the total effect on my vision would be nil, in the sense that nothing at all need change, regardless of the ontic status of the complementary field.

Since the supposed reality (or lack of it) of the limit of the visual field makes no (visible) difference, this suggests that questions concerning the visual reality of the limit are wrongheaded. In fact, to ask whether the limit itself is real *is* basically to misunderstand the significance of the concept of a limit. The answer to the question posed in the preceding paragraph is that to assert that the visual field has a limit need not be construed as a claim for the existence of an unsee-able complement to the visual field. Statements about the limit of the visual field can far better be understood as stating relational properties between various "seeings" within the visual field. When I say, for instance, that I cannot see X as clearly as Y "because X is closer to the limit of my visual field," such a state-ment employs the concept of the limit as a device with the use of which visual experiences are ordered or related. In such a case, reference to the limit need not be taken as an assertion of the existence of an (unseeable) state of affairs; the *total* significance of the statement can be accounted for solely in terms of the contents of the visual field and their properties, and no acceptance of the limit as something super-added is required. The significance of the limit is not as something independently real, but as an operational device.

Since talking about the visual field may be somewhat confusing, due to the fact that we are unavoidably close to the topic at issue, I should like to make the same point with regard to a more neutral subject matter—limits as they are used in science. As an example of such a limit, consider a modern reformulation of Newton's First Law of Motion:[1] "If the external forces F acting on a body (whose momentum along a straight line is mv) are zero, then the time-rate of change in mv (which may happen to be zero in the limiting case, so that the body is at rest relative to that line) is also zero."[2] Formulated in this manner, the axiom postulates a *limiting* motion, i.e. a state in which a body is under the influence of no forces at all. To ask whether there are *really* bodies in such a state is to miss the significance of the concept entirely. Nagel makes this point clear in the following passage:

> The first axiom formulates a complex set of facts in terms of a postulated *limiting* motion, were the series ideally prolonged without limit. However, the axiom must not be read with a sort of myopic literalness; it should not be construed as asserting that there are in fact bodies under the action of no forces, or as requiring for its validity the existence of such bodies. For the language of limits must be handled with care. In physics, as in mathematics, the assertion that a series of terms has a limit is often best construed as simply a way of stating a relational property characterizing the unquestionably existing members of the series, rather than as a statement which affirms the (possibly doubtful) occurrence of some term not initially assumed to be a member of

the series. Accordingly, the first axiom does have an empirical content, for the axiom formulates certain identifiable relational characteristics of the actual motions of bodies, all of which are under the action of forces, when these bodies are serially ordered [p. 184].

It might be added that, if there *were* a body under the influence of no forces, this would neither add to, nor detract from, the significance of the concept of limiting motion from the point of view of the series of bodies under the influence of forces. *All* of the significance of the concept as a limit derives from its use as an ordering function within the series of bodies under the influence of forces. If the limiting state is "real" it is simply not in a sense which is continuous with that of the reality of the series of bodies under force.

Furthermore, were it shown that no body *could* be under the influence of no forces, this would not mean that the series of bodies under the influence of force is not limited. I can believe, that is, that the series is limited without having to believe in the existence of a body under the influence of no force. This is even clearer in the case of another limit, absolute zero. The Third Law of Thermodynamics, if true, insures that no body can possibly have a temperature of zero degrees absolute. Yet this does not detract in the least from the significance of the limit as an ordering device for things-having-temperatures. Again, the series' being limited is completely compatible with the fact that nothing exists at absolute zero.

So far, only the "sight" side of Wittgenstein's analogy has been extended. Now the question arises, if the limit of the visual field is best treated (visually) as an ordering function, rather than as a state of affairs characterizing something, might not this treatment profitably be extended to the other side of the analogy, i.e. to death as a limit? I should like to answer in the affirmative, by suggesting that the concept of death as a state functions for us in precisely the same manner in which all of the previously mentioned limits function in relation to the members of the series which they limit. Death qua the cessation of thought and experience is not *just* a bound, although it is in itself conceptually unattainable, just as absolute zero is not *just* a limit although nothing can exist at such a temperature. In each case, the importance of the limit, and virtually *all* of its significance, derives from the fact that the limit serves as an ordering device.

To say that death functions as a limit in this sense is simply to say that we build, to a considerable extent, our conceptual lives with the *use* of it. The general, usually unconscious, realization that we are approaching the limit often impels us, e.g., to truncate projects so that we can go on to others; it forces us to pick and choose those tasks from the multitude which are more "worthwhile." In general, we form a "set," i.e. a context, from which life is viewed via the realization that life is limited, and that we are approaching the limit. All of this can be accomplished without any conception of an experienceless, literally thoughtless "self" whatsoever.

While there are many specific examples of the "mechanics" of death considered as an analogue to a limit, I shall mention only two. First, death sometimes intrudes in our lives with particular vigour. When someone slows his driving from the awareness that his driving could eventuate in a hastily-arrived-at death, he employs the concept by using it as a device which assists in the ordering of his conceptual affairs. In such a case, the individual may of course be able to conjure an image of what being involved in a crash would do to him physically, but this is not death as a limit and it does not get him closer to being able to conceive a state of experiencelessness. He cannot conceive of his (thinking and experiencing) self in a state characterized by the complete inability to think and experience, yet he reacts to precisely the possibility of attaining such a state. This again is analogous to conceiving of the temperature scale as a "reaction" to absolute zero, while existing at absolute zero is impossible.

The second and purest example of how we react to death has to do with the reactions of those who are aware that their death is imminent. A recent psychiatric study[3] suggests that individuals react to impending death in fairly regular ways. In each of the stages through which such individuals pass (denial, anger, bargaining, depression and acceptance) the individual conceives of death, not in itself, but as it bears on him while he is still alive. Death to these individuals is something to be avoided, to blame others for, to reject others in the face of, while it steadfastly resists conceptualization itself.

Because we react to death in these and many other ways, does this mean that we are implicitly committed to the existence of a self which is like our present one but cannot think or experience? Do we need, that is, some continuing "something" of which we say that it is now alive (i.e. is experiencing) and later, while persisting, will not be experiencing? The answer is no; no more than using the concept of absolute zero commits one to the existence of a body at that temperature, or using the concept of bodies under force commits one to the existence of bodies under no force. The significance of the concept of death as a limit is completely exhausted in its function as an ordering device; it requires no assumption of the existence of some super-added experienceless self.

In sum then, we have seen that, as Wittgenstein suggested, death is like a limit in the sense of being an experientially unattainable bound. But more than this, death is like a limit in deriving what significance it has from the role it plays as an ordering function with respect to the experiencing beings which it "limits."

III

Finally, I should like briefly to point out how the view of death here presented bears on other views of death.

First, the present view is strongly opposed to the view, held by many continental philosophers from Schopenhauer to the present, that we have an "awareness" of death *as such*, and that from this we come to regard death as an evil, the recognition of which points up the tragedy of the human condition, making total human happiness impossible to achieve. The view I have advanced exonerates death as the purported snake in our garden. We have, as experiencing beings, no more an "awareness" of death as such than we have, as beings which have temperatures, an awareness of absolute zero. Limits like death (i.e. limits on our powers of conception) are simply out of our league—we cannot "grasp" such limits. They are contentless and hence provide absolutely nothing for our awareness. From this point of view, death cannot diminish our human happiness, in the same way that bodies-in-motion are none the worse for having a lower bound. The bound, not being a member of the series, cannot defile it. The series is what it is, happy or unhappy, good or bad, quite independently of any bound as such.

Secondly, the view presented provides an explication of Epicurus' remark that death is nothing, "either to the living or to the dead, for with the living it is not and the dead exist no longer." Or rather, it explains the fact that his remark seems strange. Epicurus is speaking of the limit as such, and he is surely correct in saying what he does about it, particularly because it is aimed at those who hold that death is to be feared in the sense of fearing what might happen to the "self" which goes on after death. The reason why his remark seems odd is that it purposely ignores the sense in which death can be said to be *something* —which is the sense which captures all that death as a limit is. Conceiving of death as a function of life actually aids Epicurus' criticism by showing how talk of death can be so construed that the assumption of the existence of experience-less selves can be avoided.

Finally, the present view of death aids in the avoidance of pitfalls inherent in what might be called the "everyday" view of death. Consider the following formulation of such a view, provided by Paul Edwards:

> It seems quite plain that human beings not infrequently imagine and conceive of their own deaths without the least difficulty, as, for example, when they take out life insurance or when they admonish themselves to drive more carefully. Nor is it at all difficult to explain what a person imagines when he thinks of his own death.
> "When I die," wrote Bertrand Russell in a famous passage (in *What I Believe*), "I shall rot and nothing of my ego will survive"; and it is surely this that people wish to avoid or put off. A person thinking of his own death is thinking of the destruction or disintegration of his body and of the cessation of his experiences.[4]

While comfortable and ordinary, talking in this way about death is clumsy and can easily lead to quite undesirable consequences. We cannot imagine or conceive of our death as such if death is considered to be the cessation of experience. And while I might, as suggested earlier, imagine my dead *body* while driving recklessly, I imagine nothing of death *itself* when I take out life insurance. Rather, I am much more likely simply to imagine what would happen to those who depend on me were it the case that I could no longer provide for their welfare. Furthermore, it is not the fact of the cessation of the ego as such that we wish to avoid or put off, because this is simply out of our conceptual range. We cannot even *wish* to avoid it if we cannot conceive it in itself. What we wish to avoid, rather, are all of the results of applying death as a functor: separation from family and friends, inability to attain goals sought, inconvenience to others, etc. A person thinking of his own death simply cannot think of the cessation of his experience, unless this is an ellipsis for saying that he is thinking of the results of using *death* as a limit.

In summary, death treated analogously to a limit literally *is* the manner in which it is used, and to treat it in any other way is to miss its significance.

NOTES

1. Which in its original version is as follows: Every body continues in its state of rest or of uniform motion in a right line unless it is compelled to change that state by forces impressed upon it.

2. Ernest Nagel, *The Structure of Science* (New York: Harcourt, Brace, 1961), p. 159.

3. Elisabeth Kübler-Ross, M.D., *On Death and Dying* (New York: Macmillan, 1969).

4. *Encyclopedia of Philosophy*, ed. Paul Edwards (New York: Macmillan, 1967), V 416.

Existentialism and Death:
A Survey of Some
Confusions and Absurdities

PAUL EDWARDS
Brooklyn College
The City University of New York

THIS PAPER is not meant to be an exhaustive discussion of existentialist pronouncements about death. Some, like the curious notion that life is "essentially being toward death," are not dealt with at all, and others, like the view that an "authentic" mode of life is possible only for a person who "resolutely confronts death," are no more than mentioned in passing. My aim has been to cover those existentialist doctrines which are tied, in one form or another, to confused ways of thinking about death common among people in general and which occur independent of the efforts of the existentialists.[1]

DEATH AS SLEEP IN THE GRAVE

Most human beings, whether they are religious believers or not, appear *at times* to have great difficulty in regarding death as truly and really the *absence* of life. In some contexts they do treat death in this way, but at other times they think of it as a restful or gloomy or undesirable *continuation* of life. There is a very common tendency to think of a dead person as sleeping an extremely deep sleep in his grave—so deep that he will never again wake up. A famous Italian conductor was once greatly upset by the way the musicians of the New York Philharmonic were playing the movement of a Brahms symphony at a rehearsal. "If Brahms were alive," he finally exclaimed in exasperation, "he would be turning in his grave." When this story is told, it usually takes some time before people see the absurdity of the conductor's remark. If Brahms were alive he

Reprinted by permission from *Philosophy, Science, and Method*, edd. S. Morgenbesser, P. Suppes, M. White (New York: St. Martin's Press, 1969), pp. 473–505.

presumably would find better things to do than lie in a grave.[2] However, to a person vaguely thinking of Brahms as sleeping in his grave, the conductor's remark will not seem absurd.

People do not have this difficulty in the case of other absences. If a whisky bottle is empty, nobody is likely to maintain that it is filled with an ethereal liquid; and if one comes across a blank canvas, one is not tempted to describe it as an exceptionally abstract painting. Yet, this is precisely how we frequently think of death. We then refer to it more or less seriously as "the rest which may not be unwelcome after weariness has been increasing in old age" (Bertrand Russell), as "quiet consummation" (Shakespeare), or perhaps as "the cool night" which follows the hot and busy day (Heine). We also think of it as a place to which we "pass on" or depart (at the end of our "journey"), as "the harbor to which sooner or later we must head and which we can never refuse to enter" (Seneca), as "the undiscover'd country from whose bourn no traveller returns" (Shakespeare); and we tend to regard this place as dark and perhaps even terrifying, as "eternal night" (Swinburne), "a beach of darkness . . . where there'll be time enough to sleep" (A. E. Housman), the "engulfing impenetrable dark" (H. L. Mencken). It is not uncommon to speak of this place as the same one which we left when we were born. Schopenhauer speaks of birth as the "awakening out of the night of unconsciousness"[3] and he wavers between regarding our return to this state of unconsciousness as something to be welcomed and something to be dreaded. On the one hand he writes that the "heart of man rebels" against having to return to nonexistence; on the other he claims to be speaking for suffering mankind who would much rather have been "left in the peace of the all-sufficient nothing" where their days were not spent in pain or misery (op. cit., p. 389). Darrow, who shared the latter of these sentiments, spoke of life as "an unpleasant interruption of nothingness." "Not to be born is the most to be desired," in the words of Sophocles, "but having seen the light, the next best thing is to go whence one came as soon as may be." Pliny, who ridicules any belief in survival as the logically baseless "fancy" of human vanity, accuses the believers of robbing mankind of "future tranquillity." "What repose," he exclaims, "are the generations ever to have" if they cannot be "from the last day onward in the same state as they were before their first day?" Seneca, too, thought it fortunate that a person could always, by a voluntary act, "escape into safety." Advocating suicide in certain situations, he asks, "Do you like life? Then live on. Do you dislike it? Then you are free to return to the place you came from." At death, Seneca writes in another place, "you are brought back to your source." A lamp, he also observes, is no "worse off when it is extinguished than before it was lighted," and in the same way "we mortals are also lighted and extinguished; the period of suffering comes in between, on either side there is a deep peace." But not all writers who regard death as a "homecoming" think of the place to which we return as a restful abode. Thus James Baldwin, the novelist, admonishes us to negotiate the "passage" of life as nobly as possible—in this way we will obtain "a small beacon in that terrifying darkness from which we came and to which we shall return."

This tendency to think of death as a shadowy and, especially, a very painful and undesirable form of existence is reinforced by the way in which we place death at or near one end of the scale of our punishments and illnesses. Just as two years of imprisonment are more undesirable than one year and life imprisonment is worse than either, being sentenced to death is regarded by most people as a worse fate yet; and even those who consider life imprisonment worse than death regard the latter as very undesirable—at least as undesirable as, say, imprisonment for ten years. Again, just as we regard a chronic illness involving some pain as worse than a merely temporary ailment involving the same degree of pain, so we regard a mortal illness, because it is mortal, as worse than either; and although many people would regard some chronic (non-fatal) illnesses as "objectively" worse than death, almost everybody treats mortal illnesses as (necessarily) very undesirable, even if the amount of pain involved is relatively slight. Since languishing in jail and suffering a painful illness are states or processes of living organisms, it becomes tempting to regard death as another, very undesirable, state of a living organism. We see, in the words of P. L. Landsberg, a philosopher writing in the phenomenological tradition, that "death . . . must exceed all experiences of illness, suffering or old age."[4]

Another line of reflection that may lead to a similar conclusion is suggested by Landsberg in the course of discussing the "community" that two people may form—a husband and wife, for example, who not only love each other but who have braved many a storm together. If one of them dies, this "community," this "we," is destroyed. The surviving person experiences then a "bitter cold." In feeling the death of the "we," he is led into an "experiential knowledge" of his own mortality. "My community with this person," writes Landsberg, "seemed shattered, but the community was to some degree myself; and to this degree I experienced death in the very core of my own existence" (op. cit., pp. 14–16). It is tempting to proceed to the conclusion (though Landsberg in fact does not explicitly go that far) that one's own death is a more extreme instance of the same kind of thing: even more bitter and cold than the bitter cold which the survivor experiences upon the death of the "we."

FEAR, ANXIETY, AND DEATH

This common human tendency to regard death not as just the absence of life but as existence in a dark, impenetrable abode has been enshrined into a philosophical doctrine by the Christian existentialist, the late Professor Paul Tillich, in his "ontology" of Non-Being or Nothingness. Tillich's doctrine is introduced in connection with his distinction between fear and anxiety (it should be noted that although Tillich's use of these expressions is in harmony with that of other existentialists, it is significantly different from their use by most professional psychologists and psychiatrists). In fear, writes Tillich, we are always facing a definite object: It may be physical pain, the loss of a friend, the rejection by a person or a group or any number of other things, but in each case it is something "that can be faced, analyzed, attacked, endured," and met by courage.[5] In anxiety, on the other hand, the object, if it can be called an object, is "ultimate nonbeing"; the "threat" here is due not to something specific like physical pain but to nothingness. Unlike fear, anxiety cannot be met by courage and it is almost unendurable. "It is impossible for a finite being," in Tillich's words, "to stand naked anxiety for more than a flash of time. People who have experienced these moments, as for instance some mystics in their visions of the 'night of the soul,' . . . have told of the unimaginable horror of it" (CB, p. 39). Although fear and anxiety must not be confused with one another, they are closely related. Among other things, there is an element of anxiety in every fear and it is this element of anxiety which gives the fear its "sting."

Tillich applies his distinction between fear and anxiety to the "outstanding example," namely, the fear of death. There are two elements in this fear—fear proper which has an object like an accident or a mortal illness and anxiety whose "object is the absolutely unknown 'after-death,' the nonbeing which remains nonbeing even if it is filled with images of our present experience" (CB, p. 38). Tillich is very concerned that his use of the word "unknown" should not be misunderstood. It is not any unknown but the *absolutely* unknown that one faces in this "basic anxiety" of one's "ultimate nonbeing." There are "innumerable realms of the unknown" that are faced with fear but without any anxiety. Here Tillich probably has in mind the kind of thing that happens when a person is afraid of a new job in which he has to perform unfamiliar tasks or when an explorer is approaching territory about which no reports are extant. These unknowns are not in principle unknowable. The situation is altogether different in the case of the unknown "which is met with in anxiety." It is an "unknown of a special type," which "by its very nature cannot be known, because it is nonbeing" (CB, p. 37). Elsewhere, in discussing man's finitude, Tillich observes that since man is "created out of nothing," he must "return to nothing." Very much like Seneca and Pliny, he tells us that nonbeing "appears as the 'not yet' of being and also as the 'no more' of being." Like all other finite entities, human beings, while alive, are "in process of coming from and going toward nonbeing."[6] Somebody who accepts this account would presumably hold that while Shakespeare was not far wrong when he spoke of our ultimate nonbeing as the "undiscover'd country from whose bourn no traveller returns," it would have been more accurate to speak of an "undiscoverable country." Mencken was closer to the truth (as Tillich sees it) when he spoke of our death as the "impenetrable dark" that must eventually engulf us. Tillich himself indeed uses practically the same words in one place: "We come from the darkness of the 'not yet'," he writes, "and rush ahead towards the darkness of the 'no more'." Our "unavoidable end' is "impenetrable darkness."[7]

THE SEARCH FOR THE "ONTOLOGICAL CHARACTER" OF DEATH

Perhaps it would not be inappropriate to label Tillich an "agnostic ontologist." He is an ontologist in the sense that he regards death as not merely the absence of life but as a *state* toward which all human beings inevitably "rush"; and he is an agnostic in that he regards death as an unknowable state. Other existentialists, who share Tillich's view that death is a state, do not agree with him that it is *entirely* unknowable. Prominent among those who believe that human beings can, by suitable "existential" or "dialectical" techniques, achieve *some* knowledge about the nature of death are Professor John Macquarrie, the eminent Protestant theologian, co-translator of Heidegger's *Sein und Zeit,* and author of numerous influential works,[8] and the Spanish philosopher, Professor José Ferrater Mora, renowned for his monumental *Diccionario de Filosofía,* and author of *Being and Death,*[9] a work expounding a "general ontology" in which an attempt is made to "integrate" the achievements of the existentialists with the insights of the naturalists. Neither Professor Macquarrie nor Professor Mora would deny that there are grave difficulties in the way of discovering what death is, but they appear to believe that these difficulties may, to a certain extent, be overcome. We definitely need not, in Mora's words, "resign ourselves to saying nothing about death" (BD, p. 177).

Both Macquarrie and Mora engage very actively in what we may call "the ontological quest" or the search for the "ontological character" of death. To explain what this quest is, or rather what these (and various other) writers believe themselves to be doing, let us first note certain explicit disclaimers on their part. Following Heidegger, both Macquarrie and Mora regard death as more than a mere "natural happening"—as something more than could in principle be explored by the use of scientific methods. Thus, in asking the question "What is death?" or "What is the nature of death?" these philosophers are emphatic that they are not asking the kind of question that a physiologist would ask when he inquires into the nature of death. The ontologists are also not concerned with the traditional religious question of whether human beings live on after the death of their bodies. Nor are they concerned with such "metaphysical" questions as "how and why death came into the world." Heidegger and the various ontologists writing under his influence do not dismiss this last question or the question concerning survival as meaningless, but they insist that their ontological quest is more fundamental and ought to be dealt with first. Both the religious and the metaphysical question, in Macquarrie's words, presuppose "an ontological understanding of death" (ET, p. 117). We cannot hope to answer or even understand such questions until we have "clarified" the ontological nature of death (ibid.), until "the character of death . . . has been fully explored" (SCE, p. 50). These questions can be intelligently approached only after we have "grasped the existential phenomenon of death" (ibid.).

All of this tells us what the ontological quest is not. We can, I think, see what the ontological quest is or what it is supposed to be by first mentioning certain "difficulties" which our ontological explorers freely acknowledge. We cannot find out what death is by any straightforward employment of experience or of the "phenomenological method." "Death," writes Macquarrie,

> is to be investigated by the same method of phenomenological analysis that Heidegger employs in the rest of the existential analytic, [but] there are clearly difficulties here that do not attend any of the other phenomena analyzed. Understanding, moods, speech, anxiety, concern, solicitude—these are all phenomena of existence that undoubtedly go to constitute our daily living. We know them from experience and from continuous participation in them. . . .
> All this is possible because our experience of these matters is a "living through"

them, so that we are then able to reflect upon them and describe them [SCE, p. 51].

Unfortunately death is not like anxiety, concern, or solicitude: The dead person, since he is no longer alive, does not experience his death and hence the phenomenological method cannot be employed by him to study his death. In Professor Macquarrie's words, "Anyone who undergoes death seems by that very fact to be robbed of any possibility of understanding and analyzing what it was to undergo death" (ibid). The dead man's "being is no longer lit up to himself in the only way that would seem to make anything like an existential analysis possible, and so it appears that he cannot by any means understand what the undergoing of death may be like" (ibid).

Macquarrie does not abandon the search after these admissions. He attempts to get at the nature of death by a consideration of various "analogies" and by reflections about the death of others. Although he is very emphatic that the usefulness of these inquiries is limited, Macquarrie believes that they lead to a "preliminary understanding" of the nature of death. Perhaps, he asks, it is possible to compare death "to the ripeness of a fruit, which is not something added to the fruit in its immaturity, but means the fruit itself in a specific way of being" (ET, p. 118). This analogy, unfortunately, breaks down at the crucial point. For, "whereas ripeness is the fulfillment of the fruit, the end may come for man when he is still immature or it may delay until he is broken down and exhausted with his fulfillment long past" (ibid.). Although this analogy breaks down (and the same is true of others which I have not reproduced), Marquarrie believes that such considerations yield a "positive result." It becomes clear that "death belongs to my possible ways of being—though in a unique kind of way, since it is the possibility of ceasing to be. It is already a possibility present in existing . . . it shares a fundamental character of existence, and as a present possibility it is disclosed to me and can be analyzed" (ibid.).

"May information be obtained from considering the death of others?" (ET, p. 117). We cannot phenomenologically study our own death since we shall not be able to do any studying when we are dead, but perhaps we can get at the ontological character of death by paying careful attention to what happens when others die while we are yet alive to witness *their* deaths. As we mentioned previously, Macquarrie does not believe that such an inquiry is entirely fruitless, but at the same time he admits that it does not yield anything like a full answer to his original question. However, in the course of this admission he makes some very revealing remarks. He points out that when we study the death of others our phenomenological exploration is really confined to the mental states of the survivors. Our "vicarious experience" of the death of others cannot be adequate for "grasping death as an existential phenomenon" (SCE, p. 52). "The death of others is experienced as the loss sustained by those who remain behind, and not as *the loss of being which the deceased himself has sustained*" (ET, p. 118; my italics). Nor is this the only trouble. For, in addition to the fact that what we experience is *our* loss and not the loss sustained by the dead person, the latter cannot communicate to us about the loss he has sustained. He cannot "any longer communicate with us to describe that loss of being" (ibid.).

I think that we can now rephrase the ontological question as Professor Macquarrie conceives it in the following ways:

What is death like as it is to the dead?

What is the nature of the loss sustained not by the survivor but by the deceased?

How does the loss of being sustained by the dead person feel to him (not to us) or, since he feels nothing any more, how would it feel to him if he could feel it?

These questions may sound slightly mad, but they are a precise formulation of the ontological quest as conceived by Professor Macquarrie and, in varying degrees, by a number of other existentialist explorers as well.

Before leaving Macquarrie, we should note that in his opinion the study of the death of others yields an important positive result. "One positive character of death" has been ascertained: "Death is always my own since it cannot be experienced vicariously . . . it is untransferable and isolates the individual. He must die himself alone" (ET, p. 118). There are innumerable ways in which one person can represent another, "but nothing of the kind is possible in the case of death . . . no one can die for another, in the sense of taking the other's dying away from him and performing his death for him" (SCE, p. 52). This result may be "combined" with the one achieved in the course of the analogical inquiries mentioned earlier. Together, these results amount to "a preliminary understanding of death as an existential phenomenon." This preliminary understanding may be expressed by saying that "death appears as my own present untransferable possibility of being no longer in the world" (ET, p. 118). In other words, "death belongs to man's possibility—it is, indeed, his most intimate and isolated possibility, always his own" (ET, p. 119).

Like Professor Macquarrie, Professor Mora is much perturbed by the difficulties in the way of a phenomenological exploration of the nature of death. Although, he writes, "we know that there is such a thing or such an event as death, that death is inevitable, that we all must die, and so on, we still do not realize in full measure what death is and what it means until we somehow 'experience' death" (BD, pp. 175–176). But just such an experience seems to be excluded by the very nature of death.

We can "see" that people die; we can think of our own death as an event which will take place sooner or later, but we do not seem to be able to experience death in the same way as we do other "events" such as pleasure, pain, good health, illness, senility. All we can "see" of death is its "residue," for example, a corpse . . . [ibid.].

It should be noted that a dead person is here automatically regarded as more than a corpse, and it is of course this more which Professor Mora is trying to explore.

Mora agrees with Macquarrie that we cannot get a clear view of the nature of death, but he maintains that we can at least get some kind of glimpse. Although we cannot ever attain a "direct and complete grasp of the nature of death" (p. 178), our experience furnishes us with data that may serve as the basis for "drawing some inferences" (ibid.). Mora's object is to get at the *inside of death* and he thinks that he can, to some slight extent, attain this goal by studying the attitudes which people display toward death. "A description and analysis of some typical attitudes regarding death can cast some light on our subject" (pp. 192–193). It is true that in studying these attitudes we do not experience our death "exactly in the same sense in which we can experience love, friendship, sorrow, and so on" (p. 192), but in our investigation of attitudes toward death "we can place ourselves, so to speak, in front of it (or its possibility)."[10] Professor Mora then surveys different attitudes displayed by people on the point of dying—those who faced a firing squad but were reprieved at the last moment and others who appeared to be drowning but were rescued before it was too late. After enumerating the different kinds of feelings and thoughts that may be going on in people "immediately preceding impending death," Professor Mora does not hide his disappointment and concedes that the value of such a survey is severely limited as far as the purpose of his ontological inquiry is concerned. It must be granted that in attending to our and other people's attitudes, we "see our death" only "somehow from the outside" (p. 194). This is not as much as one could wish, but it is considerably more than nothing—" 'somehow from the outside' is not the same as 'completely from the outside.' In some respects we are looking at our death (or its possibility) *from the inside*; otherwise we could not even take 'an attitude' in front of our death or its possibility" (p. 194; my italics).

Like Macquarrie, Mora pays much attention to the death of others, but he is a little more sanguine in his confidence that such a study can get us to the inside of death. In the absence of a "direct and complete grasp," we can at least "use analogy and conceive of our death in terms of another's death" (p. 192). Professor Mora recounts three personal experiences which "are to be taken as examples of another's death. They cover 'cases' which, as happens in legal matters, can be considered 'precedents' " (p. 178). We shall here confine ourselves to the two which Mora himself regards as his more hopeful cases. In one of them he witnessed the sudden death of a man killed by a bullet in the course of a battle. Professor Mora had not known this man at all and although he felt the death of this man to be symbolic of "the universal and overwhelming presence of death," he experienced neither grief nor anguish. What happened was a "mere fact," something merely objective, "outside there" (p. 183). The second case deals with Professor Mora's maternal grandmother. Here the person who died was not a stranger but on the contrary was somebody whom Professor Mora had known exceedingly well and with whom he had formed "a community of participation" somewhat along the lines described by Landsberg. If the death of a given person is, in relation to a survivor, a "purely external event" then, Professor Mora believes, the survivor would not be justified in claiming that he had experienced the person's death "in the sense of *somehow* sharing it." The death of his grandmother, however, was not experienced by

Professor Mora as a merely external event. In such a case "we are not merely 'watching' someone die but we are, or are also, 'sharing' his death—at least to the degree in which we had 'shared things in common'." However, we must not allow ourselves to be carried away and claim too much. Even when the death is not a merely external event, one only "somehow" shares the deceased's death—"to conclude . . . that we are *actually* 'sharing' another's death," even when the person was terribly close to us, "would be to go too far" (p. 179; my italics). When all is said and done, Professor Mora concludes, "I knew little about the relation between my grandmother and *her* death, and still less about the relation between the man shot down in battle and *his* death" (p. 185; Mora's italics).

DEATH IS NOT A STATE

What is a person who has preserved his sanity to say to all this, more especially to the search for the ontological character of death, the "inside nature" of death as it is to the dead, the nature of the loss sustained not by the survivors but by the deceased, death not as it is observable when we see a dead body, but as it is "undergone" by the dead person? Perhaps the best way to call attention to the ludicrous confusion underlying all such ontological searches is to relate the following conversation between two German pessimists.[11] "It is much better to be dead than to be alive," said the first. "You are right," remarked the second, "but it is still better not to have been born in the first place." "That," replied the first, "is very true, but alas how few are those who achieve such a happy state." Since he regards death as a loss and not as a gain, we may, in this context at least, regard Professor Macquarrie as an optimist and we may imagine an optimist who shares his ontological views reasoning in the following way: "A man who loses both his arms sustains a greater loss than one who loses one arm only, and a man who loses his eyes and his arms sustains a still greater loss. A yet greater loss is sustained by him who loses his life. Even he, however, is not quite as badly off as the man who failed to be born in the first place. The lot of the latter is the worst of all. It is very fortunate that there are not too many who find themselves in this dreadful condition." To diagnose as clearly as possible the absurdity in the procedures of the German pessimists as well as the Macquarrian optimist let us first, following Benn and Peters,[12] distinguish between the "actions" a person performs and the "passions" he experiences or undergoes. An action is anything a person does—for example, singing a song, giving a lecture, assaulting an enemy, resigning a position. A "passion," in the broad sense in which Benn and Peters use the word, is anything that *happens* to a man—a toothache, the tortures he endures, the pleasure he experiences when drinking a glass of orange juice after a game of tennis, the feelings of constrictions he has when gagged or confined to a prison cell. No doubt the distinction is far from sharp, but it is one which all of us make in certain situations. Now, Macquarrie, Tillich, Mora, and most of the poets and philosophers mentioned in the opening section of this article recognize that the death of an individual is not an action, but they mistakenly believe or imply that it is some kind of passion, though a very special and extremely passive type of passion. In fact, however, neither death nor our nonexistence before we were born is a passion any more than it is an action. If we introduce the word "state" to mean any action or passion, then we can express our point by saying that, while feeling the coolness of the night, reaching the last stop of a journey, arriving in a strange country from which one will never return, sleep, and rest, sustaining losses (no matter how serious), undergoing pain and torture, feeling isolated and all alone and even finding oneself surrounded by impenetrable darkness are states or experiences of living human beings; death is not a state. At times, indeed, the ontological explorers themselves realize this, for example when they complain about the difficulties of a phenomenological investigation of death. At other times, however, they seriously believe that death is a state, a dark and wholly or largely inaccessible one, to be sure, but a state nevertheless. Without such an assumption they would have to admit that death is simply the absence of life and there would be nothing to explore. It should be added that these strictures do not apply to those who, when asking such questions as "What is death?" or "What are we like after death?" thereby raise the issue of survival. However, the existential ontologists whose explorations we are discussing either do not believe in survival or else explicitly stress that their ontological questions are not questions about whether we survive the death of our bodies.

The linguistic form of the sentences which we use to assert that a person is dead is similar to that of the sentences which are used to ascribe states to individuals. This similarity makes it tempting to suppose that the former sentences are also used to make state-ascriptions, but a little reflection is sufficient to show that the kind of analysis which will work for state-ascriptions does not make any sense in the case of statements asserting that somebody is dead. Let us briefly look at the following three statements:

(1) A is performing in *Don Giovanni* at the moment.

(2) Tomorrow A will be in one of his gloomy moods.

(3) A year from now A will be dead.

If we go by linguistic appearances alone, we are inclined to say that (3) no less than (1) and (2) are about A, and it is also tempting to believe that in each case we are attributing or ascribing a certain state or experience to A— in (1) an active state, in (2) one that is fairly passive, and in (3) an extremely passive one. In a sense no doubt all three statements are about A—in the sense that we are asserting some fact about A rather than about other people—B, C, etc. In another sense, however, (1) and (2) are about A while (3) is not. In (1) and (2) we *are* ascribing states to A, and we presuppose that A is or will be alive at the times in question. In (3) on the other hand we are not ascribing an extremely passive state to A: We are denying what is presupposed in all state-ascriptions. (1) can be expanded into "A is alive and is performing in *Don Giovanni* now"; (2) into "A will be alive tomorrow and will be in a gloomy state"; but (3) *cannot* be expanded into "A will be alive one year from now but he will then be in the extremely passive state of deadness." Yet those engaged in the ontological quest treat (3) as if this were the proper analysis.

THE MADNESS OF THE ONTOLOGICAL QUEST

Once death is treated as a state, it is very natural to reach Tillich's conclusion that it is something absolutely unknowable. It is then quite natural to reason along the following lines: I am now alive; I am not yet dead; hence I cannot now know from personal experience what the state of being dead is like. But this state is different from other unknowns. It is a very special unknown. Africa is also unknown to me, but others who have been there can tell me about it when they return. Again, I have never been skating, but other people can tell me what it feels like to glide across a frozen lake. Nobody, on the other hand, can tell me what death is like. For one thing, nobody can come back from the dead to tell me; but, furthermore, even if somebody did come back, this would not help, since while he was dead he would have had no experiences and could not attend to his own state of deadness. The conclusion thus seems inescapable that, as Tillich so happily put it, death "is the unknown which by its very nature cannot be known."

In arguing that death is a totally unknowable state, Tillich dimly perceived something which ontologists like Macquarrie and Mora obscure when they assert that they have *some little* knowledge of the nature of death. Tillich dimly perceived that it is *logically* impossible to attain the object of the ontological quest. The ontologists write in such a way as to suggest that they are trying to determine the characteristics of a peculiarly elusive state, but a little reflection makes it clear beyond any question that what we have here is a series of self-contradictory expressions and not any kind of state, elusive or otherwise. To an uncritical reader it may appear—and the remarks of writers like Macquarrie and Mora are specially apt to foster this impression—that the object of the ontological quest is a state which cannot *in fact* be examined by human beings because the only subjects competent to examine it are chronically absent when they are needed for the examination. It may thus be thought that the relation of human beings to the object of the ontological search is like their relation to some territory which is so extremely hot or so extremely cold that anybody wishing to explore it is annihilated before he can get to his destination. In fact, however, the situation is altogether different. The ontologists are wondering what death would feel like to the dead if they could attend to their deadness, but part of what is meant by saying that a person is dead is that he no longer has feelings or experiences. The ontological search thus amounts to the questions "How does it feel to be in a state in which one no longer has any feelings?" or "What kind of an experience does a person have who no longer has any experiences?" These questions are not one whit more sensible than such absurd questions as "How long is the fourth side of that triangle?" asked by somebody who is pointing to a perfectly ordinary triangle or "In which country is the father of this orphan living now?" where the questioner is not referring to any foster father or to any habitat in the next world. The ontological questions do not become any less grotesque by being expressed hypothetically. "How *would* Hume's death feel to him if he could attend to it?" is not any less ludicrously absurd than "How *does* Hume's death appear to him?" or "How *does* (the dead) Hume feel about his death?" Once again the reader should be reminded that the ontological explorers have ruled out questions about survival as irrelevant to their problem.

In a decision in which he enjoined the American Nazi Party from holding parades within two miles of Jewish houses of worship, a Chicago judge observed that he would similarly issue an injunction against a group of nudists if they wished to parade in their native attire outside a Presbyterian church. Puzzled by the nature of native attires, an ontologist might now engage in the following investigation: To wear one's native attire is to wear very peculiar clothes. What kind of clothes is a person wearing who is wearing his native attire? There are serious difficulties in the employment of the phenomenological method in this case. When a man is wearing a hat or a woman wearing a skirt and blouse we can perceive the clothes they are wearing. However, when we look at somebody who is wearing his native attire we cannot perceive any clothes. If we could perceive clothes on the person, he would not be wearing his native attire. At this stage a Tillichian ontologist would maintain that we must reach an agnostic conclusion—native attires consist of unknowable clothes—while somebody following Macquarrie and Mora would try to attain a "little knowledge" perhaps by a careful study of the clothes which the nudists wear when they are not wearing their native attire or by studying people who are in the process of changing from their work clothes into their native attire. Perhaps analogies might yield helpful clues—perhaps we should study oranges and apples and bananas after they have been peeled or perhaps an examination of trees, denuded of their foliage, may yield at least a preliminary understanding. The ontological investigation of the nature of death is just as ludicrous as the ontological inquiry into the nature of native attires. To every move in the latter investigation there corresponds a move occurring in the writings of the ontological explorers of death.

There is a familiar story about the boy who, before his first date, was advised by his father to discuss three subjects—love, family, and philosophy. Following his father's advice and taking up love, he first asked the girl, "Do you love noodles?" to which the answer was "no." Remembering that he should next discuss the topic of family, he asked his date whether she had a brother. The answer again was "no." This left only the subject of philosophy and the boy now asked his final question: "If you had a brother, would he love noodles?" I think it would be generally agreed that this last question is absurd, but the ontological question about death is considerably more absurd. Although it would in almost any normal circumstances be utterly pointless to inquire whether a hypothetical brother loves noodles, the question is not self-contradictory: We can describe what it would be like for a girl who in fact has no brother to have a brother and what it would be like for such a person to love or not to love noodles. We might even possess some evidence supporting the claim that a given person's brother would (or would not) love noodles. The ontological question about death, on the other hand, is self-contradictory. The question

"How would Hume feel about his death if he could attend to it?" is not merely pointless, but the very meaning of the constituent terms makes it *logically* impossible to obtain an answer. Hume (or anybody else) *cannot both be dead and attend to his deadness*: If he is dead, then he can do no attending of any kind; if he can attend to anything, he is not dead and hence cannot attend to his deadness. While we can describe what it would be like for a girl to have a brother who would (or would not) love noodles, we cannot describe what it would be like for Hume (or anybody) to experience his deadness.

Arleen Beberman, an existentialist explorer from New Haven, Connecticut, finds the ontological quest beyond her capacities. "If we think or imagine what it would be like to be dead," she remarks, "we surreptitiously introduce scenes of life and living people"[13] and thus fail to reach our objective. On the other hand, "if we do experience death," we cannot "report back from the encounter" (op. cit., pp. 18 and 22) and hence our efforts are once again defeated. Miss Beberman decides that she will not aim at anything so ambitious as a "phenomenology of death." "Such a goal," she writes, "is beyond my present intent since the method of coming to that goal requires utmost rigor, boundless creativity, and plenty of time. I lay claim to none of these" (pp. 18–19). In view of her limitations Miss Beberman concludes that her efforts will be merely "episodically phenomenological." Modesty is a most becoming human trait, but here it is out of place. In the present context even the most "creative" phenomenologist, with limitless time on his hands, could not do any better just as a person with perfect vision could not ever detect the clothes which make up a native attire and just as an observer with the most sensitive and highly developed sense of hearing could not discover the language in which somebody is silent.

Death is not a state and once this is clearly seen there is no temptation to engage in an ontological quest and equally no temptation to regard death as unknowable. Death is the absence of life and consciousness; and while in this or that instance it may of course be unknown whether a certain man is really dead (e.g., whether a Nazi leader was killed during the last days of the war or whether he is hiding in South America after undergoing plastic surgery), this is not something that is in principle undiscoverable. Nor do people, in spite of the general tendency to think of the dead as continuing in a dark abode, have in practice the slightest difficulty understanding what is meant by the assertion that somebody is dead. They understand such statements just as readily as they understand statements asserting that a certain person was not yet born at a certain time or that somebody failed to show up at a certain place or that he was silent or that a certain individual wore no clothes.

Something should perhaps be said at this stage about the widespread belief that death is unthinkable and unimaginable. In his discussion of *Grenzsituationen*, Jaspers remarks: "Death is something unimaginable, really something unthinkable. What we imagine and think of in this connection are merely negations, merely associated phenomena [*Nebenerscheinungen*] and never positivities."[14]

Jaspers is surely right in maintaining that when one thinks of such associated phenomena as funerals or the mourning of the bereaved survivors, one is not thinking of death itself, i.e., of the death of the person who died. However, if life and consciousness are in the present context taken to be "positivities," then, in thinking of death, one would *have* to think of a "negativity." If thinking of President Kennedy's life is thinking of a positivity, then thinking of his death is thinking of the termination of his life—of the absence, the nonoccurrence ever again of any actions or passions that would be part of his biography. But this is apparently not enough for Jaspers and others who are under the impression that death is a state. They presumably require that a person, in order to think of death, should be thinking of a dark presence and not merely of the termination of life and consciousness; and, since unfortunately there is no such presence (or else it is impenetrably dark), one will conclude that death itself, as distinct from side-phenomena and negativities, is altogether unthinkable.[15]

THE PSEUDO-EMPIRICAL PROCEDURES OF THE ONTOLOGICAL EXPLORERS

The full ludicrousness of the ontological search is hidden from the explorers (and presumably also from their less critical readers) by the employment of certain highly misleading strategies. The first of these to which attention should here be called is the frequent use of quasi-inductive techniques and language and the related claim, made by some ontologists, that although the nature of death must remain *largely* unknown, a certain amount of understanding has in fact been achieved by their methods. These strategies suggest that the ontologists are engaged in a quest that is not in principle different from the investigations of a scientist, however much more difficult it may be because of the peculiar nature of the subject matter.

In this connection it is worthwhile to engage in a rather full examination of the ontological "investigations" carried out by Professor Mora. It will be recalled that, according to Professor Mora, we can "somehow" get on the inside of death by studying the various attitudes which people display toward death and that we can gain a little knowledge of what death is in those cases in which there had been a community between us and the dead. Professor Mora believes that in the latter kind of case the survivor, to some extent, shares the dead person's death and that as a consequence he obtains a little knowledge of what this death is like on the inside. If a survivor and a dead person did not form a community, the death in question is merely an "external" event, but where there was a community, the death becomes more than a merely external event. It seems clear that Professor Mora is misled here by the pictures associated with the words "external" and "internal." No matter how much a person may be shaken by a given death, he cannot get at it from the inside any more than a survivor who is altogether indifferent. He does not get inside the dead person's death—not even a tiny bit—not because he lacks some special gift of empathy which other human beings possess or might conceivably possess but because *there is nothing to get into*: There is nothing to get into since death is not a state or condition "of the deceased" and since, if it were a state, it would not be one to which anybody, the dead person or any survivor, could conceivably attend.

The word "share" is commonly used in a number of different senses. For example we say that two people share a certain object, like a house or a car or a restaurant, if both of them legally own it. Again, we say that people share the same outlook or convictions—e.g., when both of them are socialists or absolute idealists or admirers of Heidegger. Here what we mean is that the two people have similar views or similar attitudes. When Professor Mora claims that on certain occasions one human being can (to some extent or somehow) share the death of another, he evidently has neither of these ordinary senses in mind. In all likelihood he is thinking of the sense in which we say of a person that he shares the grief or the suffering of somebody else if he is so sympathetic that, upon observing the other person's grief or suffering, he experiences a kind of duplication of these in himself. In general, when we use the word "share" in this last sense, we mean more than that the two people have similar feelings: We mean that the first person is so attached to the second that the feelings of the second immediately lead to similar feelings in him. A little reflection makes it quite clear that "share" can no longer be intelligibly used in this sense when a survivor is said to share the death of somebody else. For no matter what the survivor feels, he is not reproducing death in himself. One cannot be significantly said to "share" in this sense unless there is something to share—something like grief or pain—and death does not qualify as such a something. Of course, a person may in this sense share somebody else's *dying*—he may experience in himself the anguish or the serenity or whatever emotions the dying person feels; but this is totally beside the point since what the ontologist is out to explore is death and not dying.

A study of the attitudes of people toward death, whatever its intrinsic interest, does not help the ontological quest along any more than a consideration of bereavements which are classified as more than merely external events. In both cases Professor Mora seems to think that the psychological data available to us (in one case the feeling of the survivor, in the other the attitudes of the people who are thinking about their death) are related to death itself somewhat like the reflections or images of an object (in a lake or a mirror or on a photographic plate) are related to the objects whose reflections they are. However, it is not and cannot be so. Any opinion to the contrary is bound to be the product of confusion. Mora's main confusion consists in an amalgamation of two questions which are logically quite distinct. The first is the psychological question "How do people face death?" The second is the ontological question "What is death like from the inside?" or "What is deadness as it is to those who died?" Mora manages to confound these questions by an ambiguous use of the phrase "experience of death." Neither of Mora's uses can be regarded as an ordinary sense,[16] but it is easy to track down the ambiguity involved. In one context Mora refers to that experience, if such a thing were possible, which the dead person would have if he attended to his deadness. In the other sense he simply refers to the feelings and attitudes of people who contemplate their impending death. Let us call the former the "ontological" and the latter the "attitudinal" sense. Professor Mora himself in one place realizes that he is using the word "experience" in this ambiguous fashion when he concedes that "no doubt an 'attitude' is not exactly the same as an experience" (BD, pp. 193–194). This does not, however, prevent him from proceeding as if no such ambiguity existed. He argues that since people do experience death in the attitudinal sense they therefore have *some little* experience of death in the ontological sense as well. But this is a gross non sequitur and a most confusing amalgamation of two issues. To the question "Do people have experience of their death in the attitudinal sense?" the answer is clearly a ringing "yes," while to the question "Do people have experience of their death in the ontological sense?" the answer is an equally ringing "no." Professor Mora apparently thinks that by amalgamating the two questions we can reach a happy compromise and answer *the* question (suggesting that this is still just the original ontological problem) with a hesitating and soft-spoken "yes." We do not, using his favorite image, ever obtain a full inside knowledge, but equally the knowledge we have is not "wholly from the outside." Using this language, we may express the real situation by saying that if by "the nature of death" one is referring to nothing more than the ways in which people feel and think about their death, then human beings have a very good knowledge of death from the inside, while if by "nature of death" is intended what the ontologists originally set out to explore, then we do not have *even a tiny bit of inside knowledge*—or at any rate this in no way follows from our inside knowledge of death in the other sense. Mora insists that when a person thinks about his attitude he does in a sense stand "in front" of it. This is not an unnatural way of speaking, but the "in-frontness" here involved is not the in-frontness required by the ontologist. The in-frontness required by the ontologist is the kind which occurs when human beings look at a mountain or when they attend to their own feelings. In this sense, when a person attends to his attitude toward death, he is "in front" not of death but of his own feelings and thoughts about death.

Professor Mora maintains that he possesses some "little" knowledge concerning the relation between his grandmother and her death, but he nowhere tells us what this little knowledge consists of. This is not surprising for the simple reason that Professor Mora has no such knowledge and can have none. If anybody thinks otherwise this can only be due to the failure to recognize an ambiguity similar to the one described in the preceding paragraph. It should be noted that Mora does not adduce the fact that he could not achieve more than a little knowledge about the relation between his grandmother and her death as peculiar and exceptional. In other words, it is not just Professor Mora who possesses no more than a little knowledge in such a case, but all human beings are similarly handicapped and inevitably so, no matter how well they may have known the deceased, no matter how close they may have been to him or her throughout life and throughout the last days. Human beings do not even, in their own cases, have any greater access to the relation in question. The reason for this is not, as Professor Mora's language suggests, some kind of empirical limitation like that of a thief who cannot get into an apartment he wishes to rob because he finds it impossible to break through the lock. The reason is the senselessness of the expression "X's relation to his death" as this is used by the ontologist in the course of his quest. This senselessness is obscured by the fact that the expression "X's relation to his death" also has a rather clear meaning in *other* contexts. In nonontological contexts the question "What is X's relation to his death?" would be naturally interpreted to be a means of asking for information about X's attitude toward his death. Here, while we may in this or that case be very ignorant about the person's attitude, we can frequently have a *great deal* if not indeed complete knowledge; and certainly the person himself very often has more than merely a little knowledge. In this sense it seems to me that Professor Mora, having known his grandmother very well and having spent much time with her while she was dying, probably had more than a little knowledge of her relation to her death. Or if *he* did not, the ignorance is not something that is universal and inescapable. However, none of this is of any aid to the ontologist. For what the ontologist is concerned with is not how people feel about their death while they are alive but what death is, i.e., what it is to the dead, what the loss is that the deceased has sustained—not how the deceased felt prior to sustaining the loss. And if the question is taken in this ontological way, Professor Mora has not little but no knowledge whatsoever of the relation between his grandmother and her death. One would know somebody else's relation to his death when the question is asked in the spirit of the ontologist only if one were that other dead person and could then attend to that person's deadness. This, however, is a *logical* impossibility even if it were not a logical impossibility to be somebody else. It is, as we pointed out in the last section, a logical impossibility because if one is dead one cannot do any attending. Not only can Professor Mora have no knowledge about the relation between his grandmother and her death, but in the ontological sense even his grandmother herself can have no such knowledge.

It is important to realize not that Professor Mora's empirical arguments do not "happen" to be invalid, but that they are bound to fail. What is most objectionable about them is not their detailed defects but their very production in the spirit that empirical arguments of some kind might conceivably provide clues to the nature of the object of the ontological search. Much the same applies to "analogies" like that between the ripeness of a fruit on the one hand and death on the other which Macquarrie (and Heidegger) reject but whose very consideration suggests that we have here an inquiry that might conceivably be carried on by means of analogical "indications." Macquarrie and Heidegger are right in rejecting such comparisons, but they give the wrong reasons. In the case of the analogy between the fruit and death, Macquarrie and Heidegger complain that the analogy breaks down because the ripeness of the fruit is "the fulfillment of the fruit," but the end for a man may come when he is still immature or long after he has passed the peak of his powers. Let us suppose, however, that all human beings were to die precisely at the moment of their greatest fullfillment, neither too young nor too old, i.e., when their powers are at their peak. Let us suppose for example that Mozart had not died at the age of thirty-four but that he had lived on until he was sixty-five when his powers finally began to decline, and that Winston Churchill had not lived on into a state of near-senility but that he had died shortly after the successful conclusion of the war against the Nazis. Even if this sort of thing happened universally, the analogy would break down for the simple reason that the fulfillment or maturity of the fruit is a state of the fruit while the death of a man is not one of his states—mature, immature, or any other kind. It is conceivable that a certain kind of person, like Bardone in Rossellini's *Il General Della Rovere*, would experience the greatest moments of fulfillment in the course of sacrificing himself for somebody else or for a cause; but these experiences would still be states of his living organism. In such a case one may, using language loosely, say that the person's death was his greatest fulfillment. However, if one is talking sense, one is really referring to what the person did or experienced while he was dying or going to his death. It is important to bring out the proper reasons for dismissing the above and other analogies since the reason given by Macquarrie and Heidegger suggests that if only human lives were different in certain ways some of these analogies would work. Analogies in which death is compared with a state cannot work, but of course there is not the slightest need to introduce any of them in order to discover what death is. As already pointed out we know quite well what death is and we no more need "analogical clues" in the present case than we need them in order to understand the nature of silence or of native attires.

THE SHIFT FROM THE ONTOLOGICAL PROBLEM TO OTHER QUESTIONS

In both of his discussions of the ontology of death, Professor Macquarrie reaches a stage at which he claims to have achieved "a preliminary understanding" of death. This "preliminary understanding" consists in the conclusion that death "is man's untransferable possibility of being no longer in the world." I now wish to call attention to the following features of his procedure: first, whatever one may think of the assertions to which Professor Macquarrie refers as "preliminary understanding"—whether they are meaningful or not, true or not, important or not—they do not constitute any kind of relevant answer to his original question. They are in this sense not even a "preliminary" understanding. They tell us nothing about the ontological character of death—the nature of the loss sustained by the deceased, the nature of death as undergone by the dead. The statement that a person cannot transfer his death to somebody else no more tells us anything about the *content* of death than the statement that one human being cannot transfer his native attire to another tells us what native attires are. Or, to use a different illustration, in pointing out that nobody can eat or digest my food for me or that nobody can do my sleeping or resting for me, one does not explain what eating, digesting, sleeping, or resting consist in. Secondly, in the remainder of his discussions Professor Macquarrie confines himself *exclusively* to nonontological issues—chiefly to the psychological questions "How do people in fact think and feel about death?" and "Do they face it honestly or do they try to evade it and, if so, how?" and to what we may call "moral" or "practical" questions like "How ought a person to act in view of his inevitable death?" Practically the entire discussion in both books after reaching the "preliminary understanding" is devoted to an advocacy of the "authentic" attitude toward death (in which one "resolutely anticipates" one's "capital possibility" and even finds "joy in this mode of life" [SCE, p. 55]) and to an analysis and condemnation of the inauthentic approach of those who are in a "fallen" state and who "cover up" for themselves the "present possibility of death" (ibid.). Professor Macquarrie began by telling us that he is out to discover "what the undergoing of death may be like," what death is for the person who has been robbed of his being, and he rightly points out that the phenomenological method encounters difficulties here. Before long these difficulties are overcome by investigating not death but our present feelings about death. This transition is effected with the greatest ease. "Existence," we are told, "is dying, and death is present to us and, *in a way*, accessible to us" (op. cit., p. 52; my italics). And again "death is, . . . *in a sense*, already in the present. It is already accessible, as thrown possibility, to the investigation of the existential analytic" (op. cit., p. 55; my italics). Any consistent ontologist ought surely to protest that Professor Macquarrie simply abandons ontology for introspective psychology here. What is "present" and "accessible" is not death but thoughts about death and no amount of qualifications ("in a way," "in a sense," and many more I have not reproduced) can undo the difference. What becomes accessible to phenomenological study or to the existential analytic had always been accessible, and what had not been accessible (the state of deadness as distinct from thoughts about death) is no more accessible after the shift than it had been before. Macquarrie first ruled out the study of the death of others on the ground that although it "might teach us much . . . about psychological reactions in the face of death," it "can never disclose death as an existential phenomenon," but he ends up studying precisely such psychological reactions.

It should be emphasized that Professor Macquarrie is by no means alone in shifting from ontological to psychological and practical issues, and it should also be noted that these psychological and practical questions are not usually senseless. The failure to detect the shift and the intelligibility of the questions to which the ontologists transfer their attention are perhaps as much responsible for their not perceiving ludicrousness of the initial ontological quest as the use of such quasi-inductive techniques as we described in the last section. In Macquarrie's case the main mechanism of the shift is an ambiguity in the word "existential" as it is used in such expressions as "existential character" or "existential phenomenon." All existentialists are agreed that death is more than a biological phenomenon; and to this "more" they refer as the "existential character" or the "existential aspect" of death. However, different existentialists and sometimes the same existentialists at different times have different things in mind when they speak of this "more." Sometimes when we are told that the existential character of death must escape the biologist, what is meant is indeed the "ontological character" of death—the object of what we have been calling the ontological quest; but at other times, when the limitations of the public methods of biology are stressed, the writers refer to the inner[17] feelings of anguish, horror, serenity, or whatever people experience when they think about their death. Since the word "existential" is used in both of these ways, Professor Macquarrie can maintain that all his answers are answers to questions about the existential character of death and anybody who is not attentive to the ambiguity just described would not notice the shift that has taken place.

In Mora's case the mechanism of the main shift is an ambiguity in the word "understand." Professor Mora sets out to "understand" death and originally this means finding out what death is on the inside in the ontological sense. But he is also concerned with the question "Does death ever (and perhaps always) have meaning or is it always or at least sometimes an absurd happening?" To this latter question Professor Mora proposes the answer that "human death is never completely meaningful, nor is it entirely meaningless—it is meaningful and meaningless in varying degrees" (BD, p. 186). I do not profess to understand what he means either by this question or by his answer, but this does not affect the possibility of tracking down his shift. It seems quite clear that when we say about something, x, that we know what it means, it is permissible to express this by saying that we understand x, whether x is a word, a phenomenon, or a theory. It is thus quite natural for Professor Mora to believe that he has answered his original ontological question after concluding that death is always meaningful in varying degrees and that this meaning can be ascertained. Whatever the merits of these last contentions may be, they do not constitute any kind of answer to his original question—they do not make death "comprehensible" or "understood" in the sense in which these words must be used when they express the ontological problem.

THE CLAIM THAT DEATH IS MORE THAN A "NATURAL" PHENOMENON

All existentialists agree that death is more than a natural phenomenon and that some nonscientific technique (variously called the "phenomenological method" or the "existential analytic") is required for the study of its nonnatural aspects. This conviction is shared by existentialists who actively pursue the ontological quest and by those who only occasionally show some slight inclinations in that direction without ever setting out on a full-fledged expedition. Professor John Wild, who belongs to the latter group, offers the following considerations in support of the view that death is not merely a natural phenomenon:

> The existentialist thinkers have performed an important service in recalling our attention to the actual phenomenon of personal death. They have shown with great cogency and clarity that this is something more than the objective biological stoppage which can be observed from the outside. The limited methods of science can shed no light on this inner existential phenomenon which is open only to philosophical description and analysis.[18]

> The existentialist contributions to the phenomenology of death are also of major importance. They have certainly shown the incapacity of naturalistic and pan-objectivistic interpretations to account for the more important existential phases of this mysterious and long-neglected phenomenon. In this sense, death is not something universal. It concerns me as an individual. It is not a replaceable, interchangeable function, but something I must face by myself alone. It is not an event that I will observe in the future, but something that I must either evade or face authentically here and now.[19]

There is a great deal that is objectionable in all this. With the claims that death is a "mysterious" phenomenon and that I *must* face death "by myself alone" I shall deal in later sections. Right now, however, it is necessary to observe that although some of Professor Wild's remarks are true, they do not in any way imply his main conclusion about the existence of aspects of death which cannot be studied by the "limited methods of science." To begin with, Professor Wild is quite right in calling attention to the difference between what one may call the statistical and the personal perspectives. It surely cannot be denied that a person's state of mind is very different when he gives his assent to the proposition that all men are mortal from what it is when he realizes that he himself is one of those who will inevitably die. Although this is certainly not something that existentialists have discovered, people do perhaps on occasions forget it and it may well be salutary to be reminded of it from time to time. To this, however, it must be added that the differences are not peculiar to the subject of death. It is exactly the same with thousands of other things—e.g., suffering imprisonment unjustly or contracting a chronic and painful disease. The state of mind of a person who reads in a book that 10 per cent of all people condemned to prison sentences are in fact innocent is very likely to be significantly different from what it would be if he became one of those convicted for a crime he did not commit; and the state of mind of somebody who reads about what patients suffering from chronic arthritis go through is likely to be very different from what it would be if he himself became such a sufferer. Convictions, just and unjust, are phenomena that can be studied by the methods of science and so can the feelings of those convicted; and the same is true of arthritis and the states of mind of those suffering from this disease. It is not easy to see why the admission that there is a genuine difference between the personal and the statistical viewpoints should imply that either the subject in question (be it arthritis, convictions, or death) or the mental states which make up the personal viewpoint fall outside the scope of scientific inquiry.

Professor Wild, like other existentialists, has a tendency to define "science" in a misleadingly narrow way. It may be granted that death is "something more than the objective biological stoppage which can be observed from the outside." Death is also the termination of consciousness. However, for this insight it is not necessary to appeal to phenomenology or to the existential analytic. Professor Wild no doubt in this context also thinks of *dying*; and again it may be granted that the biologist, in studying the physiological processes that go on in a dying organism, does not thereby study the experiences of the individual which, from the human point of view, are usually the most poignant aspect of the situation. Again, however, from this it does not follow that science cannot study these inner experiences; and in fact Feifel and other contemporary psychologists[20] have amassed a good deal of interesting material which is not one whit less scientific than the work of other psychologists who rely on the introspective reports of their subjects. Some of Heidegger's own most interesting comments about human attitudes toward death, which carry the wholehearted endorsement of Professors Macquarrie and Wild, would, if true, be part of this branch of scientific psychology.

Somebody might admit all of this but maintain that science cannot tackle the practical and moral issues about death—how human beings *ought* to face it and conduct their lives in the light of their inevitable doom. This may be admitted, although it is an exaggeration to say that scientific information can *never* have *any* bearing on such moral questions. It may be conceded that science cannot answer these questions without, however, conceding that there are some nonnatural features of death which require investigation by the "existential analytic." There are many other practical questions which also cannot be answered (simply) by using scientific techniques. If a man is contemplating marriage and the question before him is which of two women he should choose, or, to take a less momentous example, if a person asks himself which tie he should wear with his new blue shirt, science too does not provide the answers. However, it does not follow from any of these admissions that the choice of a wife or of a tie are phenomena with aspects that can be investigated only by some nonscientific technique.

DYING ISOLATED AND ALONE

One of the most pervasive confusions in the writings of the existentialists is their failure to distinguish between death and dying.[21] The existentialists themselves on occasions endorse this distinction in a *general* way. Thus both Macquarrie and Mora quote, with apparent approval, Wittgenstein's dictum that "death is not an event of life"[22]—at any rate if they think that Wittgenstein was wrong they nowhere give us their reasons. Such admissions in general terms do not, however, prevent these writers from constantly confounding death and dying in discussions of specific topics. Unlike death, dying *is* a process or, in our use of the word, a state or succession of states, and many of the existentialist pronouncements cease to be senseless when they are interpreted as statements about dying. Thus it is not nonsense to maintain that a person finds his greatest fulfillment in dying, although cases of this sort are certainly very rare. It is not nonsense, but frequently true, that a person while dying is *undergoing* a great deal of suffering. Again, if we have in mind the anguish or the other feelings experienced by a person who knows that he is dying, then it is conceivable that others may share his dying in the same sense in which one sympathetic human being may share the emotions of other human beings. Or, to take one of Tillich's favorite statements, it is indeed absurd to maintain that a person finds himself, after death, engulfed by an impenetrable darkness, but similar remarks about dying are not only not absurd but may well be true. Thus a German physician, Johannes Lange, who studied patients dying very gradually of degenerative diseases, reports that as their life was slowly ebbing away, they felt that they became more and more surrounded by darkness.[23] In our ordinary thinking we also frequently fail to keep death and dying clearly apart, and this is one reason why the full ludicrousness of the ontological quest is not always noticed. When the existentialists mean death (and I am here referring to situations in which they must mean death if they are to do ontology), many an innocent reader tacitly substitutes "dying" and the resulting statements, though frequently false, are no longer senseless.[24]

The confusion between death and dying is unquestionably one of the factors responsible for the extremely misleading assertions, endlessly repeated by all existentialists, that all of us must die isolated and alone. "No one can die my death for me," writes Professor Wild; "this thing at least I *must do alone*" (op. cit., p. 82; my italics). Death, he later remarks, "is an actual act to be lived through by an individual *alone*" (p. 83; my italics). Again, in a passage quoted previously, we are told that death is "something I must face by myself alone" (p. 239; my italics). Professor Macquarrie expresses this doctrine of what we may call "the privacy of death" by declaring that death "*isolates* the individual. He must die himself *alone*" (ET, p. 118; my italics). In a similar vein, though not using the word "alone," Professor William Barrett writes: "Death is not a public fact occurring out there in the world; it is something that happens within my own existence."[25] When these writers maintain that human beings die isolated and alone (and this of course is asserted not of some but of all human beings), they presumably wish to claim more than merely that all human beings eventually die. They give the impression and they themselves undoubtedly believe that they are not merely redescribing the latter familiar fact. However, if "alone" is used in any sense in which "all human beings die alone" asserts more than that they all eventually die, it is quite clearly false. In one natural sense of this expression, somebody dies alone if he is physically isolated as in the case of a man who gets lost on an Arctic expedition and freezes or starves to death before the rescuers arrive. There is another sense in which one may quite naturally speak of somebody as dying alone or in solitude, although the person need not be physically isolated like the man lost in the Arctic. What we then mean is that, while dying, the person is psychologically or emotionally isolated—he does not greatly care about anybody else and nobody else cares much about him. It is in this latter sense that Ivan Ilyich in Tolstoy's moving story dies alone although he has a dutiful wife and daughter. Now, it is clear beyond any doubt that, while some people die alone in one and some in both of these senses, others do not die alone in either sense. Winston Churchill, Louis XIV, and David Hume, to cite some familiar cases, did not die alone in either of these senses.

The existentialists suggest that there is a third sense in which "dying alone" means more than just "dying" and in which all human beings necessarily die alone. It is easy to show that there is no such further sense and that the only sense in which it is true that all human beings necessarily die alone is one in which "dying alone" is logically equivalent to "dying." As the existentialists use "alone" (or rather as it must be interpreted if their statement is not to be plainly false), it is *logically inconceivable* for a person not to die alone. Let us suppose that a human being is not dying in either physical or emotional isolation but is, on the contrary, experiencing the greatest and deepest love and happiness of his entire life during his last days.[26] As the existentialists use "alone" in the present context, such a person would still have to be described as dying alone for the simple reason that he is dying. If "alone" had some additional content, then it would be possible to describe what it would be like for a person to die without dying alone; but as the existentialists use these words, such a description is not possible. The existentialists *seem* to be saying something novel and of interest here and they also *seem* to be saying something that is plainly true. However, the upshot of our discussion is that if their statement is interpreted in such a way that it says something interesting, then it is clearly false; while if it is interpreted so as to make it true, it becomes nothing more than a rhetorical way of asserting the exceedingly familiar fact that everybody dies some day.

Much the same comment is applicable to the other formulation that is commonly given to what we called the doctrine of the privacy of death. We are told that nobody can get another human being to die for him, to act as his substitute or representative in the matter of death; and this is put forward as a statement asserting more than the familiar fact that everybody eventually dies. However, the key expressions in these formulations are ambiguous: When used in one sense, the statement to the effect that nobody can die somebody else's death is not platitudinous and goes beyond the assertion that everybody eventually dies, but in this sense it is false; when used in another sense the statement is true, but then it becomes a platitude simply reasserting that everybody dies some day. There is a perfectly natural sense in which people can get others to die as their substitutes. During the French Revolution the authorities in Paris would occasionally allow a man who had been sentenced to death to leave his prison in order to attend to urgent business provided that somebody else took his place as a kind of human bail. If the person sentenced to death did not return by a given time, the man substituting for him would be guillotined in his place. Heidegger and his followers point out that in such a case the evil day is postponed and not ultimately avoided: The person who absconded will some day die and then he will not be able to have somebody else die in his place. In Heidegger's own words: "No one can die for another. He may give his life for another, but that does not in the slightest deliver the other from his own death."[27] To keep these two senses apart, let us insert the adjective "ultimately" whenever we use the expressions in the sense in which it is clearly true that nobody can get somebody else to die as his substitute or representative. Now, it seems clear that what prevents a person from *ultimately* getting a substitute is simply the fact that he will eventually die. It is part of the meaning of "he will die" that he cannot ultimately get a substitute. It is not one fact that all human beings eventually die and a further fact that they cannot ultimately get a substitute for their death: These are two different ways of referring to *the same fact.* Suppose there were a tremendously powerful tyrant who has for many years been in the habit of getting other people to do the most varied things in his place. Whenever an unpleasant task comes up—e.g., to meet a foreign dignitary, to attend the opening of a boring play, or to receive an honorary degree—he sends somebody else. When he is challenged to a duel, he sends a substitute, and when he wishes to get rid of dangerous opponents, he sends other people to do the killing for him. After many years of this, he comes to believe that he can also (in our second sense, i.e., "ultimately") get somebody else to die for him. How would we, if this were possible, convince the tyrant that he was mistaken? In effect he believes that he will never die and to show him that here he cannot ultimately get a substitute we would have to convince him that, like all others, he will eventually die: We do not have to convince him first that he will eventually die and then, separately, that he cannot ultimately get a substitute in the matter of dying.

To the above criticisms of the doctrine of the privacy of death, it may be replied that although not everybody is necessarily alone while dying, *in death* this is the fate of all human beings; and this contention will appear plausible to all, whether they are ordinary people or philosophers engaged in the ontological quest, who are under the influence of the notion that the dead person is sleeping in the grave or that he somehow continues to exist in a dark abode. The man who is lying in his coffin is there all alone and his loneliness would not be remedied even if we put a few corpses or perhaps a few living people into the same coffin since he would not be able to converse with them. Somebody under the sway of this picture might exclaim that the dead are in fact more alone than any living person can be. For, unlike the living they cannot obtain any of the relief that comes from talking about one's losses. The dead cannot talk to the living or to their fellow dead or even to themselves. Their loneliness is thus seen to be truly staggering! Once this is spelled out in full, the absurdity becomes quite obvious; while it is *false* to assert that everybody dies alone in any sense in which this asserts more than that people eventually die, it is *senseless* to say about anybody that he is alone in his death. To be alone, one has to be alive, and the dead are neither alone nor not alone for the same reason that Julius Caesar is neither an even nor an odd number and that feelings of anger are neither blue nor red. As for Professor Barrett's statement that death is not a "public event," it is appropriate to remark that unless death is taken as the inner state of the deceased in which he has the experience of having no experiences—and we saw that there were "difficulties" in conceiving death in this way—death *is* a public event, though not one which the dead person can witness. What is not or not exclusively a public event is dying, or more specifically the experiences of the dying person; but these, it should be added, are no more private than other feelings and thoughts.

THE "MYSTERY" OF DEATH

Almost as frequently as they assert that each person must die his death alone, the existentialists make remarks to the effect that death is something mysterious. They do not merely mean that this or that man's death is a mystery but that all deaths anywhere, at all times, and under all imaginable circumstances are, and are necessarily, mysterious. Thus Professor Wild, in a passage quoted previously, speaks of "this mysterious and long-neglected phenomenon" (op. cit., p. 238) and earlier in the same work he observed that "harsh, mysterious, and inexorable, death places all else in question and reveals the uncanny strangeness of the world" (p. 84). In several places Wild also asserts that death is "opaque to theoretical analysis" (p. 82) or "opaque to understanding" (p. 81). Professor Tillich, needless to say, since he regards death as the "end . . . with its impenetrable darkness," concurs in this opinion and adds that time too is a mystery.[28] Professor Macquarrie complains that people who treat death as an impersonal phenomenon are thereby taking the "mystery and imminent threat" out of it (ET, p. 121). The remarks about the mysterious nature of death just quoted are rather cryptic, but there is a much fuller statement in a recent work by an English writer who, while not calling himself an existentialist, expresses great sympathy for the movement. In his *Existentialism—For and Against*, Paul Roubiczek praises the existentialists for offering valuable correctives of errors associated with positivism and the thinkers of the Enlightenment. "The

mystery of death," he writes, "even more than that of birth, is bound to in-
validate all the false convictions which survive from the Age of Reason." To
this he adds:

> Purely rational thought, though it can explain the causes of death in scientific
> terms, can never account for the fact that we can die at any moment and are
> beings who, in any case, must die sooner or later. The length of our lives
> seems to be fixed in a purely arbitrary way which, being inexplicable, defeats
> the power of reason [p. 113].

Perhaps none of the existentialist theses about death strikes a more responsive
chord in ordinary readers than this claim that death is mysterious; and it is
echoed in countless statements found among poets, novelists, orators, religious
writers, and even psychologists.[29] The feelings of helplessness and horror which
death inspires in most people seem to lead very naturally to the remark that
death is a mystery or to other remarks along the same lines. It is probably
sacrilege of the most damnable kind to subject such statements to a critical
examination, but those who prefer clear thinking to nebulous rhetoric will not
wish to shirk this task.

Of the various senses in which the word "mystery" has been used, either
in ordinary life or by philosophers and theologians, there seem to be only two
in which the statement that death is a mystery could make any sense. We refer
to something as a mystery in one of these senses if we do not know its cause
or if we are ignorant of certain of its features. It is in this sense that various
diseases are mysteries even at the present time and it is in this sense that somebody, accustomed to the beautifully simple arrangement of streets and avenues
in midtown Manhattan, is liable to find parts of Brooklyn or the North Side
of Chicago baffling mysteries. Although this or that death may well be mysterious in this first sense, it cannot be reasonably maintained that the same is
true of every death: We frequently do know the causes of death as well as
the surrounding circumstances. In any event, as Mr. Roubiczek remarks quite
explicitly, this is not the sense in which he or the existentialists declare death
to be a mystery.

In the other sense we say of something that it is a mystery if it conflicts, or
at least if it appears to conflict, with some proposition that is neither well established nor extremely probable nor at least fervently adhered to. Let us suppose
that a man whom we thought happy and exceptionally stable suddenly suffers
a psychotic breakdown or that he commits suicide. We would be inclined to
describe his breakdown or his suicide as mysterious. By this we would mean
that they cannot be reconciled with the proposition, apparently based on very
strong evidence, that he was happy and stable. It is in this sense that believers
in an all-powerful and all-good God frequently use the word "mystery," when
they concede that evil or at least certain forms of evil found in the world are a
mystery. Now, if somebody believes in such a God and if he regards death as
something evil and as the kind of evil which an all-powerful and all-good God
might have been expected to prevent, then *his* statement that death is a mystery
makes perfectly good sense. One may think that he is irrational in not abandoning his belief in an all-powerful and all-good God in view of the facts of evil that

cannot be reconciled with such a belief, but that is another matter with which we are not here concerned. What does concern us here is that it is *not open* to those existentialists who are not believers in such a God to regard death as a mystery in the sense under discussion. And to this it should be added that, as far as one can judge from their writings, those existentialists who are believers in an all-powerful and all-good God do not mean this either. Although they may in fact be perplexed by the problem of evil, they are not discussing this problem in any of its forms and shapes when they describe death as a mystery.

I may of course be mistaken in thinking that the two senses just discussed are the only ones in which the word "mystery" can be understood if the declaration that death is a mystery is to make any sense. If I am mistaken, I hope than an existential ontologist will come forward and tell us what other sense there is in which death can be intelligibly characterized as a mystery. If, however, I am right and the above two senses are the only ones to be considered in this context, we may reach the following conclusion: It is meaningful but false to maintain that death is always a mystery in the first sense; religious believers could say something sensible by calling death a mystery in the second sense, but the existentialists are not, and many of them cannot be, using "mystery" in this sense.

We can perhaps obtain some understanding of what these writers are doing by comparing their statements about the mystery of death with what I have elsewhere called the "quasi-theological why."[30] People who do not or who no longer believe in God nevertheless quite frequently ask such apparent questions as "Why do I have to suffer so much?" or "Why is it that, although I try so hard and mean so well, happiness in the end always eludes me?" As asked by somebody who believes in a just and good God, these are genuine questions, asking how the initial theological assumption can be reconciled with the injustice and suffering experienced by the questioner. However, when an unbeliever uses such language, we no longer have anything that can be treated as a genuine question. What we have before us are *complaints* about the nature of the universe, expressions of disappointment and perhaps despair that the operations of the world are not in accordance with the individual's moral demands. Similarly, when somebody like Mr. Roubiczek speaks of death as a mystery and excludes from the start as irrelevant any information that science might provide, he may well be using the word "mystery" in a quasi-theological way. He does not seem to be raising a question but to be complaining about the "absurdity" of death: He seems to be complaining that death occurs at all and, furthermore, that there is no correspondence between the length of a human life and the moral caliber of the particular human being.

It is a pity that Mr. Roubiczek does not identify the thinkers of the Age of Reason whose "false convictions" he wishes to demolish. It is more than doubtful that philosophers like Hume or Diderot would ever have wished to dispute the assertion that death is a contingent fact or that the lack of any correspondence between the length of a human life and the moral qualities of the person in question is a feature of the world which cannot be further explained. What they would probably have added to these admissions is that one is not advancing the understanding of anything by referring to such contingent facts as "mysteries."

CONCLUSIONS

It may be helpful to bring together the main conclusions reached in this article:

1. There is a real difference between what we called the "statistical" and the "personal" perspectives. This, however, is not peculiar to the subject of death; and the feelings and thoughts which constitute the personal perspective can be made the object of scientific inquiry no less than other psychological phenomena.

2. Death is the absence of life and is no more inconceivable than other absences—e.g., the absence of sound or of clothes. Not only is death not inconceivable, but in fact people conceive of it constantly and without the slightest difficulty.

3. Although this or that death may be a mystery, it is not true that all deaths are necessarily mysterious—at any rate the only people who could justly make such a claim are believers in an all-powerful and all-good God provided they also regard death as an evil which such a God might have been expected to prevent.

4. The doctrine of the privacy of death, whether it is expressed by the statement that everybody dies isolated and alone or by the statement that in the matter of death one cannot have a representative, is either false or platitudinous, asserting no more than that everybody eventually dies.

5. The writings of the existentialists are pervaded by a confusion of death with dying. Many of their pronouncements which are absurd when interpreted as statements about death cease to be absurd when treated as statements about dying.

6. It is claimed by many existentialists that *their* question "What is death?" is distinct from scientific questions about the nature of death, from religious questions about survival, and from such metaphysical questions as "Why does death occur at all?" Their question is said to be concerned with the "ontological character" of death. However, we found that when they discuss the "ontological character" of death, the existentialists do one of two things: They either address themselves to certain psychological and practical issues in which case the use of the word "ontological" is highly misleading, or else they engage in what we called the "ontological quest" which amounts to asking "What does death feel like to the dead?" and this turned out to be a grotesque pseudo-inquiry. It would perhaps be claiming too much to say that there is no genuine ontological question here, but if there is one, this has yet to be demonstrated.

NOTES

1. I wish to thank my friends Martin Lean, Donald Levy, Margaret Miner, Mary Mothersill, and Elmer Sprague for reading an earlier version of this manuscript and for making helpful suggestions.

2. The only person known to me who habitually slept in his coffin was "Lord" Timothy Dexter, an illiterate Yankee trader who made a fortune during the Revolutionary War and who subsequently settled in Newburyport, Massachusetts. There he built a Hall of Fame containing statues of Napoleon, Benjamin Franklin, George Washington, George III, and himself as well as a mausoleum with an enormous coffin painted white and green. To enjoy the coffin while he was still alive, Dexter had a couch put into it and not infrequently he took his nap on the couch. Brahms was an eccentric man, but it was not his habit to sleep in a coffin.

3. *The World as Will and Idea*, III 382.

4. *The Experience of Death*, p. 13.

5. *The Courage to Be* (referred to as CB), p. 36.

6. *Systematic Theology*, I 188–89.

7. "The Eternal Now," in H. Feifel (ed.), *The Meaning of Death*, pp. 30–31.

8. Macquarrie's discussions of death are contained in his *An Existentialist Theology* (abbreviated as ET) and *Studies in Christian Existentialism* (abbreviated as SCE).

9. Referred to as BD.

10. There is a constant shift in Mora's discussion from talk about death to talk about the possibility of death. I am ignoring this here because experiences of the "possibility of death" have nothing to do with the original ontological aim which, in Professor Mora's words, is "to scrutinize in detail the nature of human death" (p. 170). In a later section of this article I shall provide a detailed account of the chronic shifts of existentialists from ontological issues to psychological and moral questions.

11. Adapted from Bertrand Russell's *Portraits from Memory*, p. 147.

12. *Social Principles and the Democratic State*, p. 200. Needless to say, Benn and Peters are not the first to make this distinction. It is already found in Aristotle and Descartes.

13. "Death and My Life," *The Review of Metaphysics*, 1963, p. 22.

14. *Psychologie der Weltanschauungen*, p. 261.

15. For a discussion of the peculiar arguments in support of the claim that although the death of others is conceivable and imaginable, one's own death is not, see my article "My Death," *The Encyclopedia of Philosophy*, V, 416–19.

16. The only ordinary sense known to me in which we ever say of somebody that he "experiences death" occurs in connection with people, like doctors, nurses, and coroners, who frequently observe dead bodies (and dying patients). By saying that these people "experience death" we mean that they habitually observe human beings as they are dying and their dead bodies shortly after death has taken place.

17. The word "inner" is used ambiguously in much the same way as "existential." Biology, we are told, cannot explore the "inner" nature of death; and sometimes this means the inner nature as it would appear to the deceased if he could attend to it while at other times it just refers to attitudes toward death on the part of the living.

18. *The Challenge of Existentialism*, p. 218.

19. *Op. cit.*, pp. 238–39.

20. See H. Feifel, "Death—Relevant Variable in Psychology," in R. May (ed.), *Existential Psychology*, the same author's "Death" in N. L. Farberow (ed.), *Taboo Topics*, and the contributions by C. W. Wahl, N. H. Nagy, R. Kastenbaum, H. Feifel, A. A. Hutschnecker, G. J. Aronson, and E. S. Shneidman and N. L. Farberow to H. Feifel (ed.), *The Meaning of Death*. Feifel's own contribution to this volume contains a valuable bibliography.

21. One notable exception is Jaspers who is hardly ever guilty of this confusion and who in fact makes a clear distinction between them on several occasions. Thus he writes: "Death cannot be an experience. Whoever has an experience is still alive" (*General Psychopathology*, p. 477). Again: "Every report on dying persons refers to their attitude to death, not to death itself" (p. 478).

22. The full text is as follows: "Death is not an event of life—death is not lived through" (*Tractatus Logico-Philosophicus*, 6.4311).

23. Quoted by Jaspers in his *General Psychopathology*, p. 478.

24. In one place Macquarrie remarks (SCE, p. 237) that although a "sinless" person cannot avoid death any more than one who is "fallen" or living inauthentically, their deaths are significantly different—"the end of the 'sinless' person would be somehow different from death as we ordinarily know it." Macquarrie, it should be emphasized, is not in any way referring to some differences in the afterlife; but, if so, what he says can make sense only if he means "dying" and not "death." In the absence of an afterlife, the deaths of the sinless and the sinful man are *not* "somehow" different. When they are dead, neither of them is alive and neither can take any satisfaction in anything or suffer any regrets about a previous inauthentic existence.

25. *What is Existentialism?*, p. 63.

26. Cases of this sort are found both in literature and in real life. Thus Hume, while close to death, wrote referring to the days of his final illness: "Were I to name the period of my life which I should most choose to pass over again, I might be tempted to point to this later period." Matthias Clausen, in Gerhardt Hauptmann's magnificent play, *Vor Sonnenuntergang*, is experiencing his greatest love and his deepest feelings during his last months. Many other such examples could be cited.

27. *Sein und Zeit*, p. 240.

28. "We speak of time in three ways or modes: the past, present and future. Every child is aware of them, but no wise man has ever penetrated their mystery. . . . The mystery of the future and the mystery of the past are united in the mystery of the present. . . . The mystery is that we *have* a present; and even more, that we have *our* future. Also because we anticipate in the present; and that we have *our* past; also because we remember it in the present. The present, our future and our past are *ours*" ("The Eternal Now," *op. cit.*, pp. 31–36, 37). One cannot help wondering what is troubling Tillich: Under what circumstances would time no longer be a mystery? Unless Tillich can answer this question, it is not easy to see what is meant by saying that time is a mystery.

29. Herman Feifel, the psychologist, who seems otherwise a sensible man and not given to nebulous pronouncements, cannot refrain from speaking of death as "the eternal mystery" ("Death—Relevant Variable in Psychology," in Rollo May [ed.], *Existential Psychology*, p. 61).

30. See my article "Why?" *The Encyclopedia of Philosophy*, VIII 296–302.

4

Death

Thomas Nagel
Princeton University

> The syllogism he had learnt from Kiesewetter's logic: "Caius is a man, men are mortal, therefore Caius is mortal," had always seemed to him correct as applied to Caius, but certainly not as applied to himself. . . . What did Caius know of the smell of that striped leather ball Vanya had been so fond of?
>
> TOLSTOY, *The Death of Ivan Ilyich*

IF, AS MANY PEOPLE BELIEVE, death is the unequivocal and permanent end of our existence, the question arises whether it is a bad thing to die. There is conspicuous disagreement about the matter: some people think death is dreadful; others have no objection to death *per se*, though they hope their own will be neither premature nor painful.

Those in the former category tend to think that those in the latter are blind to the obvious, while the latter suppose the former to be prey to some sort of confusion. On the one hand it can be said that life is all one has, and the loss of it is the greatest loss one can sustain. On the other hand it may be objected that death deprives this supposed loss of its subject, and that if one realizes that death is not an unimaginable condition of the persisting person, but a mere blank, one will see that it can have no value whatever, positive or negative.

Since I want to leave aside the question whether we are, or might be, immortal in some form, I shall simply use the word "death" and its cognates in this discussion to mean *permanent* death, unsupplemented by any form of conscious survival. I wish to consider whether death is in itself an evil; and how great an evil, and of what kind, it might be. This question should be of interest even to those who believe that we do not die permanently, for one's attitude toward immortality must depend in part on one's attitude toward death.

Clearly if death is an evil at all, it cannot be because of its positive features, but only because of what it deprives us of. I shall try to deal with the difficulties surrounding the natural view that death is an evil because it brings to an end all the goods that life contains.[1] An account of these goods need not occupy us

Reprinted from *Moral Problems*, ed. James Rachels (New York: Harper & Row, 1971), pp. 361–70; by permission of the author and the original publisher, the Editor of *Noûs*, 4 (1970), 73–80.

here, except to observe that some of them, like perception, desire, activity, and thought, are so general as to be constitutive of human life. They are widely regarded as formidable benefits in themselves, despite the fact that they are conditions of misery as well as of happiness, and that a sufficient quantity of more particular evils can perhaps outweigh them. That is what is meant, I think, by the allegation that it is good simply to be alive, even if one is under-going terrible experiences. The situation is roughly this: There are elements which, if added to one's experience, make life better; there are other elements which, if added to one's experience, make life worse. But what remains when these are set aside is not merely *neutral*: it is emphatically positive. Therefore life is worth living even when the bad elements of experience are plentiful, and the good ones too meager to outweigh the bad ones on their own. The additional positive weight is supplied by experience itself, rather than by any of its contents.

I shall not discuss the value that one person's life or death may have for others, or its objective value, but only the value it has for the person who is its subject. That seems to me the primary case, and the case which presents the greatest difficulties. Let me add only two observations. First, the value of life and its contents does not attach to mere organic survival: almost everyone would be indifferent (other things equal) between immediate death and immediate coma followed by death twenty years later without reawakening. And second, like most goods, this can be multiplied by time: more is better than less. The added quantities need not be temporarily continuous (though continuity has its social advantages). People are attracted to the possibility of long-term suspended animation or freezing, followed by the resumption of conscious life, because they can regard it from within simply as a *continuation* of their present life. If these techniques are ever perfected, what from outside appeared as a dormant interval of three hundred years could be experienced by the subject as nothing more than a sharp discontinuity in the character of his experiences. I do not deny, of course, that this has its own disadvantages. Family and friends may have died in the meantime; the language may have changed; the comforts of social, geographical, and cultural familarity would be lacking. Nevertheless these inconveniences would not obliterate the basic advantage of continued, though discontinuous, existence.

If we turn from what is good about life to what is bad about death, the case is completely different. Essentially, though there may be problems about their specification, what we find desirable in life are certain states, conditions, or types of activity. It is *being* alive, *doing* certain things, having certain experiences, that we consider good. But if death is an evil, it is the *loss of life*, rather than the state of being dead, or nonexistent, or unconscious, that is objectionable.[2] This asymmetry is important. If it is good to be alive, that advantage can be attributed to a person at each point of his life. It is a good of which Bach had more than Schubert, simply because he lived longer. Death, however, is not an evil of which Shakespeare has so far received a larger portion than Proust. If death is a disadvantage, it is not easy to say when a man suffers it.

There are two other indications that we do not object to death merely because it involves long periods of nonexistence. First, as has been mentioned, most of us would not regard the *temporary* suspension of life, even for substantial intervals, as in itself a misfortune. If it develops that people can be frozen without reduction of the conscious lifespan, it will be inappropriate to pity those who are temporarily out of circulation. Second, none of us existed before we were born (or conceived), but few regard that as a misfortune. I shall have more to say about this later.

The point that death is not regarded as an unfortunate *state* enables us to refute a curious but very common suggestion about the origin of the fear of death. It is often said that those who object to death have made the mistake of trying to imagine what it is like to *be* dead. It is alleged that the failure to realize that this task is logically impossible (for the banal reason that there is nothing to imagine) leads to the conviction that death is a mysterious and therefore terrifying prospective *state*. But this diagnosis is evidently false, for it is just as impossible to imagine being totally unconscious as to imagine being dead (though it is easy enough to imagine oneself, from the outside, in either of those conditions). Yet people who are averse to death are not usually averse to unconsciousness (so long as it does not entail a substantial cut in the total duration of waking life).

If we are to make sense of the view that to die is bad, it must be on the ground that life is a good and death is the corresponding deprivation or loss, bad not because of any positive features but because of the desirability of what it removes. We must now turn to the serious difficulties which this hypothesis raises, difficulties about loss and privation in general, and about death in particular.

Essentially, there are three types of problem. First, doubt may be raised whether *anything* can be bad for a man without being positively unpleasant to him: specifically, it may be doubted that there are any evils which consist merely in the deprivation or absence of possible goods, and which do not depend on someone's *minding* that deprivation. Second, there are special difficulties, in the case of death, about how the supposed misfortune is to be assigned to a subject at all. There is doubt both as to *who* its subject is, and as to *when* he undergoes it. So long as a person exists, he has not yet died, and once he has died, he no longer exists; so there seems to be no time when death, if it is a misfortune, can be ascribed to its unfortunate subject. The third type of difficulty concerns the asymmetry, mentioned above, between our attitudes to posthumous and prenatal nonexistence. How can the former be bad if the latter is not?

It should be recognized that if these are valid objections to counting death as an evil, they will apply to many other supposed evils as well. The first type of objection is expressed in general form by the common remark that what you don't know can't hurt you. It means that even if a man is betrayed by his friends, ridiculed behind his back, and despised by people who treat him politely to his face, none of it can be counted as a misfortune for him so long as he does not suffer as a result. It means that a man is not injured if his wishes are ignored by the executor of his will, or if, after death, the belief becomes current that all the literary works on which his fame rests were really written by his brother, who died in Mexico at the age of 28. It seems to me worth asking what assumptions about good and evil lead to these drastic restrictions.

All the questions have something to do with time. There certainly are goods and evils of a simple kind (including some pleasures and pains) which a person possesses at a given time simply in virtue of his condition at that time. But this is not true of all the things we regard as good or bad for a man. Often we need to know his history to tell whether something is a misfortune or not; this applies to ills like deterioration, deprivation, and damage. Sometimes his experimental *state* is relatively unimportant—as in the case of a man who wastes his life in the cheerful pursuit of a method of communicating with asparagus plants. Someone who holds that all goods and evils must be temporarily assignable states of the person may of course try to bring difficult cases into line by pointing to the pleasure or pain that more complicated goods and evils cause. Loss, betrayal, deception, and ridicule are on this view bad because people suffer when they learn of them. But it should be asked how our ideas of human value would have to be constituted to accommodate these cases directly instead. One advantage of such an account might be that it would enable us to explain *why* the discovery of these misfortunes causes suffering—in a way that makes it reasonable. For the natural view is that the discovery of betrayal makes us unhappy because it is bad to be betrayed—not that betrayal is bad because its discovery makes us unhappy.

It therefore seems to me worth exploring the position that most good and ill fortune has as its subject a person identified by his history and his possibilities, rather than merely by his categorical state of the moment—and that while this subject can be exactly located in a sequence of places and times, the same is not necessarily true of the goods and ills that befall him.[3]

These ideas can be illustrated by an example of deprivation whose severity approaches that of death. Suppose an intelligent person receives a brain injury that reduces him to the mental condition of a contented infant, and that such desires as remain to him can be satisfied by a custodian, so that he is free from care. Such a development would be widely regarded as a severe misfortune, not only for his friends and relations, or for society, but also, and primarily, for the person himself. This does not mean that a contented infant is unfortunate. The intelligent adult who has been *reduced* to this condition is the subject of the misfortune. He is the one we pity, though of course he does not mind his condition—there is some doubt, in fact, whether he can be said to exist any longer.

The view that such a man has suffered a misfortune is open to the same objections which have been raised in regard to death. He does not mind his condition. It is in fact the same condition he was in at the age of three months, except that he is bigger. If we did not pity him then, why pity him now; in any case, who is there to pity? The intelligent adult has disappeared, and for a creature like the one before us, happiness consists in a full stomach and a dry diaper.

If these objections are invalid, it must be because they rest on a mistaken assumption about the temporal relation between the subject of a misfortune and the circumstances which constitute it. If, instead of concentrating exclusively on the oversized baby before us, we consider the person he was, and the person he *could* be now, then his reduction to this state and the cancellation of his natural adult development constitute a perfectly intelligible catastrophe.

This case should convince us that it is arbitrary to restrict the goods and evils that can befall a man to nonrelational properties ascribable to him at particular times. As it stands, that restriction excludes not only such cases of gross degeneration, but also a good deal of what is important about success and failure, and other features of a life that have the character of processes. I believe that we can go further, however. There are goods and evils which are irreducibly relational; they are features of the relations between a person, with spatial and temporal boundaries of the usual sort, and circumstances which may not coincide with him either in space or in time. A man's life includes much that does not take place within the boundaries of his body and his mind, and what happens to him can include much that does not take place within the boundaries of his life. These boundaries are commonly crossed by the misfortunes of being deceived, or despised, or betrayed. (If this is correct, there is a simple account of what is wrong with breaking a deathbed promise. It is an injury to the dead man. For certain purposes it is possible to regard time as just another type of distance.) The case of mental degeneration shows us an evil that depends on a contrast between the reality and the possible alternatives. A man is the subject of good and evil as much because he has hopes which may or may not be fulfilled, or possibilities which may or may not be realized, as because of his capacity to suffer and enjoy. If death is an evil, it must be accounted for in these terms, and the impossibility of locating it within life should not trouble us.

When a man dies we are left with his corpse, and while a corpse can suffer the kind of mishap that may occur to an article of furniture, it is not a suitable object for pity. The man, however, is. He has lost his life, and if he had not died, he would have continued to live it, and to possess whatever good there is in living. If we apply to death the account suggested for the case of dementia, we shall say that although the spatial and temporal locations of the individual who suffered the loss are clear enough, the misfortune itself cannot be so easily located. One must be content just to state that his life is over and there will never be any more of it. That *fact*, rather than his past or present condition, constitutes his misfortune, if it is one. Nevertheless if there is a loss, someone must suffer it, and *he* must have existence and specific spatial and temporal location even if the loss itself does not. The fact that Beethoven had no children may have been a cause of regret to him, or a sad thing for the world, but it cannot be described as a misfortune for the children that he never had. All of us, I believe, are fortunate to have been born. But unless good and ill can be assigned to an embryo, or even to an unconnected pair of gametes, it cannot be said that not to be born is a misfortune. (That is a factor to be considered in deciding whether abortion and contraception are akin to murder.)

This approach also provides a solution to the problem of temporal asymmetry, pointed out by Lucretius. He observed that no one finds it disturbing to contemplate the eternity preceding his own birth, and he took this to show that it must be irrational to fear death, since death is simply the mirror image of the prior abyss. That is not true, however, and the difference between the two explains why it is reasonable to regard them differently. It is true that both the time before a man's birth and the time after his death are times when he does not exist. But the time after his death is time of which his death deprives him. It is time in which, had he not died then, he would be alive. Therefore any death entails the loss of *some* life that its victim would have led had he not died at that or any earlier point. We know perfectly well what it would be for him to have had it instead of losing it, and there is no difficulty in identifying the loser.

But we cannot say that the time prior to a man's birth is time in which he would have lived had he been born not then but earlier. For aside from the brief margin permitted by premature labor, he *could* not have been born earlier: anyone born substantially earlier than he was would have been someone else. Therefore the time prior to his birth is not time in which his subsequent birth prevents him from living. His birth, when it occurs, does not entail the loss to him of any life whatever.

The direction of time is crucial in assigning possibilities to people or other individuals. Distinct possible lives of a single person can diverge from a common beginning, but they cannot converge to a common conclusion from diverse beginnings. (The latter would represent not a set of different possible lives of one individual, but a set of distinct possible individuals, whose lives have identical conclusions.) Given an identifiable individual, countless possibilities for his continued existence are imaginable, and we can clearly conceive of what it would be for him to go on existing indefinitely. However inevitable it is that this will not come about, its possibility is still that of the continuation of a good for him, if life is the good we take it to be.[4]

We are left, therefore, with the question whether the nonrealization of this possibility is in every case a misfortune, or whether it depends on what can naturally be hoped for. This seems to me the most serious difficulty with the view that death is always an evil. Even if we can dispose of the objections against admitting misfortune that is not experienced, or cannot be assigned to a definite time in the person's life, we still have to set some limits on *how* possible a possibility must be for its nonrealization to be a misfortune (or good fortune, should the possibility be a bad one). The death of Keats at 24 is generally regarded as tragic; that of Tolstoy at 82 is not. Although they will both be dead forever, Keats's death deprived him of many years of life which were allowed to Tolstoy; so in a clear sense Keats's loss was greater (though not in the sense standardly employed in mathematical comparison between infinite quantities). However, this does not prove that Tolstoy's loss was insignificant. Perhaps we record an objection only to evils which are gratuitously added to the inevitable; the fact that it is worse to die at 24 than at 82 does not imply that it is not a terrible thing to die at 82, or even at 806. The question is whether we can regard as a misfortune any limitation, like mortality, that is normal to the species. Blindness or near-blindness is not a misfortune for a mole, nor would it be for a man, if that were the natural condition of the human race.

The trouble is that life familiarizes us with the goods of which death deprives us. We are already able to appreciate them, as a mole is not able to appreciate vision. If we put aside doubts about their status as goods and grant that their quantity is in part a function of their duration, the question remains whether death, no matter when it occurs, can be said to deprive its victim of what is in the relevant sense a possible continuation of life.

The situation is an ambiguous one. Observed from without, human beings obviously have a natural lifespan and cannot live much longer than a hundred years. A man's sense of his own experience, on the other hand, does not embody this idea of a natural limit. His existence defines for him an essentially open-ended possible future, containing the usual mixture of goods and evils that he has found so tolerable in the past. Having been gratuitously introduced to the world by a collection of natural, historical, and social accidents, he finds himself the subject of a *life*, with an indeterminate and not essentially limited future. Viewed in this way, death, no matter how inevitable, is an abrupt cancellation of indefinitely extensive possible goods. Normality seems to have nothing to do with it, for the fact that we will all inevitably die in a few score years cannot by itself imply that it would not be good to live longer. Suppose that we were all inevitably going to die in *agony*—physical agony lasting six months. Would inevitability make *that* prospect any less unpleasant? And why should it be different for a deprivation? If the normal lifespan were a thousand years, death at 80 would be a tragedy. As things are, it may just be a more widespread tragedy. If there is no limit to the amount of life that it would be good to have, then it may be that a bad end is in store for us all.

NOTES

1. As we shall see, this does not mean that it brings to an end all the goods that a man can possess.
2. It is sometimes suggested that what we really mind is the process of *dying*. But I should not really object to dying if it were not followed by death.
3. It is certainly not true in general of the things that can be said of him. For example, Abraham Lincoln was taller than Louis XIV. But when?
4. I confess to being troubled by the above argument, on the ground that it is too sophisticated to explain the simple difference between our attitudes to prenatal and posthumous nonexistence. For this reason I suspect that something essential is omitted from the account of the badness of death by an analysis which treats it as a deprivation of possibilities. My suspicion is supported by the following suggestion of Robert Nozick. We could imagine discovering that people developed from individual spores that had existed indefinitely far in advance of their birth. In this fantasy, birth never occurs naturally more than 100 years before the permanent end of the spore's existence. But then we discover a way to trigger the premature hatching of these spores, and people are born who have thousands of years of active life before them. Given such a situation, it would be possible to imagine *oneself* having come into existence thousands of years previously. If we put aside the question whether this would really be the same person, even given the identity of the spore, then the consequence appears to be that a person's birth at a given time *could* deprive him of many earlier years of possible life. Now while it would be cause for regret that one had been deprived of all those possible years of life by being born too late, the feeling would differ from that which many people have about death. I conclude that something about the future prospect of permanent nothingness is not captured by the analysis in terms of denied possibilities. If so, then Lucretius' argument still awaits an answer.

5

Existentialism and the Fear of Dying

Michael A. Slote
Trinity College, Dublin

In this paper I shall present a fairly systematic "existentialist" view of human anxiety about death and human responses to that anxiety, based on the work of Pascal, Kierkegaard, Heidegger, and Sartre. My main purpose is constructive, rather than exegetical. What seems to me most distinctive and important about the work of these existentialist authors is their approach to the fear of dying—or at least the relevance of what they say to that subject, for sometimes, when they deal with other topics, what they say can (I shall attempt to show) be used to illuminate the nature of human responses to the fear of death. But I think that much of what these authors say about the fear of dying is inchoate, confusing, or incomplete, and requires supplementation, clarification, and systematization of the kind I shall be attempting to provide here.[1]

I

Perhaps the central locus of discussion, by an Existentialist, of human attitudes toward and responses to death is the section of Kierkegaard's *Concluding Unscientific Postscript* called "The Task of Becoming Subjective." According to Kierkegaard, becoming subjective is "the most difficult of all tasks in fact, precisely because every human being has a strong natural bent and passion to become something more and different."[2] But what is it to be subjective or to be objective, and why is the former so difficult and the latter so tempting? Part of Kierkegaard's explanation involves him in a contrast between the subjective and objective acceptance of Christianity. But Kierkegaard also applies the subjective/objective distinction to attitudes toward life and death generally. And what unites Kierkegaard in the "Becoming Subjective" section of the *Postscript* with such non-religious Existentialists as Heidegger and Sartre is the fact that he has something to say about human attitudes toward life and death that presupposes no particular form of religiosity and that has not, I think, been said by

Reprinted by permission from *American Philosophical Quarterly*, 12 (1975), 17–28.

anyone outside the existentialist tradition. And it is this aspect of Kierkegaard's work that I shall be examining.

According to Kierkegaard, to have an objective attitude toward one's life is to have the kind of attitude toward one's life encouraged by an Hegelian view of the world. On such a view, one is part of a larger "world-historical" process of the self-realization of Reason or Spirit, and one's life takes on significance if one plays a role, however minor, in that world-historical process. One does not have to be an Hegelian to think in this kind of way. One can be thinking in a similar way if, as a scientist or philosopher, e.g., one devotes oneself to one's field in the belief or hope that one's life gains significance through one's contribution to something "bigger."

Kierkegaard says that people with such an attitude have an objective attitude toward their lives; and he wants each of us to dare to become subjective and renounce this "loftily pretentious and yet delusive intercourse" with the world-historical.[3] Those who live objectively are, according to Kierkegaard, under a delusion or illusion, and if so, then surely he has a real argument in favor of being subjective. For Kierkegaard, at least part of the illusion is, I think, the belief that by living objectively, one's dividend, what (good) one gets from life, is greater.[4] In the first place, even if a certain world-historical process of development is a great good, it is a good that is divided up among those participating in that development into many parts, none of which, presumably, is large in relation to the whole, and so perhaps the good to be derived from participating in that development will be less than the good to be gained by living subjectively. But Kierkegaard then seems to question whether indeed there is *any* good to be gained from living for some world-historical process, since one who does so may not be around when it comes to fruition. But it is not clear that the good of such a process of development must all come at the end of that development, so I think Kierkegaard has still not given us any very strong reason for believing that one who lives objectively is under some kind of illusion that his life is better.

However, in the *Postscript* Kierkegaard attempts to tie up his discussion of living objectively, i.e., of living for the world-historical, with certain illusory "objective" attitudes toward death. One who lives world-historically will sometimes say: "What does it matter whether I die or not; the work is what is important, and others will be able to carry it forward." But this is to think of one's death as nothing special, as just one death among others, as a "something in general." And Kierkegaard seems to believe that one who thinks this way is under an illusion, the illusion that his own death has no more significance *for him* than the death of (random) others, or, to put it slightly differently, that he *should be* no more concerned about his own death than about that of others. However, various Stoic philosophers would, I think, tend to argue that it is Kierkegaard's belief that one should be especially concerned about one's own death that is an illusion, an illusion born of irrational self-centeredness. So it is not obvious that Kierkegaard is correct about the illusory nature of objective living, or about the advisability of living subjectively. In any case, the attitude of people who live for the world-historical toward their own deaths is of some interest: they are, at least at some level, not as afraid of dying as they might be or as some people are. And I think there are interesting implications to be drawn from this fact that have some of the spirit of what Kierkegaard says in the *Postscript*.

II

Those who live world-historically for some enterprise like science or philosophy seem not to be very anxious about dying. And I would like to suggest, what Kierkegaard never actually says, that we may be able to *explain* the tendency to live for the world-historical as resulting from our characteristically human fear of dying. For no one wants to live in fear, and since one who lives objectively, for the world-historical, does not feel the fear of dying that some of us do, there is reason and motive for people who have experienced anxiety or fear at the prospect of dying to (try to) adopt an objective existence, including an objective attitude toward their own deaths. But what are the psychological mechanisms by which living world-historically assuages someone's fear of death? Here I can only suggest, not establish, an answer, and what I shall say is intended as exploratory and somewhat speculative.

Consider the claim that people who live for the world-historical sometimes make that they will *be or become immortal through their works*, or that they will *live on through their works*. Why do people ever say such things; if what they are saying is just metaphorical, why do they use *that* metaphor and why do they seem to take the metaphor seriously?[5] It seems to me that such claims of immortality or living on are not (if there is no afterlife along traditional religious lines) literally true. It is not even literally true to say that part of one lives on in one's works, for books, e.g., are not literally parts of those who write them. Moreover, even if there is a traditional religious type of afterlife, one presumably does not live on *through one's works*.[6]

When we say that we shall live on or be immortal through our writings, e.g., I think we sometimes make that claim in a serious spirit. We are not just joking or deliberately speaking loosely. But when someone points out that what we are saying is not literally true, I think that most of us are willing to admit that what we have said is not literally true. How is this possible? It is my conjecture that someone who says he will live on, at least unconsciously believes that what he has said is (literally) true. Part of the evidence for the *unconsciousness* of the belief, if it exists, is the fact that when someone brings it to our attention that it cannot literally be true, we are ready, at least on a conscious level, to admit that this is so. What (further) supports the idea that the belief exists on some unconscious level is the fact that we at first express it in a serious vein and are not fully conscious that what we are saying is not literally true. We have to be reminded that what we have said is not literally true, and in this respect are not like someone who says that a certain person has a heart of gold. In the latter case, one is quite clear in one's mind *ab initio* that what one is saying is not the literal truth. One is, I think, often less clear, and in some sense more confused, about the literal falsehood of what one says when one says that one will live on in one's works. And this unclarity or confusion, as compared with the "heart of gold" case, is some evidence that one who speaks of living on in his works unconsciously believes that he will do so, inasmuch as the existence of such an unconscious belief is one very obvious possible explanation of that unclarity or confusion.[7] But what lends the greatest support to the view that such an unconscious belief exists in those who live world-historically and say they will live on in their works is the generally accepted fact that human beings naturally tend to fear dying. It is to be expected that men will try to avoid that fear and repress it, if possible. One way of doing this would be to convince oneself that one was immortal through one's works, so that death was not really or fully the end of one's existence. It would be hard to convince oneself of such a claim on a conscious level, just because of its literal falseness. But such belief in one's immortality could perhaps survive on an unconscious level where it would be less subject to rational scrutiny, and perhaps be capable of counteracting one's fear of death. The unconscious delusion of one's immortality (or living on) through one's works can, if we adopt Freudian terminology, be thought of as an unconscious defense mechanism of the ego that protects us from conscious fear about death by repressing that fear and counterbalancing it in such a way that it for the most part remains unconscious.[8] And this would explain why people who live for the world-historical are not consciously afraid of dying much of the time, and, in effect, why people so often live for the world-historical.[9]

Let me carry my speculation further. At one point in the *Postscript* (p. 274), Kierkegaard says that to live for the world-historical is to forget that one exists. This curious claim is, I think, more plausible or forceful than it may seem at first. Consider a person who lives objectively and unconsciously believes that he will live on through his books. Such a belief is not just false, but necessarily false, since it involves both the idea that one is alive and the idea that the existence of certain works like books is sufficient for one's continued existence; and nothing whose continued existence is entailed by the existence of such works can be *alive*. Moreover, the belief that one's books' existence is sufficient for one's continued existence seems to involve the idea that one has roughly the same kind of being as a book or series of books. So I think there is something to the idea that one who lives objectively somehow thinks of himself as not existing as a person, and as not being alive. But he presumably does not think this on a conscious level, for much the same reason that one does not on a conscious level think that one is going to live on through one's works. On the other hand, the *unconscious* delusion that one is not alive (or is of the same kind as a series of books) would seem capable of counteracting and allaying anxiety about dying just as easily as the unconscious belief that one is immortal through one's works does so. If one is going to live on in books, one is not going to lose one's life and there is nothing to fear from death, so that fears about dying may be prevented from becoming conscious by being allayed on an unconscious level. Similarly, if one is not really alive, or is of the same "stuff" as books, then one also has nothing to fear from dying; and one's ceasing to be, if it occurs, will be no more tragic than the ceasing to be of a book.[10] So if one believes this kind of thing on an unconscious level, it is again not hard to see how one's fear of death may be allayed and kept unconscious.[11] Thus it would seem that people so often live for the world-historical because such living involves unconscious beliefs (delusions) that help them, more or less successfully, to avoid conscious fears about dying.[12]

According to Kierkegaard, however, not only does one who lives for the world-historical forget that he exists, but such a person at least to some extent ceases to exist as a person, ceases to live.[13] For if we use our lives as a means to the existence of certain works and/or to be mentioned in some paragraph or footnote of some authoritative history of our field of endeavor, then we are valuing our lives no more than we value the existence of certain works or our being mentioned in paragraphs or footnotes. And when we unconsciously think of ourselves as immortal through our works, we are in effect thinking that what we lose when we die cannot be that important or valuable. And to do and think in this way is to put a low value on one's living. But if one places a low value on actual living, one will not take full advantage of one's life (living) and that is a bit like already being dead, or not alive. So I think there really is something to Kierkegaard's claim that to live world-historically is to some extent to cease to exist as a person, to cease to be alive. The claim constitutes, not literal truth, but a forceful and penetrating metaphor.

It is well known that the fear of dying is a prime source of much of human religiosity. Belief in an afterlife of the traditional religious sort is one way that men can assuage their anxiety about dying. What is perhaps not so well known is how the fear of dying can give rise to (and explain) certain attitudes and activities of people who are not in any ordinary way religious, and perhaps also certain attitudes and activities of religious people that are not generally associated with religion. What I have tried to show here is that there are in Kierkegaard's *Concluding Unscientific Postscript* insights about our attitudes toward life and death that can be used to help us understand how certain non-religious aspects of human life result from the fear of dying.

In doing so, I have assumed that people who live objectively and say that they are not terribly anxious about dying are nonetheless afraid of dying at some level. And this may seem high-handed. However, I am inclined to think that in general people living world-historically (who do not believe in some traditional religious type of life after death) continue to be subject to a certain welling-up of death anxiety that can overtake them in the midst of their daily lives.[14] Despite my own tendencies toward the world-historical, I have often experienced this sudden welling-up of death anxiety, and I think that the fact that this phenomenon is widespread among non-religious world-historical people (and indeed among people in general) is evidence that fear of dying never entirely ceases to exist in (such) people, but always continues to exist at least on an unconscious plane. For it is easier to imagine such a sudden welling-up of fear as the "return of the repressed" and as indicating a certain inefficiency of one's repressive mechanisms than to think of it as resulting from the sudden regeneration of death fears within one. What could plausibly explain such a sudden rebirth of death anxiety *in medias res*? Moreover, the earlier-mentioned fact that world-historical people (people who live for the world-historical) sometimes seriously say that they will be immortal through their works, without being clear in their own minds that this is just a metaphor, is, as I have already argued, evidence that such people unconsciously believe that they are immortal through their works (or that they are not alive). But why should they have such unconscious beliefs, except as part of a mechanism to relieve and keep repressed their fear of dying? So even such seemingly innocuous locutions as that we shall be immortal through our works indicate the existence of death fears even on the part of people who live for the world-historical and claim not to be afraid of dying. Let us now turn to Pascal's *Pensées* to see how the fear of dying affects other aspects of human life.

III

There is a famous long passage in the *Pensées* where Pascal talks about diversion, its role in human life, and its sources. Men "cannot stay quietly in their own chamber" alone and meditating, for any length of time.[15] We need or think we need diversion and activity and cannot be happy without diverting ourselves from ourselves because of the "natural poverty of our feeble and mortal condition, so miserable that nothing can comfort us when we think of it closely."[16] Now, Pascal does not go on to decry the vanity of human diversion and claim that life would be less vain if we thought more about ourselves and our mortality. He is not arguing for the vanity of worldly human concerns in the time-worn manner of Ecclesiastes. He has an entirely new perspective on where the vanity of human life really lies. The vanity of our lives consists, for Pascal, in the fact that when we divert ourselves (from ourselves), we typically deceive ourselves about our motives for behaving as we do.[17] For example, a man who gambles often convinces himself that obtaining the money he is gambling for would make him happy (at least for a while). He focuses on the getting of the money and forgets that his real or main purpose is to divert himself. Thus if he were offered the money on condition that he not gamble, he would be (at least temporarily) unhappy, because he seeks diversion. On the other hand, if he were offered the diversion, say, of playing cards without being able to gamble for money, he would also be unhappy. For it is not just diversion he seeks; he must also have some imagined goal which he focuses on in such a way that he does not see that diversion is his real or main goal. Pascal does not, however, explain why men cannot simply seek diversion without fooling themselves about their goal. But an explanation can be given along lines that Pascal might have approved. Imagine that we divert ourselves in order not to have to think of ourselves, and also realize that this is so. Shall we not *ipso facto* be thrust back into that very awareness of self which we sought to avoid through diversion? To realize that one wants not to think of oneself because it is unpleasant to dwell on one's feeble and mortal condition is *ipso facto* to be thinking of oneself and opening oneself up to the very unpleasantness one wishes to avoid. And if those who want to avoid thinking of themselves must remain ignorant of that fact if they are to succeed in not thinking of themselves, how better to accomplish this than by focusing on something outside themselves and thinking of it as their goal?

This explanation of human striving and activity applies not just to gambling, but, as Pascal says, to the waging of campaigns in love or in war and to many other human activities. Many of us fool ourselves about our motives much of the time when engaged in such activities. One objection to this analysis, however, would be that to explain so much human activity in terms of the fear of, or desire not to be, thinking of oneself is to offer a gratuitous explanation of our behavior. Why not just say that as animals we have an instinctive desire for certain activities which typically involve a lack of self-consciousness and which are called "diversions"? But the instinct theory of the origin of our diversions has, as it stands, no obvious way of explaining the self-deception Pascal points out. If we simply have an instinct for certain activities, activities that in fact tend to divert us from ourselves, why do some of us much of the time and many of us some of the time deceive ourselves into thinking that it is winning a certain victory or honor or woman that is our main goal, when it is the diverting activity leading up to that winning that is our main goal? On the theory that we do not like thinking about ourselves, however, the fact of self-deception can be explained along the above lines; so the assumption of a desire not to think of oneself is not gratuitous.

Furthermore, there is good independent evidence that people do not like to think about themselves. There is, for example, an experience that I have sometimes had, and that I think the reader will probably also have had; in the middle of thinking about something else I have all of a sudden thought to myself: "All this is being done by *me* and all these people are talking about *me*." I hope this description will suffice to convey the kind of experience I have in mind. What is interesting, but also perplexing and distressing to me, are the following facts. When I have this experience of myself, there seems to me to be something precious about it; and I think: "This is the moment when I am most alive; it is very good to have this experience." (There is, after all, a long tradition in which self-consciousness is a great, or the greatest, good.) I usually also think that though I am at that moment too busy to prolong the self-consciousness, I shall definitely set aside a good deal of time in the future to take full advantage of this kind of experience of self-awareness. But somehow that never happens. And when I am again momentarily self-conscious in the way I have been describing, I again put off a long bout of such self-consciousness to the future, despite my typical accompanying conviction that the experience of being self-conscious is a wonderful one that I really should and shall take greater advantage of. All this needs explaining, and the obvious explanation, I think, is that I really do not like the experience of self-consciousness, as Pascal suggests.

But why, in the end, should we not want to think about ourselves? Pascal suggests that the reason is that thinking about ourselves makes us think of our feeble and mortal condition. He also says about man: "to be happy, he would have to make himself immortal; but, not being able to do so, it has occurred to him to prevent himself from thinking of death."[18] Presumably, then, Pascal thinks that there is a connection between thinking about oneself and thinking unpleasant thoughts about one's death; and this seems to me to be quite plausible. For at least while we are absorbed in things outside us, we do not think of ourselves, or thus, it would seem, of our death; whereas if and when one does think about oneself, one might very easily think about one's death. It would seem, then, that the explanation of our diverting ourselves from (thinking about) ourselves is that this at least to some degree enables us to avoid thinking anxiously about our mortality. And so we have now clarified two general areas or aspects of human life in terms of the fear of dying. Let us turn next to Heidegger.

IV

Men's attitudes toward death are a major theme in Heidegger's *Being and Time*.[19] For Heidegger, in everyday life we exist in a mode that Heidegger calls the "they" (*das Man*). Heidegger characterizes this mode of existence as inauthentic, at least in part because in it, one is forgetful of the fact that death is one's ownmost possibility and cannot be outstripped. By this he means something close to the Kierkegaardian idea that one's own death has greater significance for one than does the death of others. Heidegger says that such a mode of existence is tempting because it tranquilizes one's anxiety in the face of death.[20] So it would seem that Heidegger can be thought of as providing a psychological explanation of certain aspects of human life, which he calls collectively "(being lost in) the 'they'," and thus that Heidegger is doing something similar to what we have seen Kierkegaard doing in the *Postscript* and Pascal doing in the *Pensées*.[21]

According to Heidegger, one important aspect of our average everyday lostness in the "they" is its typical modes of discourse, chatter, and idle talk, and the busy-body curiosity that characterizes such discourse. Heidegger points out that when people are idly and curiously talking about whether John and Mary will get divorced, the actual event, the divorce, if it occurs, actually disappoints the idle talkers; for then they are no longer able to conjecture about and be in on the thing in advance. The curiosity of everyday idle talk is concerned with the very latest thing(s), with novelty; and what interests in anticipation may be "old hat" or out of date when it occurs. Horse races and even pennant races in baseball seem to me to be good examples of this tendency. We have the keenest interest in who will win, but it is hard to maintain much interest in such races once we know their outcome; there is even a certain disappointment or let-down sometimes when the results of such things finally become known.[22] Heidegger's discussion here seems to have a good deal in common with what Pascal says about diversion, for one way of diverting ourselves from ourselves would be to be constantly curious about the latest things. But why not be interested in things that are not new and be diverted by them? The answer here—though it is not one that Heidegger actually gives—seems to me to lie precisely in the desire not to think of oneself that Pascal lays such emphasis on. What is newer is less well known, and the more there is to learn about something, the less likely one is to get bored with it or to cease being absorbed in it, and so be thrust back into thoughts about oneself. Furthermore, our earlier discussion of Pascal can help us to explain why we are sometimes let down when a certain event we have (only) conjectured about occurs, even though in advance we thought that "nothing would make us happier" than to know exactly when and how the event would occur. For if our goal is distraction from ourselves through conjecturing, we cannot very well admit this to ourselves without (running a grave risk of) defeating that goal; so we somehow fool ourselves into thinking that what we want is to know for sure about the character of the event we are conjecturing about, as a means to our real goal of diverting ourselves through conjecturing about something or someone outside ourselves; and when we cannot conjecture any more, then of course we are let down.

There may be a further reason why the desire for novelty is so pervasive in human life—though what I shall now be saying is perhaps more speculative than anything else I have to say here. As Heidegger says (p. 217), when one has the desire for novelty, it is as if one's motive were to have known (seen) rather than to know (see); for as soon as one has known (seen) something, one no longer wants to know (see) it. And there seems to be a certain vanity in such a way of dealing with things. Now consider what is implicitly involved in wanting, say, to have seen Rome, but not to see (keep seeing) Rome. There are tours whose advertising has the feeling of: "Come to Europe with us and you will see 8—count 'em, 8—countries in 8 days"; and such advertising and such tours appeal to many people who want to (say that they) have been, e.g., in Rome, but who do not much want to *be* in Rome. When one makes such a tour, one often even wishes the tour were already over so that one (could say that one) had already been to Rome in Italy (and to the other seven countries). The actual touring, with its "inconveniences," is often not desired or enjoyed. But to want the eight days and the trip to be already over with is in a certain sense to want a part of one's life over with in exchange for a being able to say one has been. This desire is in many cases unconscious. Sometimes some of us say, with an air of seriousness, that we wish that a certain trip or period of time were already over. But when confronted with the implications of what we have said, we almost inevitably recoil from what we have said and say that of course we do not *really* want a certain part of our life to be already over, perhaps adding that we were only speaking loosely or jokingly in making our original remark. In that case our desire to have a certain part of our life over with exists, if at all, only on an unconscious level. Evidence that there *is* such an unconscious desire comes from the fact of our original seriousness in saying that we wished a certain trip over with and from the fact that we are by no means clear in our own minds that we do not mean our statement literally, the way a hungry man is, for example, when he says that he could eat a mountain of flapjacks. I think this initial unclarity is best explained by (and thus evidence for) the existence of an unconscious desire to have a certain part of our life over with.[23] And perhaps for the very purpose of keeping this desire out of consciousness, we convince ourselves at least temporarily that we really want to *be* in Rome, or *feel* its living antiquity, etc. But then, after we have spent the tour rushing about, impatient with tarrying in one place too long, we *may*, upon reflection, recognize that we wanted the having seen more than the seeing of the places, like Rome, that we visited.

The logical extension of the wish to have a certain portion of one's life already over with is the wish to have one's whole life over with, and I would like now very tentatively to argue that at some deep level many of us have this latter wish, and so want not to be alive. Part of the reason for thinking so consists in the way we deceive ourselves about the extent of our desires to have portions of our lives over with. We sometimes think: if only it were a week from now so that I knew whether p, everything would be all right. But then when the time comes at which everything is supposed to be going to be all right, we soon find another reason for thinking things are not all right and for wishing other parts of our lives over with. I think that the initially implausible assumption that some people unconsciously wish their whole lives over with, wish not to be alive, provides the best explanation of this whole perplexing phenomenon. For if one has the unconscious desire to have one's whole life over with, there will be mechanisms in force to prevent it from becoming conscious. If one were conscious that one wanted *many different parts* of one's life over with *seriatim*, one would be dangerously close to being conscious that one wanted one's *whole life* over with. So it might reasonably be expected that someone with the unconscious wish or desire that his whole life be over with would be (made to be) unaware of the extent to which he wanted particular portions of his life over with before they were lived. Thus I think there is reason to believe that people who deceive themselves in this way unconsciously wish not to be alive.[24]

It will perhaps seem more plausible to hold that such a wish exists if I can show how it is explained by our fear of dying. One way of allaying fear of the loss of something is a kind of denial that one might call the technique of "sour grapes in advance." We can convince ourselves that the thing we may lose is not worth having or that we do not really want it. (This recalls the studies psychologists have done on the resolution of "cognitive dissonance.") An unconscious desire not to be alive might, then, help us to counterbalance or to keep repressed our fear of dying. The existence of such a desire can thus be supported in various ways and fits well into the kind of theory about our attitudes toward death so far proposed. But there is no time to speculate further in its favor.[25]

We argued earlier that if someone thinks of himself as not alive, he will not take full advantage of his life and it will be as if he is not (fully) alive. The same can be said for someone who wants not to be alive. We saw earlier the force of the metaphor that some of us are dead. Since it is as if some of us are dead because of what we have, unconsciously, done to ourselves, there is also force to the metaphor that some of us have killed ourselves. To live for the having seen and known of things is, metaphorically speaking, not to be alive, and to have killed oneself.[26] And one can also say this about those who live for the world-historical. I have a tendency to put myself entirely into my work and to live for something "bigger," philosophy. But sometimes I recoil from such an existence and from myself, and I feel that I have really just thrown my life away, have been personally emptied, through world-historical living. At such a time the metaphor of killing oneself seems particularly compelling.

We have thus far characterized those who live world-historically as assuaging the fear of dying via the *beliefs* that they are immortal and/or that they are not alive. But I think that such people also sometimes unconsciously wish not to be alive in the manner of those who divert themselves with novelties.[27] (Of course, those who live world-historically can be diverting themselves as well, e.g., with busy research or advocacy of causes.) For one thing, as we have already seen, people who live world-historically unconsciously think that they are not alive. And they want to think this, at least unconsciously, as a means to less fear or anxiety. But presumably if one wants to think one is not alive, that is because one wants not to be alive. This kind of inference from what one wants to think to what one wants is surely *usually* in order. Secondly, there is evidence that world-historical people tend to want parts of their lives over with in much the same way that seekers after novelty do. Someone writing a book that is intended to advance some field in the long run will often wish that the next six months of his life were already over so that he could see the book in finished form and have the writing of it over with. If only this were possible, everything would start being all right, he thinks, and he would be ready really to live his life again. Such a person, however, will, in many cases, be fooling himself about the extent to which he wants to "put off living" by missing parts of his life. As soon as there is another book to write, or academic appointment in the offing, he may very well once again want some part of his life already over with. Saying that such a man really wants to live, but only wants to avoid certain tense or burdensome parts of his life, does not really allow us to understand why he so often on such slight pretexts (is writing a book really so unpleasant and tense, considering the rest of the things that can be going on in one's life at the same time?) thinks up reasons for wanting to postpone living by omitting some part of his life. Just as a man who is always *just about* to take a vacation and really live (it up) for a change, but who never does, can be plausibly suspected of preferring his work to a vacation or to "life" despite his protestations to the contrary, the perplexing behavior of one who lives world-historically and keeps wanting parts of his life over with while remaining unconscious or unaware of the extent to which this is so can, I think, only be made sense of in terms of an unconscious desire not to be alive.[28] Such a desire is strange and perplexing, perhaps, but no more so than the behavior it is supposed to explain.

Heidegger says many more interesting things about the "they." Idle talk and curiosity seem to be interested in anything and everything, though in fact, unbeknown to us, limits have been set on what we are to be interested in. For example, one is not, in the midst of curious talk, supposed to bring up the tragedy of life or the inevitability of death. Anyone who brings up such things is told not to be "morbid." Heidegger suggests that idle talk and curiosity function as a way of keeping us from thinking of our own death. For one thing—if I may borrow again from our discussion of Pascal to supplement what Heidegger is saying here—the illusion of interest in everything is an excellent means for blocking off thought about dying and its consequent anxiety, since if we believed, while we were engaged in idle talk, that we were not supposed to be deeply talking about death, we might very easily be thrust back into the very anxiety that idle talk was supposed to avoid. Moreover, the very self-assurance and harshness with which someone who brings up death in the midst of idle talk is branded as morbid tends to encourage and rationalize our avoidance of the topic of death.

Another device by which everyday living in the "they" keeps us from fears of death is by branding such fears as cowardly. Heidegger, however, thinks that it is more cowardly *not* to face death anxiously. Now there certainly seems to be room for disagreement on this issue. Some of the Stoics seem to have thought that it was irrational, rather than courageous, to be anxious about one's own death because death was a matter of indifference. And this latter philosophy of death may be correct; but it might be interesting at this point to make some educated guesses about the psychology of those who have advocated the "Stoic" view of death. For to my mind there is something strange and suspicious about (holding) the view that one's own death is not an evil. I have already discussed the fact that despite our best repressive mechanisms, the fear of dying sometimes comes upon (some of) us suddenly in the midst of life. When others tell us that it is morbid or cowardly to worry about death, we are given an excuse or motive not to worry about death, and such advice may well help us to get rid of the conscious fear of death at least temporarily. The philosophical view that it is irrational to worry about death because death is a matter of indifference may have a similar function to play in the psychic lives of those who propound it. Philosophers pride themselves on being rational, and by branding the fear of dying as "irrational" they may give themselves a motive for ceasing consciously to worry about death and actually help themselves to get rid of the conscious fear of dying. I am inclined to think, then, that the view that it is irrational, and not courageous, to fear death, because death is no evil, may well be motivated, in many of those who propound it, by the fear of death itself, a fear that they are consequently able to repress, but not to get rid of. If so, then those who are helped to repress their fear of dying by holding a "Stoic" view of death are under an illusion when they claim as rational philosophers to be totally indifferent to death. But it might be better to live under such an illusion without consciously worrying about death than to know that one was not indifferent to death because one *was* consciously afraid of death. In the light of these complexities, it would seem hard to decide between Heidegger, on the one hand, and the Stoics and the "they," on the other, as to whether it is courageous to be (consciously) anxious in the face of dying.

Heidegger suggests yet further ways in which existence in the "they" tranquilizes our anxiety about dying. In the "they" there is an emphasis on keeping busy doing things, as the means to, or sign of, a full and good life. When someone suggests that one might do better to be more reflective and less busy, the response of the "they" is that by keeping busy, one is living "concretely" and avoiding self-defeating and morbid self-consciousness; this encourages the person who hears this to keep busy and not reflect on himself, and thus functions as a means to keeping us from the conscious fear of dying. (Consider, in particular, how the old, who are especially subject to fears of death, are told to keep busy and active.)

Heidegger points out that someone lost in the "they" will *admit* that death is certain and that one (everyone) dies in the end. According to Heidegger, in speaking of what happens to "everyone" or to "one" eventually, we "depersonalize" and "intellectualize" death. In thus depersonalizing death, it is as if the person were saying that death has nothing to do with *him right now*, and this enables him to talk about death without focusing on himself or having that particularly intimate experience of self-awareness described earlier or, thus, having fearful thoughts about death. Also talk about the inevitability or certainty of death, etc., may be part of a process of "isolation of affect" in which one intellectualizes (about) a certain phenomenon to keep away from (consciousness of) certain related feelings.[29] Heidegger also points out that social scientists often seek to create "typologies" and systematic theories about humanity in the belief that they are thereby penetrating to the deepest level on which one can understand humanity and oneself, but that such intellectual "hustle and bustle" may entirely ignore the question of the significance for men of their own death and death anxiety; such intellectualization, he suggests, may serve to keep one from anxious thoughts about death by convincing one that one has reflected as deeply as it is possible to do. And the very stuffiness and detachment with which some sociologists, psychologists, etc., sometimes declare their desire to plumb the depths of the human spirit is, I would think, some evidence that they have a deeper need to avoid the *feeling* of their own mortality.

An important further point that is due to Kierkegaard rather than to Heidegger is that one can even overintellectualize one's response to a work, like that of Kierkegaard or Heidegger, which attempts to reveal in an "existential" manner the importance of our attitudes toward dying.[30] Spinoza has said that "passive" feelings like fear tend to dissipate when we scrutinize them, and this may well mean that it is difficult at one and the same time both intellectually to focus on and learn the significance of death anxiety and to *feel* that significance. And so there seems to be a real danger that someone who reads the writings of Existentialists will only intellectually understand and agree with what they say, and thus fail to derive all the benefit one could or should get from reading them. Of course, Spinoza's dictum also implies that it is difficult to think intellectually about death anxiety while feeling such anxiety. And one reason why I and others may be so interested in thinking and writing about death anxiety is that such thinking and writing may, in effect, involve an isolation of affect about death.[31]

In discussing Heidegger, we have brought in Kierkegaard and Pascal to help "deepen" his analysis of how death anxiety affects large portions of human life. I would like now to make use of certain ideas of Sartre's (in ways that Sartre undoubtedly would not approve) to point out yet another aspect of human life that can be explained in terms of the fear of dying. (However, I shall not discuss Sartre's own views on death, which in fact run counter to much of what we have to say on that subject.)

V

Being and Nothingness is perhaps most famous for its discussion of what Sartre calls "bad faith," which consists in being or putting oneself under the illusion that one is not free and cannot do other than what one in fact does.[32] For Sartre, one is in bad faith when one says: I have to get up and get to work; I can't stay in bed, I have a family to feed. Bad faith is involved because one does not *have* to get up and go to work.

Some people will immediately object to what Sartre is saying on the grounds that if determinism about human behavior is true and a certain person in fact will not stay in bed, then he is under no illusion when he says that he cannot stay in bed. Since, despite anything Sartre says, it is by no means obvious to me that such determinism is not (approximately) true or that human beings possess free will, I would like now to (re)interpret Sartre's "bad faith" in such a way as to avoid assuming either human indeterminism or human free will.

Someone who says he has to go to work in the morning will sometimes say: "I have no choice in the matter." But I think that he does have a choice, even if a determined and unfree one, and that if he cannot stay at home, that is in part *because* of his (perhaps determined and unfree) choice. Moreover, I think that someone who is reminded of these facts will typically be willing to take back his original claim to have no choice in some matter, will grant that he had been speaking loosely or metaphorically. But it seems to me that such a person will typically not have been clear in his own mind about all this at the time when he originally claimed to have "no choice." And for reasons we have already gone into at length, I think this indicates that the person making such a claim unconsciously believes that he has no choice in a certain matter, even though he really does have a (possibly determined and unfree) choice in that matter and can be brought to conscious awareness of that fact. Such a person is under an illusion about the part he (and his choosing or deciding) plays in certain events or situations, and it is *this kind* of illusion that *I* shall call "bad faith."

Bad faith in this new sense is clearly related to bad faith in Sartre's sense. And, assuming that the new kind of bad faith does exist, it would be good if we could give some sort of explanation of it. Sartre's explanation of bad faith in the old sense will not be of much help to us here, since it assumes not only that human behavior is undetermined but also (implausibly enough) that human beings basically realize (believe) that this is so. My suggestion is that we explain bad faith in my new sense in much the same way that we have been explaining various other phenomena—namely, in terms of the fear of dying. (Indeed, Heidegger hints at this idea in *Being and Time*, p. 239.) I think that we can explain bad faith in terms of the fear of dying, if we suppose that the illusion of bad faith helps to repress such fear and if we borrow one further idea of Sartre's. According to Sartre, someone in bad faith (in his sense) who denies his own freedom is, in effect, thinking of himself as a thing or object, since things and objects are unfree, etc. I would like tentatively to claim that people who unconsciously believe that they have no choice, say, about getting up in the morning are, in effect, thinking of themselves as things or objects,[33] since things and objects really do lack choice. If we make this assumption, we can explain how bad faith in my sense enables one to relieve or repress death fears. For objects cannot die, and so unconsciously thinking of oneself as an object is unconsciously to think that one has nothing to fear from death.[34] (And if one passes away but is a mere object, then that is no more tragic than the passing away of a rock.)

Bad faith in the new sense seems to have much in common with living for the world-historical. In the latter case, one thinks of oneself as not alive; in the former, one thinks of oneself as a mere thing; and one might wonder whether there is much difference here either in the content of these unconscious beliefs or in the way they act on the fear of dying. Furthermore, just as one who lives for the world-historical can aptly be described metaphorically as not alive[35] and as having killed himself, one who lives in bad faith is, metaphorically speaking, a mere thing and not alive, and since he has (unconsciously) done this to himself, he has, metaphorically speaking, turned himself into a thing. And given the fact that the only way a person really can turn himself into a thing is by turning himself into a corpse, it is perhaps metaphorically appropriate to describe someone who is (constantly) in bad faith as having killed himself. Sartre holds that someone who thinks of himself as a mere thing wants (among other things) to *be* a mere thing. And I think we could argue that people in bad faith in my sense sometimes unconsciously want to be things in something like the way we earlier argued that people living for the world-historical want not to be alive. Furthermore, the unconscious desire to be an object would seem capable of countering the fear of dying in much the same way that the unconscious desire not to be alive does so, and so there is this further similarity between living in bad faith and living for the world-historical.

VI

If what has been said here is on the right track, then it would seem that Pascal, Kierkegaard, Heidegger, and Sartre all describe phenomena that pervade our lives and that are best explained in terms of their efficacy in relieving or repressing the fear of dying. Our explanation has made use of a Freudian type of view of repression and of the unconscious. This will certainly make our arguments here suspect in the eyes of some people. I have in effect been "practicing" a kind of "existential psychoanalysis," and though this term is one that was originally used by Sartre in *Being and Nothingness* to describe some of his own procedures, it may well apply more accurately to the kinds of things I have been doing here. For Sartre does not posit an unconscious, but I have followed Freud in doing just that.[36] In any case, I hope that this paper may bring to light an area, or areas, where Existentialism and Psychoanalysis can be mutually enlightening.

Of course, in addition to using psychoanalytic ideas, I have also frequently appealed to my own experience and intuitions, to how things strike me and to the "feel" of certain ideas. Though some things, I trust, will strike readers the way they have struck me, this will no doubt not always be the case; and when it is not, my appeals to how things feel to me, etc., are bound to seem like special pleading. Perhaps I *am* guilty of this, but I do not know how to avoid it in a paper like this where personal experience may be more relevant to seeing certain points than abstract arguments. And perhaps some of the ideas or intuitions I have relied on will seem more palatable to the reader if he "lives with them" and takes the time to see whether they do not, perhaps, make sense in and of his experience of himself and the world. For it is in something like this way that many of the ideas and intuitions of this paper have become acceptable to me.

In this paper, I have pieced together various ideas from Pascal, Heidegger,

Sartre, and Kierkegaard, as well as extrapolated beyond what any of them has said, to provide a fairly general picture of how the fear of dying accounts for many aspects of human life. The explanatory "theory" we have presented links together phenomena that the various Existentialists discussed separately, and as such should, given any standard account of scientific method, be more plausible than the accounts of the various Existentialists taken separately. So I hope I have helped to support and fill out the basically existentialist notion that the quality of a (non-religious) man's life greatly depends on his attitude toward his own death. And even if this idea is not particularly prevalent in Sartre, we can use things Sartre says to substantiate it.

Some people will complain that I have only been doing psychology, not philosophy. But it may not be important whether this accusation is true. And I also think that when psychology is general enough and speaks directly to the human condition, it can also count as philosophy. If, as we have argued, the main motive for world-historical (or busily self-distractive) participation in certain enterprises comes from (desire to avoid) the fear of dying, then a good many intellectuals, scientists, and others may be less pure in motive, less selfless, than they are often thought to be.[37] And this fact, if it is one, is surely very relevant to our understanding of the human condition, and so counts in favor of calling what we have been doing philosophy.[38]

NOTES

1. I shall by no means, however, be discussing all the things these authors say on the topic of death.

2. *Concluding Unscientific Postscript* (Princeton, 1960), p. 116.

3. *Ibid.*, p. 133.

4. *Ibid.*, pp. 130ff.

5. Horace in the *Odes* (3, xxx) seems to be an example of someone who takes the metaphor seriously.

6. I think that people who talk of gaining immortality through their children also say what is literally false, and their psychology is, I think, significantly similar to the psychology of those who talk of living on through their books.

7. Kierkegaard hints at the idea that world-historical people believe they live on through their works when he implies (*Postscript*, p. 140) that such people need to be reminded that "in the world-historical process the dead are not recalled to life."

8. For examples of reasoning similar to that just used that appear in the psychoanalytic literature, see, e.g., S. Freud's "Splitting of the Ego in the Defensive Process" (in his *Collected Papers* [London, 1956], 372–75) and Otto Fenichel's *The Psychoanalytic Theory of Neurosis* (New York, 1945), pp. 479–84. For another *philosophical* use of an argument like mine above, see M. Lazerowitz' *The Structure of Metaphysics* (London, 1955), pp. 69ff. and *Studies in Metaphilosophy* (London, 1964), pp. 225ff., 251. I am indebted to Lazerowitz' account for some of the structure of my own analysis.

9. J. P. Sartre (in *Being and Nothingness* [New York, 1956], p. 543) says that "to be dead is to be a prey for the living." And Thomas Nagel (in "Death," Ch. 4) has tentatively claimed that a man can be harmed or unfortunate as a result of things that happen after his death, e.g., if his reputation suffers posthumously. I wonder

whether these views are not, perhaps, indicative of some sort of unconscious belief that people live on in their works.

10. The unconscious belief that one is going to live on and the unconscious belief that one is not alive seem to counteract the unconscious belief or fear that one is going to die in contradictory ways, the former with the "message" that we are not really going to lose what we have, the latter with the "message" that we really have nothing to lose. But we have already seen that the unconscious belief that one lives on in books is itself contradictory or necessarily false, so it should not, perhaps, be so surprising that the unconscious uses mutually contradictory means to repress death-fears. On this see Freud's *The Interpretation of Dreams*, ch. 2. For similar use of the (metaphorical?) notion of unconscious "messages," see Otto Fenichel's *Outline of Clinical Psychoanalysis* (New York, 1934), esp. pp. 13, 30, 33, 52, 250, 260, 275f.

11. In "A Lecture on Ethics," *The Philosophical Review*, 74 (1965), 8ff. Ludwig Wittgenstein speaks of the feeling people sometimes have of being safe whatever happens. He claims that such a feeling or belief is nonsensical; but perhaps this occasional feeling is better thought of as the expression of a meaningful, but necessarily or clearly false, unconscious belief that we are safe whatever happens, a belief that counteracts the fear of dying and that is roughly equivalent to the unconscious belief that one is not alive. For one is absolutely safe (from death) if and only if one is not alive.

12. I do not want to claim that everyone dedicated to some "cause," to something "bigger" than himself, is living world-historically. Such dedication may result from altruism or "conviction" and may not involve the world-historical psychology if it is not accompanied by delusions of immortality through one's works or actions, or the view that one's own death is unimportant.

13. *Ibid.*, pp. 118, 175, 271, 273.

14. See Heidegger's *Being and Time* (New York, 1962), pp. 233f.

15. (New York, 1958), p. 39.

16. *Ibid.*

17. *Ibid.*, p. 40.

18. *Ibid.*, p. 49.

19. Our discussion here will be based on sections 27, 35–42, and 47–53 of *Being and Time*.

20. Heidegger uses "fear" only with respect to things in the world. For death "anxiety" is reserved; but this is not necessarily dictated by ordinary usage.

21. Of course, some philosophers will say that by treating Heidegger as an explanatory psychologist, I am treating him as if he were operating on the "ontic" level, whereas Heidegger thinks of himself as operating on an "ontological" level deeper than the "ontic" level on which science, psychology, and most pre-Heideggerian philosophy typically function. However, despite many efforts, I myself have never been able to make satisfactory sense of the ontic/ontological distinction. If the distinction is viable, Heidegger may have a good deal more to say than I shall be giving him credit for; but we can at least credit him with insights on a level with those of a Pascal or a Kierkegaard.

22. Of course, some people constantly dwell on past (sporting) events (and their part in them), but I do not think this is incompatible with the general tendency I am describing.

23. Compare here our earlier argument for the existence, in world-historical people, of an unconscious belief in their immortality through their works.

24. Our earlier argument that we do not like thinking about ourselves can be

strengthened along the lines of our present argument for the existence of an unconscious wish not to be alive. Similar self-deception occurs in the two cases.

25. I have posited the wish not to be alive as an unconscious defense mechanism of the ego that responds to (prior) fear of dying. Freud, on the other hand, late in his career posited a basic (id-based) death instinct to account for various phenomena. See *Beyond the Pleasure Principle* (New York, 1950). The two sorts of views are incompatible, and so the explanation given just now in the text may be mistaken. However, there is some reason to prefer it. Our ego-theory of the death wish fits in better with our earlier-discussed theories about the ego's unconscious handling of the fear of dying. Moreover, other things being equal, it is better to treat a phenomenon as a derived phenomenon, within a theory, than to treat it as basic, within that theory. In addition, there is the sheer unintuitiveness of supposing that we have death wishes *ab initio*, rather than acquiring such (irrational) wishes in the *neurotic* process of repression. Finally, it is by no means clear that a basic death instinct is needed to account for clinical phenomena. On this see Otto Fenichel's "A Critique of the Death Instinct" in *The Collected Papers of Otto Fenichel*, first series (New York, 1953), pp. 363–72.

26. I think we have some inkling of this metaphorical killing when we speak of "killing time" at moments when we want to have something over with, want a certain (perhaps boring) part of our lives over with. Use of that phrase may be a disguised conscious expression of the unconscious desire not to be alive.

27. Kierkegaard's claim in the *Postscript* (p. 137) that one whose eye is on world-historical things has perhaps found "a highly significant way of . . . killing time" seems to indicate some awareness on his part that world-historical people want not to be alive and have, metaphorically speaking, killed themselves. Whose time, after all, does one kill except one's own? And one's time is one's life. Incidentally, it is natural to say that world-historical people "bury themselves in their work," and this metaphor seems to suggest the very same things that our use of the metaphor of killing time does.

28. Cf. Emerson's remark in his *Journals* (April 13, 1834) that "we are always getting ready to live, but never living."

29. Cf. O. Fenichel's "Outline of Clinical Psychoanalysis," *op. cit.*, pp. 190f., for ideas about "isolation of affect" that are related to some of the things we have said here and earlier in the paper.

30. *Postscript*, pp. 166f.

31. Heidegger also points out that the force of living in the "they" is such as to make people lost in the "they" scoff at his analysis of such lostness. Once one is aware of one's tendencies to cover up certain anxieties, it may be harder to use the mechanisms one has previously used in doing so; so one who wishes at some level to keep covering up his anxiety has a motive to reject Heidegger's analysis and, indeed, our analysis here.

32. See *Being and Nothingness*, Pt. 1.

33. I hope I shall be forgiven for ignoring plants.

34. This recalls the Simon and Garfunkel song that goes: "I am a rock, I am an island; and a rock feels no pain, and an island never cries." The idea that we sometimes want to think of ourselves as things to avoid the pain of life or of facing death is not new or silly. Moreover, even if people in bad faith only think of themselves, unconsciously, as *similar to* mere things, that thought may itself be capable of relieving the fear of death.

35. Kierkegaard says that such a person is also a "walking stick," which suggests the similarity of such a person to someone in bad faith who exists as a mere object.

36. Sartre rejects the unconscious for reasons that seem to me to be interesting, but ultimately unacceptable.

37. This is not to say that such people should stop doing science, etc., with their present motives. They may be happier than they are otherwise likely to be, and may be contributing to the intellectual or practical good of other people. Also see note 12, above.

38. I am indebted to G. Boolos, E. Erwin, B. Jacobs, D. Levin, S. Ogilvy, and M. Wilson for helpful comments on earlier drafts of this paper.

6

Suicide and Rationality

JOHN DONNELLY

University of San Diego

> There is but one truly serious philosophical problem, and that is
> suicide. Judging whether life is or is not worth living amounts to
> answering the fundamental question of philosophy.
>
> ALBERT CAMUS, *The Myth of Sisyphus*

A MAJOR CONCERN of contemporary epistemologists (of whom Roderick Chisholm is an exemplar) has been the problem of the criterion.[1] The puzzle is as follows: there seem to be two basic epistemological questions, namely, (A) What do we know? and (B) How are we to decide whether we know?, or What are the criteria of knowledge? Traditionally, three philosophical stances can be assumed toward these queries. The *Skeptic* argues that the answers to either (A) or (B) are mutually reciprocal, so that, given this interdependency, we can have no knowledge whatsoever. The *Methodist*, traditionally an empiricist, opts for (B) as the means finally to solve (A). But Chisholm (I believe correctly) argues for the *Particularist* position, maintaining that we first answer (A) and then establish an answer to (B).

Needless to say, Chisholm has provided valuable spadework on this interesting epistemological turf with his development of various systems of epistemic logic. Quite obviously I shall not be concerned with the merits of any such system in this paper; rather, my purpose is to borrow some proffered epistemic locutions from Chisholm's book *The Problem of the Criterion* and apply them to a topic of considerable importance in the practical sphere, namely, suicide. Working with the primitive concept of "epistemic preferability" (which Chisholm maintains embodies an *objective* relation independent of the personal predilections of the subject), Chisholm offers among others the following epistemic rules: (*a*) P is *evident* to S at t provided believing P at t is epistemically preferable for S to withholding P (e.g., On a sunny day, the proposition "it is

Parts of this paper are taken from my article "Suicide: Some Epistemological Considerations" in *Analysis and Metaphysics*, ed. Keith Lehrer (Dordrecht: Reidel, 1975), pp. 283–98. I wish to acknowledge a debt to C. Wade Savage's unpublished paper "Death and the Rationality of Suicide." Much of what I say in section IV of my paper parallels his own view on the topic. However, I suspect Savage would not wish to carry out the thesis into the extended areas of sections V–VII.

sunny outside" is evident to a normal observer); (*b*) P is *presumable* for S at t provided believing P is epistemically preferable for S at t than S's believing not-P (e.g., that "I will not be poisoned by my food at tonight's dinner" is a presumable proposition); and (*c*) P is *unreasonable* for S at t provided withholding P is preferable for S at t than believing P (e.g., the proposition "All politicians are inherently honest" is [sadly enough] unreasonable).

My intention in this paper is to apply some of the Particularist's insights (i.e., those core beliefs of common sense) to a matter of considerable practical importance—suicide. Despite Camus' deification of suicide[2] as a (the?) legitimate philosophical (and thereby presumably rational) option, a particularist framework would suggest that suicide *not* be a legitimate philosophical alternative, and accordingly judge such acts irrational and/or arational on an epistemological level, and possibly immoral and/or amoral on an ethical level.[3] In short, if the proposition P in question is "Suicide is not philosophically justified," then my thesis will be that such a proposition is at worst presumable and at best evident, but in all cases its negation is unreasonable.

The systematization of epistemic concepts usually proceeds in a context of formulating a viable theory of empirical evidence. Accordingly, my claim in the above paragraph should be qualified inasmuch as my paper will attempt to rule out any personal justification of suicide on *logical* as well as on empirical grounds. In short, in the language of the problem of the criterion, my thesis is that we know (as an article of commonsensism) that suicide is not rational, and my aim is to uncover the philosophical reasons why we make such a knowledge claim.

I fully realize that my claim that suicide is not rational is bound to strike many philosophers as obviously false and naïve. I would hope that no reader or commentator characterizes my position as "the Catholic view" or "the Conservative view," although the latter caricature does not really disturb me, albeit my conservative outlook is more realistic than optimistic. If there is an official, communally received and accepted Catholic view on any subject of moral importance today (and I am not sure it is at all obvious that there is), then doubtless with regard to suicide it is the view of Thomas Aquinas. However, I believe the usually astute Aquinas offered a woefully inadequate defense of the unreasonableness of suicide. Aquinas basically suggested that suicide could not be justified philosophically because it was (1) contrary to nature; (2) harmful to the community; and (3) a violation of that love of self which leads one in Locke's words not "to quit his station wilfully."

Since my thesis that suicide is not rational is not tied to any historical figure or school, I shall not comment at length on the Thomistic stance. Suffice it to say that point (1) is questionable in light of Freudian views on the unconscious and clearly self-defeating (for St. Thomas if true) for it would rule out celibacy as well; point (2) is obviously false in most instances whether one be a consequentialist or not; and the last point simply begs the question.

I

One of Wittgenstein's many contributions to philosophy was to conceive of philosophy as having a decidedly therapeutic function. Despite some unfortunate cases of suicide in his own family and some personal attempts on Wittgenstein's own part deliberately to take his life, it strikes me that a worthwhile way to demonstrate philosophical therapy is ironically enough to analyze the issue of suicide and dispel its alleged justification. We are told by many philosophers today, especially the existentialists,[4] that suicide (what Kant termed "the intention to destroy oneself") is a noble activity, well worth the serious consideration of those so inclined. Indeed, such a panegyric is not confined to continental writers. David Hume, for example, spoke of suicide as "laudable":

> That suicide may often be consistent with interest and with our duty to ourselves, no one can question who allows that age, sickness, or misfortune may render life a burden, and make it worse even than annihilation. . . . both prudence and courage should engage us to rid ourselves at once of existence when it becomes a burden.[5]

It seems fair to say, then, that many modern writers have suggested the possibility, indeed even the viability, of a philosophical justification of suicide. To be sure, the practice of suicide permeates widely diverse categories such as nations, races, and age-groups, as witnessed by its high incidence in Sweden, Hungary, West Germany, among American Indians, and college students. Sociological data which would suggest that suicide is not widely practiced can be deceptive. Humanistic considerations for the dead and the deceased's family, understandably enough, often cause medical examiners to list genuine suicides as accidental deaths. This practice of coroner's reports has reached peaks of morbid, comical absurdity as in the case of an English coroner's report that described the "accidental" death of a man who just happened to shoot himself while cleaning the muzzle of his gun with that most efficient feline cleansing device—his tongue![6] Euphemisms also abound when it comes to suicides, as attested by the use of such expressions as "removing oneself from life," "saying 'nay' to one's existence," "passing away by one's own hand," "authentically terminating one's existence," etc. However, no matter how widespread suicide is as an empirical practice, I nonetheless wish to challenge its alleged philosophical legitimacy, for if I am not mistaken, acts of suicide are irrational at worst, arational at best. That is, propositions of the form "Suicide is the rational action for a person to perform" are, I want to say, in the language of the problem of the criterion neither evident nor presumable. In short, careful heed to the logic of suicide will show, I believe, how both language (especially in section IV) and logic have gone on holiday for those who attempt to justify such an act. I would warn the reader that in sections VI and VII of this paper, I am far less sure of such a bald claim that suicide is not rational. Philosophical caution advises me to base my case on sections IV and V, but I will venture to disregard this admonition and press on with my thesis in sections VI and VII.

It should be underscored that my inquiry is not concerned *per se* with the (ethical) issue of whether suicide is right or wrong, but rather whether it is rational (justifiable) or not. However, if the moral ascriptions of "right" and "wrong" to various actions are in order, then it seems to follow that the agents who perform such moral acts are responsible for such acts, and consequently responsible for the supervenient moral evaluation involved. But, inasmuch as responsible acts are also rational acts, then it would seem that, if I am successful in making my thesis hold, I may also be obliquely arguing a case for the (moral) wrongness of suicide. That is, given this somewhat Aristotelian conceptual framework, if an act of some significance is irrational (unreasonable), then it is also irresponsible, and, assuming it has some bearing on ethics, it is also an immoral act. If this point is correct, then, at least from a deontological standpoint, acts of suicide are morally blameworthy, although, to be sure, there are gradations of moral blame. Quite obviously, from a teleological standpoint, such acts *could* still be judged as morally praiseworthy. If my thesis can only support the weaker claim—that acts of suicide are arational—then, again, such actions are not responsible, and accordingly not assignable moral credit (at least from a deontological standpoint). Wittgenstein, in a tantalizing cryptic saying, put it well:

> If suicide is allowed then everything is allowed. If anything is not allowed then suicide is not allowed. This throws a light on the nature of ethics, for suicide is, so to speak, the elementary sin.[7]

It is here necessary to add the important qualification to the above that, even if suicide can be established as non-rational, and indeed immoral as well, it does not necessarily follow that the suicidist is blameworthy, because his objectively wrong action *ex hypothesi* may be *excusable*—for example, he may be adjudged temporarily insane as specified in the M'Naghten and Durham rules.

What I have just said, nevertheless, needs to be taken with a fair amount of caution. The term "responsible" is clearly equivocal. Under a *normative* interpretation of the term, "responsible" is more properly an attribute of the action itself and not of the agent who performs the action. To say of an action X that it is a *responsible* action is to ascribe right-making characteristics to it. To say of an act Y that it is an irresponsible act is to ascribe wrong-making characteristics to Y.

But the term "responsible" also has a *metaphysical* interpretation. Here "responsible" is a predicate of the agent, and not of the act itself. We speak of A as responsible (accountable) for X or Y in circumstances C if A freely chose to do X or Y, when A could have chosen to do otherwise in C.

In light of this equivocation, we might note the following: (*a*) An action could be a responsible one (in the normative sense) even if the agent was not responsible (in the metaphysical sense) for bringing it about. Also, (*b*) an agent could be responsible (in the metaphysical sense) even if the act brought about by his choice was wrong (and hence not responsible in the normative sense). Accordingly, the locution "responsible acts are also rational acts" is usually true in the normative sense of the term "responsible" (on the assumption that the performance of a good act is ideally the rational thing to do), but quite often false in the strictly metaphysical sense of "responsible," for an agent voluntarily and intentionally could perform a deed which is not rational.

Of course, just because in a normative sense of "responsible," "responsible

acts are rational" may be true, it hardly follows that all rational acts are responsible (i.e., an agent acting quite rationally could bring about an evil action) in
a normative sense. But to say "responsible acts are rational" does seem to
imply that all non-rational acts are non-responsible, in a normative sense.

One lesson to learn from contemporary work in epistemic logic is that even
our basic epistemic terms are not purely descriptive, but instead embody normative features as well.

II

Contemporary work in philosophy of mind is fraught with debate between
materialists and non-materialists. Some philosophers argue that the experience
of psychological states is nothing but a series of cerebral events, while others
attempt to effect a program of logical behaviorism to eradicate deceptive psychological statements that purport to describe an elusive, ghost-like realm of
inner, private processes. Of course, on the other side of the ledger, the dualists
strive to show the falsity of such reductive materialistic programs, and thereby
in turn develop a defense of man as a psycho-physical being. My aim in this
paper is not to discuss the relative merits or debits of such opposing conceptual
frameworks. Indeed, I believe that my claim that suicide is not a rational activity can be sustained on the assumption of the truth of either a materialistic
or non-materialistic schema. If I am correct, then philosophers are surely mistaken in arguing that what is called a reason for living is also an excellent reason
for dying.

Before defending my thesis, however, it will be necessary to clarify some
fundamental terms. Is *death* a univocal concept? Is *suicide* a univocal concept?
Indeed, what exactly is meant by the terms "suicide" and "death"?

Suppose we consider the term "death." I believe that the concept of death is
clearly equivocal as outlined in (D^1) and (D^2).

(D^1) Here the term "death" refers to the strict materialistic view to the effect
that death marks the irreversible cessation of the life processes. Given this
conception of death, death is the end of life, the total annihilation of all life
processes. Such a conception rules out any form of post-mortem existence. I
shall henceforth refer to this sense as death$_1$.

(D^2) Here the term "death" refers to the non-materialistic view to the effect
that death is but an event in life and not the extinction of life. Much as the
patient who receives sodium pentathol undergoes only a partial extinction
of the life processes, so too on such a conception of a person's death, despite
bodily cessation, a mental remnant will survive in some form of post-mortem
existence. I shall refer to such a sense of death as death$_2$. I fully realize the
many difficulties attendant upon such a concept as death$_2$. Some philosophers
argue that the concept of death$_2$ is meaningless. Others raise interesting logico-
metaphysical puzzles concerning the description of such a post-mortem world,
as well as questions concerning the personal identity of *soma pneumatikon*,
the issue of resuscitation or reconstitution on a theistic resurrection-world

model, doubts as to whether parapsychological data cannot be interpreted purely naturalistically, and not merely as confirmatory evidence for some transcendental realm, etc.

Moreover, if *death* is an open-textured concept, so too is the concept of *suicide*. I propose that we distinguish two senses of the term "suicide" which, logically distinct, are often interwoven in the at-times-complex decision procedure to commit an act of suicide.

(S^1) Here the term "suicide" describes an action which is egotistical in nature, so that the act of a person's taking his own life is performed primarily in order to satisfy certain basic needs, goals, desires, and purposes of a selfish sort. Any act of deliberately taking one's own life with such a motivational component I shall label an act of suicide$_1$.

(S^2) Here the term "suicide" describes an action which is altruistic in scope, so that the act of a person's taking his own life is performed primarily in order to bring about some achievement of the basic needs, goals, desires, and purposes of others. Any act of deliberately taking one's own life with such a motivational component I shall label an act of suicide$_2$.

It might be contended that the concept of suicide$_2$ under either death$_1$ or death$_2$ is a muddle, that the concept of altruistic suicide is incoherent. Suicide$_2$, this objection maintains, is heroic action, however rational or not, and hence not properly labeled suicide. I believe my remarks in sections VI and VII will somewhat dispel such an objection, although I confess to having considerable reservations with regard to my denial of such an objection. However, much as there is a fine line between the colors blue and green, yet blue is not green, so too the genuine difficulty of demarcation with regard to suicide$_2$ and heroic action does not necessarily obliterate the distinction. I would underscore, though, the factual claim that most suicides offer impressive psychiatric evidence of being properly classified as suicide$_1$, and I feel fairly confident about my arguments against the rationality of egocentric suicide under either death$_1$ or death$_2$ in sections IV and V.

Lastly, I shall use the term "suicide" to refer to a specific action whenever the following conditions are satisfied: S performs an act of suicide X provided S directly and deliberately wills, either through his own causal efficacy or that of others, that his life be totally or partially preternaturally extinguished for reasons of an egoistic and/or altruistic sort *except* in cases where: (1) S can only preserve his life by performing a morally dishonorable act where such an act is adjudged dishonorable by anyone who is willing to take the moral point of view, and/or cases in which (2) S is in a state of terminal illness such that without extraordinary (artificial) medical apparatus S would die in a rather brief period of time.

Quite obviously the moral point of view is a somewhat fuzzy concept. However, I use this expression to refer to anyone who reaches an evaluative judgment by being impartial, conceptually clear, factually correct, willing to universalize, etc.

I am assuming that the mode of committing suicide is inapposite, it making no major (or minor) philosophical difference to my argument whether the suicidist takes his life by such self-imposed methods as hanging, slitting his wrists, taking an overdose of pills, knifing, drowning, etc. I believe that a similar irrelevance, although less obviously, applies to a description of the circumstances surrounding the act of suicide. That is, from an epistemological standpoint the context surrounding the act is topic-neutral—we have a case of suicide whenever such a definition is satisfied—albeit, from a moral standpoint, there are surely important gradations of moral blame depending on the description of the circumstances surrounding the act. That is, we tend to be lenient in our ethical judgment concerning, say, an oppressed ghetto mother who takes her own life, while we do not ordinarily hesitate to admonish the conduct of a Hollywood starlet who frivolously commits suicide. It might also be noted that such a definition of suicide has the effect of stressing the importance of a person's inner life, which sociologists (such as Durkheim) tend to neglect often in classifying all instances of "death resulting directly or indirectly from a positive or negative act of the victim himself which he knows will produce this result"[8] as suicidal. The absurdity of such a sociological account is easily demonstrated by noting that if the sociological hypothesis were true, then, from the truism that any intelligent person recognizes he is closer to death each passing second of his life (the existentialists speak of persons as "beings-toward-death"), it would be appropriate to conclude (with the manifestly absurd statement) that we are all suicidists (in some tenseless sense)!

Some philosophers, such as Jacques Choron, have suggested that euthanatic suicide as a proposed solution to escape a prolonged but impending death has a different logic than $suicide_1$ or $suicide_2$ as proposed solutions to escape a miserable life. "Considering suicide the wrong cure for the ills of living does not necessarily exclude the possibility that it may be the right cure for the ills of dying."[9]

To be sure, I do not think that *all* cases of suicide are cases of euthanasia, nor do I think that all cases of euthanasia are arational at best, irrational at worst. I do however think that such epistemic appraisals hold of $suicides_1$ and $suicides_2$ (as I will attempt to demonstrate), where these cases properly involve actions and not just events—that is, where we are dealing with the concept of *Bilanzselbstmord*, "balance-sheet suicide."

The German word for suicide (*Selbstmord*, "self-murder") raises many interesting questions concerning the semantics of suicide which I will have to pass over in this paper. However, let me at least raise the basic linguistic puzzle connected with the use of the term *Selbstmord*. Why is it most people are reluctant to call suicide "self-murder" (the German notwithstanding)? In a case of intentional and voluntary but indirect suicide, that is, a case in which A asks B to kill A and B does kill A, B is labeled a murderer and A is not. Note that if A asked B to kill C and B did kill C, then both A and B would be labeled murderers. Since it is not part of my paper to label suicidists as murderers, I suggest that the discrepancy just noted is due to the fact that murder, unlike homicide, involves the willful violation of a person's right to life, and, since the suicidist consents to have his right to life so abrogated, it is not murder.

Choron also suggests that there are few balance-sheet suicides, whereas there are many "rational suicides," where this implies "not only that there is no psychiatric disorder but also that the reasoning of the suicidal person is in no way impaired and that his motives would seem justifiable, or at least 'understandable' by the majority of his contemporaries in the same culture or social group."[10] Unfortunately, Choron's distinction (between balance-sheet suicides and rational suicides) has the infelicitous consequence of equating the term "justifiable" not so much with the concept of rationality, as with the concept of understandability. But surely, I may *understand* how a person was driven to suicide, but nonetheless find that person's action unjustified!

Moreover, where a proposed case of euthanasia satisfies, as many do, my definition of suicide outlined in this section (cf. "living wills"), then Choron's distinction (between euthanatic suicide and suicide proper) marks no *de facto* difference. That is, given the existentialist's sense of the person as a being-toward-death, then surely our contingency is apparent, so that even suicide may be described as a response to the ills of dying as well as to the ills of living. It may be true that the right to die is as inalienable as the right to life, but the exercise of it (in committing suicide) is, I believe, not as rational.

III

Given the preceding terminological equipment, any thesis which wishes to maintain that suicide is irrational (or at best non-rational) must analyze the attempted lines of justification for the following four possible types of suicide.

Case 1: $Suicide_1$ under $death_1$
Case 2: $Suicide_1$ under $death_2$
Case 3: $Suicide_2$ under $death_1$
Case 4: $Suicide_2$ under $death_2$

Again, before proceeding to an analysis of each of these cases, it needs to be emphasized that my definition of suicide in section II can recognize *mixed* cases of suicide in which the motivational component is simply not just primarily egotistic or altruistic. Nonetheless, what holds for each of these cases also holds, I believe, for any combination of these cases.

The delicate epistemological issue as to how one ascertains the inner episodes of a person's state of consciousness (in the case of a suicidist, his prior intendings, motives, deliberations, etc.) I shall here pass over. There is no need for such a psychological autopsy, given my forthcoming arguments in sections IV–VII. Also, in claiming that acts of suicide are arational at best, irrational at worst, I do not mean to suggest that all suicidists are deranged. Surely, one can voluntarily and intentionally bring about a particular action that is unjustifiable, without being neurotic or psychotic.

IV

Cases of $suicide_1$ under $death_1$ typically involve a person whose fortunes are at an all-time low. Every attempt to rectify his plight ends in further humiliation, frustration, and eventual depression, and each new crisis suggests no way out except suicide. On the brink of such an act, some philosophers would argue that the agent in question could justify his contemplated action by arguing that "I would be better off dead than alive" or something similar, such as "I will take my life and finally attain some consolation in death." But this type of reply is senseless inasmuch as it presupposes that a corpse can be the subject of various *psychological* predicates. To be sure, it makes sense to attribute various physiological properties to corpses—we can speak of "the remains" as weighing two hundred pounds, being located on a metal slab in a mortuary drawer, emitting an offensive odor, etc.—but it is nonsensical to say "this cadaver is at peace with the world," etc. Dostoevsky had it wrong, then, when he claimed that without a theistic concept of death$_2$ being operative, suicide was an "inevitable necessity for any man who, by his mental development, has even slightly lifted himself above the level of cattle." Accordingly, the defense of suicide$_1$ under death$_1$ discussed so far is simply a muddle. I might quickly add that not all existentialists shared Dostoevsky's view. Sartre, for instance, wrote that "suicide is an absurdity which causes my life to be submerged in the absurd."[11]

Undaunted, our would-be suicide victim might try to avoid the above counter by arguing "It would be better if I were dead," and thus avoid the charge of attributing a psychological state to a cadaver. But the question now arises: "Better for whom?" And the answer is obvious: "Me, of course!" But again, albeit somewhat more deviously, this leaves us with the indefensible position that death, a non-state, is a state, having certain assignable psychological characteristics. There can, of course, be third-person ascriptions of psychological states to a person who has died in this strict sense of death$_1$, viz., "he is better (or worse) off dead than alive," etc. But the latter statement interpreted either as a distinctly moral judgment (i.e., "His action of committing suicide was the right thing to do") or as an epistemic claim (i.e., "His action of committing suicide was the rational thing to do") is, I believe, false. However, interpreted to read "He is happier dead than alive," it is not just false, but meaningless.

To avoid the blatant logical howlers contained in the above attempted justifications of suicide$_1$ under death$_1$, we might test the explanatory possibilities of a more sophisticated description of a suicide attempt. Consider a prisoner of war who is not only incarcerated but about to be subjected to a brutal torture. The captors inform the prisoner of what lies in store for him, namely, how a particular punishment will be administered over an extended period of time until he reveals some desired military secrets, or, should he not so confess, how he will be killed at the end of the designated torture period. Suppose it is also the case that both the captive and his captors know that the secrets in question are a matter of public record, so the captured soldier realizes that this is all a cruel hoax—for the enemy intend to kill him anyway at a certain date. Surely, the defenders of suicide$_1$ under death$_1$ might argue, it would be a paradigm case of rational action for our prisoner to commit suicide as soon as possible (i.e., conveniently enough, he has a capsule containing potassium cyanide lodged in his dentures). To make the case more difficult, let us suppose that our prisoner makes *no* attempt to justify his conduct by arguing "I would be better off dead than alive" or some such variant locution. Instead, he opts to commit suicide under no such pretensions. Would not our captive be justified in committing suicide? It is important to note that the situation before us is a different one from that described in the preceding two paragraphs. Whereas the two previous attempted justifications ended in the obvious muddle of talking of death₁ as a state which is a non-state, as an experienceless episode which is experienced (even for the better!), the present attempted justification can meaningfully employ the concept of death₁ to serve as a limit which acts as an ordering function to guide our conceptual endeavors. James Van Evra writes: "The significance of the limit is not as something independently real, but as an operational device." [12]

Despite this *prima facie* evidence, I believe that the contemplated action would be nevertheless not rational. For one, it is a somewhat dubious hypothesis to argue that pain is cumulative over time, such that a person would be better off killing himself at t than at t + n. Returned Vietnam prisoners of war offer elaborate psychiatric evidence to the contrary, where the will to live was made bearable (and in some instances actually strengthened) by excessive torture. It is also interesting to note that the rate of suicide was extremely low in Nazi concentration camps.[13] Secondly, it might very well be a poor inductive risk to commit suicide in such a situation, for the captors may have a change of heart and end their malicious frivolity, or they may themselves be captured by the enemy, etc. Lastly, and more importantly, if our prisoner in such a situation is faced with a choice between undergoing torture for a certain amount of time and then murder, or taking his own life by biting his teeth into a capsule and being poisoned, then it might be replied that the choice confronting him is not truly a "live option" (no pun intended). In which case, it may be simply a case of recalling that not all choices involve free acts, for some choices, as in this case, are compatible with coercion, and so are more properly described as events rather than actions. But a veridical instance of suicide involves an action and not an event. R. F. Holland writes: "Taking hemlock does not, in the context of an Athenian judicial execution, amount to slaughtering oneself: in this circumstance it is no more an act of suicide than the condemned man's walk to the scaffold in our society." [14] One needs to be reminded that statements of the form "I wish that death might come" or "I hope to die soon" do not necessarily entail "I opt for suicide."

Suppose the situation described by suicide₁ under death₁ involves the case of an artist who has exhausted all his creative energies, and who now (correctly) perceives himself unable to continue living the distinctly human lifestyle he has led in the past. Suppose, to make matters worse, he is a famous sculptor who as a result of an auto accident has had amputated both his arms. Undaunted in his choice to commit suicide, he says neither "I will be better off dead than alive" nor "It will be better if I were dead." Also, unlike our captive, the artist is confronted with a live option. Rather he concludes "It is false that I will be miserable when dead" if I commit suicide (whereas he is sure to remain miserable in his current ante-mortem state deprived of his artistic abilities).

Now, "It is false that I will be miserable when dead" implies "I will be non-miserable dead." But being non-miserable is either a state of the artist at death (and hence a contradictory predication), or the artist is opting for nothing over something.

But why would one choose nothing over something? To say "I just would" is no justification at all, and at best makes the artist's choice for suicide arational. For the artist to reply "It is better for me to opt for nothing" again leads to a contradiction, namely, that a state of non-being is a state of being, that nothingness is better for me!

V

Having found no justification for suicide$_1$ under death$_1$, let us turn to consider the case of suicide$_1$ under death$_2$. The typical situation here involves a person about to commit suicide for various prudential reasons of a self-centered sort, and who is such that he believes in some form of post-mortem existence. To begin with, this proffered justification can take a few different stances.

Suppose the would-be suicide victim views death$_2$ under a non-theistic interpretation of the post-mortem state. Such a non-theistic dualist could argue, so it would seem, that it would be the rational thing to do in his oppressed situation to extinguish his bodily processes so that his true *self* could find unhindered joy in the post-mortem state of disembodied existence. Quite obviously, no charge of logical contradiction can be adduced against such a suicidist, for he makes no attempt to ascribe psychological states to a cadaver. However, the notion of disembodied existence is fraught with philosophical difficulties (the concept of the soul as the repository of certain psychological factors is replete with difficulties concerning identity/individuation) to such an extent that, if Aquinas is correct in claiming *anima mea non est ego*, then it is simply erroneous to believe that the prudential considerations motivating the act of suicide$_1$ will be satisfied under a non-theistic view of death$_2$. [Cf. *Philosophical Investigations* #281: ". . . only of a living human being and what resembles (behaves like) a living human being can one say: it has sensations; it sees; is blind; hears; is deaf; is conscious or unconscious."] How can a person be relieved of his misery in the post-mortem realm when the disembodied existent that survives is not he? Moreover, the contents of such a post-mortem state would be principally experiences of memories and acts of imagination, etc. But the memory of the ante-mortem life which drove the man to attempt suicide is sure to prove just as recalcitrant in the post-mortem state. Accordingly, it seems presumptuous to believe that the suicidist would be better off in the post-mortem realm. At worst, he (it?) would be less well off, and at best, he (it?) would be no better off.

On the other hand, death$_2$ under a theistic interpretation involves the institution of divine retribution, so that the suicidist would in all likelihood be far worse off than had he withstood his ante-mortem misery. I shall not go into the theological rationale behind the theistic prohibition on suicide: suffice it to say that such a prohibition principally involves the belief that man must work out his own destiny, and part of that salvific process involves a purification through suffering. Standing resolute in the face of evil and not succumbing to its mundane blandishments is the task of the theist. Other reasons behind the theistic prohibition have also been offered, such as suicide's adverse affect on the community, its unnaturalness, its usurping of divine providence, its violation of the fifth commandment, etc.

I am not suggesting that these theological arguments against suicide are cogent. Indeed, the philosophical assessment of them in this paper is not even apropos. The important point is that our would-be suicidist believes in a theistic concept of death$_2$ with all its attendant theological trimmings. And for him, given this set of beliefs (which *ex hypothesi* are true), surely it would be nonrational to commit suicide.

Kant put the matter well: "God is our owner; we are his property; his providence works for our good. A bondman in the care of a beneficent master deserves punishment if he opposes his master's wishes."[15] Accordingly, given the logical and epistemic considerations outlined, I cannot understand how a case can be made for the rationality of suicide$_1$ under death$_2$.

VI

Let us turn to consider cases of suicide$_2$ under death$_1$. We are now dealing with a case where a person wishes to take his life for reasons of an altruistic nature, and does not believe that death is merely an event in life. For such a man, death is the end of life. Consider a man whose every effort results in abject failure, who sees his family suffer as innocent victims to his misfortune, and who resolves to kill himself for their benefit. Here the utilitarian justification involved may work, but it is so risky that good inductive judgment cautions against it. Suppose, furthermore, that our suicidist is utterly miserable, a failure in whatever endeavor he attempts, but also a person who has recently taken out a life insurance policy which will bring both financial relief and security to his family. Would not it be reasonable for him to commit suicide$_2$ under death$_1$? I think not! For one, it is difficult to judge the epistemic consequences of such an action. His family may experience intense guilt and so not escape but have compounded the misery inflicted on them; they may find that they would rather have their father alive than financial security. Secondly, as if the first points were not distressing enough, the planned suicide$_2$ is irrational when one considers the fact that insurance companies do not honor suicides within the first two years of issue of the contract! I confess that my argument here is somewhat vulnerable, given the non-detection of, say, potassium chloride by autopsy.

Such considerations as the first example suggests would hold even in cases in which the suicidist had a long-standing insurance policy, naming his family as beneficiaries. It seems a necessary condition of a rational act that it be an act which the agent is prepared to stand by, to back up or support with argument. A case of suicide$_2$ under death$_1$ rules out such a self-justification. Such a justification could not be given *prior* to the suicide by the agent since his action's success is dependent upon its results, and his epistemic ability to judge those results in advance is greatly restricted, making his suicide at best arational. And if he were to ask the beneficiaries in advance how they would feel if he committed suicide for them, and they responded favorably, this revelation would doubtless squelch his suicide$_2$, making it a suicide$_1$ if performed.

Again, some subtle legal act-descriptions surface, as the insurance company lawyer argues that the beneficiaries merit no payment, for the victim committed suicide by taking an overdose of pills in order to annihilate himself, while the family's counsel argues that the beneficiaries do merit the policy windfall in question inasmuch as the victim accidentally died while *inadvertently* taking an overdose of sleeping pills. Here the words of Mark Antony seem to ring true that the evil that we do lives on while the good is often interred with our bones.

The matter of insurance companies' not honoring the policies of suicidists in the first two years is an interesting but complicated matter. One might argue against my central thesis that, in the case of either suicide$_2$ under death$_1$ or suicide$_2$ under death$_2$, it might be quite possible to feign an accidental death which in reality involved suicide. I take it that such disguises would not be apropos to cases of suicide$_1$ but only to suicide$_2$. Conceivably, it might be somewhat pertinent to cases of suicide$_1$ under death$_2$ given a theistic post-mortem model, but such an attempted justification would involve conceptual confusion —duplicity *cannot* work on an Omniscient Deity.

For instance, a person not previously known to be depressed or melancholic, etc., could skillfully simulate an accidental death which in fact was a suicide by driving his car off a mountain road onto the canyon floor below, and the insurance company involved might well conclude that it was an accidental death caused by meteorological conditions, brake failure, etc. Since suicide$_2$ is motivated by an altruistic component, would this not be a rational case of suicide?

I would think that if we are talking of suicide$_2$ under death$_1$ it would not be rational. The suicidist would have no way adequately to determine beforehand that his plan would be successful, with the result that it would be arational, albeit perhaps not an irrational act.

Suppose we have a case of a congenital sex maniac, who, as if he were wearing Gyges' Ring, manages to rape woman after woman with perfect immunity from arrest and prosecution. He *reasons* that he will take his own life (for the good of society) rather than carry out his base urges, and so decides to take his life.

The case of the congenital sex maniac happens to be R. F. Holland's own example. It would seem that there is obviously a less drastic solution to his dilemma, i.e., he could have himself castrated by undergoing a bilateral orchidectomy. However, it might be argued that not all rapists are primarily concerned with a *sexual* assault on women so much as they are concerned with the forceful brutalization and dehumanization of women. In short, Holland's rapist, even if gelded, could still be a malicious misogynist. So the example remains instructive.

However, granted the above, it might be argued: why does the rapist not simply commit himself to a mental asylum? This suggestion, I believe, is ruled out because our rapist is currently disposed to perform another rape, so that in the interval between his *decision* to commit himself and his actual confinement, there is reason to believe that another rape will take place.

Surely, it might be argued, such a case of suicide$_2$ under death$_1$ is rational. Indeed, I would argue that the action is rational, but that it is inappropriately described as suicide. Our rapist chooses not to kill himself or have himself killed; rather he does what he considers it his obligation to do. His is an heroic action, not a suicidal act. (Strictly speaking, not all actions called "suicidal" are cases of suicide. The hero who with reckless abandon sacrifices his life in order to do a courageous and virtuous act may be said to perform a suicidal action but not be a suicidist. However, to avoid any needless complications, I shall refer to all cases of suicide as suicidal actions.) Accordingly, it is fallacious to maintain that there is a strict entailment relationship between "R knowingly and deliberately brought about his death" and "R committed suicide." Kant put the point well: "If, then, I cannot preserve my life except by disgraceful conduct, virtue relieves me of this duty because a higher duty here comes into play and commands me to sacrifice my life."[16] Incidentally, I believe the same line of argumentation might apply in the case of the so-called "revolutionary suicide" victim (e.g., a liberation army member), provided he did not directly will to annihilate himself or have himself annihilated, but rather primarily intended to fight "to the death" for his cause. However, if the cause or end-in-view in question is highly suspect, one might still make a case for listing the revolutionary's action as irrational, and possibly suicidal.

R. F. Holland would not agree with my analysis of the sex maniac's case. Holland writes: "This is manifestly a doing and not a suffering; hence it was false to claim that 'all he really does is to preserve someone else.' That is not all, for he kills himself."[17] However, Holland's verdict overlooks the distinction between direct and indirect acts of killing. Ironically, while Holland labels the sex maniac a suicide victim, he contends that Captain Oates, Antarctic explorer, is not, inasmuch as he died by leaving his expedition while injured so as not to be a burden to his fellow itinerants. I find this verdict somewhat paradoxical, for in Holland's recital of the narrative portrayal of Oates, it is related how Oates hoped not to wake from his night sleep (which in this context at least has intimations of being a conscious Freudian death-wish), yet Holland contends that Oates did not kill himself—the blizzard killed him! This assessment seems absurd. If I suffer from vertigo, and in addition my current lot in life is a miserable one leading me to wish to be dead, but I am frightened to take my own life out of deference to various social pressures, yet I nonetheless decide to go jogging on a major highway on a foggy afternoon, does it follow that it might be truly said of me that I did not commit suicide because in fact the car killed me? I believe the question answers itself.

Holland seems to have second thoughts about his original verdict.

> But then of course neither is it absurd to claim that he [Captain Oates] killed himself by going out into the blizzard. And there is much to be said for a description that is midway between the two: "He let the blizzard kill him." To call one of these descriptions the right one is to say little more than "That's how I look at it."[18]

I cannot agree. Holland's neutral description "He let the blizzard kill him" brings in the notion of deficient causality which is at least logically distinct from the concept of efficient causality, but which in certain circumstances proves not to be *de facto* distinct from the notion of efficient causality. For example, consider the case of a person who is freely able to prevent an act of homicide from occurring, and yet chooses to allow it to happen. There seems a sense in which it is appropriate to say that the actions of the bystander (deficient causality) brought about the homicide as much as the criminal (efficient causality) who brought it about. In short, agents exercising deficient causality are often just as directly responsible (and morally blameworthy) for certain actions as agents exercising efficient causality are for those same acts. Yet Holland claims that it is not arbitrary to claim that Oates was killed by the blizzard because of the "spirit" and "surrounding" of his case. Presumably the *spirit* of his act is to save his companions from needless delay and the caring for an injured colleague, while the *surrounding* of his act is such that in all probability Oates will die anyway on the expedition. Nonetheless, if I am not mistaken, the melancholic, vertigo jogger's case involves *mutatis mutandis* a rather similar spirit and surrounding, yet it is absurd to describe his case in the above manner.

Could not someone who agreed with me on the sex maniac's situation argue that Oates's action was also rational, heroic, and *not* suicidal? I think not! What distinguishes the sex maniac from the Antarctic explorer (Oates) is that the explorer could have opted for continuing with his fellow itinerants *without* violating any moral canons (his act would be socially dishonorable only by the code of English Gentlemen), whereas the sex maniac would not escape the performance of a morally forbidden act in carrying out his base urges and raping yet another victim.

VII

Finally, let us consider cases of suicide$_2$ under death$_2$. If the situation being described here is akin, *mutatis mutandis*, to that described in the first paragraph of section VI, then I would argue that the contemplated act of suicide is not rational. Again, it is important to distinguish here between non-theistic and theistic interpretations of death$_2$. Under the non-theistic interpretation, the victim despite his utilitarian intentions may be haunted by eternal guilt feelings if through some form of telepathic communication he learns of the resultant unhappiness of his relatives, etc.[19] Even if he subsequently learns of the resultant *happiness* of his relatives (a revelation, I suspect, which cannot be all that comforting), it would seem that he would still be haunted by memories of his ante-mortem experiences which led him to commit suicide. Of course, he may never learn the results of his action, a situation that would likely turn even pure altruism into egoistic frustration. To suggest by way of rebuttal that a person might control his memories (and thus avoid any post-mortem discomfort) in the absence of any evidence for ascribing rational capabilities to him (it?) in his (its?) discarnate state (e.g., his occipital cortex is non-existent) seems highly questionable. Of course, under a theistic interpretation of death$_2$, he will suffer eternal damnation and the forfeiture of any peaceful reunion with his loved ones.

I take it that for a theist even the most altruistic action can never be such as to involve any separation of self from God.

If, on the other hand, we are describing the act of a hero (or martyr), then properly speaking we have not suicide₂ but a supererogatory act. Consider the case of a bus-driver beginning his daily route whose occupant-free vehicle's brakes fail while descending a hill. In front of the bus at the bottom of the hill is the town's central shopping area where several hundred pedestrians are congregated. He knows that if he descends the hill many people will be killed, so he elects to steer his bus off the road where it overturns—killing only himself. Here we have, I believe, heroic action on a grand scale, which involves not a doing of evil so much as a suffering of it. Moreover, to argue as I have attempted to do that suicide is unjustified epistemically (as well as morally) is not to imply that there are not times when life ought to be terminated. Situations may arise when, in order to preserve my life, I must violate certain duties to myself such that I instead choose to sacrifice my life, favoring death to dishonor. "To live is not a necessity; but to live honourably while life lasts is a necessity." [20] Like Kant, I am maintaining that one's personhood is the supreme value, so that one may be called upon to sacrifice one's life in order to save one's humanity. [21] But this can in no way be construed as an act of suicide₂.

One might here reply that my thesis is merely verbal, an example of linguistic stipulation—that is, I have (perhaps subtly) been recommending that if X is a suicidal act then X is irrational or arational for S to perform. Statements of the form "Acts of suicide are not rational" then become analytic on my thesis, telling us that "acts which are not rational are not rational."

Has not this indeed been my stratagem: namely, to reply, when a most plausible counter-example is suggested to show that a proposed act Y is both rational and suicidal, that the proposal is epistemically appealing to be sure but mistakenly labeled a case of suicide? I believe that this objection is misplaced, because I have tried to offer some justification for labeling a particular action suicidal rather than heroic, other than simply invoking (as Holland ultimately does) an appeal to self-evidence.

Of course, if by suicide is meant simply *self-annihilation*, the deliberate taking of one's own life, then of course I would agree that suicide in at least some cases is rational (i.e., *evident* or *presumable* in the language of the problem of the criterion): e.g., cases of euthanasia, heroic self-sacrifice, etc. However, it is the task of philosophy to analyze basic concepts of fundamental importance to human experience, and such a definition of suicide as self-annihilation is far too facile, nebulous, and open-textured.

VIII

It might be suggested by someone who is sympathetic to my thesis that the view just presented has involved much ado about nothing. That is, because the person contemplating suicide is in a highly emotional state, and not in Butler's "cool hour," then the suicidist's psychological state is such that he cannot discern available alternative courses of action, and, while yet remaining sane, he is still not capable of being rational under such duress. Psychologists tell us that the extremely depressed person (who may be contemplating suicide) has a highly intensified view of his plight which is likely to distort any remaining (and possibly viable) alternative courses of action. In the philosophical language of the problem of the criterion, he may not be able to establish what is *epistemically preferable* for him. Accordingly, suicide is not rationally justified. To be sure, this view raises interesting psychological questions, issues which are perhaps beyond the province of the philosopher. However, while this psychological view may be largely true (and ultimately supportive of my thesis), I have been willing to assume, possibly contrary to fact, that the would-be suicidist could deliberate *coolly* about his future free action(s).

The analysis of suicide raises many philosophical puzzles. It can also arouse great wrath as well as considerable sorrow for those who have been emotionally affected by suicide. To be sure, it is important from an ethical standpoint to distinguish between degrees of culpability attaching to *bona fide* suicides. We have understandable pity for the oppressed, the miserable, and the downtrodden who ultimately resort to suicide, and considerable anger for those who are whimsical and frivolous perpetrators of suicide. Nonetheless, despite our various emotions toward suicide, from an epistemological standpoint, individual acts of suicide remain, I believe, irrational and/or arational.[22]

NOTES

1. *The Problem of the Criterion* (Milwaukee: Marquette University Press, 1973).

2. Cf. "There is but one truly serious philosophical problem, and that is suicide." *The Myth of Sisyphus and Other Essays*, tr. J. O'Brien (New York: Knopf, 1955), p. 21. I should quickly add that, although Camus was greatly convinced of life's absurdity, it did not follow, as a result, that he claimed a philosophical justification for suicide. Indeed, Camus is careful to point out that it is fallacious to argue that "refusing to grant meaning to life necessarily leads to declaring that it is not worth living" (*ibid.*, p. 7).

3. To question the particularist framework and its epistemological stance of "epistemic preferability" is obviously possible. Here again, though, my sympathies lie with the Chisholmian reply to such an objection: "What few philosophers have had the courage to recognize is this: we can deal with the problem only by begging the question. It seems to me that, if we do recognize this fact, as we should, then it is unseemly for us to try to pretend that it isn't so" (*The Problem of the Criterion*, p. 37). Cf. Camus in *The Myth of Sisyphus*: "In a subject at once so humble and so heavy with emotion, the learned and classical dialectic must yield, one can see, to a more modest attitude of mind deriving at one and the same time from common sense and understanding" (*The Fabric of Existentialism*, edd. R. Gill & E. Sherman [Englewood Cliffs: Prentice-Hall, 1973], p. 538).

4. Cf. Nietzsche's encomium: "Free to die and free in death, able to say a holy No when the time for Yes has passed: thus he knows how to die and to live." *Thus Spoke Zarathustra* in *The Portable Nietzsche*, ed. W. Kaufman (New York: Viking, 1954), p. 185.

5. *Essays: Moral, Political and Literary* (London: Oxford University Press, 1963), p. 595. I detect similar considerations in Bernard Williams, *Problems of the*

Self (Cambridge: Cambridge University Press, 1973), pp. 85ff. (see Ch. 17). Looking back, one can also cite Epictetus, Seneca, Baron d'Holbach, and Rousseau as believers in the rational justification of suicide.

6. Cf. A. Alvarez, *The Savage God* (New York: Random House, 1972), p. 82.

7. *Notebooks, 1914–16*, edd. G. E. M. Anscombe, R. Rhees, G. H. Von Wright (London: Oxford University Press, 1961), p. 91e. Cf. Arthur Schopenhauer's *The World as Will and Idea*, tr. T. B. Haldane, J. Kemp (London: Routledge and Kegan Paul, 1883), I 362: "Whoever is oppressed with the burden of life, whoever desires life and affirms it, but abhors its torments, such a man has no deliverance to hope from death, and cannot right himself by suicide."

8. *Suicide*, tr. J. A. Spaulding, G. Simpson (New York: Free Press, 1951), p. 43.

9. *Suicide* (New York: Scribner, 1972), p. 106.

10. *Ibid.*, p. 97.

11. *Being and Nothingness*, tr. H. Barnes (New York: Philosophical Library, 1956), p. 540.

12. "On Death as a Limit," Ch. 2.

13. Cf. J. Tas, "Psychical Disorders Among Inmates of Concentration Camps and Repatriates," *Psychiatric Quarterly*, 25 (1951).

14. "Suicide," in *Moral Problems*, ed. J. Rachels (New York: Harper and Row, 1971), p. 348. I might add that Holland's treatment of suicide, unlike mine, deals with suicide primarily as an ethico-religious problem.

15. *Lecture on Ethics*, tr. L. Infield (New York: Harper and Row, 1963), p. 150.

16. *Ibid.*, p. 157.

17. Holland, *op. cit.*, p. 352. Actually it is not clear whether Holland wants to label the action of the sex maniac rational and suicidal or suicidal and non-rational. It is clear that he views it unfavorably from a moral standpoint.

18. *Ibid.*, p. 353.

19. "If psychoanalysts are right, there is such a thing as a desire to be punished. Most people, we are told, have guilt-feelings which are more or less repressed; we have desires, unacknowledged or only half-acknowledged, to suffer for the wrongs we have done. These desires too will have their way in the next world . . . and will manifest themselves by images which fulfil them. It is not a very pleasant prospect. . . . But it looks as if everyone would experience an image-purgatory which exactly suits him." H. H. Price, "Survival and the Idea of 'Another World'" (Ch. 13).

20. Kant, *op. cit.*, p. 152.

21. "Humanity in one's own person is something inviolable." *Ibid.*, p. 151.

22. I am indebted to D. Goldblatt, M. Kohl, K. Lucey, T. Machan, D. Palmer, J. Sadowsky, and M. Schagrin for helpful comments on earlier versions of this paper.

7

The Absurd

THOMAS NAGEL
Princeton University

MOST PEOPLE FEEL ON OCCASION that life is absurd, and some feel it vividly and continually. Yet the reasons usually offered in defense of this conviction are patently inadequate: they *could* not really explain why life is absurd. Why then do they provide a natural expression for the sense that it is?

I

Consider some examples. It is often remarked that nothing we do now will matter in a million years. But if that is true, then by the same token, nothing that will be the case in a million years matters now. In particular, it does not matter now that in a million years nothing we do now will matter. Moreover, even if what we did now *were* going to matter in a million years, how could that keep our present concerns from being absurd? If their mattering now is not enough to accomplish that, how would it help if they mattered a million years from now?

Whether what we do now will matter in a million years could make the crucial difference only if its mattering in a million years depended on its mattering, period. But then to deny that whatever happens now will matter in a million years is to beg the question against its mattering, period; for in that sense one cannot know that it will not matter in a million years whether (for example) someone now is happy or miserable, without knowing that it does not matter, period.

What we say to convey the absurdity of our lives often has to do with space or time: we are tiny specks in the infinite vastness of the universe; our lives are mere instants even on a geological time scale, let alone a cosmic one; we will all be dead any minute. But of course none of these evident facts can be what *makes* life absurd, if it is absurd. For suppose we lived forever; would not a life that is absurd if it lasts seventy years be infinitely absurd if it lasted through eternity? And if our lives are absurd given our present size, why would they be any less absurd if we filled the universe (either because we were larger or because the universe was smaller)? Reflection on our minuteness and brevity ap-

Reprinted by permission from *The Journal of Philosophy*, 68 (1971), 716–27.

pears to be intimately connected with the sense that life is meaningless; but it is not clear what the connection is.

Another inadequate argument is that because we are going to die, all chains of justification must leave off in mid-air; one studies and works to earn money to pay for clothing, housing, entertainment, food, to sustain oneself from year to year, perhaps to support a family and pursue a career—but to what final end? All of it is an elaborate journey leading nowhere. (One will also have some effect on other people's lives, but that simply reproduces the problem, for they will die too.)

There are several replies to this argument. First, life does not consist of a sequence of activities each of which has as its purpose some later member of the sequence. Chains of justification come repeatedly to an end within life, and whether the process as a whole can be justified has no bearing on the finality of these end-points. No further justification is needed to make it reasonable to take aspirin for a headache, attend an exhibit of the work of a painter one admires, or stop a child from putting his hand on a hot stove. No larger context or further purpose is needed to prevent these acts from being pointless.

Even if someone wished to supply a further justification for pursuing all the things in life that are commonly regarded as self-justifying, that justification would have to end somewhere too. If *nothing* can justify unless it is justified in terms of something outside itself, which is also justified, then an infinite regress results, and no chain of justification can be complete. Moreover, if a finite chain of reasons cannot justify anything, what could be accomplished by an infinite chain, each link of which must be justified by something outside itself?

Since justifications must come to an end somewhere, nothing is gained by denying that they end where they appear to, within life—or by trying to subsume the multiple, often trivial ordinary justifications of action under a single, controlling life scheme. We can be satisfied more easily than that. In fact, through its misrepresentation of the process of justification, the argument makes a vacuous demand. It insists that the reasons available within life are incomplete, but suggests thereby that all reasons which come to an end are incomplete. This makes it impossible to supply any reasons at all.

The standard arguments for absurdity appear therefore to fail as arguments. Yet I believe they attempt to express something that is difficult to state, but fundamentally correct.

II

In ordinary life a situation is absurd when it includes a conspicuous discrepancy between pretension or aspiration and reality: someone gives a complicated speech in support of a motion that has already been passed; a notorious criminal is made president of a major philanthropic foundation; you declare your love over the telephone to a recorded announcement; as you are being knighted, your pants fall down.

When a person finds himself in an absurd situation, he will usually attempt to change it, by modifying his aspirations, or by trying to bring reality into better accord with them, or by removing himself from the situation entirely. We are not always willing or able to extricate ourselves from a position whose absurdity has become clear to us. Nevertheless, it is usually possible to imagine some change that would remove the absurdity—whether or not we can or will implement it. The sense that life as a whole is absurd arises when we perceive, perhaps dimly, an inflated pretension or aspiration which is inseparable from the continuation of human life and which makes its absurdity inescapable, short of escape from life itself.

Many people's lives are absurd, temporarily or permanently, for conventional reasons having to do with their particular ambitions, circumstances, and personal relations. If there is a philosophical sense of absurdity, however, it must arise from the perception of something universal—some respect in which pretension and reality inevitably clash for us all. This condition is supplied, I shall argue, by the collision between the seriousness with which we take our lives and the perpetual possibility of regarding everything about which we are serious as arbitrary, or open to doubt.

We cannot live human lives without energy and attention, nor without making choices which show that we take some things more seriously than others. Yet we have always available a point of view outside the particular form of our lives, from which the seriousness appears gratuitous. These two inescapable viewpoints collide in us, and that is what makes life absurd. It is absurd because we ignore the doubts that we know cannot be settled, continuing to live with nearly undiminished seriousness in spite of them.

This analysis requires defense in two respects: first as regards the unavoidability of seriousness; second as regards the inescapability of doubt.

We take ourselves seriously whether we lead serious lives or not and whether we are concerned primarily with fame, pleasure, virtue, luxury, triumph, beauty, justice, knowledge, salvation, or mere survival. If we take other people seriously and devote ourselves to them, that only multiplies the problem. Human life is full of effort, plans, calculation, success and failure: we *pursue* our lives, with varying degrees of sloth and energy.

It would be different if we could not step back and reflect on the process, but were merely led from impulse to impulse without self-consciousness. But human beings do not act solely on impulse. They are prudent, they reflect, they weigh consequences, they ask whether what they are doing is worth while. Not only are their lives full of particular choices that hang together in larger activities with temporal structure: they also decide in the broadest terms what to pursue and what to avoid, what the priorities among their various aims should be, and what kind of people they want to be or become. Some men are faced with such choices by the large decisions they make from time to time; some merely by reflection on the course their lives are taking as the product of countless small decisions. They decide whom to marry, what profession to follow, whether to join the Country Club, or the Resistance; or they may just wonder why they go on being salesmen or academics or taxi drivers, and then stop thinking about it after a certain period of inconclusive reflection.

Although they may be motivated from act to act by those immediate needs with which life presents them, they allow the process to continue by adhering to the general system of habits and the form of life in which such motives have their place—or perhaps only by clinging to life itself. They spend enormous quantities of energy, risk, and calculation on the details. Think of how an ordinary individual sweats over his appearance, his health, his sex life, his emotional honesty, his social utility, his self-knowledge, the quality of his ties with family, colleagues, and friends, how well he does his job, whether he understands the world and what is going on in it. Leading a human life is a full-time occupation, to which everyone devotes decades of intense concern.

This fact is so obvious that it is hard to find it extraordinary and important. Each of us lives his own life—lives with himself twenty-four hours a day. What else is he supposed to do—live someone else's life? Yet humans have the special capacity to step back and survey themselves, and the lives to which they are committed, with that detached amazement which comes from watching an ant struggle up a heap of sand. Without developing the illusion that they are able to escape from their highly specific and idiosyncratic position, they can view it *sub specie aeternitatis*—and the view is at once sobering and comical.

The crucial backward step is not taken by asking for still another justification in the chain, and failing to get it. The objections to that line of attack have already been stated; justifications come to an end. But this is precisely what provides universal doubt with its object. We step back to find that the whole system of justification and criticism, which controls our choices and supports our claims to rationality, rests on responses and habits which we never question, which we should not know how to defend without circularity, and to which we shall continue to adhere even after they are called into question.

The things we do or want without reasons, and without requiring reasons—the things that define what for us is a reason and what is not—are the starting points of our skepticism. We see ourselves from outside, and all the contingency and specificity of our aims and pursuits become clear. Yet when we take this view and recognize what we do as arbitrary, it does not disengage us from life, and there lies our absurdity: not in the fact that such an external view can be taken of us, but in the fact that we ourselves can take it, without ceasing to be the persons whose ultimate concerns are so coolly regarded.

III

One may try to escape the position by seeking broader ultimate concerns, from which it is impossible to step back—the idea being that absurdity results because what we take seriously is something small and insignificant and individual. Those seeking to supply their lives with meaning usually envision a role or function in something larger than themselves. They therefore seek fulfillment in service to society, the state, the revolution, the progress of history, the advance of science, or religion and the glory of God.

But a role in some larger enterprise cannot confer significance unless that enterprise is itself significant. And its significance must come back to what we can understand, or it will not even appear to give us what we are seeking. If we learned that we were being raised to provide food for other creatures fond

of human flesh, who planned to turn us into cutlets before we got too stringy—
even if we learned that the human race had been developed by animal breeders
precisely for this purpose—that would still not give our lives meaning, for two
reasons. First, we would still be in the dark as to the significance of the lives of
those other beings; second, although we might acknowledge that this culinary
role would make our lives meaningful to them, it is not clear how it would make
them meaningful to us.

Admittedly, the usual form of service to a higher being is different from this.
One is supposed to behold and partake of the glory of God, for example, in a
way in which chickens do not share in the glory of coq au vin. The same is true
of service to a state, a movement, or a revolution. People can come to feel, when
they are part of something bigger, that it is part of them too. They worry less
about what is peculiar to themselves, but identify enough with the larger enterprise to find their role in it fulfilling.

However, any such larger purpose can be put in doubt in the same way that
the aims of an individual life can be, and for the same reasons. It is as legitimate
to find ultimate justification there as to find it earlier, among the details of individual life. But this does not alter the fact that justifications come to an end
when we are content to have them end—when we do not find it necessary to look
any further. If we can step back from the purposes of individual life and doubt
their point, we can step back also from the progress of human history, or of
science, or the success of a society, or the kingdom, power, and glory of God,[1]
and put all these things into question in the same way. What seems to us to confer meaning, justification, significance, does so in virtue of the fact that we need
no more reasons after a certain point.

What makes doubt inescapable with regard to the limited aims of individual
life also makes it inescapable with regard to any larger purpose that encourages
the sense that life is meaningful. Once the fundamental doubt has begun, it cannot be laid to rest.

Camus maintains in *The Myth of Sisyphus* that the absurd arises because the
world fails to meet our demands for meaning. This suggests that the world
might satisfy those demands if it were different. But now we can see that this
is not the case. There does not appear to be any conceivable world (containing
us) about which unsettleable doubts could not arise. Consequently the absurdity of our situation derives, not from a collision between our expectations and
the world, but from a collision within ourselves.

IV

It may be objected that the standpoint from which these doubts are supposed to
be felt does not exist—that if we take the recommended backward step we will
land on thin air, without any basis for judgment about the natural responses we
are supposed to be surveying. If we retain our usual standards of what is important, then questions about the significance of what we are doing with our
lives will be answerable in the usual way. But if we do not, then those questions

can mean nothing to us, since there is no longer any content to the idea of what matters, and hence no content to the idea that nothing does.

But this objection misconceives the nature of the backward step. It is not supposed to give us an understanding of what is *really* important, so that we see by contrast that our lives are insignificant. We never, in the course of these reflections, abandon the ordinary standards that guide our lives. We merely observe them in operation, and recognize that if they are called into question we can justify them only by reference to themselves, uselessly. We adhere to them because of the way we are put together; what seems to us important or serious or valuable would not seem so if we were differently constituted.

In ordinary life, to be sure, we do not judge a situation absurd unless we have in mind some standards of seriousness, significance, or harmony with which the absurd can be contrasted. This contrast is not implied by the philosophical judgment of absurdity, and that might be thought to make the concept unsuitable for the expression of such judgments. This is not so, however, for the philosophical judgment depends on another contrast which makes it a natural extension from more ordinary cases. It departs from them only in contrasting the pretensions of life with a larger context in which *no* standards can be discovered, rather than with a context from which alternative, overriding standards may be applied.

v

In this respect, as in others, philosophical perception of the absurd resembles epistemological skepticism. In both cases the final, philosophical doubt is not contrasted with any unchallenged certainties, though it is arrived at by extrapolation from examples of doubt within the system of evidence or justification, where a contrast with other certainties *is* implied. In both cases our limitedness joins with a capacity to transcend those limitations in thought (thus seeing them as limitations, and as inescapable).

Skepticism begins when we include ourselves in the world about which we claim knowledge. We notice that certain types of evidence convince us, that we are content to allow justifications of belief to come to an end at certain points, that we feel we know many things even without knowing or having grounds for believing the denial of others which, if true, would make what we claim to know false.

For example, I know that I am looking at a piece of paper, although I have no adequate grounds to claim I know that I am not dreaming; and if I am dreaming then I am not looking at a piece of paper. Here an ordinary conception of how appearance may diverge from reality is employed to show that we take our world largely for granted; the certainty that we are not dreaming cannot be justified except circularly, in terms of those very appearances which are being put in doubt. It is somewhat far-fetched to suggest that I may be dreaming; but the possibility is only illustrative. It reveals that our claims to knowledge depend on our not feeling it necessary to exclude certain incompatible alternatives, and the dreaming possibility or the total-hallucination possibility are just representatives for limitless possibilities most of which we cannot even conceive of.[2]

Once we have taken the backward step to an abstract view of our whole system of beliefs, evidence, and justification, and seen that it works only, despite its pretensions, by taking the world largely for granted, we are *not* in a position to contrast all these appearances with an alternative reality. We cannot shed our ordinary responses, and if we could it would leave us with no means of conceiving a reality of any kind.

It is the same in the practical domain. We do not step outside our lives to a new vantage point from which we see what is really, objectively significant. We continue to take life largely for granted while seeing that all our decisions and certainties are possible only because there is a great deal we do not bother to rule out.

Both epistemological skepticism and a sense of the absurd can be reached via initial doubts posed within systems of evidence and justification that we accept, and can be stated without violence to our ordinary concepts. We can ask, not only why we should believe there is a floor under us, but also why we should believe the evidence of our senses at all—and at some point the framable questions will have outlasted the answers. Similarly, we can ask, not only why we should take aspirin, but why we should take trouble over our own comfort at all. The fact that we shall take the aspirin without waiting for an answer to this last question does not show that it is an unreal question. We shall also continue to believe that there is a floor under us without waiting for an answer to the other question. In both cases it is this unsupported natural confidence that generates skeptical doubts; so it cannot be used to settle them.

Philosophical skepticism does not cause us to abandon our ordinary beliefs, but it lends them a peculiar flavor. After acknowledging that their truth is incompatible with possibilities that we have no grounds for believing do not obtain —apart from grounds in those very beliefs which we have called into question— we return to our familiar convictions with a certain irony and resignation. Unable to abandon the natural responses on which they depend, we take them back, like a spouse who has run off with someone else and then decided to return; but we regard them differently (not that the new attitude is necessarily inferior to the old, in either case).

The same situation obtains after we have put in question the seriousness with which we take our lives and human life in general and have looked at ourselves without presuppositions. We then return to our lives, as we must, but our seriousness is laced with irony. Not that irony enables us to escape the absurd. It is useless to mutter: "Life is meaningless; life is meaningless . . ." as an accompaniment to everything we do. In continuing to live and work and strive, we take ourselves seriously in action no matter what we say.

What sustains us, in belief as in action, is not reason or justification, but something more basic than these—for we go on in the same way even after we are convinced that the reasons have given out.[3] If we tried to rely entirely on reason, and pressed it hard, our lives and beliefs would collapse—a form of madness that may actually occur if the inertial force of taking the world and life for

granted is somehow lost. If we lose our grip on that, reason will not give it
back to us.

VI

In viewing ourselves from a perspective broader than we can occupy in the flesh,
we become spectators of our own lives. We cannot do very much as pure spectators of our own lives, so we continue to lead them, and devote ourselves to
what we are able at the same time to view as no more than a curiosity, like the
ritual of an alien religion.

This explains why the sense of absurdity finds its natural expression in those
bad arguments with which the discussion began. Reference to our small size and
short lifespan and to the fact that all of mankind will eventually vanish without
a trace are metaphors for the backward step which permits us to regard ourselves from without and to find the particular form of our lives curious and
slightly surprising. By feigning a nebula's-eye view, we illustrate the capacity
to see ourselves without presuppositions, as arbitrary, idiosyncratic, highly
specific occupants of the world, one of countless possible forms of life.

Before turning to the question whether the absurdity of our lives is something
to be regretted and if possible escaped, let me consider what would have to be
given up in order to avoid it.

Why is the life of a mouse not absurd? The orbit of the moon is not absurd
either, but that involves no strivings or aims at all. A mouse, however, has to
work to stay alive. Yet he is not absurd, because he lacks the capacities for self-
consciousness and self-transcendence that would enable him to see that he is
only a mouse. If that *did* happen, his life would become absurd, since self-
awareness would not make him cease to be a mouse and would not enable him
to rise above his mousely strivings. Bringing his new-found self-consciousness
with him, he would have to return to his meager yet frantic life, full of doubts
that he was unable to answer, but also full of purposes that he was unable to
abandon.

Given that the transcendental step is natural to us humans, can we avoid absurdity by refusing to take that step and remaining entirely within our sublunar
lives? Well, we cannot refuse consciously, for to do that we would have to be
aware of the viewpoint we were refusing to adopt. The only way to avoid the
relevant self-consciousness would be either never to attain it or to forget it—
neither of which can be achieved by the will.

On the other hand, it is possible to expend effort on an attempt to destroy the
other component of the absurd—abandoning one's earthly, individual, human
life in order to identify as completely as possible with that universal viewpoint
from which human life seems arbitrary and trivial. (This appears to be the
ideal of certain Oriental religions.) If one succeeds, then one will not have to
drag the superior awareness through a strenuous mundane life, and absurdity
will be diminished.

However, insofar as this self-etiolation is the result of effort, will-power,
asceticism, and so forth, it requires that one take oneself seriously as an indi-

vidual—that one be willing to take considerable trouble to avoid being creaturely and absurd. Thus one may undermine the aim of unworldliness by pursuing it too vigorously. Still, if someone simply allowed his individual, animal nature to drift and respond to impulse, without making the pursuit of its needs a central conscious aim, then he might, at considerable dissociative cost, achieve a life that was less absurd than most. It would not be a meaningful life either, of course; but it would not involve the engagement of a transcendent awareness in the assiduous pursuit of mundane goals. And that is the main condition of absurdity—the dragooning of an unconvinced transcendent consciousness into the service of an immanent, limited enterprise like a human life.

The final escape is suicide; but before adopting any hasty solutions, it would be wise to consider carefully whether the absurdity of our existence truly presents us with a *problem*, to which some solution must be found—a way of dealing with prima facie disaster. That is certainly the attitude with which Camus approaches the issue, and it gains support from the fact that we are all eager to escape from absurd situations on a smaller scale.

Camus—not on uniformly good grounds—rejects suicide and the other solutions he regards as escapist. What he recommends is defiance or scorn. We can salvage our dignity, he appears to believe, by shaking a fist at the world which is deaf to our pleas, and continuing to live in spite of it. This will not make our lives un-absurd, but it will lend them a certain nobility.[4]

This seems to me romantic and slightly self-pitying. Our absurdity warrants neither that much distress nor that much defiance. At the risk of falling into romanticism by a different route, I would argue that absurdity is one of the most human things about us: a manifestation of our most advanced and interesting characteristics. Like skepticism in epistemology, it is possible only because we possess a certain kind of insight—the capacity to transcend ourselves in thought.

If a sense of the absurd is a way of perceiving our true situation (even though the situation is not absurd until the perception arises), then what reason can we have to resent or escape it? Like the capacity for epistemological skepticism, it results from the ability to understand our human limitations. It need not be a matter for agony unless we make it so. Nor need it evoke a defiant contempt of fate that allows us to feel brave or proud. Such dramatics, even if carried on in private, betray a failure to appreciate the cosmic unimportance of the situation. If *sub specie aeternitatis* there is no reason to believe that anything matters, then that does not matter either, and we can approach our absurd lives with irony instead of heroism or despair.

NOTES

1. See Robert Nozick, "Teleology," *Mosaic*, 12 No. 1 (Spring 1971), 27–28.
2. I am aware that skepticism about the external world is widely thought to have been refuted, but I have remained convinced of its irrefutability since being exposed at Berkeley to Thompson Clarke's largely unpublished ideas on the subject.
3. As Hume says in a famous passage of the *Treatise*: "Most fortunately it hap-

pens, that since reason is incapable of dispelling these clouds, nature herself suffices to that purpose, and cures me of this philosophical melancholy and delirium, either by relaxing this bent of mind, or by some avocation, and lively impression of my senses, which obliterate all these chimeras. I dine, I play a game of backgammon, I converse, and am merry with my friends; and when after three or four hours' amusement, I would return to these speculations, they appear so cold, and strain'd, and ridiculous, that I cannot find in my heart to enter into them any farther" (Book 1, Part 4, Section 7; Selby-Bigge, p. 269).

4. "Sisyphus, proletarian of the gods, powerless and rebellious, knows the whole extent of his wretched condition: it is what he thinks of during his descent. The lucidity that was to constitute his torture at the same time crowns his victory. There is no fate that cannot be surmounted by scorn" (*The Myth of Sisyphus*, Vintage edition, p. 90).

8

Death and Ivan Ilych

JOHN DONNELLY

University of San Diego

> His mental sufferings were due to the fact that that night, as he looked at Gerasim's sleepy, good-natured face with its prominent cheek-bones, the question suddenly occurred to him: "What if my whole life has really been wrong?"
>
> It is as if I had been going downhill while I imagined I was going up. And that is really what it was. I was going up in public opinion, but to the same extent life was ebbing away from me. And now it is all done and there is only death.[1]

I

IT IS A CURIOUS PARADOX that the meaning of life is often found in the meaning of death. Presumably a man's death takes place when he suffers irreversible loss of those characteristics essential to his personhood, so that in determining when such a loss occurs, one is also determining what properties are regarded as essential to constitute a person's life. Leo Tolstoy's *The Death of Ivan Ilych* vividly depicts such a paradox through the dramatic unfolding of the moral reappraisal of Ivan Ilych's life in his dying stages. Ilych as the vernacular has it *found himself in dying*, discovering what existentialists term *authenticity* upon careful reflection on the meaning of death. Despite what appeared to be an agonizing, painful dying process,[2] replete with pathetic self-pity on the part of his hypocritical loved ones[3] and professional insensitivity on the part of his attending physicians,[4] Ilych had dominion over death at the end. " 'Let the pain be. And death . . . where is it?' He sought his former accustomed fear of death and did not find it. 'Where is it? What death?' There was no fear because there was no death. In place of death there was light. 'So that's what it is!' he suddenly exclaimed aloud. 'What joy!' [pp. 155–56]"

I suspect readers of Raymond Moody's *Life After Life* will locate some interesting comparisons between Moody's clinical account of "near-death experiences" and the subsequent confrontation with a "Being of Light," and Ilych's "in place of death there was light." Such a comparison and many more doubtlessly invite themselves (compare but Elisabeth Kübler-Ross's psychiatric analysis of the various stages of dying with Tolstoy's narration of Ilych's dying process), but I do not wish to pursue here a parapsychological or psychiatric analysis of Ilych's death.

Instead, if I am not mistaken, both Tolstoy and Ilych (that is, the Ilych in the last two hours of his drawn-out dying period) were much too sanguine about the human condition and the prospects for attaining moral integrity in this life. In short, I believe the Tolstoyan lesson to be drawn from Ilych's dying is not a realistic expectation, although it is devoutly to be wished. "At that very moment Ivan Ilych fell through and caught sight of the light, and it was revealed to him that though his life had not been what it should have been, this could still be rectified" (p. 155).

Tolstoy seems to be suggesting that a man is dead not just when he suffers irreversible loss of neocortical activity, or when he satisfies the 1968 Harvard Medical School criteria for brain death—but most importantly a person is dead when stripped of his autonomy regardless of how operative his cerebral functions. While there is clearly a normative element in any proposed definition of death, the normative component of Tolstoy's suggestion is all-pervasive. Remindful of Chisholm's earlier discussion of coming-into-being and passing-away, Tolstoy seems to be saying that a person may have ceased long before a human being does—even if that same human being is physiologically well-functioning.

Tolstoy appears to be maintaining then that questions about whether a man has a soul or not, or whether a man is dead or not, are not simply empirical inquiries but rather questions about the kind of life he is living. Offering a somewhat secularized version of Kierkegaard's *Purity of Heart*, death is viewed as alienation from virtue; immortality as union with various conduct. There are obviously theological analogues to Tolstoy's account of death as in the Pauline words that "to be carnally minded is death; but to be spiritually minded is life and peace." I choose to quote Paul because I do not wish to side with those philosophical theologians (e.g., D. Z. Phillips, Ilham Dilman) who maintain that belief in immortality when associated with belief in some form of post-mortem existence rests on a mistake, that *eternity* involves no form of post-mortem bodily resurrection but only a pre-mortem life of commitment to moral and religious ideals. What is overlooked in such accounts is that granted an eschatology (i.e., Paul also offered the caveat that if Christ is not risen, then we are of all men most miserable) without such a moral and spiritual orientation would surely be blind, *but* so too would the latter be empty without the former. Nicholas Berdyaev writes:

Eternal and immortal life may be objectified and naturalized, and then it is spoken of as life in the world beyond. It appears as a natural realm of being though different from ours. Man enters it after death. But eternal and immortal life regarded from within and not objectified is essentially different in quality from the natural and even the supernatural existence. It is a spiritual life, in which eternity is attained while still in time. . . . The unfolding of spirituality, the affirmation of the eternal in life and participation in a different order of being mean transcendence of death and victory over it.[5]

Yet Berdyaev admonishes those who would offer *only* a moral, non-metaphysical religious account (the spiritual, non-objectified view) of immortality that "man is both mortal and immortal, he belongs both to the death-dealing time and to eternity, he is both a spiritual and a natural being. Death is a terrible tragedy, and death is conquered by death through Resurrection. It is conquered not by natural but by supernatural forces."[6]

A man is dead for Tolstoy, I suggest, when he either chooses to renounce his integrity and the complex set of moral practices and beliefs associated with and constitutive of that integrity, or when he has his integrity violated against his wishes. Given such a state of affairs we say "the man has lost his soul"—even though in the descriptive and more properly metaphysical sense his soul (incorporeal substance, discarnate personality, etc.) may be quite intact.

There are obviously some difficulties attached to such a normative definition of death, the most obvious being the host of slippery-slope pitfalls contained therein. However, any justified fears about such thin-edge-of-the wedge arguments seem more forceful with regard to currently formulated biological definitions of death than to Tolstoy's highly normative definition. That is, current biological accounts of death all speak of *irreversible* cessation of either neocortical activity or spontaneous brain function, etc., and consequently add a note of finality to their practical ramifications. But Tolstoy's account remains more tentative inasmuch as the man who loses his autonomy may not have suffered an irreversible loss, as but witness Ilych's moral conversion.

My intent in this paper is to explore why I believe, *given* Tolstoy's proposed analysis of death, that it would be unrealistic for most persons to expect to attain moral integrity (except for death-bed moral conversions where any cause for optimism is quickly relinquished by recalling Aristotle's caveat that one swallow does not make a spring, and I take it Tolstoy considers it merely fortuitous that Ilych was in that situation), so that in some sense *pace* Ilych death has dominion over us.

II

J. L. Austin writes: "In philosophy it is *can* in particular that we seem so often to uncover, just when we had thought some problem settled, grinning residually up at us like the frog at the bottom of the beer mug."[7] There is a widely accepted deontic principle in philosophical circles to the effect that "*ought* implies *can*." That is, if it is appropriate to say of someone that he ought to do a particular act X, or ought not to perform a particular action Y, then surely in making such third-person judgments it must be the case that the person in question presented with such diverse moral demands can do or can refrain from doing the particular actions elicited. Contrapositively, it is held that if a person cannot do what is morally required, or cannot refrain from doing what is morally forbidden, then it is appropriate to say that it is not the case that he ought to do that which is required, or it is not the case that he ought not to do that which is morally forbidden. In short, inability to perform a moral action or refrain from performing an immoral action removes a person from the ethical sphere.

For example, we normally claim we have an obligation to be honest, considerate, charitable, temperate, etc.—in short, an obligation to be virtuous, to develop the requisite traits of character for leading a distinctly human lifestyle. On the negative side of the coin, we maintain that we ought not to be unjust toward our neighbors, ought not to punish the innocent, ought not to be dishonest—in short, that we have an obligation to avoid the development of a vicious character. It seems fair to say that our ordinary concepts of responsibility, and the consequential ascriptions of praise and blame rest on this fundamental deontic principle. To be sure, *ought* implies *can* as a significant deontic principle must utilize a sense of *can* not confined to mere logical possibility. Obviously, it is (logically) possible for a person to do anything that does not violate a law of logic, so that the *can* of logical possibility is not here the appropriate meaning. Nor is the *can* of physical possibility necessarily the most important sense, although it is usually thought to be. I suggest the interesting *can* here operative is what I term the *"can of expectability."* This *can of expectability* governs those situations in which traditional morality or the moral law expect it to be the case that a person will perform a specific action given the absence of any logico-physical incapacity to do the required action or refrain from the forbidden action. It needs to be pointed out that I am not going to question this basic deontic principle on the grounds that some form of psycho-physical determinism is true. Indeed, my thesis suggests that the principle is questionable even postulating the truth of some version of metaphysical libertarianism.[8] The principle that *ought* implies *can* is questionable not only because there may be cases where I cannot do X, yet ought to do X (e.g., I am not excused from providing for my ailing mother which I promised my father on his deathbed to do, just because I am now bankrupt, having gambled away all my inheritance) but also because there may be cases where I cannot do X (i.e., in the *can of expectability* sense *only*), yet it may still be true to say that it is false that I ought to do X. The latter case—if the *can of expectability* is recognized and included in the fundamental deontic principle—does not make the principle false but only questionable in the sense that it renders morality far too onerous an enterprise to expect most people to engage in.

Let me attempt to illustrate this new and interesting sense of *can* by the following question asked by, say, a fifteen-year-old-boy to his mother, namely: (1) "Can I go out and play basketball with the guys?" The question lends itself to *at least* three diverse interpretations.

(1a) Is it logically possible for me to play basketball while at the same time baby-sitting for my younger brother in the playground adjacent to the basketball court?

(1b) Do you think I am capable of performing on a competitive level with my friends at basketball?

(1c) Is it consistent with commonly accepted practice to play basketball with the guys? This question might be asked by someone who is inquisitive about what society expects with regard to recreational pursuits in time of dire economic recession (i.e., perhaps the boy's father is unemployed). Or, he might be inquiring whether the Parks Department allows basketball playing in the public playground after 6:00 P.M.

It is this last question (1c) which deals with the *can of expectability*. Now, shifting to a situation involving moral choice, suppose one asks: (2) "Can I perform the morally required action X?" Again this question lends itself to *at least* three diverse interpretations.

(2a) Is it logically possible for me to do X?[9]

(2b) Do I have the requisite character or physical ability to do X?

(2c) Is it consistent with commonly accepted practice to do X?

Again, it is this last question (2c) which deals with the *can of expectability*, and which I believe provides the most interesting use of *can* in our deontic principle. As Austin reminds us, "*can*" is a very protean word.

III

The upshot of this use and recognition of the *can of expectability* is that our time-honored deontic maxim, if carried through to its logical conclusion, under this interpretation of *can* suggests the infelicitous thesis that most people cannot be expected to be moral in the high-blown Platonic sense Tolstoy's analysis favors. Indeed, I would maintain the even more skeptical thesis that no person could be expected to be moral if it were not for the sociological fact that some people find themselves as a result of *fate* or *fame* or *fortune* to be so situated in life that they *can* be expected to be moral. In somewhat Marxist terms, morality is distinctly bourgeois and not for the likes of us ordinary folk who suffer the deprivation of fate, fame, and fortune.

To comment now on the defeasibility clause dealing with the fated, the famous, and/or the fortunate: My basic point is that *ought* implies *can* is a perfectly true but rather uninteresting and insignificant claim when dealing with the fated, the famous, and/or the fortunate. For the truly *fated*, moral conduct is just the done thing, and in the absence of any conditions governing contra-causal freedom not really a subject for consequential ascriptions of praise and responsibility. I agree with Chisholm when he writes: "The author had said of Cato, 'He was good because he could not be otherwise,' and Reid observes: 'This saying, if understood literally and strictly, is not the praise of Cato, but of his constitution which was no more the work of Cato than his existence.' "[10]

With regard to the *famous*, I am here thinking not only of generally recognized important public figures (like Ivan Ilych), but of people who are in quieter ways able because of great wealth, power, or accomplishment to exert considerable influence on the mores of society. They *can* be moral (and unfortunately often are not) in the interesting sense of the *can of expectability* because they are beyond the reach of society's punitive grasp.

The *fortunate* are those moral agents who are so blessed by assorted contingent factors (and who need not be *fated* or *famous*) that they *can* be moral, even insouciantly so, and society's powerful sanctions are ineffective or inoperative against them. Legally, the *fortunate* may be protected by seniority-status, contract, etc., or pragmatically they may be judged instrumentally valuable to society and hence tolerable in their (moral) behavior. Or like Gyges, they may just be lucky. Ivan Ilych could be placed in either of the last two categories for "on the whole his life ran its course as he believed life should do: easily, pleasantly and decorously." [11]

Whereas philosophers have traditionally raised the questions "Why should I be moral?" or "What is the morally appropriate act to do in this situation?" and proposed various solutions to such questions, I am suggesting that such queries have neglected the more fundamental question whether most people *can* be moral. My thesis is that some persons can be expected to be moral but it would be unreasonable to demand this of everyone or more importantly for most people to demand this of themselves. The situations I envision are cases where an agent *can* (logically and physically) choose the morally appropriate action-patterns, *can* (logically and physically) select the morally appropriate means to such ends (and indeed would do so in the best of all possible worlds), but *cannot* be reasonably expected to do so basically because society (or a subclass of it) will not tolerate the performance of such action-patterns and will take severe retaliative steps against violators of its wishes and expectations— even if society's official position is in favor of such lip-service to moral demands. As D. Z. Phillips has wisely remarked: "Deceit depends to a large extent on a pre-established stock of goodwill." [12]

It might be suggested that because a person cannot do X in the *can of expectability* sense, he is justified in not doing X. On the other hand, there are some cases where I cannot do X in the sense that I cannot be expected to do X, and yet it still seems true to say that I ought to do X. This latter view suggests that our fundamental deontic maxim is false. Nonetheless, deontological considerations notwithstanding, I would suggest that such a person has a possible excuse for not doing X so that it may be permissible for him not to do X. If so, then this raises doubts about traditional accounts that if X ought to be done, it is not permissible not to do X. That is, if I cannot do X in the *can of expectability* sense only, that is I cannot be expected to do X, then in some such cases it is false that I ought to do X, so that doing X becomes supererogatory on a possibly heroic scale. The fundamental deontic principle is still true, but Tolstoy's somewhat Platonic ethic suffers a setback.

To illustrate this thesis I will cite some fairly general cases from the fields of education, business, politics, and religion. I have no specific cases in mind in my illustrations, although I have no doubt that such examples cited below are fairly standard in practice.

Case One: Educational institutions in their public relations output like to impress the public with their recognition of a person's basic constitutional guarantees—particularly, freedom of speech. In fact, all too often such is not the case. For example: non-tenured faculty may have certain basic constitutional rights, and certain moral scruples, but they soon learn (except for the fated, famous, or fortunate few) that the actual exercise of these rights and moral demands (specifically on a matter not shared by their senior colleagues) is occasionally frowned upon. Of course, they can do the morally required action in such a frowned-upon situation, but then their job or career is imperiled. It is an unfortunate fact that the American Association of University Professors documents over a thousand complaints yearly on the part of non-tenured faculty claiming infringement of their basic right to academic freedom, but rarely, if ever, are there reports of alleged cases of discrimination toward the tenured—and yet few question the obvious disparity. Nathan Glazer recently wrote: "It is a devastating fact that no faculty has ever moved against a fellow faculty member to take away tenure, for any reason. Even the American Medical Association and the American Bar Association have a better record than that"![13] Here again, the high cost of moral conduct turns morality into supererogatory performance.

Case Two: In the business world an employee may fully know that his company's product is defective and/or overpriced, yet such a person is unable to protest his reasoned conclusion for fear of job loss and resultant professional damage. As occasional media coverage has noted, employees who question the business ethics of certain real estate companies with regard to land fraud often find their protestations a direct ticket to the grave. We should bear in mind here the Orwellian admonition against double-think or Newspeak. It is a mistake to think that the expression "professional misconduct" is synonymous with "unethical conduct." Indeed, often the morally appropriate mode of conduct is exactly the performance of the so-called unprofessional deed. (What the Pentagon termed unprofessional conduct was to Daniel Ellsberg a conscientious action.) But of course few want ever to appear unprofessional, so morality takes a holiday.

Case Three: When one turns to the political realm, it is more than obvious that similar considerations apply. In serving the needs of one's constituency, compromise and expediency are the orders of the day. Pragmatic considerations which are often non-moral and occasionally immoral become the determining norms for tolerable conduct. Skepticism about politics is so pervasive that I need not, in Kierkegaard's words, pursue the matter, "by reason of the loud tones with which actual events speak to the same effect."[14]

Case Four: In religious life, there are often clashes of authority. The religious man may want to serve God, but the dogma of a particular religious sect or the advice of a superior may demand obedience to a particular precept which is adjudged wrong by such a man. Too often, the religious man is forced to choose the culture over God. Indeed, for many religious believers the rituals, practices, tenets, and institutional sanctions of a particular religion become paramount, and not that transcendent force to which all religion is but a particular human response. Recall the wise counsel of Russell: "I can respect the men who argue that religion is true and therefore ought to be believed, but I can feel only profound reprobation for those who say that religion ought to be believed because it is useful, and that to ask whether it is true is a waste of time."[15]

IV

In an extremely insightful essay, "What Violence Is," Newton Garver[16] points out that we too often tend (mistakenly) to identify violent acts as any action directed against the status quo, and overlook the fact that violence can be performed in defense of the status quo as well.

Garver suggests that what is essential to (immoral) violent conduct is not so much the idea of physical *force* directed against the innocent but rather the notion of *violation* which robs a person of his autonomy and dignity. Most social commentators would agree that we have an abundance of violence in the former sense in our world today, but not in the latter sense. If I am not mistaken, however, it is the cruel ambiance of violence as violation of personal autonomy that is suffocating our society and in return rendering moral conduct beyond the reach of most of us.

I am mindful that this is a strongly stated thesis. I shall not, perhaps to the reader's disappointment, support empirically such a generalization with a wealth of sociological data. Indeed, I suspect such statistical data would be hard to come by, much as they are in cases of sociological inquiry into the occurrences of suicide, child molestation, etc. Nonetheless, despite my reliance here on philosophical intuition, I intend my thesis—that violence as violation of personal autonomy is permeating our present age—to be an empirical claim.

Garver draws a distinction between four types of (immoral) violence: (1) *overt personal violence* (e.g., muggings, rapes); (2) *covert personal violence* (e.g., violating the autonomy of innocent persons); (3) *overt institutionalized violence* (e.g., wars, political repression, industrial lay-offs); (4) *covert institutionalized violence* (e.g., sexism, racism).

Garver focuses his analyses on the neglected areas of (2) and (4), and indeed the range of the *can of expectability* primarily surfaces within these less-marked-off ranges. I want to say that the violence exhibited in (2) and (4) can often cause a man who is able to do X (even where X is what is morally required) to choose not to do X, so that in some sense to fight the good fight (by doing X), to buck either the covert personal or covert institutionalized form of violence being perpetrated (as a result of doing X), would involve supererogatory conduct. In short, apart from the fated, the famous, and the fortunate, a person in some sense cannot be expected to do X, and therefore it may be false that he ought to do X.

To be sure, our agent *abstains*. He does not decide that he ought not to do X. Ironically enough, he abstains with full knowledge that it is not that difficult to become herd-like. This is the great irony but also the great tragedy, because the pressures of covert institutionalized and covert personal violence make our present age an epoch of lethargic amorality. Kierkegaard writes: "For it is not so great a trick to win the crowd. All that is needed is some talent, a certain dose of falsehood, and a little acquaintance with human passions. But no witness for the truth . . . dare become engaged with the crowd."[17]

Suppose we pursue this alleged depiction of our present age by turning to a case of *covert personal violence.* Consider a person who is a candidate for tenure in a university department. *Ex hypothesi,* our candidate has satisfied all the objective norms governing the conferral of tenure (i.e., he has a proven record of scholarship; strong evaluations of his teaching ability; and marked contributions to the university and the professional community at large). Suppose further that among the tenured members of the department deciding on his candidacy few have any expertise in his field, and some for personal reasons decide to inveigh against the candidate.[18] The vendetta is begun. One member reads a paper written by the candidate and accuses him of misinterpreting an important academician in the paper, and urges his tenured colleagues to reject this candidate's tenure application. The candidate knows he never wrote such a paper (and even if he had, could one not dispute a standard interpretation of a particular author?), but he is powerless. It is well to recall here that no candidate is officially represented at tenure meetings. Another member claims he was labeled a homosexual by the candidate in a private conversation; the candidate learns of the allegation, disavows such an outrageous allegation, but to no avail. The candidate even apologizes for the obvious misunderstanding but again to no avail. Kierkegaard writes: "Alas, often enough such an unfortunate person, in addition to his heavy, innocent suffering must bear the severe judgment of the arrogant, the busy, and the stupid, who are indeed able to irritate and hurt him, but who can never understand him."[19]

The reader might here insist that this is obviously a straw-man case; logically conceivable perhaps for those with a somewhat paranoid imagination, but far too desert-islandish to illustrate the moral ills, if any, of our present age. I think not. Walter Kaufmann insightfully writes:

> This is not the place to document timidity, conformity, intolerance, and the lack of high standards of honesty in academia. . . . But consider meetings of committees, academic departments. . . . A considerable amount of courage is required to raise objections or suggest alternatives that others plainly do not want to hear, and it is extraordinary how often that which is not gladly heard remains unspoken. Some professors, of course, are luminous examples of integrity. . . . But they pay the usual price.[20]

Here we have a case of what Garver would call the "Freudian-rebuff." Garver writes:

> This type of Freudian rebuff has the effect of what John Henry Newman called "poisoning the wells." It gives its victim no ground to stand on. If he tries to advance facts and statistics, they are discounted and his involvement is attributed to Freudian factors. If he attempts to prove himself free of the aberration in question, his very protest is used as evidence against him. To structure a situation against a person in such a manner does violence to him by depriving him of his dignity; no matter what he does there is no way at all, so long as he accepts the problem in the terms in which it is presented, for him to make a response that will allow him to emerge with honor.[21]

Indeed, no matter what the candidate does to defend himself against such fabricated allegations only serves further to brand him as a trouble-maker. (One is reminded here of Ivan Ilych's thought upon witnessing the artificial mannerisms of Praskovya Fëdorovna and the doctor attending their dying patient: "He felt that he was so surrounded and involved in a mesh of falsity that it was hard to unravel anything" [pp. 142–43].) If the tenured faculty members would only recall some basic logic, they would realize that their charges are vacuous, because unfalsifiable. Everything counts against the candidate; nothing for him.

The insidious violence of such an imaginable case can well lessen the exaggerated rhetoric of Kierkegaard's otherwise sagacious admonition to decent men that "even if every individual, each for himself in private, were to be in possession of the truth, yet in case they were all to get together in a crowd—a crowd to which any sort of *decisive* significance is attributed, a voting, noisy, audible crowd—untruth would at once be in evidence."[22]

With regard to *covert institutionalized violence*, I would recount a case where the local municipal housing authority was trying to remove a destitute man from a building slated to be demolished. The old man was homesteading in the publicly condemned building and delaying its razing. No public official, including representatives of the media covering the story, could understand why the old man would live in such squalor when he could be placed by the housing authority into a new development for the aged. The reason the old man tried to resist his eviction was not based on any love for squalor or filth. He was neither deranged nor a misanthrope. He was, however, not fated, fortunate, or famous. What led the man to choose to remain in the condemned building was a housing authority ordinance that prohibited a person from maintaining pets in the newly constructed apartment complex for the aged, and the old man in question clung to life in his present dwelling with his two best friends—a dog and a cat. The bureaucrats could not understand the man and had him forcefully evicted from the condemned dwelling. His pets were placed in the local animal shelter, where the dog died a few days later of a broken heart and the cat was "put to sleep." The old man was placed under observation in the local state hospital, where he was declared sane, and then released to take up domicile in the new housing project. He did not fight the system; he did not get rid of his pets; he simply resigned himself to the situation.

The reader who correctly perceives my sympathies to be with the old man and consequently accuses me of maudlin romanticism is in my judgment a speciesist.[23] I believe that we have in both these cases I have outlined violence of great proportion which in Garver's words is "as real, and as wicked, as the thief with a knife."[24] What is more, I do not think these two cited cases to be isolated phenomena, for the sword of covert personal and covert institutionalized violence is farther reaching than it is normally perceived to be. If I am not mistaken, its cruel steel permeates our present age.

V

In short, I am suggesting that a cynical but realistic attitude is in order toward moral practice which results in a despairing attitude toward Tolstoy's true morality which sadly enough requires supererogatory performance for most of us.

It might be said that morality is not a "constitutionally iffy" affair, but I am afraid it is just that, *unless* of course one is a member of that exclusive club which comprises the fated, the famous, and/or the fortunate few. And since the majority of us (like Gerasim) do not belong to this exclusive club, therein lies the difficulty of advocating moral integrity when one cannot expect moral conduct in return. I would quickly add that introduction of the *can of expect-*

ability does not excuse cowardice, for the coward is an agent who could be expected to do the required act, but chooses not to do it.

It needs to be noted that the difficulties of moral choice I have outlined in sections II, III, and IV did not involve any moral dilemmas. One's moral choice was always quite evident. However, the consequences of acting on that choice would prove disastrous for the agent. It might be argued that the truly conscientious person will do the moral deed in question and find recourse in that supposedly blissful state of virtue providing its own reward. This strikes me as a thin shelter unless a transcendental foundation for such a haven is invoked and defended—namely, that God has reserved a reward for the truly virtuous. In short, I am inclined to think that the virtuous life not only ought to but does in fact constitute a good for the virtuous man. No doubt, it will be suggested that my view reduces morality to expediency. But this puts the cart before the horse. Surely, it is societies' policies that have made morality demand supererogation, and in not having morality serve humanity have made virtuous conduct often too high a price to be paid.

Stewart Sutherland relates a case of overt institutional violence involving the Austrian peasant Franz Jäggerstätter who was beheaded by the Nazis for refusal to pay taxes or be conscripted into the German Army. Jäggerstätter knew the likely effects of his action—misery for his family and loved ones, and the political ineffectiveness of his defiance—yet he could not compromise his integrity. As Kierkegaard writes, "in eternity, conscience is the only voice." Sutherland rightly applauds all of this, and suggests in typical neo-Wittgensteinian fashion that Jäggerstätter attained immortality by his act of defiance—even if there be no God: ". . . what a man does may *transcend* the limitations of finite existence: it may reflect or show one of the ways in which men may have independence of the vicissitudes of spatio-temporal existence, one of the ways in which they may escape the fear that some contingency may trivialise or wholly remove the significance which they give to, or find in, the disparate parts of their experience."[25] Sutherland's description of Jäggerstätter's plight suggests that those who are influenced by the *can of expectability* must make all their moral decisions in light of their perceived vulnerability, with the result that they have "no ultimate independence of the limitations of finitude." I agree. That is why they are dead in Tolstoy's highly normative sense. But it strikes me as a mistake to conclude from this (as Sutherland does) that: ". . . what is of fundamental significance in his [Jäggerstätter's] life and what gives fundamental significance to his life is something which cannot be rendered trivial, pointless, by what can befall him. In that sense his life does give expression, or show, 'something eternal in man, . . . able to exist and be grasped within every change.' "[26]

I greatly admire men like Jäggerstätter. Sutherland, however, views him as only doing his duty, much like Kierkegaard, who says: "In the eternal order, if the circumstances are difficult the obligation to speak is doubled."[27] *Pace* Sutherland, the action of Jäggerstätter is reasonably regarded as supererogatory. Whereas Sutherland sees Jäggerstätter attaining immortality in the ethical by not "suffering trivialisation" at the "vicissitudes and contingencies of spatio-temporal existence,"[28] such immortality seems but a token prize unless (to quote a neglected passage from Kierkegaard): "There is still a place in the next world where there is no more evasion than there is shade in the scorching desert."[29] My point is a Kantian one: without the hope of post-mortem survival, Jäggerstätter's extraordinary heroism is rendered meaningless.

It would be incorrect to think that I am espousing moral relativism in this paper of either a cultural or conceptual variety. On the contrary, I believe in the objectivity of morals, only I am afraid that given our current societal policies the conduct required by morality is for most people a matter of supererogation. I would genuinely hope that the less fated, less famous, and less fortunate among us not have their personal autonomy so violated that they become organization men who, as Kierkegaard said, find it too dangerous to be themselves, "far easier and safer to be like the others, to become an imitation, a number, a cipher in the crowd." That at least is my hope, but it is not a very realistic expectation.

Most people, I suspect, will become functionaries who will continue through life much like Tolstoy's Ivan Ilych did as "capable, cheerful, good natured, and sociable—though strict in the fulfillment of what [they] considered to be [their] duty; and [they] considered [their] duty to be what was so considered by those in authority" (p. 105).

I hope, however, that that rare moment may arise (only sooner) when like Ivan Ilych (on his deathbed) each person may ask if his heteronomous life (if applicable) had not been a mistake.

> It occurred to him that what had appeared perfectly impossible before, namely, that he had not spent his life as he should have done, might after all be true. It occurred to him that his scarcely perceptible attempts to struggle against what was considered good by the most highly placed people, those scarcely noticeable impulses which he had immediately suppressed, might have been the real thing, and all the rest false. And his professional duties and the whole arrangement of his life and of his family and all his social and official interests might all have been false. He tried to defend all these things to himself and suddenly felt the weakness of what he was defending. There was nothing to defend [p. 152].[30]

It may be true, as Tolstoy's normative portrayal of Ilych implies, that Ilych lived dying and died living, but for most of us, if there be no God, our lot in all likelihood will be to live dying and eventually to die.

Kierkegaard writes: "To live in the unconditional, inhaling only the unconditional, is impossible to man; he perishes, like the fish forced to live in the air. But on the other hand, without relating himself to the unconditional, man cannot in the deepest sense be said to 'live'."[31]

NOTES

1. Leo Tolstoy, *The Death of Ivan Ilych* (New York: New American Library, 1960), pp. 152, 148.
2. "He slept less and less. He was given opium and hypodermic injections of morphine, but this did not relieve him. The dull depression he experienced in a

somnolent condition . . . became as distressing as the pain itself or even more so" (p. 135).

3. "Praskovya Fëdorovna came in self-satisfied but yet with a rather guilty air. She sat down and asked how he was, but, as he saw, only for the sake of asking and not in order to learn about it. . . . Their daughter came in in full evening dress, her fresh young flesh exposed (making a show of that very flesh which in his own case caused so much suffering), strong, healthy, evidently in love, and impatient with illness, suffering, and death, because they interfered with her happiness" (p. 144).

4. "Ivan Ilych knows quite well and definitely that all this is nonsense and pure deception, but when the doctor, getting down on his knee, leans over him, putting his ear first higher then lower, and performs various gymnastic movements over him with a significant expression on his face, Ivan Ilych submits to it all as he used to submit to the speeches of the lawyers, though he knew very well that they were all lying and why they were lying" (pp. 141–42).

5. Nicholas Berdyaev, "Death and Immortality" in *Philosophy of Religion*, edd. George L. Abernethy *et al.* (New York: Macmillan, 1968), pp. 572–73.

6. *Ibid.*, p. 570.

7. "Ifs and Cans" in *New Readings in Philosophical Analysis*, edd. H. Feigl *et al.* (New York: Appleton-Century-Crofts, 1972), p. 641.

8. I am inclined to think, however, that metaphysical libertarianism is false. Perhaps my major difficulty with metaphysical libertarianism (often called agency-theory) centers on the "primitive causal relationship" of an agent's putting forth of an effort or causally contributing to a certain effect. Indeed Roderick Chisholm (the principal defender of agency-theory today) once expressed skepticism on this very point: "For it seems impossible to conceive what the relation is that . . . holds between the 'will,' 'self,' 'mover,' or 'active-power' on the one hand, and the bodily events this power is supposed to control, on the other—the relation between the 'activities' of the self and the events described by physics" ("Responsibility and Avoidability" in *Determinism and Freedom in the Age of Modern Science*, ed. S. Hook [New York: Collier, 1961], p. 159). To be sure, if metaphysical libertarianism is correct, it must be true that (*a*) the agent brings about X as opposed to X's simply happening to him, and (*b*) the agent could have done something other than X. That is, human actions must be genuinely "substitutable" so as to avoid being either random accidents or inevitable effects of causal ancestors. Given the theory of non-occurrent causation, the agent causes some cerebral event (libertarians speak of a "primitive causal relation") which in turn by occurrent causation makes X happen. However, this view seems to conflict with requirement (*a*), for if there is no change within the agent, nothing distinguishes *his* doing X from X's happening to him. That is, agency-theory seems consistent with indeterministic accounts. In short, just as there are uncaused microscopic events, such as the emission of alpha particles and gamma rays by radioactive material, so too on the macro-level there are capricious happenings, in this case, actions. Maintaining an analogy with quantum mechanics, it seems a physicist could be such that he inevitably "predicts" the orbital movement of electrons within an atom, not on the basis of any statistical laws of probability, but simply by clairvoyance. Just as our physicist does not causally *explain* such random movements, so too the libertarian's agent does not causally explain the action X in question. One wonders what is added to the assertion that X happened when it is asserted that an agent caused X to happen? No doubt the libertarian could here respond that there is an analogous problem with respect to occurrent causation, namely, what is the difference between asserting that an event Y caused the event

Z, and asserting that the event Y happened and then the event Z happened? Of course, the difference in this case, it is often pointed out, is a matter of counterfactual support. Indeed; but if the analogy is tight, then this suggests that if the libertarian's agent were acting under a similar set of circumstances at another time, X would again happen. But this implies a (at least soft) deterministic framework and violates condition (b).

Consequently, the agency-theorist seems faced with one of two horns of a dilemma: to violate requirement (a) or requirement (b), which is to accept either indeterminism or determinism, which in turn is to render the agency theory in the words of C. D. Broad "self-evidently impossible."

9. That is, I may be so infelicitously situated geographically that there is a rape going on 100 ft. south of me, and a mugging taking place 100 ft. north of me. I know of both events. I could break up one but not both, and yet both actions seem equally demanding and obligatory.

10. Roderick M. Chisholm, "Freedom and Action" in *Freedom and Determinism*, ed. K. Lehrer (New York: Random House, 1966), p. 14.

11. Tolstoy, p. 117. Compare Tolstoy's penetrating satiric description of Ilych's father who was a Privy Councillor and "superfluous member of various superfluous institutions"; ". . . an official who after serving in various ministries and departments in Petersburg had made the sort of career which brings men to positions from which by reason of their long service they cannot be dismissed, though they are obviously unfit to hold any responsible position, and for whom therefore posts are specially created, which though fictitious carry salaries . . . that are not fictitious, and in receipt of which they live on to a great age" (p. 104).

12. "Does it Pay to be Good?" in *Ethics*, edd. J. Thomson and G. Dworkin (New York: Harper and Row, 1968), p. 264. On societal double standards, Tolstoy writes: "It all came under the heading of the French saying: 'Il faut que jeunesse se passe.' It was all done with clean hands, in clean linen, with French phrases, and above all among people of the best society and consequently with the approval of people of rank" (p. 106).

13. "The Torment of Tenure" in *The Idea of a Modern University*, edd. S. Hook *et al.* (Buffalo: Prometheus Books, 1974), p. 250.

14. *The Point of View for My Work as an Author* (New York: Harper & Row, 1962), p. 120.

15. Bertrand Russell, *Why I Am Not a Christian* (New York: Simon & Schuster, 1957), p. 197.

16. In *Moral Problems*, ed. James Rachels (New York: Harper & Row, 1971), pp. 242–49.

17. " 'The Individual': Two 'Notes' Concerning my Work as an Author" (n. 14), p. 115. Followers of current best-seller lists may have noticed the popularity of books that serve as "do it yourself" manuals on the acquisition of power and the manipulation of other persons. Cf. Tolstoy, p. 107.

18. "But the autonomous human being who chooses to make his own decisions instead of bowing to authority or going along with the crowd alienates his fellow men without ever having thought of doing that. . . . alienation is the price of sensitivity, self-consciousness, and autonomy." Walter Kaufmann, *Without Guilt and Justice* (New York: Peter Wyden, 1973), p. 157. Cf. ". . . one can admire from a distance some of those who have lived freer lives, while one detests nonconformists near at hand. Socrates was a great man—as long as more than twenty centuries lie between him and us. At that safe distance one can even speak well of the prophets" (p. 212).

19. Søren Kierkegaard, *Purity of Heart* (New York: Harper & Row, 1956), pp. 124–25.

20. "Without Guilt and Justice" (n. 14), pp. 194–95.

21. Garver, p. 247. Cf. Kierkegaard: ". . . for how could it be possible for an individual to make a stand against the crowd which possesses the power! And he could not wish to get the crowd on his side for the sake of ensuring that his view would prevail, the crowd, ethico-religiously regarded, being the untruth—that would be mocking himself" (" 'The Individual'," p. 119).

22. *Ibid.*, p. 110.

23. Cf. Peter Singer's defense of the rights of animals in "Animal Liberation," *The New York Review of Books*, 20 (April 5, 1973), 17–21.

24. Garver, p. 249.

25. "What Happens After Death?" *Scottish Journal of Theology*, 22 (1969), 415.

26. *Ibid.*, p. 416.

27. *Purity of Heart*, p. 213.

28. Cf. "Immortality cannot be a final alteration that crept in, so to speak, at the moment of death as the final stage. On the contrary, it is a changelessness that is not altered by the passage of the years" (*ibid.*, p. 35).

29. *Ibid.*, p. 197; see also p. 190.

30. Cf. the words of Pablo Ibbieta in Sartre's *The Wall*: "My life was in front of me, shut, closed, like a box and yet everything inside of it was unfinished. . . . I had spent my time counterfeiting eternity." In *Existentialism*, ed. W. Kaufmann (New York: New American Library, 1975), p. 292.

31. Kierkegaard, "The Point of View" (n. 14), p. 158. See also *Purity of Heart*, p. 190: "And in eternity, you will not be asked inquisitively and professionally, as though by a newspaper reporter, whether there were many that had the same—wrong opinion. You will be asked only whether you have held it, whether you have spoiled your soul by joining in this frivolous and thoughtless judging, because the others, because the many judged thoughtlessly. You will be asked only whether you may not have ruined the best within you by joining the crowd in its defiance, thinking that you were many and therefore you had the prerogative, because you were many, that is, because you were many who were wrong. In eternity it will be asked whether you may not have damaged a good thing, in order that you also might judge with them that did not know how to judge, but who possessed the crowd's strength, which in the temporal sense is significant but to which eternity is wholly indifferent."

9

De Anima

Richard Taylor
University of Rochester

SOME PHILOSOPHERS SAY that each of us has, or indeed *is*, a personal self, ego, or soul, related some way or other to his body and to the rest of the world. Just what those relationships are is much debated; but it is considered beyond doubt that there is at the very center of things this self or ego. Such, at least, is the teaching of a long and respectable philosophical tradition. It is said that this personal self came into being at a certain moment in time, and that, alas, it is going to perish at some approaching moment of time, never to exist again in the whole of eternity. Theologians say it arose as a result of God's creating it and that, if certain of God's expectations are lived up to, it can hope to go right on existing forever in some place specially reserved for it.

Other philosophers say that there is no such thing at all, that a man is nothing more than his body and that his ultimate fate, therefore, is simply the fate of his body, which is known to be dust and ashes. This teaching has the advantage of simplicity and seems generally more scientific, but since it is rather depressing, it is not so widely held.

Both schools of thought seem agreed in this, however: that a man is a finite being, distinct from everything that is not himself; that he came into being at a certain more or less identifiable moment; and that, apart from the hope nourished by religion, he is going to perish at some future moment not yet known.

Both points of view are basically mistaken on that point, though it is not easy to demonstrate this through philosophical arguments. That should be no cause for embarrassment, for philosophers have never proved anything about this, one way or another, anyway. Each imagines that he has, and dismisses those of a contrary opinion as too dense to follow his demonstrations, but in fact all any philosopher has ever done here is to arrange his presuppositions and prejudices in an orderly way, then step back and say, "Behold what I have proved."

Nor is it easy to show in any other way what is wrong here. Proofs seem to accomplish nothing, except to stimulate controversy. Nothing can be counted on, but we might have some luck with

Reprinted by permission from Professor Taylor's *With Heart and Mind* (New York: St. Martin's Press, 1973), pp. 122–33.

WALTER'S AMOEBIARY:
A PHILOSOPHICAL FABLE

Walter had an engrossing interest in microscopy, but this eventually evolved into an interest in micro-organisms and, more particularly, amoebae, not merely
as subjects of microscopic study, but for their own sakes. That is, he grew fond
of them, studied sympathetically their individual traits and personalities, and
in time got to the point of spending hours upon hours in their company. Of
course he gave them names: Alice, Henry, and so on. The choice of the name
was in no way guided by the sex of its possessor, for amoebae are not distin-
guishable by sex, but this did not matter. Walter found it natural and easy to
think of Alice as female, for instance, Henry as male, and so on, considering
that an amoeba's name was a perfectly reliable guide in determining whether
to refer to a given animal as *he* or *she*.

From the many hours he spent with them, Walter eventually came to know
his animals with astonishing understanding. He could pick out Alice at once,
for example, knew the circumstances of her birth and something of her achievements, frustrations, and failures. When any amoeba seemed sluggish or ill, he
felt genuine concern, and when one perished, it was for Walter not just the
loss of something easily replaced. The amoebae, to be sure, showed little re-
ciprocation for this devotion and in fact exhibited no more fidelity to their
owner than does a cat, but this made no difference to Walter.

It was a harmless little hobby until Walter decided to breed the tiny animals,
with a view to improving the strain, and this led him almost to the madhouse.
Amoebae multiply rather quickly, but Walter's problem did not arise from this.
They were instead metaphysical. There were perfectly straightforward questions, the answers to which he needed for his records, and while those answers
lay right under his nose, he somehow could not find them. He became more ob-
sessed with metaphysics than with his amoebae. He was beginning to think himself deficient in intellect, but this was unjustified, for, as he eventually discovered,
the questions that plagued him were questions that could not arise.

His frustrations arose in the following way. The breeder of any stock needs
to know its ancestry. This would at first seem to be utterly simple for the amoeba
breeder, for an amoeba has only one parent. Instead, then, of the usual family
histories, with their numberless branches and ramifications, which in a few
generations baffle all comprehension, the amoeba breeder would need only a
simple linear record of successive parents and offspring. The breed would be
improved by encouraging those with the desired traits to multiply, and by inhibiting the rest. It all seemed utterly simple. There would be no need at all to
pair off prospective parents and then hope for the best, meanwhile becoming
mired in the complexities of bisexual genetics.

But then arose the first problem. The amoeba reproduces simply by splitting
in two. So if Henry thus divides himself, the question arises, which of the two
resulting amoebae is really Henry and which is his offspring? Walter at first
answered that in what seemed a perfectly straightforward, unarbitrary way.

The parent, he thought, would be the larger of the two; and the offspring, the smaller. In fact it was usually quite obvious when he was on hand to witness the birth, for the offspring first appeared as a tiny bud on the parent, gradually grew larger, and then split off. There was then no problem.

But then Walter got to wondering: Why do I record the small bud as breaking off from the larger one to become its offspring, instead of thinking of the large bud as breaking away from the smaller one to become *its* offspring? Is identity a mere function of size? How do I know, to begin with, that a small bud appears on the parent amoeba? Perhaps the parent amoeba withdraws into a small bud and leaves behind the larger remains, its offspring; the parent then eventually recovers its original size and resembles its offspring. How would I ever know, in case that actually happened? How do I know it does not happen every time? So perhaps my records are all backwards, exhibiting a total confusion between parents and offspring?

Walter lost many hours and quite a bit of sleep too, pondering this question, until he hit upon a technique whereby he could, he thought, unfailingly identify any one of his animals, once and for all. He would tag them, he decided. So he developed a technique for imprinting minute but indelible colored spots on them, which could be combined in various configurations. With each animal so marked, he could then know for certain just which amoeba was before him, by checking its markings. Being thus able to distinguish any amoeba from any other, he could thereby distinguish it from any offspring, including its own. He found this particularly useful in those cases of an amoeba's reproducing by dividing itself through the middle, resulting in two animals of the same size. Had it not been for the markings, it would have been utterly impossible to tell which was the offspring, which the original. With the marking system, Walter had only to check to see which animal bore the identifying mark. That would be the parent; and the other, the offspring. He particularly rejoiced at having this system when several times he found that the offspring was in fact the larger of the two divisions, for it was in these cases the bud which bore the identifying marks. This of course confirmed his earlier fear that the larger part might sometimes be the bud that breaks off from the smaller original, so that in truth the larger of the two is the offspring and the smaller one is the parent.

This was all fine, and Walter felt entirely secure in the accuracy of his records and pedigrees, until one day a strange thing happened. One of his amoebae gave birth, but retained only half of the identifying marking, passing the other half to its offspring. Walter found himself totally unable to tell which was which. Without knowing which was the parent, his record of lineage, with respect to that particular family of amoebae, had to come to a dead end, to his dismay.

At first he thought he had minimized the chance of this ever happening again, by making the markings so tiny that it would be very unlikely that they would be divided in any fission of their bearers. But then there arose the following question, which suggested to Walter that the entire system of markings might be unreliable. What if, he thought, a parent amoeba, in shedding some and perhaps even most of its substance to give rise to a totally new individual, should at the same time shed its identifying mark, so that the very mark which was supposed to identify the parent should now be sported by its offspring? Would that not throw the records into a confusion which would be metaphysically impossible to clarify?

For quite a while Walter tried to banish this doubt by insisting that, since marks had been introduced as the very criteria of identity, no question could arise of one amoeba's transmitting its marks to another. The amoeba bearing the marks criterially distinctive of Henry, for example, would have to be Henry. It is by those very marks, after all, that we pick Henry out in the first place. To speak of another amoeba as having Henry's marks is to speak unintelligibly.

But like so much that passes for incisive philosophical thinking, this was soon seen to be an arbitrary fiction, from the most elementary consideration. For clearly, if one could regard a given animal as that one upon which a certain mark was bestowed, making its identity entirely a function of this, then one could by the same logic regard a given animal as one upon which a certain name is bestowed. Thus, Henry would be whichever animal one called "Henry," and that would be the end of the matter. But surely such a solution to the problem would be worthy only of children and the most dull-witted philosophers. Our common sense tells us that there would be nothing under the sun to prevent one from flushing Henry down a drain and henceforth calling another amoeba by that name. No animal's continuing identity is ensured by a resolution to continue applying its name. But as an animal can shed its name, so also it can shed its markings—and with that obvious reflection Walter found himself back where he had begun, and on the brink of madness.

After such frustrations, Walter finally destroyed all his records, convinced they must be filled with errors. He tried other systems, but with no better luck. He had long since noted, for example, that his different amoebae displayed different personality traits, different preferences and habits, though all these were of course rather simple. When observing his amoebiary he could quite reliably distinguish one from another by these traits of character, and had in fact been partly guided by these observations in bestowing individual names in the first place. So for a time he used distinctive character traits as his guide, deciding which amoeba was Henry, which Alice, and so on, simply by how they behaved. It was not difficult, once he got to know them sufficiently well. But then one of the amoebae split, and each of the two resulting animals exhibited the character traits of the original to about the same degree. So it was again impossible to tell which was the pre-existing parent and which the offspring just come into being. It was equally impossible to regard both as having been there from the start, and just as impossible to say that each had arisen with the coming into being of the other. In fact it was impossible to say anything that had any sense to it.

If amoebae only had fingers, Walter thought, so that one could make fingerprints. But were not the distinctive marks the equivalent of fingerprints? And they did not do much good. Or if only one could communicate with amoebae at even the most rudimentary level. That would settle any doubts. If there are two similar dogs, for example, and one wants to know which is Rover, one needs only to say "Rover" and see which dog picks up his ears. But then, what if an amoeba named Henry divided into two, and each half responded to the name of Henry?

Walter finally gave up the whole enterprise of records, pedigrees, and family histories, deciding that any resolution of the problems they presented would be achieved only by metaphysicians. He went back to enjoying his pets for their own sakes, inspired by thoughts of the grandeur of even the lowliest of God's creatures, and he tried to banish metaphysical puzzles from his mind. Some of the old problems did from time to time unsettle his peace and trouble his sleep, but he resisted fairly well any temptation to try solving them.

In time the truth of things did finally dawn on Walter, however; not in the sense that any of his problems were solved, but rather, that he realized there had never been any problems there to begin with. They were all just problems that could never arise in the first place.

This enlightenment began when Walter started receiving instruction in metaphysical thinking. One of the first things he learned was that all men have souls. This is what makes them persons. If they did not have souls, they would be nothing but bodies, in principle no different from amoebae. More complicated, to be sure, but otherwise of the same order of being. Philosophers refer to this inner soul as the *self*. Since it is what thinks, it is also called the *mind*. Amoebae do not think, because they do not have any minds to think with. It is also this soul which gives men their dignity. That is why amoebae have no dignity. They lack the necessary souls. All this was of course very clear, and Walter began seeing everything in a new and much better light.

What was particularly significant for Walter, of course, was that it is on the basis of the inner self that it makes sense to distinguish one person from another in the first place. This distinction has to begin with the distinction between the self and what is not the self, which of course brings us right back again to the soul. When someone refers to *himself*, he is really referring (though he may not realize it) to his self. He as much as says so. That is, he is not referring to his body, which is only a gross physical thing, continuously changing into other things, continuously arising and perishing. He is referring to his *self*. Therefore this must be something that is not physical. It is related somehow or other to the body, no doubt. It possesses and commands the body, for example. Thus when the self commands the arm to rise, the arm does rise, and in a similar way (readily understood in one's own case) it commands the tongue to speak, instructs it in what it should say, and so on. It (the self) retains its unalterable identity throughout all the changes occurring around it in the world at large and particularly in that part of the outside world which the self refers to as its body.

The birth of the body is therefore not the origination of the person, for everyone knows that the body does not spring into being at birth. It existed before then, as part of another body. Indeed, it has always existed, mingled with other things, unlike the self itself. The person begins when there comes into being a brand new self, or what theologians appropriately call the soul, and philosophers, the mind, the ego, or simply the self. Without such minds or souls, there would only be the corporeal realm, where everything is constantly changing, where nothing is ever created or utterly perishes and where all distinctions between things are relative, as they are in the case of amoebae. In the world considered solely as corporeal, there could be no absolute distinctions between one self and another, for in such a world there would be no selves to distinguish. Hence, in such a world there could be no ultimate distinction between me and thee, mine and thine, for there would be not even the most fundamental and precious of all distinctions, that between onself and everything else.

Walter saw, of course, that such distinctions as these, so obvious to one who has mastered the fundamentals of metaphysics, do not apply at the level of amoebae. Amoebae are not possessed of egos, selves, or souls. *That*, Walter perceived, must be why the distinction between parent and offspring was so elusive. It must be a distinction which at that level does not exist. There one finds only life assuming successive forms, wherein nothing is really born and nothing really dies—unlike that which is discovered, through metaphysics, at the higher personal level.

All this enabled Walter to see pretty clearly what had gone wrong with his attempts to keep records of amoeban ancestry. If his amoebae had possessed souls, as we do, there would have been no difficulty whatsoever. He would only have needed to keep track of souls and to record the relations of the different souls to each other.

Punch line: "Then," thought Walter, "everything would have been straightforward, perfectly simple, and above all, of course, clear."

10

On the Observability of the Self

RODERICK M. CHISHOLM
Brown University

I

> A traveller of good judgment may mistake his way, and be un-
> awares led into a wrong track; and while the road is fair before
> him, he may go on without suspicion and be followed by others;
> but when it ends in a coal-pit, it requires no great judgment to
> know that he hath gone wrong, nor perhaps to find out what mis-
> led him.
>
> THOMAS REID, *Inquiry into the Human Mind*, Ch. I sect. VIII

THE TWO GREAT TRADITIONS of contemporary Western philosophy—"phenomenology" and "logical analysis"—seem to meet, unfortunately, at the extremes.
The point of contact is the thesis according to which one is never aware of a
subject of experience. The thesis in question does not pertain to the perception
of one's body. If we are identical with our bodies and if, as all but skeptics hold,
we do perceive our bodies, then, whether we realize it or not, we also perceive
ourselves. The thesis has to do, rather, with what we find when we consult the
data of our immediate experience, or when, as Hume puts it, we enter most
intimately into what we call ourselves. Thus Sartre seems to say that, although
we may apprehend things that are *pour-soi*, things that are manifested or presented to the self, we cannot apprehend the self to which, or to whom, they are
manifested—we cannot apprehend the self as it is in itself, as it is *en-soi*.[1] And
Russell has frequently said that the self or subject is not "empirically discov-
erable"; Carnap expressed what I take to be the same view by saying that "the
given is subjectless."[2] I say it is unfortunate that the members of the two great
philosophical traditions happen to meet at this particular point, of all places. For
at this particular point, if I am not mistaken, both groups have lost their way.

Both traditions trace their origins, in part, to Hume.[3] I suggest that, if we
are to find out what went wrong, we should turn back to the doctrines of Hume,
where we will find a number of obvious, but disastrous, mistakes.

Reprinted by permission from *Philosophy and Phenomenological Research*,
30 (1969), 7–21.

II

The first mistake was a very simple one. Consider the following remark which may be found in Hume's "Abstract of a Treatise of Human Nature": "As our idea of any body, a peach, for instance, is only that of a particular taste, color, figure, size, consistency, etc., so our idea of any mind is only that of particular perceptions without the notion of anything we call substance, either simple or compound."[4] This seems to me to be very obviously false, but many philosophers, I am afraid, tend all too easily and unthinkingly to assume that it is true.

Is it true that our idea of a peach is an idea only of a particular taste, color, figure, size, consistency, and the like, and analogously that our ideas of such things as ships, trees, dogs, and houses are ideas only of the particular qualities or attributes that these things are commonly said to have? One is tempted to say instead that our idea of a peach is an idea of *something that has* a particular taste, color, figure, size, and consistency; and analogously for the other familiar physical things. But even this is not quite right. Our idea of a peach is not an idea of something that *has* the particular qualities, say, of sweetness, roundness, and fuzziness. It is an idea of something that *is* sweet and round and fuzzy.

More pedantically, our idea of a peach is an idea of an individual x such that x is sweet and x is round and x is fuzzy. By thus using variables and adjectives, we express the fact that the object of our idea is not the set of qualities sweetness, roundness, and fuzziness, but the concrete thing that *is* sweet and round and fuzzy. We also make clear, what is essential to our idea of a peach, that the thing that is round is the *same* thing as the thing that is sweet and also the *same* thing as the thing that is fuzzy.

Leibniz saw the point very clearly when he criticized Locke's *Essay Concerning Human Understanding.* When we consider any person or thing, he said, what comes before the mind is always a *concretum* and not a set of abstract things or qualities; we may consider something as knowing, or something as warm, or something as shining, but we do not thereby consider knowledge, or warmth, or light. The abstract things, he noted, are far more difficult to grasp than are the corresponding *concreta.*[5]

I cannot help but think that the point is a simple-minded one. "Our idea of a peach is not an idea of sweetness, roundness, and fuzziness . . . ; it is an idea of something that is sweet and also round and also fuzzy. . . ." One would not have even thought of mentioning it, had not philosophers denied it and constructed fantastic systems on the basis of its negation. A small mistake at the outset, as the Philosopher said, turns out to be a great one in the end.

If the first part of Hume's observation is wrong, then so is the second. Our idea of "a mind" (if by "a mind" we mean, as Hume usually does, a person, or a self) is not an idea only of "particular perceptions." It is not the idea of the perception of love or hate and the perception of cold or warmth, much less an idea of love or hate and of heat or cold. It is an idea of that which loves or hates, and of that which feels cold or warm (and, of course, of much more besides). That is to say, it is an idea of an x such that x loves or x hates, and such that x feels cold and x feels warm, and so forth.

III

I would say that a second error we find in Hume's writings, and in the writings of those who follow him with respect to the observability of the self, has to do with the interpretation of certain data or evidence. The Hume argued, it will be recalled, that he and most of the rest of mankind are "nothing but a bundle or collection of different perceptions." And in support of this "bundle theory," he cites a kind of *negative* evidence. He tells us, with respect to a certain proposition, that he *has* certain evidence for saying that he has *no* evidence for that proposition. But when he cites the evidence he *has* for saying that he has *no* evidence for the proposition, he seems to presuppose, after all, that he *does* have evidence for the proposition.

What Hume said was this: "For my part, when I enter most intimately into what I call *myself*, I always stumble on some particular perception or other, of heat or cold, light or shade, love or hatred, pain or pleasure. I never can catch *myself* at any time without a perception, and never can observe anything but the perception."[6] As Professor Price once observed, it looks very much as though the self that Hume professed to be unable to find is the one that he finds to be stumbling—to be stumbling onto different perceptions.[7] How can he say that he does not find himself—if he is correct in saying that he finds himself to be stumbling and, more fully, that he finds himself to be stumbling on certain things and not to be stumbling on certain other things?

We must take care not to misinterpret the difficulty. The difficulty is *not* that, in formulating his evidence for the "bundle theory" of the self, Hume presupposes that there *is* a self. For this presupposition, that there is a self, is not contrary to what Hume wishes to say. The "bundle theory," after all, is not intended to *deny* that there is a self. It is intended merely to say *what* the self is and what it is not. There is a self, or there are selves, according to Hume, and what selves are are "bundles of perceptions."

The difficulty is that Hume appeals to certain evidence to show that there are only perceptions, and that when he tells us what this evidence is, he implies not only (i) that there is, as he puts it in his example, heat or cold, light or shade, love or hatred, but also (ii) that there is *someone* who finds heat or cold, light or shade, love or hatred, and moreover (iii) that the one who finds heat or cold is *the same as* the one who finds love or hatred and *the same as* the one who finds light or shade, and finally (iv) that this one does not in fact stumble upon anything but perceptions. It is not unreasonable to ask, therefore, whether Hume's report of his fourth finding is consistent with his report of the second and the third. If Hume finds what he says he finds, that is to say, if he finds not only perceptions, but also that *he* finds them and hence that there is *someone* who finds them, how can his premises be used to establish the conclusion that he never observes anything but perceptions?

One may protest: "But this is not fair to Hume. It is true that, in reporting his data, he used such sentences as 'I stumble on heat or cold' and 'I never observe anything but perceptions.' He did not need to express himself in this way. Instead of saying 'I stumble on heat or cold' or 'I find heat or cold,' he could have said, more simply, 'Heat or cold is found.' And instead of saying 'I never observe anything but perceptions,' he could have said, more simply, 'Nothing but perceptions are found.' He could have reported his data in this way; and had he done so, he would not have presupposed that there exists an x such that x succeeds in finding certain things and such that x fails to find certain others."

But *could* Hume have reported his data in this selfless way? Let us recall that his findings are both positive and negative and let us consider just the negative ones. It is one thing to say, modestly and empirically, "I find nothing but impressions or perceptions." It is quite another thing to say, rashly and nonempirically, "Nothing but perceptions or impressions are found." The point will be clearer, perhaps, if we consider another type of example. I may look around the room and, from where I stand, fail to see any cats or dogs in the room. If I express this negative finding modestly and empirically, I will simply say "I do not see any cats or dogs." But if I say, solely on the basis of my negative observation, "No cats or dogs are seen," then I will be speaking rashly and nonempirically and going far beyond what my data warrant. How do I know what other people or God may find? And how can I be sure that there are no unseen dogs or cats? Clearly Hume would not have been justified in saying "Nothing but impressions are to be found." And in fact he made no such subjectless report. He said, referring to himself, that *he* found nothing but impressions.

The difficulty may be put briefly. It is essential to Hume's argument that he report not only what it is that he finds but also what it is that he fails to find. But the two types of report are quite different. The fact that a man finds a certain proposition p to be true does warrant a subjectless report to the effect that p is true. For finding that p is true entails that p is true. But the fact that he fails to find a certain proposition q to be true does not similarly warrant any subjectless report about q. For one's failure to find that q is true entails nothing about the truth of q. The fact that a man fails to find that q is true entitles him to say only that *he*, at least, does not find that q is true. And this would not be a subjectless report.

What Hume found, then, was not merely the particular perceptions, but also the fact that *he* found those perceptions as well as the fact that *he* failed to find certain other things. And these are findings with respect to himself.

Referring to the view that the self is a substance persisting through time, Hume said that we have no "idea of self, after the manner it is here explain'd. For from what impression cou'd this idea be derived?" Given our first two general points, could the proper reply be this—that one may derive the idea of such a self from any impression whatever?[8]

IV

Why, then, is it so tempting to agree with Hume in his report of his negative findings?

I think we tend to reason as follows. We suppose—mistakenly, it seems to me—that if we do perceive or apprehend ourselves in our immediate experience, then such perception or apprehension must resemble in essential respects the way in which we perceive or apprehend the familiar external things around us. And then we find, in fact, that we do *not* perceive or apprehend ourselves in our immediate experience in the way in which we apprehend or perceive the familiar external things around us.

Thus whenever we perceive—say, whenever we *see*—a spatial object, then the object that we perceive has certain proper parts that we perceive and certain proper parts that we do not perceive. Suppose, for example, that I see a cat. Then we may say of that side of the cat that faces me that I see certain parts of *it*. But I do not see *all* the parts of the side that faces me (I do not see those parts I would see if I took a closer look or used a microscope) and I do not see *any* of the parts of the insides or any of the parts of the sides that face away. One of the results in changes of spatial perspective is that certain parts become seen that had not been seen before and certain parts cease to be seen that had been seen before. And so, if the distance between our body and the perceived object is not too great, we may now look over this part and now look over that. We may look more closely and scrutinize—and this means that we may now see smaller parts that we had not seen before. And analogously for the nonvisual senses. But whatever our perspective upon the perceived object may be, there will always be certain parts of the perceived object that we do perceive and certain other parts of the perceived object that we do not perceive. Moreover, and this is the important point about external perception, if we know that we are perceiving a certain physical thing, then we are also capable of knowing that we are perceiving something that is just a proper part of that thing. But the situation is different when we perceive ourselves to be thinking.

I may perceive myself to be thinking and know that I am doing so and yet be unable to know whether I am perceiving any proper part of anything that I am perceiving. It may be, for all anyone knows, that whenever I perceive myself to be thinking, I *do* perceive some part of myself. This would be the case, for example, if I could not perceive myself to be thinking without perceiving some part of my body, and if, moreover, I were identical with my body or with that part of my body. But it is not true that, whenever I perceive myself to be thinking I thereby perceive what I can *know* to be a part of myself. (Whether or not I am identical with my body or with some part of my body, I do not *know* that I am.) In short, to know that I perceive the cat to be standing, I must know that I perceive a proper part of the cat, or of the cat's body; but to know that I perceive myself to be thinking I need *not* know that I perceive what is a proper part of myself. Sartre said that the ego is "opaque"; I would think it better to say that the ego is "transparent."[9]

Ordinarily if a man can be said to perceive *that* the cat is standing, then he may also be said, more simply, to perceive *the cat*. But the locution "S perceives that *a* is F" does not entail the simpler locution "S perceives *a*."[10] Compare "Jones perceives that Smith is no longer in the room" and "Jones perceives that the lights are on next door." Could it be, then, that a man might be aware of himself as experiencing *without* thereby being aware of himself? Let us approach this question somewhat obliquely, by recalling still another familiar source of philosophical perplexity.

During the first third of this century, British and American philosophers were perplexed about the status of what they called "sense-data" or "appearances." They thought, for example, that if a man were to walk around a table, while focusing upon the white tablecloth on the top, he could experience a great variety of sense-data or appearances. Some of these entities would be rectangular like the table-top itself; they would be the ones he would sense if he were able to get his head directly above the table and then look down. Most of them, however, would be rhomboids of various sorts. If the lighting conditions were good and the man's eyes in proper order, most of the appearances would be white, like the table-cloth. But if the man were wearing rose-colored glasses, he might sense appearances that were pink, or if he were a victim of jaundice, he might sense appearances that were yellow. The other senses, as well as imagination, were thought to bring us into relation with still other types of appearances or sense-datum.

The nature and location of these strange entities, as we all know, caused considerable puzzlement, and imposing metaphysical systems were constructed to bring them together with the rest of the world. I am sure that it is not necessary now to unravel all the confusions that were involved in this kind of talk, for the sense-datum theory has been ridiculed about as thoroughly as any philosophical theory can be ridiculed. But we should remind ourselves of one of these confusions—another very simple mistake. It was the mistake that H. A. Prichard had in mind, I think, when he used the expression, "the sense-datum fallacy."[11]

It was assumed that, if a physical thing appears white or rhomboidal or bitter to a man, then the man may be said to sense or to be aware of an appearance that *is* white, or an appearance that *is* rhomboidal, or an appearance that *is* bitter. It was assumed that if a dog presents a canine appearance, then the dog presents an appearance that *is* canine. (Thus Professor Lovejoy wrote: "No man doubts that when he brings to mind the look of a dog he owned when a boy, there is something of a canine sort immediately present to and therefore compresent with his consciousness, but that it is quite certainly not that dog in the flesh."[12]) And then it was assumed, more generally, that whenever we have a true statement of the form "Such-and-such a physical thing appears, or looks, or seems - - - to Mr. Jones," we can derive a true statement of the form "Mr. Jones is aware of an appearance which is in fact - - - ." But this assumption is quite obviously false.[13] Consider the following reasoning, which would be quite sound if the assumption were true: "I know that Mr. Simione is an Italian and that he is also old and sick. I saw him this morning and I can assure you that he also appeared Italian, and he appeared old and sick as well. Therefore Mr. Simione presents an appearance which, like himself, really is Italian, and he also presents an appearance which, like himself once again, is old and sick." It is absurd to suppose that an appearance, like a man, may be Italian or old or sick; it is absurd to suppose that an appearance may be a dog; and, I think, it is equally absurd to suppose that an appearance, like a tablecloth, may be rectangular, or pink, or white.

When the philosophers thus talked about sense-data or appearances, they were, however inadequately, reporting *something* that is very familiar to us all, and we should not let their philosophical theories blind us to the fact that there is such a going-on as sensation and that the experiences we have when we observe the familiar things around us may be varied merely by varying the conditions of observation. Suppose now we were considering this fact on its own, and without any thoughts about Hume's theory or about Hume on the observability of the self. How would we describe it if we are to avoid the absurdities of the sense-datum fallacy?

I think we would do well to compare the "grammar" of our talk about appearances with that of our talk about feelings. Consider the sentence "I feel depressed." It does not imply that there is a relation between me and some other entity; it simply tells one *how* I feel. The adjective "depressed," in other words, does not describe the *object* of my feeling; rather, if I may put the matter so, it describes the *way* in which I feel. It could be misleading, therefore, to use the longer sentence "I have a depressed feeling" in place of the shorter "I feel depressed." For the longer sentence, "I have a depressed feeling," has a syntactical structure very much like that of "I have a red book." Hence one might be led to suppose, mistakenly, that it implies the existence of *two* entities, one of them *had* by the other. And taking "a depressed feeling" as one would ordinarily take "a red book," one might also be led to suppose, again mistakenly, that the feeling which the person is said to have resembles the person in being *itself* depressed. I say one *might* be misled in these ways by the sentence "I have a depressed feeling," though I do not know of anyone who ever *has* been misled by it.

It is quite obvious, I think, that in such sentences as "I feel depressed" the verb is used to refer to a certain type of *undergoing*. This undergoing is what traditionally has been called being in a conscious state, or being in a sentient state. And the adjective, in such sentences as "I feel depressed," is used to qualify the verb and thus to specify further the type of undergoing to which the verb refers. The adjective could be said to function, therefore, as an adverb. Thus the sentences "I feel depressed" and "I feel exuberant" are related in the way in which "He runs slowly" and "He runs swiftly" are related, and not in the way in which "He has a red book" and "He has a brown book" are related. In short, *being depressed* is not a predicate of the feeling; rather, *feeling depressed* is a predicate of the man.

I suggest that the sentences "I am aware of a red appearance" and "I am experiencing a red sensation" are to be interpreted in the way in which we interpreted "I have a depressed feeling" and "I feel a wave of exuberance." Despite their grammatical or syntactical structure, neither sentence tells us that there are *two* entities which are related in a certain way. They, too, ascribe a certain type of undergoing to the person. The adjective "red," in "I am aware of a red appearance" and "I am experiencing a red sensation," is used adverbially to qualify this undergoing. It would be useful, at least for the purposes of philosophy, if there were a verb—say, the verb "to sense"—which we could use to refer to this type of undergoing. Then we could say that such a sentence as "I am aware of a red appearance" tells us *how* the subject is sensing. Or, better perhaps, it tells us in what *way* he is sensing. For to be aware of "a red appearance," presumably, is to sense in one of the ways that people do when, under favorable conditions, they look at objects that are red.[15] (If we may say that a man "senses redly," may we also say that he "senses rhomboidally," or "senses rectangularly"? There is no reason why we may not—especially if we can identify one's sensing rhomboidally, or one's sensing rectangularly, with one of the ways in which a person might be expected to sense if, under favorable conditions, he were to observe objects that are rhomboidal, or rectangular.)

We may summarize this way of looking at the matter by saying that so-called appearances or sense-data are "affections" or "modifications" of the person who is said to experience them.[16] And this is simply to say that those sentences in which we seem to predicate properties of appearances can be paraphrased into other sentences in which we predicate properties only of the self or person who is said to sense those appearances. If this is correct, then appearances would be paradigm cases of what the Scholastics called "*entia entis*" or "*entia per accidens.*" These things are not entities in their own right; they are "accidents" of other things. And what they are accidents *of* are persons or selves.

It is interesting to note, in passing, that Hume himself criticizes the view that appearances are modifications of persons or selves—and that, in doing so, he provides us with an excellent example of the sense-datum fallacy. First he notes the absurdity of Spinoza's view, according to which such things as the sun, moon, and stars, and the earth, seas, plants, animals, men, ships, and houses are in fact only "modifications" of a single divine substance. And then he argues that, if this Spinozistic view is absurd, then so, too, is the view that "impressions" or "ideas" are only modifications of the self. But the reason he cites for this seems clearly to be based upon the sense-datum fallacy. For, he says, when I consider "the universe of thought, or my impressions and ideas," I then "observe *another* sun, moon, and stars and earth, and seas, covered and inhabited by plants and animals; towns, houses, mountains, rivers . . ."[17] In other words, if a real dog cannot be a modification of God, then an appearance of a dog cannot be a modification of me!

Why this way of interpreting appearances? For one thing, it seems to me, we multiply entities beyond necessity if we suppose that, in addition to the person who is in a state of undergoing or sensing, there is a certain *further* entity, a sense-datum or an appearance, which is the object of that undergoing or sensing. And for another thing, when we do thus multiply entities beyond necessity, we entangle ourselves in philosophical puzzles we might otherwise have avoided. ("Does the red sense-datum or appearance have a back side as well as a front side? Where is it located? Does it have any weight? What is it made of?")

And now we may return to the question that brought us to this consideration of appearances: "Could it be that a man might be aware of himself as experiencing without thereby being aware of himself?" If what I have suggested is true, then the answer should be negative. For in being aware of ourselves as experiencing, we are, *ipso facto*, aware of the self or person—of the self or person as being affected in a certain way.

This is not to say, of course, that we do not *also* perceive or observe external physical things. It is in virtue of the ways in which we are "appeared to" by the familiar things around us, of the ways in which we are affected or modified by them, that we perceive them to be what they are. If, under the right conditions, the fields should appear green to me, then I would *see* the fields to be green.[18] And at the same time I could become directly aware of—immediately acquainted with—the fact that I myself am modified or affected in a certain way.

If what I have been saying is true, then there are two rather different senses in which we may be said to apprehend ourselves.

The first type of apprehension was what Hume himself reported—that *he* found heat or cold, that *he* found light or shade, and that *he* did not find himself, at least in the sense in which he found heat or cold and light or shade. He found, to repeat, that there was *someone* who found heat or cold, that this same someone found light or shade, and that this same someone did not in the same sense find himself. That we apprehend ourselves in this first sense would seem to be clear whatever view we may take about the nature of appearances, or of being appeared to.

And if the particular view of appearances that I have proposed is true, then we apprehend ourselves in still another sense. For if appearances, as I have said, are "accidents" or "modifications" of the one who is appeared to, then *what* one apprehends when one apprehends heat or cold, light or shade, love or hatred, is simply oneself. Whether one knows it or not, one apprehends *oneself* as being affected or modified.

The two points may be summarized by returning to the figure of the bundle theory. One may ask, with respect to any bundle of things, what is the nature of the bundle and what is the nature of the bundled. What is it that holds the particular items together, and what are the particular items that are thus held together? Now, according to the second of the two points that I have just made, the items within the bundle are nothing but states of the person. And according to the first point, as we may now put it, what ties these items together is the fact that that same self or person apprehends them all. Hence, if these two points are both correct, the existence of particular bundles of perceptions presupposes in two rather different ways the existence of selves or persons that are not mere bundles of perceptions.

v

And there is one more simple mistake that we may note briefly.

One may grant everything that I have said ("Yes, there are those senses in which one may be said to observe the self") and yet insist, at the same time, that we really know nothing about the self which we do thus observe ("Knowing what states the self is in does not entitle you to say that you know anything about the self"). What kind of reasoning is this?

Let us recall what Kant says about the subject of experiences—about the I which, as he puts it, we "attach to our thoughts." Whenever we find ourselves thinking or judging, he said, we attach this I to the thinking or judging, and then we say to ourselves, or think to ourselves, "I think" and "I judge." Yet, although we manage somehow to "attach" the I to the thinking or judging, we do so "without knowing anything of it, either by direct acquaintance or otherwise." The I is known, he says, "only through the thoughts which are its predicates, and of it, apart from them, we cannot have any concept whatever."[19]

Kant seems to be telling us this: even if there is a subject that thinks, we have no acquaintance with it at all and we can never know what it is. And his *reason* for saying we have no acquaintance with it at all and can never hope to know what it is, would seem to be this: the most we can ever hope to know about the subject is to know what predicates it has—to know what properties it exemplifies; and apart from this—apart from knowing what predicates it has or what properties it exemplifies—we can never know anything of it at all.

During the latter part of the nineteenth century and the early part of the twentieth century, there were philosophers in the idealistic tradition who reasoned in a similar way. They seemed to say that we can never hope to have any genuine knowledge of reality. The most we can hope to know about any particular thing is to know what some of its properties or attributes are. But, they said, we can never know what the thing is that has those properties or attributes.[20] In the present century, Jean-Paul Sartre has despaired because we seem to have no access to the *en-soi*—to the self as it is in itself. Whatever we find is at best only *pour-soi*—the self as it manifests itself to itself.[21]

Despite the impressive tradition, should we not say that this is simply a muddle? The reasoning seems to be as follows.

It is noted (i) that a person can be acquainted with the subject of experience to the extent that the subject manifests itself as having certain properties. (And this we can readily accept—provided we take care not to commit at this point the first of the errors on our list above. What we should say is not merely that the subject manifests certain qualities; it is rather that the subject manifests itself *as having* certain qualities.)

Then one adds an "only" to what has just been said. One now says (ii) that a person can be acquainted with the subject of experience *only* to the extent that the subject manifests itself as having certain qualities. The "only" is thought to express a limitation. (But consider the limitation expressed by the "only" in "One can see what is only an object of sight" and "Trees are capable of growing only below the timberline.")

From these two premises one then deduces (iii) that no one has acquaintance with the self as it is in itself.

But it is not difficult to see, it seems to me, that (ii) does not add anything to (i), and that (iii), moreover, does not follow from (i) and (ii). Indeed I would say, not only that (iii) does *not* follow from (i) and (ii), but also that the *negation* of (iii) *does* follow from (i) and (ii). From the fact that we are acquainted with the self as it manifests itself as having certain qualities, it follows that we are acquainted with the self as it is in itself. Manifestation, after all, is the converse of acquaintance: x manifests itself to y, if, and only if, y is acquainted with x. How can a man be acquainted with *anything* unless the thing manifests or presents itself to him? And how can the thing manifest or present itself unless it manifests or presents itself as having certain qualities or attributes?[22]

The muddle was neatly put by Wittgenstein. We are all naked, he said, underneath our clothes.

NOTES

1. Jean-Paul Sartre, *L'être et le néant* (Paris: Gallimard, 1948), pp. 134, 145, 652–53.

2. Bertrand Russell, *Logic and Knowledge* (London: Allen & Unwin, 1956), p. 305; Rudolf Carnap, *Der logische Aufbau der Welt* (Berlin: Weltkreis, 1928), pp. 87–90.

3. Husserl wrote of Hume: "Dessen genialer *Treatise* hat bereits die Gestalt einer auf strenge Konsequenz bedachten struckturellen Durchforschung der reinen Erlebnissphäre, [ist] in gewisser Weise also der erste Anhieb einer 'Phänomenologie'." E. Husserl, *Phänomenologische Psychologie* (The Hague: Nijhoff, 1962), p. 264. The members of the Vienna Circle traced the "scientific world-outlook" to the same source; see *Wissenschaftliche Weltauffassung* (Vienna: Wolf, 1929), p. 12.

4. Hume, *An Enquiry Concerning Human Understanding*, ed. Charles W. Hendel (New York: Liberal Arts Press, 1955), p. 194.

5. *New Essays Concerning Human Understanding*, Book II, Ch. 23, sec. 1. ". . . c'est plutôt le *concretum* comme savant, chaud, luisant, qui nous vient dans l'esprit, que les *abstractions* ou qualités (car se sont elles, qui sont dans l'object substantiel et non pas les Idées) comme savoir, chaleur, lumière, etc. qui sont bien plus difficiles à comprendre" (Leibniz, *Opera philosophica*, ed. Erdmann, p. 272).

6. *A Treatise of Human Nature*, Book I, Part iv, sec. vi ("Of Personal Identity").

7. H. H. Price, *Hume's Theory of the External World* (Oxford: Clarendon, 1940), pp. 5–6; compare P. F. Strawson, *Individuals* (London: Methuen, 1959), pp. 96–97.

8. Compare Brentano's remark about the concept of substance: "Those who say that this concept is not included in any perception are very much mistaken. Rather it is given in every perception, as Aristotle had said . . ." (Franz Brentano, *Versuch über die Erkenntnis* [Leipzig: Meiner, 1925], p. 30). Referring to the thesis according to which we know only "phenomena" and not "things in themselves," he wrote: "But what does it mean to say that one apprehends something as a *phenomenon*? Simply that one apprehends it as a phenomenon to the one for whom it is a phenomenon. This means, in other words, that one apprehends that one is presented with or intuits the phenomenon in question and hence that one apprehends the one to whom it is presented, the one who intuits. But this is a thing that one apprehends in itself" (*Die vier Phasen der Philosophie* [Leipzig: Meiner, 1926], p. 92; my italics). But Brentano also held, unfortunately, that so-called external perception is "blind."

9. Jean-Paul Sartre, *The Transcendence of the Ego*, trans. Forrest Williams and Robert Kirkpatrick (New York: Farrar, Straus & Cudahy, 1957), p. 51.

10. I am indebted to Keith Lehrer for this point. I am also indebted to him and to Charles Caton for criticisms enabling me to correct an earlier version of this paper.

11. See H. A. Prichard, *Knowledge and Perception* (Oxford: Clarendon, 1950), p. 213. Compare his much earlier *Kant's Theory of Knowledge* (Oxford: Clarendon, 1909) and his "Appearances and Reality," first published in *Mind* in 1906 and republished in *Realism and the Background of Phenomenology*, ed. R. M. Chisholm (Glencoe: Free Press, 1960), pp. 143–50.

12. A. O. Lovejoy, *The Revolt Against Dualism* (New York: Norton, 1930), p. 305.

13. "The general rule which one may derive from these examples is that the propositions we ordinarily express by saying that a person *A* is perceiving a material thing *M*, which appears to him to have the quality *x*, may be expressed in the sense-datum terminology by saying that *A* is sensing a sense-datum *s*, which really has the quality *x*, and which belongs to *M*." A. J. Ayer, *The Foundations of Empirical Knowledge* (New York: Macmillan, 1940), p. 58.

14. Compare Thomas Reid: "When I am pained, I cannot say that the pain I feel is one thing, and that my feeling of it is another thing. They are one and the same thing and cannot be disjoined even in the imagination" (*Essays on the Intellectual Powers*, Essay I, Chapter 1).

15. But there are still two alternative interpretations of such expressions as "sensing red" or "sensing redly." (i) We might define "sensing redly" in such a way that our definiens makes explicit reference to things that are red. Using the expression in this way, we may say that no one can *know* that he is sensing redly unless he *also* knows something about red things and the ways in which they appear. Or, more empirically, (ii) we might take "sensing redly" as undefined, in which case we may say that a man who knows nothing about red things may yet know that he is sensing redly. For in this second case, the proposition connecting his sensing redly with one of the ways in which people are appeared to by things that are red would be a proposition that is synthetic.

16. And so are "thoughts." Consider a man who is thinking about a unicorn. We may say, if we choose, that he has a thought and that his thought is about a unicorn. Whether or not we say, as Meinong did, that the situation involves a relation between an existent man and a nonexistent unicorn, we should not say that the situation involves a relation between a man and a certain independent entity which is his thought. There is not *one* relation between a man and a thought, and then a *second* relation between the thought and a nonexistent unicorn. Though we say, quite naturally, that the unicorn is the object of the man's thought, it would be less misleading to say that the unicorn is the object of the man to the extent that he is thinking. For thinking, like feeling and like what we may call "sensing," is an affection, modification, or state of the man. Compare Leibniz's assertion that ideas are "affections or modifications of the mind," in his "Thoughts on Knowledge, Truth, and Ideas" in Erdmann's edition of Leibniz's *Opera philosophica*, p. 81. Sartre, too, has said that the appearance is "the manner in which the subject is affected [la manière dont le sujet est affecté]," but he adds, unfortunately, that "consciousness has nothing of the substantial [la conscience n'a rien de substantiel]." *L'être et le néant*, pp. 13, 23.

17. *Treatise of Human Nature*, Book I, Part IV, sec. v; my italics.

18. I have tried to say what these conditions are in *Theory of Knowledge* (Englewood Cliffs: Prentice-Hall, 1966), Chapter Three, and in *Perceiving: A Philosophical Study* (Ithaca: Cornell University Press, 1957). An excellent summary of this view of perception may be found in Keith Lehrer, "Scottish Influences on Contemporary American Philosophy," *The Philosophical Journal*, 5 (1968), 34–42.

19. "Durch dieses Ich oder Er oder Es (das Ding), welches denkt, wird nun nichts weiter als ein transcendentales Subject der Gedanken vorgestellt = X, welches nur durch die Gedanken, die seine Prädicate sind, erkannt wird, und wovon wir abgesondert niemals den mindesten Begriff haben können. . . . Es ist aber offenbar, dass das Subject der Inhärenz durch das dem Gedanken angehängte Ich nur transcendental bezeichnet werde, ohne die mindeste Eigenschaft desselben zu be-

merken, oder überhaupt etwas von ihm zu kennen oder zu wissen." *Kritik der reinen Vernunft*, A346, A355 (ed. N. Kemp Smith, pp. 331, 337).

20. Compare A. E. Taylor: "What we call one *thing* is said, in spite of its unity, to have many *qualities*. It is, *e.g.*, at once round, white, shiny, and hard, or at once green, soft, and rough. Now, what do we understand by the *it* to which these numerous attributes are alike ascribed, and how does it possess them? To use the traditional technical names, what is the substance to which the several qualities belong or in which they inhere, and what is the manner of their *inherence*? . . . The notion *that* things have a that or substance prior to their *what* or quality . . . is thus unmeaning as well as superfluous" (*Elements of Metaphysics* [5th ed.; London: Methuen, 1920], pp. 128, 133).

21. "Ainsi le Pour-soi en tant qu'il n'est pas *soi* est une présence à soi qui manque d'une certaine présence à soi et c'est en tant que manque de cette présence qu'il est présence à soi." *L'être et le néant*, p. 145.

22. Compare Leibniz again: "En distinguant deux choses dans la substance, les attributs ou prédicats et le sujet commun de ces prédicats, ce n'est pas merveille, qu'on ne peut rien concevoir de particulier dans ce sujet. Il le faut bien, puisqu'on déjà séparé tous les attributs, où l'on pourroit concevoir quelque détail. Ainsi demander quelque chose de plus dans ce pur *sujet en général*, que ce qu'il faut pour concevoir que c'est la même chose (p. e. qui entend et qui veut, qui imagine et qui raisonne) c'est demander l'impossible et contrevenir à sa propre supposition, qu'on a faite en faisant abstraction et concevant separément le sujet et ses qualités ou accidens" (*Opera philosophica*, ed. Erdmann, p. 272). *New Essays Concerning Human Understanding*, Book II, Ch. 23, sec. 2.

11

Biology and the Soul

JOHN HICK
University of Birmingham

THROUGHOUT THE HISTORY of the relation between science and religion the scientific theories that have proved most stimulating or most challenging to religious thought have arisen at different times within different aspects of the study of nature. In the sixteenth century, for example, the main source was astronomy; in the nineteenth century, paleontology and zoology. Fifty years ago, when Sir Arthur Eddington was writing on the nature of the physical world, his own subject of physics was the science with the most striking implications for philosophy and religion. New concepts of matter and energy, relativity theory, the principle of indeterminacy, the concept of complementarity were raising issues and suggesting speculations transcending the physicist's strict field of enquiry. Since then the biological sciences have taken a great leap forward and it is from that quarter that many of the most intriguing and disturbing new questions, and hints of possible theoretical reformulations, are coming today. Accordingly in this paper I want to look at certain aspects of contemporary biological theory in so far as these may be relevant to the religious understanding of man.

At first sight it might seem that the focus of religious interest in biology should be within the field of bio-medicine. For this has recently given rise to books with such dramatic titles as *The Biological Time-Bomb, The Bio-Medical Revolution*, and *Fabricated Man*. The reference here is to startling new methods, actual and prospective, of controlling the human genetic material, with such possibilities opening before us as the deliberate deletion of defective or unwanted genes, the cloning of human beings by producing any number of individuals with precisely the same genetic code, and even the engineering of a structure of chromosomes to a chosen specification, thereby determining in advance the characteristics which members of the next generation are to have. Within the sphere of bio-medicine itself this sudden explosion of both theory and technology can no doubt properly be described as a revolution. But whilst these new developments throw light on the nature of the human being they do not appear to throw *new* light. They dramatise facts that were already available

Reprinted by permission from Professor Hick's *Biology and the Soul* (Cambridge: Cambridge University Press, 1972).

to us, even though it may well be that many, at any rate in the theological world, had not sufficiently taken account of these facts and are now being prompted for the first time to give serious thought to their implications. But we already knew, or should have known, that the individual's psycho-physical nature is determined by a particular contingent knot, as it were, in the criss-crossing threads of genetic material as it passes down the generations. What is novel is the possibility of deliberate interference with some of the details of the process. But this new technological capability, immensely important though its practical consequences must be, does not call for a new and different picture of human nature. Men have always to some extent influenced the selection of genetic material which was to form their successors. The general fact of the transmission of characteristics has been evident from time immemorial and people have long taken account of it, in so far as they wished to, in their choice of mates. And long before there was a science of genetics mankind knew of the effects of in-breeding and had evolved prohibitions against incest and against marriage within the same tribe or extended family. Again, the thought of cloning, although revolutionary indeed as a new bio-medical technique, is not new as a fact; for we have long been familiar with the phenomenon of identical twins, and identical twins as two expansions of the same genetic code are natural clones.

Thus whilst the bio-medical revolution represents a tremendous development in technology, bringing with it immense new ethical and social problems, it does not appear to me that it revolutionises our conception of man—unless this had remained largely unaffected by the implications of the wider advances in biology during the last thirty or so years.

What then are the aspects of modern biological knowledge that bear upon the religious conception of man's nature? The particular aspect which I propose to single out for consideration is the rapidly growing understanding of the genetic process by which each of us has been uniquely formed.

What, I think, particularly strikes a layman like myself as he attends to the geneticists' descriptions of the formation of an individual, with his particular set of characteristics, is the enormous number of possible genetic codes out of which the one that is actualised has been apparently randomly selected. Behind each of us there lies an astronomical number of other possible arrangements of the same genetic material. If we confine attention for the moment to the father's contribution, there are some three to six hundred million sperm which he has launched on their race to reach and fertilise the ovum. These, say, four hundred million sperm are not however completely alike, as identical copies of each other. On the contrary, each one is unique. In each case of the millions of formations of sperm cells, through the complex process of meiotic division, a partial reshuffling of the parental genes takes place, producing unpredictable results. For a slightly different course is taken each time in the selection and arrangement of the twenty-three out of the father's forty-six chromosomes that are to constitute his sperm's contribution to the full genetic complement of a member of the next generation. The ordering of the chromosomes in the sperm cell is itself partly a matter of chance, depending upon which out of each pair of chromosomes happens to be on one side and which on the other when the two sets separate to form new daughter cells. But the degree of randomness thus

introduced (calculated as at least eight million potentially different arrangements of the chromosomes) is multiplied by scattered breaks and re-formations
in many of the chromosomes in the "crossing over" stage of meiosis. So it is
that, of the four hundred or so million sperm cells, each carries, in its details,
a different genetic code. But only one out of these four hundred million can win
the race to the ovum. Nevertheless this vast number is needed if the ovum is to
be fertilised. A single sperm, unsupported by its millions of companions, would
not be able to make its way across the mucus area at the entry to the uterus,
up the Fallopian tube, and through the membrane protecting the egg. For each
sperm produces only a minute quantity of the enzyme which digests the material to be penetrated, and so only by the combined action of many is a way
made through to the target. Thus hundreds of millions of sperm perish in enabling one of their number to continue in the life of a new organism.

Approximately half of the four hundred million or so sperm carry the Y sex
chromosome which will result in a male embryo whilst the other half carry
the X chromosome which will produce a female. And each of these two hundred or so million possible or notional males, and likewise each of the two hundred or so million possible females, is unique, differing from its potential
brothers and sisters in a number of ways, mostly slight but some, arising from
major mutations, far from slight.

But this family of some four hundred million potential children, only one of
whom, normally, will actually be conceived and born, is really only a family
of four hundred million half-children! For the sperm carries only half the total
complement of human chromosomes. Meanwhile the mother has been producing egg cells, though not nearly as many as the father produces sperm cells,
and usually only one at a time. Each of these eggs contains its own unique
arrangement of chromosomes, and the vast range of possibilities which lies behind the formation of a particular sperm cell likewise lies behind the formation
of a particular egg cell. Thus there is a further enormous multiplication in the
possibilities out of which a particular genetic code is selected when it is actualised by the union of a particular sperm with a particular egg. And it is out of
this astronomical number of different potential individuals, exhibiting the kinds
of differences that can occur between children of the same parents, that a single
individual comes into being.

Thus the process whereby a particular genetic code begins to be actualised
includes, according to the geneticists, crucial elements of randomness. I pre-
sume, however, that this is not randomness in the sense in which the term is
used in quantum physics. The units with which the geneticist is dealing are not
the sub-atomic particles to which indeterminacy is ascribed in quantum physics,
but complex molecular structures; and I take it that their individual behaviour
is not unpredictable in principle, as is apparently the case with electrons, but
only unpredictable in fact. I assume, then, that the "shuffling" of the chromosomes in the formation of sperm cells, and again the selection of one sperm
out of some four hundred million different ones to fertilise the ovum, are random processes only in the sense that they fall outside the scope of human
predictability. Presumably the continuity of cause and effect, and hence of pre-

dictability in principle, is not suspended; but the processes involved are so complex that their outcome is unpredictable in practice, and in that sense random from the human point of view. In the ensuing discussion, I shall accordingly be using the term "random" in this weaker sense.

What, then, are the implications for the nature and status of the human being of this area of randomness in the selection of a genetic code for actualisation?

From a religious point of view the randomness out of which we have come is an aspect of the radical contingency of our existence. We are not "self-made men" but products of forces at work outside and prior to ourselves. Our dependent status is ultimately traced by religious thought back to the dependence of the entire natural order upon the creative will of God. Thus far, then, our emergence out of the bewildering randomness of the genetic process is not in tension with the basic theological conception of man's absolute contingency as a created being. But on the other hand, when we stress the randomness of the process whereby we, rather than countless other possible human beings, have come into existence, we must ask how well this agrees with our traditional religious conception of the human being as an immortal soul. Let us therefore now turn to this idea of the soul and to the bearings of modern biological knowledge upon it.

Many different concepts of soul occur across the world and through the centuries; but in this paper I must confine myself very largely to the one prevalent in our Western and Christian culture. Here the soul has generally been equated with the individual self-conscious mind or ego, together (as we must add today) with such unconscious mental life as is able directly to influence it. Whether the soul as self is mental and in principle detachable from the body as the more Platonic strands of Western thought have affirmed, or whether it is a psycho-physical entity with indissoluble mental and bodily aspects as the more Biblical and Aristotelian strands of thought claim, is thus far an open question, and one which I shall not in this paper make any moves towards settling. This means leaving open also the issue between two different conceptions of human immortality, one attributing it to the mind, separated from the body at death, and the other attributing it to a re-created body–mind totality. Although I cannot defend this view here, I believe that both ideas are in fact conceptually viable: however, this is not the subject of the present paper. What is important at the moment is that in Christian thought the soul, whether detachable from the body or including the body, is the conscious, responsible ego which earns rewards and deserves penalties, which becomes or fails to become conscious of God by faith, and which is to enjoy hereafter the blissful life of heaven or (in the patristic and medieval tradition) to suffer eternal loss of heaven. For it is clear from Jesus' parables that the self which faces judgment after death is the same self that has lived on earth in the body. Dives and Lazarus remember their former lives and are aware of the moral appropriateness of the consequences which they encounter after death. In the parable of the sheep and the goats those who stand before the King for judgment are conscious of being the same persons who had served or who had rejected "the least of his brethren" in their earthly need. In short, the self that is to be judged hereafter and rewarded or punished in respect of choices made in this life is the conscious, responsible personal mind and will who has made those fateful choices.

Leaving aside, as I am doing in this discussion, the question of immortality, there is thus far nothing in the religious way of speaking about the self that need disturb the biologist; for the conscious personal self undoubtedly exists, and all that is so far in question is the proposal to call it (together with its unconscious depths) the soul. But a doctrine has been historically connected with this which the biologist may well feel obliged to question, namely that the soul is a metaphysical entity which has become linked with a developing human body either at conception or at some point between conception and birth. The religious heart of this doctrine is that souls—or selves—have been individually created by God for eternal fellowship with Himself. As one of the documents of the First Vatican Council of 1869–70 declared, in reaffirmation of an ancient doctrine, "God creates a new soul and infuses it into each man" (Schema of the Dogmatic Constitution on the Principal Mysteries of the Faith, Ch. 2). The point that I want to make about this traditional doctrine is that if it is to have any substance at all, so as to be worth either affirming or denying, it must entail that there are characteristics of the self which are derived neither from genetic inheritance nor from interaction with the environment. If the divinely infused soul is to have a function in the economy of human existence it must form the inner core of individuality, the unique personal essence of a human being, providing the ultimate ground of human individuation. For there would be no value in postulating a soul without content, as a mere qualityless psychic atom. Souls would not then differ from one another except numerically. Such a conception of the soul as featureless would deny all point to the notion that God has specifically created each individual human soul and endowed it with a body. For it would then be the body rather than the soul that acts as the principle of individuation, constituting one person as different from another. Everything that is distinctive of the individual would be a product of heredity and environment, and the soul would be a needless concept. It would refer at most to a metaphysical substratum, in Locke's disparaging phrase a "something, I know not what," underlying our mental life, but not to an essential self carrying the unique characteristics of the individual.

If then there is to be any point to the traditional claim that souls are special divine creations, they must be the bearers of some at least of the distinctive characteristics of the individual. These characteristics must however be ones which do not arise from the inherited genetic code. For the picture of God creating souls and infusing them into bodies involves a distinction between those characteristics that are carried by the soul and those that are already built genetically into the developing structure of the body. Thus to speak of the divinely inserted soul as any kind of real entity, playing a real part in the makeup of the human being, is to commit oneself to the claim that there are innate personal qualities which have not been inherited from one's parents but which have been implanted by God.

However, this idea of innate but not inherited qualities is highly problematic. It has long been clear, even without benefit of special scientific knowledge, that children are almost as often like a parent in basic personality traits as in purely physical characteristics. Thus it is evident that some aspects at least of one's innate character are inherited even if there should be still other aspects which represent a special divine creation. And the delimiting of the boundaries of the soul thus called for by common observation is now carried much further by the modern science of genetics. For many characteristics which might have been supposed to be attributes of the soul are now believed to be part of our genetic inheritance. Dr. Darlington lists as follows those characteristics of the human individual to which there is an important genetic contribution:

> Our hormone systems and hence our temperament, whether sanguine, melancholy or choleric; timid or courageous; observant, reflective, or impulsive. Hence our social habits, whether solitary or gregarious; affectionate or morose; settled or nomadic, useful, deranged, or criminal; hence also the company we keep, and our capacities and directions of love and hatred. Our perception and appreciation of taste, touch and smell, sound and colour, harmony and pattern. Our capacities and qualities for memory, whether for sound, sight, number or form. Our kinds and degrees of imagination, visualization and reason. Hence our understanding of truth and beauty. Hence also our educability in all these respects, or lack of it, and our capacity and choice in work and leisure.[1]

It is also maintained by many geneticists that various special aptitudes, such as those for mathematics and for music, are inherited. But if our temperamental type and character structure, our intelligence, our imaginative range and special aptitudes, all develop in directions and within limits that are genetically prescribed, it seems that this pre-established framework of possibility must be distinct from the divinely infused soul, as part of its earthly environment. The body to which the soul is said to be attached already contains genetic information selecting the personal characteristics that can and cannot be developed; and this information is part of the range of environmental factors amid which the soul is placed when it is inserted into the body. In other words we must bracket inheritance and environment together as jointly constituting the soul's world. Inheritance provides the more immediate and individual setting of the soul's life, whilst the external world provides its less immediate and more public environment—the two being of course in continual interaction and jointly constituting the concrete situation within which the soul carries on its own life of spiritual progress or regress.

The problem facing the traditional soul–theorist, then, is to indicate an adequate content and function for the soul after genetics has pared so much away.

It might be suggested, for instance, that the soul is the locus of our personal and moral freedom. The question of freewill, like that of immortality, is an immensely intricate and important subject which I cannot attempt to discuss adequately in passing. I must be content to say that I am here presupposing a real though limited human freedom; for it appears to me that however strong the arguments for universal determinism may be, the claim to know that one is totally determined must always be a self-refuting claim, since the concept of knowledge embedded in our language presupposes that the cognising mind is not totally determined. Assuming, then, the (limited) freedom of the will, might we not identify the soul with this freedom? The answer, I think, is that freedom as a purely formal condition would not be sufficient to constitute the soul as the principal of individuation. We must add to it at least the basic personal nature in virtue of which the individual exercises his freedom in one way rather than in another. We should then identify the soul with certain fundamental dispositional characteristics—presumably our basic moral and religious attitudes. Thus a contemporary believer in the soul as a special divine creation seems led to the position that the attributes of the soul are the moral and spiritual dispositions which operate in worshipping, in valuing, in making ethical choices, and in adopting purposes and selecting ends. He will add that the material and social world of which we are a part sets the problems in the tackling of which the soul's earthly career consists, whilst our genetic inheritance, together with our acquired training and experience, furnish the tools with which we tackle those problems. Of course this distinction between problems and tools, or between the outer and inner layers of the soul's environment, is only a relative one; for the tools can themselves create problems by giving rise both to good opportunities (for example, to develop an artistic talent) and to evil temptations (for example, to be dominated by some animal drive or passion). Nevertheless on this view the soul remains as the core of the individual's being, his essential nature, consisting in a structure of personal and ethical characteristics which inhere, presumably, in some kind of persisting substratum or frame.

This notion coincides to a striking extent with the Indian idea of the *linga śarīra*, or "subtle body," as the bearer of a structure of moral and spiritual dispositions which are progressively reincarnated in a succession of psycho-physical individuals; and it may be instructive at this point to take note of this important Eastern conception.

The complex and profound philosophy of Advaita Vedanta, which represents the most influential school of Hindu thought today, speaks of innumerable eternal *jīvātmans* (or *jīvas*), which are ultimately identical with the Absolute, *Brahman*, but which now exist in a state of illusory separation from *Brahman*. And in this state of illusory separation the *jīvātman* has a number of bodies, thought of on the analogy of a series of sheaths enclosing the blade of a sword. One of these is the gross or physical body (*sthūla śarīra*) which begins to be formed at conception and begins to disintegrate at death. Another is the *linga śarīra*, usually translated, in a way that can easily mislead the Western reader, as the "subtle body." This is not a body at all in the customary Western sense of something occupying space (although in some Western esoteric and theosophical thought it is identified with an etheric or astral body). It is however bodily in the traditional Indian philosophical sense of lacking consciousness. It consists of a developing structure of moral and spiritual dispositions which is reincarnated by becoming successively associated with a series of physical bodies, whose growth it influences. As regards its content the Eastern *linga śarīra* is thus the equivalent of the Western soul when this latter has been reduced by the pressures of genetic science. It differs however in that in the West the soul is not usually thought of as reincarnating in a series of bodies; and also in that the soul, as the phenomenal ego, has the quality of self-consciousness. The *linga śarīra*, on the other hand, is a constellation of basic dispositional characteristics which goes on from life to life but which is other than a person in that it lacks consciousness and memory. Thus the idea of the *linga śarīra* or subtle body is akin to the late C. D. Broad's concept of the psychic factor.[2] Broad developed this notion largely to provide a possible explanation of the phenomenon of trance mediumship. When an individual dies the mental aspect of his being persists, not however as a complete conscious personality but as a constellation of mental elements—dispositions, memories, desires, fears, etc.—constituting a "psychic factor," which may hold together for a considerable time or may perhaps quickly disintegrate into scattered fragments. Broad suggested that such a psychic grouping, sufficiently cohesive to be identified as consisting of the memories and dispositional characteristics of a particular deceased individual, may become connected with a medium in a state of trance, thus generating a temporary conscious personality which is a conflation of certain persisting mental elements of the deceased together with the living structure of the medium. The theory of reincarnation can be seen as taking this concept further—as indeed Broad himself noted[3]—and claiming that the psychic factor which separates itself from the body at death subsequently becomes fused, not with the developed life-structure of a medium but with the still undeveloped life-structure of a human embryo. It then influences the growth of the embryo as a factor additional to its physical inheritance and its external environment.

This Indian concept of the *linga śarīra* agrees with the Western idea of the soul in that both postulate the existence of innate dispositional characteristics which are not part of the individual's genetic inheritance; and the same biological comment will be relevant to both. To what extent then, let us ask, is such an idea compatible with the account of man given today by the biological sciences?

The answer seems to be that whilst it cannot be proved that the two factors of heredity and environment between them account for the entire range of the individual's character traits, it certainly seems that they do and that there is no need to postulate in addition the influence of a soul or of a *linga śarīra* carrying basic dispositional characteristics either supplied directly by God or developed in previous earthly lives. There is a good deal of established correlation, for example, between experiences in early childhood and later moral attitudes; and without spelling this out in detail it can be said to give rise to a reasonable and fairly strong presumption that a man's moral character is formed during this life, partly through learning and partly through his reactions to environmental events. His inherited physical makeup enters into the process, of course, as its necessary basis, but there is so much evidence of the formation of moral character through the individual's interaction with environmental circumstances that there is no need to postulate either ethical genes or innate ethical dispositions carried in a soul or in a *linga śarīra*. From this point of view such hypotheses are redundant. At the same time, so long as we assume the reality of human freedom it must be impossible decisively to rule out these ancient conceptions. For the basic moral and spiritual dispositions which are said to inhere in the *linga śarīra*, or in the soul, presumably actualise themselves in our fundamental choices as free beings. And so long as one man freely differs from another in his moral and spiritual attitudes it will be impossible to disprove the claim that this difference is due to basic dispositions which were either formed in previous lives or implanted by God at conception.

In view of the empirically unverifiable and unfalsifiable nature of the hypothesis the main debate has to take place on other grounds; and I shall pursue it, to the limited extent that time allows, in relation to the Western idea of the soul as a metaphysical reality which God individually creates and attaches to the body. Let us ask what hangs upon the traditional insistence on the special divine creation of each soul. What has been the significance of this idea within the Western religious understanding of man? This understanding, as it has developed through the centuries and as it has worked itself out in Western theology and philosophy, social theory and the arts, and as it has been expressed in the organisation of human life in the West, sees the human being as a unique individual who is valued and sustained by his Creator and who in virtue of his relationship to the Eternal may enjoy an eternal life. Religiously the high point in the development of the idea occurred in Jesus' teaching about God as our heavenly Father, who knows each of His human children so that the very hairs of our heads are numbered. He cares for each like a shepherd seeking a lost sheep, or a needy widow searching for a lost coin, and He lavishes His love upon each like a father welcoming back a long-lost son. Philosophically, the high points are Plato's *Phaedo*, affirming the immortality of the rational soul; Descartes' *cogito ergo sum*, taking the existence of individual self-consciousness as the necessary starting point for thought; and Kant's founding of ethics upon the free, autonomous person seen as an end in himself. In politics the idea of the inherent value of the individual human being has worked itself out in the demise of feudalism, the eventual abandonment of slavery, the gradual growth of democracy, and in the advance of women towards full social equality with men. The common theme here is the idea of the unique value of the human person as a child of God, made in the divine image, and destined to an eternal life in fellowship with God.

Now how does this Western religious valuation of man agree with the random character of the process of meiosis in the formation of the individual sperm cell, and again with the randomness of the process by which one out of some four hundred million sperm, carrying their variant genetic codes, is selected to fertilise an ovum?

We have seen the difficulty of basing the traditional Christian valuation of man upon a doctrine of the special divine creation of the soul, defined as a metaphysical entity which God infuses into the body. Are we then to justify the high value of the human individual by saying that the hand of God has been secretly at work guiding the details of the meiotic division of cells, or in aiding one particular divinely favoured sperm in its race to the ovum? To suppose this would be to invoke the "God of the gaps" in a way which recent Christian thought has for the most part renounced. God, we have been saying, is the Lord of the natural order, not merely of the gaps in the natural order. To be sure, such miraculous divine interventions cannot be disproved. If there were sufficient other grounds for maintaining such a doctrine one could maintain it. But are there good grounds for insisting upon the special divine determination of the initial genetic makeup of each human person? Is there not on the contrary a strong theological motive for *not* wanting to maintain this? For do we really want to claim that God has specifically bestowed upon each individual the basic good and bad tendencies of character with which he is born? Would not this make Him the direct author of evil as well as good? Is it not therefore theologically preferable, as well as being in accordance with the picture indicated by the human sciences, to say that the genetic process includes a genuine element of unpredictable contingency?

We are not here in the realm of strict proof and disproof but of an informal process of probing in search of a more adequate conceptualisation of the data. As well as setting aside, as I think we must, the temptation to locate God's activity in the still unmapped intricacies of the genetic process we have also seen reasons to abandon the notion of the soul as a divinely created and infused entity. This does not however necessarily mean that the term "soul" can no longer have any proper use, but only that it should not be used as the name of a spiritual substance or entity. But we also commonly use the word as an indicator of value. "Save Our Souls," for example, the time-honoured distress signal at sea, is not only a call for help but at the same time a reminder of the value of those in danger, as fellow human beings and children of God. "You have no soul," said to an uncultured philistine, means that he lacks the capacity to appreciate value. When something is "soul-destroying" it is not the person but his values that are in danger of destruction. "Soul food" indicates the meaning of the food as a symbol of the values of the black community in its search for human justice and civil rights. And indeed I think it will be found that the word normally has a valuational connotation. It could well be that this feature of our ordinary use of the term points to its primary meaning within human communication and that the metaphysical theories of the soul are secondary, as speculative or mythological ways of affirming the unique value of the individual human person. If we accept this suggestion we shall not be opposed to the continued use of soul-language, or even to speaking of human beings as souls, or as having souls, in distinction perhaps from the lower animals; for such language will express that sense of the sacredness of human personality and of the inalienable rights of the human individual which we have already seen to be the moral and political content of the Western idea of the soul. Nor need the Church cease to strive to save souls; but the souls to be saved are simply people and not some mysterious religious entity attached to them. To speak of man as a soul is, then, to speak mythologically, but in a way which is bound up with important practical attitudes and practices. The myth of the soul expresses a faith in the intrinsic value of the human individual as an end in himself.

But let us now ask whether this valuation of humanity can continue to be religiously based once the metaphysical conception of the soul has been abandoned? In attempting to answer this question it will perhaps be best to speak from within the context of Christianity, as the faith which has historically particularly cherished and taught the idea of the sacredness of human personality and the value of men and women as rational and moral ends in themselves. Speaking, then, as a Christian theologian it appears to me that the time has come to complete the shift of emphasis in theological anthropology from the question of origins to the question of ends. It is not what man has come from but what he is going to that is important. We must assume that the picture being built up by the natural sciences of the origin of man, both individually and as a species, is basically correct and is progressively becoming more adequate and accurate as research continues. According to this picture, life on this planet began with natural chemical reactions occurring under the influence of radiations falling upon the earth's surface. Thus began the long, slow evolution of the forms of life, a process which has eventually produced man. And each human individual comes about through the partially random selection of a specific genetic code out of the virtually infinite range of possibilities contained even in the portion of genetic material lodged in his parents. This is, in broadest outline, the picture of man's beginning as it emerges from the physicists', chemists', and biologists' researches. And Christianity does not offer a different or rival account of our human origins. It says, in its Hebraic myth of man's genesis, that he has been created out of the dust of the earth; but the details of the creative process, from dust to the immensely complex religious and valuing human animal, are for the relevant sciences to trace.

If soul-language expresses a valuation of mankind, so that the soul is the human person seen and valued in this special way, then we must be prepared to renounce the idea that whereas the body has been produced by natural processes the soul has been produced by a special act of divine creation. We have to say that the soul is a divine creation in the same sense as the body—namely through the instrumentality of the entire evolution of the universe and within this of the development of life on our planet. Distinctively human mentality and spirituality emerges, in accordance with the divine purpose, in complex bodily organisms. But once it has emerged it is the vehicle, according to Christian faith, of a continuing creative activity only the beginnings of which have so far taken place.

The Biblical myth of Adam and Eve and their fall from grace, as it came to be interpreted in the mainstream of Christian tradition, cannot readily accommodate this conception. If we insist upon continuing to use the language of that tradition we have to qualify the meanings of our key terms until we no longer mean what other people hear us say. We find ourselves speaking of a fall which did not take place at any point in time, from a paradisaical condition which did not exist at any place. But on the other hand the alternative strand of Christian theology, which began as early as the second century A.D. in the work of some of the Greek Fathers, such as Irenaeus and Clement of Alexandria, can readily absorb the new empirical knowledge. Irenaeus distinguished between what he called the image of God and the likeness of God, and suggested a two-stage conception of the divine creation of man. The *imago dei* is man's nature as a rational, personal, and moral animal. Thus man in society, man the ethical being, man the creator of culture, exists in the image of God. It has taken many hundreds of millions of years of biological evolution to produce him, and yet even so he is only the raw material for the second stage of the creative process, which is the bringing of man, thus fashioned as person in the divine image, into the finite likeness of God. This latter state represents the fulfilment of the potentialities of our human nature, the completed humanisation of man in a society expressing mutual love. Whereas the first stage of creation is an exercise of divine power, the second stage is of a different kind; for the creatures who have been brought into existence in God's image are endowed with a real though limited freedom, and their further growth into the finite divine likeness has to take place through their own free responses within the world in which they find themselves. Human life as we know it is the sphere in which this second stage of creation is taking place; though it seems clear that if the process is to be completed it must continue in each individual life beyond our earthly three-score years and ten, whether by the survival of the mind after the death of the body or through the reconstitution of the total psycho-physical being. I have already declared my belief that both of these futures are conceivable— though I must in this context simply say this, without supporting arguments.

Such a religious interpretation of human existence is teleologically and indeed eschatologically oriented. The final meaning of man's life lies in the future state to which, in God's purpose, he is moving. And from this point of view man's lowly beginnings are not in contradiction with his high destiny. The origin of life out of the dust of the earth—or rather, in the scientifically preferred metaphor, out of the primeval soup; the emergence of the human species from lower forms of life to form the apex of the evolutionary procss; the programming of the individual genetic code through an unpredictable rearranging of the chromosomes; and again the unpredictable selection of one out of hundreds of millions of sperm to fertilise an ovum, are the ways in which man has been brought upon the stage. They do not in themselves tell us what he is here for or what his future is to be. The religions, however, do profess to tell us this. The Christian faith, in the Irenaean version of its theology, suggests that this complex process whereby man has been created as a personal being in God's image makes possible his cognitive freedom in relation to his Maker. Finding himself as part of an autonomous natural order, whose functioning can at all points be described without reference to a creator, man is not compelled to be conscious of God. He has an innate tendency to interpret his experience religiously, but if he gives rein to this tendency his resulting awareness of the divine is the kind of partially free awareness that we call faith. Thus man's existence as part of the natural order ensures his status as a relatively free being over against the infinite Creator. The finite creature is able to come as a (relatively) free person to know and worship God because his embeddedness in nature has initially set him at an epistemic distance from the divine Being. Thus the process by which men and women are formed may be understood, theologically, as an aspect of the self-governing natural order on which man's cognitive freedom in relation to his Creator depends. God wills to exist an autonomous physical universe, structured towards the production of rational and personal life—an organisation of matter which may well be developing not only on this earth but on millions of planets of millions of stars in millions of galaxies. The virtually infinite complexity of the cosmic process makes it to us, as finite minds existing within it, a law-governed realm which however includes randomness and unpredictability in its details; and as such it constitutes an environment within which we may grow as free beings towards that fullness of personal life, in conscious relationship to God, which (according to Christianity) represents the divine purpose for us.

NOTES

1. C. D. Darlington, *Genetics and Man* (London: Allen & Unwin, 1964), p. 241.
2. *The Mind and Its Place in Nature* (London: Routledge & Kegan Paul, 1925), pp. 536ff.
3. *Ibid.*, p. 551.

12

The Conquest of Death

Roland Puccetti
Dalhousie University

Old age is a shipwreck.

Charles de Gaulle

But think of the alternative.

Maurice Chevalier

Death, thou shalt die!

John Donne

EXCEPT FOR THE RELIGIOUSLY INCLINED, like Donne, it seems fatuous to talk of conquering death. Death is not the last disease mankind will have to overcome. It is what follows when the organism finally succumbs to disease or injury, the absence of life where there was life before. One does not, after everything else has happened, catch death too: if that were the case people would sometimes recover from death; but in this world, at least, they never do.

Does that mean men *must* die? This cannot be a logical "must." The familiar premiss "All men are mortal" is hardly analytic, since children who understand they are human are sometimes surprised to learn they will die. The statement must be empirical, an inductive generalisation of some sort. What evidence do we have for its truth? Just that all men we have known have died except those now living. Could anyone *know* it is true? I do not see how. The last man alive could know he is dying, but never that he had died.

However, this point cuts both ways. There seems no way a man could know he is not mortal, either. If Zeus or a voice from the heavens proclaimed to me that I had been given the gift of immortality, accompanied by suitable displays of miraculous powers, I might have good psychological reasons for expecting an open-ended personal future. But no amount of assurances could make this a necessary truth. There never could be a time when, having survived so long, I could be sure of living on still another day.

But then what shall we say about the notion of conquering death? If it does not convey immortality because nothing can logically guarantee this, is it an empty phrase? I shall take it to mean just the indefinite prolongation of life.

This essay is dedicated to the memory of William Arthur Sewell. Reprinted by permission from *The Monist*, 59 (1976), 249–63.

And since as I argued nothing in our logical conventions or even our conceptual scheme rules this out, it is a meaningful concept.

But is it theoretically as well as logically possible? Here the analogy with disease may not be entirely misleading. For we do speak of, and understand, the "conquest" of diseases like malaria and cholera where we do not mean they have been wholly eradicated, but that in some parts of the world at least they have been brought under medical control to a degree that few people ever have fatal encounters with them. Similarly, the notion of conquering death can be pared down to this: the idea that we might some day be able so to prolong life that few of us would die over very long time-spans, and then only by bizarre accidents. Is this conceivable? Could death itself become as rare as, say, death by tetanus or influenza is today? And would that be desirable?

I want to discuss this possibility at length, but first we have to get clear what the death of a human being amounts to.

THE PHYSIOLOGY OF DEATH

Looked at biologically, a human being like any organism above unicellular level is an integrated four-dimensional clone of cells. Obviously if all the cells constituting a human being die, he is dead too. But this cannot be our criterion of death, since some cells (e.g. cartilage cells) go on living for hours after a man's death; and no one would say we are burying him alive because part of, say, his left knee is living as we lower him into the grave. For the same reason we do not say a man is dead when a peripheral part of his body has died, e.g. a foot after severe frostbite. In both cases there has not been involvement of the central integrating organs, the life or death of which determines our judgment of the individual's continued survival.

What are these organs? First, there are the major supporting organs that keep the brain alive and conscious: heart and lungs. Second, the brain itself. Normally these function so interdependently that there is little point in distinguishing them with regard to the death of a man. Lung failure or heart failure or both together prevent oxygen-carrying blood from reaching the brain; hypoxia in the brain causes rapid destruction of tissue; and when the reticular core of the brainstem is damaged, there can be no recovery of consciousness. However, it must not be thought that these organs have a rough parity of importance to human life. Strictly speaking, it is not true that men die of heart attacks or drowning or lung cancer. Rather, these events cause paralysis or destruction of respiratory and cardiac functions, which causes anoxia in the brain; and it is *this* which in turn causes death of the brain and person. The point can be made this way: a bullet through the heart kills within minutes, but a bullet through the upper brainstem kills instantaneously. Admittedly, the distinction will seem picayune to someone facing a firing squad; but as we shall now see, it can have great importance in some controversial medical contexts.

NEOCORTICAL DEATH

In 1968 the Ad Hoc Committee of the Harvard Medical School issued a report intended to provide a definition of irreversible coma.[1] The authors were no doubt aware they were doing more than that: in effect the report sets out criteria of brain death which, if accepted, allow the physician to pronounce a terminal patient dead while his body, or the rest of it, is still living. The connection of this with the problem of justifying organ transplantation is too obvious to require discussion. Briefly summarized, these are the criteria:

1. Total lack of receptivity or responsiveness to externally applied stimuli, even what would be most painful stimuli, in the form of speaking or groaning, withdrawing a limb or quickening of respiration.
2. No spontaneous movements or breathing when the mechanical respirator is turned off for three minutes (long enough to see if the brainstem is functioning but not long enough to cause brain damage by anoxia).
3. No reflexes: pupil fixed and dilated, unresponsive to bright light; no ocular movements, postural activity, swallowing, yawning, tendon or muscular reflexes.
4. Flat electroencephalogram during ten minutes of recording, and no EEG response to noise or to pinching.
5. All of the above tests to be repeated twenty-four hours later with negative results.
6. Provided conditions of hypothermia (below 32° C.) and pharmacological depression (such as barbiturates) have been excluded, these indications of irreversible cerebral damage are conclusive.

Now, it is interesting that within the medical profession itself, and among others concerned with bioethical problems, there has been considerable disagreement about whether irreversible cerebral damage is itself tantamount to death of the person. In one sense, of course, it is not, because the person's body when on a heart and lung machine is still living, albeit artifically. But these days no one but a primitive Aristotelian would suppose the heart is the seat of consciousness; if it is agreed the brain is dead then we know the patient's conscious life has ended forever. Why should there by any difficulty here? So far as I can see, what has disturbed some people is just the fact that in a few, fortunately very rare, cases one can have neocortical death without brainstem death.[2] When this happens the patient, though permanently unconscious, is able to breathe spontaneously and exhibit reflex actions, thus passing the Harvard test for being alive, for as long as six months. One concerned group has said: "While an isoelectric EEG may be grounds for interrupting all forms of treatment and allowing these patients to die, it cannot itself be the basis for declaring dead someone who is still spontaneously breathing and who still has intact cerebral reflexes. It is inconceivable that society or the medical profession would allow the preparation of such persons for burial."[3] All I can say to this is that it is not inconceivable to me. When reasonably assured of a loved one's neocortical death, it would not have the slightest interest for me that this person was still breathing when prepared for burial, however grisly it might seem to those who have to do that. And I should hope those close to me would feel the same way in my own case. If someone suggested to me that my body might survive death of the neocortex for several months or years, provided it were fed and cleaned properly, etc., that would have no greater appeal to me than preservation of my appendix in a bottle of formaldehyde. For in the sense in which life has value for human beings, I would have been dead all that time. What we are talking about is not a living person but a breathing corpse. And if the notion of burying a breathing corpse is repulsive, then I suggest we simply stop it from breathing.

These morbid reflections do, however, provide us with some gain in physiological specificity. While a functioning reticular formation in the upper brainstem is necessary to consciousness accompanying neocortical functions, without the neocortex such paleocortical structures can maintain only the crudest sort of wakefulness,[4] and nothing like conscious human life. So at a bare minimum the conquest of death must mean indefinite prolongation of neocortical function—sustained and altered, normally, by those lower brain centres.

THE LOGIC OF SENESCENCE

All things get older; only living things age. A bacterium may live indefinitely under the right conditions, but more complex organisms cannot. If they manage to survive long enough, they all deteriorate and then die. They do not die *of* age; no one, really, succumbs to the burden of his years. But beyond maturity there always lies decline, greater and greater vulnerability to stress, injury, disease. It is interesting that in industrialised societies with high standards of medical care the number of people who achieve old age increases constantly, but the life span of men does not. It has been estimated that if cancer were extirpated this would add only 1.5 years to the allotted human span; even today only 1 in 100 of us will reach 90 years of age, and 1 in 1000 age 100. As of 1963 the oldest known man whose birth was fully authenticated died at 113 years 100 days, and that was back in 1814.[5]

The notion of a relatively fixed life-span in almost all forms of life above unicellular level suggests that we are somehow genetically programmed to age and die. However, there is no empirical evidence to support this idea, and upon reflection one sees it is superfluous. Darwinian principles apply to species, not to individuals; if the evolutionary rationale of individual decline and death is to avoid overpopulation and to assure dominance of new generations, who, by random mutation, will be better adapted to changing environmental circumstances, it is sufficient that members of the species *not* be programmed to go on sustaining size, strength, and physiological efficiency beyond maturity and reproductive activity. Bidder puts the point well:

> If primitive man at 18 begat a son, the species had no more need of him by 37, when his son could hunt for food for the grandchildren. Therefore the dwindling of cartilage, muscle and nerve cell, which we call senescence, did not affect

the survival of the species; the checking of growth had secured that by ensuring a perfect physique between 20 and 40. Effects of continued negative growth after 37 were of indifference to the race; probably no man ever reached 60 years old until language attained such importance in the equipment of the species that long experience became valuable in man who could neither fight nor hunt.[6]

If this is a substantially correct account of the logic of senescence, then the human situation is deplorable in two respects. First, the rising life expectancy of individuals in medically privileged societies, coupled with a fairly fixed total life-span for the species as a whole, means we are condemned to spending more and more of our lives in progressively debilitating bodily condition. Whereas primitive and even medieval European man probably lived less than ⅕ of his life in senescence, we are approaching a curve in which most of us will pass ½ of our lives that way. A study made some years ago with 400 males shows what we can expect.[7] Between the ages of 30 and 75 a man loses, on the average, the following: brain weight, 44%; blood flow to the brain, 20%; cardiac output, 30%; kidney plasma flow, 50%; the number of nerve trunk fibres, 37%; nerve conduction velocity, 10%; the number of taste buds, 64%; the maximum oxygen uptake during exercise, 60%; the maximum voluntary breathing capacity, 57%; strength of hand grip, 45%; basic metabolic rate, 16%; and total body weight, 12%. Since all these changes are gradual over 45 years, the ageing person does not feel suddenly deprived; if, however, they took place very quickly, one would have no hesitation describing this as a catastrophic loss.

Secondly, and perhaps more important, the complete waste of human ability and experience that accompanies the termination of senescence is a constant, recurring loss to all of society. Imagine a digital computer with 10^{10} units which builds up an extremely sophisticated programme for solving equations over several years, constantly improving the programme as it goes along, adding to its memory store, etc., until one day it breaks down, destroying within minutes all its circuitry and memory banks and simply disintegrating into metallic scrap. But something not entirely unlike that occurs every time a trained or educated human being dies. We spend the first two decades of our lives growing up, learning the language, acquiring basic knowledge and skills. Then we spend two more decades developing whatever special abilities we have to full productive potential. It is precisely at this point, the beginning of the plateau of maximum service to society, when incipient bodily deterioration becomes noticeable.[8] From here on the continued refinement of our skills and growth of our knowledge and judgment proceed side by side with physical decline for two or three decades, until we are forced into retirement, waiting quietly for the end. This pattern, whereby the occupational and intellectual worth of the individual continues to increase in inverse proportion to the ability of the organism to sustain this physically, is the price we pay for our evolutionary origins.

VARIOUS PANACEAS

Given these unpalatable facts, it is not surprising that men have always sought some magical way of staving off senescence and death, though usually from in-

dividual concerns rather than social ones. King David, among others, was coun-
seled to lie between two young girls; according to Marsilio Ficino (1498), the
old man should drink milk from the breast of a young girl.[9] No doubt these are
pleasant enough remedies, though probably too stressful for the elderly. Pope
Innocent VIII (1432–1492), showing perhaps a different predilection, had the
blood of young men transfused into his veins; since nothing was then known of
incompatible blood-types, he promptly died. Voronoff (1866–1951) attempted
grafting monkey testicles onto his aged male clients; Metchnikoff (1845–1916)
recommended yogurt and removal of the large intestine. Even today the search
goes on. In Bucharest, one can get injections of H-3 and KH-3; and in Switzer-
land, injections of living cells, usually from a lamb embryo.[10] Unfortunately it
is unclear how any of these measures would add to the genotype what is not
there, i.e. instructions to the body's cells to sustain their functions indefinitely
when this is unnecessary to species survival.

Perhaps aware of the fundamental problem, many people these days are opting for an entirely different kind of solution, what might be called the Great
Postponement. Here the idea is that what we cannot do today will certainly be
possible tomorrow, or the day after, or the day after that. All we individuals
need concern ourselves with is being around when the currently impossible becomes possible, i.e. in some indefinite future state of scientific and technological
progress. And the way to do that, they say, is by getting yourself frozen. But
there are two, in some ways opposed, schools of thought on the subject, and in
fairness they must be separated.

The first and more radical school is the "Freeze Dead" school, which pins its
faith on eventual thawing out and *reanimation*. For about $10,000 you can
arrange to have your corpse perfused with glycerol or DMSO and cryogenically
interred in a liquid nitrogen environment; robot surgeons of the future will
obligingly "reconstruct" the damaged brain so that you will live again, perhaps
unendingly.[11] Certainly this proposal will do no harm, if you can afford $10,000
and particularly like the idea of permanent embalmment: the advantage of believing in any kind of resurrection is that you will never find out you were wrong.
However, there can be no serious expectation of surgeons' "restoring" thousands
of millions of destroyed and missing neurons with all the precise interconnec-
tions they had before you died so that *you*, an individual person, would live
again; how could they, since the pattern of neocortical connections disappeared
before you were frozen?

The second school, recognising this fact, is more modest. It urges research in
cryogenics so that some day *suspended animation* may be achieved in mammals,
eventually in men, without the present-day hazards of ventricular fibrillation,
cellular destruction by formation of ice crystals, and other problems. It is, in
other words, the "Freeze Alive" school of thought. But it, too, banks on one's
being reawakened centuries later when, in one author's words, "All disease and
aging are cured—relegated to history."[12] Here, of course, there is an explicit
assumption that genetic engineering will allow us to change the genotype itself.
Without this being achieved, "hybernauts" of the future will not gain greater
longevity by suspended animation; seventy or so years of conscious life is still

no more than seventy years if you live half of it in the twentieth century and half in the twenty-second.

Can the genotype be changed? Sir Macfarlane Burnet, discussing the publicity accompanying Kornberg's successful synthesis of DNA in 1967, has this to say:

> What they [Kornberg and Tatum] were envisaging in principle was that in due course it could become possible to extract from normal human cells the sequence of DNA that was missing from or wrongly made in the patient. Once isolated these could be used as the pattern, the template, for the synthesis by bacterial enzymes of numerous replicas of itself. This is acceptable as a possibility of the foreseeable future. The next step would be the crucial and probably impossible one: to incorporate the gene into the genetic mechanism of a suitable virus vehicle in such a fashion that the virus in its turn will transfer the gene it is carrying to cells throughout the body and in the process precisely replace the faulty gene with the right one. I should be willing to state in any company that the chance of doing this will remain infinitely small to the last syllable of recorded time.[13]

But Sir Macfarlane was talking only of *one* faulty gene responsible, say, for a specific hereditary defect like harelip. If senescence and hence greater vulnerability to fatal injury or disease is due to most of the human body's organs' not being programmed to sustain optimum efficiency beyond maturity, then to "cure" ageing would involve altering a vast number of genes such that all these organs never falter or wear out. I conclude, always tentatively, that as long as we have bodies we shall grow old and die, and that no amount of scientific optimism will change this.

CYBORG MAN

But must we have bodies? I said earlier that conscious human life—the only sort worth having—is rooted in neocortical function, sustained and alerted to consciousness by the reticular formation in the brainstem and associated structures. It follows that an intact human brain kept *in vitro* but nourished by a properly oxygenated and glucose-supplied blood flow mechanically pumped into it through the severed arteries could support conscious life; indeed there is partial support for this claim in the fact that monkey brains have been kept alive for several days *in vitro*: the EEG recordings indicated periods of consciousness.[14]

However, an isolated human brain, devoid of neural inputs and unable to affect anything with its motor commands, would have an unenviable life. It would see nothing, hear nothing, feel nothing. When conscious it could only feed on its memories of an embodied past and, eerily, talk to itself, an endless silent monologue. (Theologians will recognise in this description the physiological analogue of continued existence as a disembodied soul.) It would appear that to live a genuinely human life, a body is necessary after all.

But need it be a *human* body, hence vulnerable to ageing and death? Need it even be a *living* body? I do not see why. After all, the body is just the means by which our brains interact with the extrabodily environment. In principle, though it is technologically very far-fetched, we could someday build prosthetic bodies housing portable, miniaturised heart-and-lung machines that keep the brain— comfortably installed in the head cavity—well-nourished with blood and glucose, etc. Descending neural pathways from the brain would end at, say, the medulla oblongata, where the electrical charges they emit could activate a miniaturised digital computer to perform limb movements. Conversely, receptors in the prosthetic body would send messages up to the computer, which could in turn fire the proper sequence of ascending nerve fibres that transform these into proprioceptive, kinesthetic, somesthetic, and tactile sensations in the brain. It is important to note that these sensations would be qualitatively indistinguishable from those we now experience. A touch or caress upon the surface of the prosthetic body would be felt by the person whose brain it is as *his* bodily sensation: One must not think one would be sacrificing all the pleasures of having a body by exchanging the one he now has for an inanimate replica body. And indeed for aesthetic and psychological reasons, as well as satisfying third-person criteria of personal identity, this prosthetic body should be modeled on his own: he might, however, introduce one or two long-desired cosmetic changes.

What I have just described is technically outrageous, but it does not require overriding any physiological realities.[15] Even vision and hearing could be achieved with a prosthetic body of sufficient sophistication, by having mechanical sensors fire the appropriate neurons in the visual and auditory cortices directly, thus bypassing the normal optic and auditory nerve pathways: indeed in the case of vision that would only be an extension of present research.[16] But I shall leave further details to the imagination. I am not sure, for example, whether it would be worthwhile to develop mechanical digestive and excretory systems, just in order not to forgo the pleasures of the table; or whether one should sacrifice some surface sensitivity in the prosthetic body to avoid risk of activating pain mechanisms in the brain. These are complications we can afford to neglect.

AGEING IN CYBORG MAN

The idea of escaping the evolutionary limitations of our present bodies by having our brains transplanted at postmaturity into bodies which, being inorganic, do not age or deteriorate, has a prima facie attractiveness about it. If I am correct that death amounts to destruction of the neocortex, then the most common causes of this—failure of supportive organs due to conditions like heart disease or lung cancer—would not kill cyborg man. Indeed a great number of widely held theories about the mechanisms of senescence in higher animals would have no application to him. These include those which emphasise the increase of collagen, a fibrous protein, in the body;[17] the theory that capillary breakdown due to circulatory deficiency is the culprit;[18] the decline-in-endocrine-gland approach; that version of the waste product theory which blames faulty metabolism and the increase of toxic substances in the blood;[19] and the theory that failing autoimmunological surveillance related to a diminishing thymus is responsible.[20] Even such general restrictions on longevity as the "Hayflick Limitation," which limits the number of times an embryonic human cell can divide in tissue culture (about fifty),[21] seems irrelevant to the postmitotic cells of the brain. Radiation, of course, can destroy the chromosomal integrity of any cell, including those of the human brain, but at less than cytoxic levels it does not seem to have any effect on ageing.[22]

The greatest challenge to any hope of vastly prolonging human life by corporeal prosthesis is found in *Abnutzungstheorie*, the "wear and tear" view of ageing. For if this is right the brain of cyborg man would, just like any bodily organ, wear out in time. And certainly the large (statistically established) loss of brain weight between ages thirty and seventy-five mentioned earlier supports this pessimism. However, it is far from clear how, if at all, this loss contributes to death. For one thing, cellular fallout appears to begin at puberty rather than middle age, while both physical strength and intellectual growth are still increasing. What is more, it seems to *taper off* in the last decade of a normal lifespan. A recent study by Tomlinson suggests that there is no significant difference in the proportionate brain weight of intellectually unimpaired people who die at sixty-five and those who die at seventy-five. Speaking of twenty-eight cases, he says: "As a group, loss of brain weight and the degree of cerebral atrophy was relatively slight, and the lateral ventricles were only slightly larger than those of normal young adults. Indeed all the brain weights fell within the normal limits for young adults and many brains showed no apparent cortical atrophy or significant ventricular dilation." [23]

Dayan has made a thorough review of evidence for pathological change in the ageing human brain and it is surprising how difficult it is to say in what these changes consist. Atrophy clearly occurs, but the nature of the loss is unknown since suggested anatomical sites for the loss have been disproven at almost every place where exact counts have been made. Argyrophilic plaques appear in the cortex in the sixth or seventh decade of life, and neurofibrillary tangles at about the same time: these are independent idiopathic degenerative processes, but they do not appear to affect the most important neuronal processes. Neuro-axonal dystrophy is another invariable finding, but of very limited functional significance; and the same appears to be true of amyloid deposits around small blood vessels in the cortex and of intra-neuronal inclusions.[24] Other types of brain lesions associated with ageing are too variable to be significant. It is true that lipofucins build up in brain cells (and in heart muscle cells) with age; another version of the waste product theory holds this to be responsible for senescence. However, artificially induced concentrations of these substances in rats did not alter their life-span,[25] and there is some evidence this pigment can be decreased by chemical treatment.[26]

But even if cellular fallout and cortical atrophy are not themselves clearly fatal, it is true that with age our brains become more and more susceptible to disorders of cerebral blood flow that can cause fatal brain trauma such as atheroma of the arteries, thrombosis, embolisms, aneurysms, sclerosis, etc. However, it is not known to what degree circulatory deficiencies reflect degenerative changes in the ageing brain, or are due primarily to failing cardiac/respiratory support systems in an ageing body.[27] If the latter is the case, cyborg man's brain might very well retain efficient blood circulation indefinitely, because of superior artificial (and easily replaceable) support systems. Even if, as now appears the case,[28] cerebrovascular insufficiency in the elderly is due to malfunctioning central ganglion cells, leading to decreased oxygen and glucose uptake, it has been shown that brain metabolism is responsive to pharmaceutical treatment.[29] In cyborg man autoregulatory mechanisms of the brain could be monitored by computer and appropriate chemicals injected into the blood stream when needed. About all one can say in our present state of knowledge is that we just do not know whether, under these idealised conditions, the human brain could survive the ageing process for an indefinite period of time.

THE INTELLECT OF CYBORG MAN

Senility is so often associated with senescence in our experience of elderly people that one might legitimately wonder if, even if cyborg man's brain did not die with age, it would not become so intellectually deteriorated that the whole exercise would be futile. What is the point of keeping a man alive and conscious in a youthful-looking prosthetic body if he becomes doddering, absent-minded, amnesic, cranky, etc., *anyway*?

Bromley[30] and Welford[31] have independently shown that there *is* a decline in intellectual ability with normal ageing, which they attribute to deterioration in the central processing functions of cognition. However, this relates to intelligence testing of a large number of individuals from all walks of life. One would expect that in the creative professions the gain from experience, learning, and refinement of judgment outweighs this mild decline in general capacity. After all, the value to us of a playwright or paleontologist or painter is not measured by his performance on the WAIS over the years, but on the quality and quantity of his output. Even if this also declines between, say, ages fifty and sixty-five, that may not be disconnected from the fact that he is then becoming but two-thirds or so of the man he was in terms of organic, physiological efficiency. Cyborg man would not show physiological deterioration like this; it remains to be proved that he would *nevertheless* decline intellectually. Even Bromley admits that effects of ageing appear to be *less* conspicuous in the brain than some other systems of the body.[32] Without deleterious changes in the body at all, why should the brain begin to fail?

And indeed if not, if cyborg man's brain neither died nor deteriorated with age, think of what this could mean to society. Imagine that we had been able to do hundreds of years ago what I am suggesting we may be able to do hundreds of years from now. Who can say that the geniuses of the seventeenth century would not have done two, three, any number of times as much great work had they lived on in good health to age 200, 300, or more years? Shakespeare might not have gone into voluntary retirement; Newton's life might have overlapped with Einstein's; and Beethoven might be with us still. True, even cyborg man could perish in the accidents of life. A hard enough blow to the prosthetic head would dispatch him as easily as it does us. He could still drown or get run over or have an irate husband shoot him. But once the principal causes of human mortality are eliminated, the genius has as good an opportunity to live half a millennium as to live half a hundred years.

IS DEATH DESIRABLE?

Leon Kass has said that death is "not only inevitable, but also biologically, psychologically, and spiritually desirable."[33] I hope I have said enough to show that one may rationally doubt whether it is inevitable. Dr. Kass offers no argument for the rest of his statement. That death should be *biologically* desirable suggests Weismann's old argument that "Worn-out individuals are not only valueless to the species, but they are even harmful, for they take the place of those which are sound."[34] Alex Comfort's rejoinder to this is worth quoting: "This argument both assumes what it sets out to explain, that the survival of an individual decreases with increasing age, and denies its own premiss, by suggesting that worn-out individuals threaten the existence of the young."[35] However, Kass may only have meant that in most species *overpopulation* would result from this. That is true; but the difficulty and expense of creating cyborg men are such that either (1) only few individuals of great promise would be preserved this way, somewhat like the system of academic tenure today, *or* (2) in a society which could afford to give every mature male and female this option, overpopulation would have been solved by birth control, planetary and stellar migration, etc., long before.

That death is *spiritually* desirable is incomprehensible to me since in many of the great living religions, at least, it is the (other-worldly) conquest of death which gives them much of their attraction and *rationale*. But of course in another sense what Kass says is true: for some religions it is terribly important that you experience complete *physical* death before, with luck and merit, you are allowed to live again. But since I am not concerned in this essay with spiritual matters, I shall let that pass.

That death is *psychologically* desirable is a more interesting suggestion. On the surface it has a certain appeal. There are certainly moments when, peering vaguely ahead into our lives, Marcus Aurelius' plaintive question "*Quousque tandem?*" takes on real meaning. Death appears as the darkness at the end of a cone of diminishing light, and it is not unwelcome. It equals perfect rest, the end of tribulations. But apart from those unfortunates whose continued lives have become circled in pain or stress, we show a remarkable reluctance to step into the shadows. We cling on, and scream against the dying light. Perhaps that is just selfishness; but how many of us, in good health and with undiminished intellectual powers, would really say: "Well, tomorrow is all right with me"? Surely on the morrow we would want to say the same. It is only because the cone stretches far ahead that the shadows seem welcome.

But I do not like to think of death just in my own case. We must all have had friends, or at least one friend, who was personally so valuable to us that his decline and death seems an irreparable loss to ourselves and everyone who knew him. Such a person, bright and warm and enriching to the end, was in fact based in a well-functioning neocortex being slowly more threatened with death from an ageing supportive body system. We need only ask ourselves this question: If I could have *him*, or *her*, sitting here with me in my study tonight, joking and commenting on the latest news or theory or what have you, would it matter greatly that he or she was there in a prosthetic body? And if he or she could have been installed in such a body when he or she was thirty-five or forty, would that be worse than the cruel image Shakespeare etched in our racial memory with these words?

> . . . and his big manly voice
> Turning again toward childish treble, pipes
> And whistles in his sound. Last scene of all,
> That ends this strange eventful history,
> Is second childishness and mere oblivion—
> Sans teeth, sans eyes, sans taste, sans everything.
>   —*As You Like It*

NOTES

1. *Journal of the American Medical Association*, 205 (1968), 337–40.

2. J. B. Brierly et al., "Neocortical Death After Cardiac Arrest," *Lancet*, 2 (1971), 560–65. Neuropathological examination confirmed death of the neocortices in these patients.

3. Task Force on Death and Dying, The Institute of Society, Ethics, and the Life Sciences, "Refinements in Criteria for the Determination of Death: An Appraisal," *Journal of the American Medical Association*, 221 (1972), 48–53.

4. P. Bard and M. B. Macht, "The Behaviour of Chronically Decerebrate Cats," *Neurological Basis of Behaviour* (London: Churchill, 1958), pp. 55–75.

5. Alex Comfort, *Ageing: The Biology of Senescence* (London: Routledge & Kegan Paul, 1964), fig. 72 p. 272, pp. 275, 88.

6. G. P. Bidder, "Senescence," *British Medical Journal*, 11 (1932), 5831; see also Comfort, *Ageing*, Ch. 8.

7. Nathan W. Shock, "The Physiology of Aging," *Scientific American* (January 1962), 100–10.

8. It is true that the maximum work rate drops 30% between ages 30 and 75, and the maximum work rate for short bursts as much as 60% (Shock, 101). But that is *physical* work. My remarks obviously do not apply to unskilled manual labour, or to professional sports.

9. Comfort, *Ageing*, p. 183.

10. *Theory and Therapeutics of Aging*, ed. Ewald W. Busse (New York: Medcom Press, 1973), Chap. 1.

11. R. C. W. Ettinger, *The Prospect of Immortality* (New York: Doubleday, 1964), pp. 29–30.

12. Robert W. Prehoda, *Suspended Animation* (Philadelphia: Chilton, 1969), p. 126.

13. Macfarlane Burnet, *Genes, Dreams and Realities* (New York: Penguin, 1973), p. 81.

14. Robert J. White, Maurice S. Albin, and Javier Verdura, "Preservation of

Viability in the Isolated Monkey Brain Utilizing a Mechanical Extracorporeal Circulation," *Nature*, 202 (1964), 1082–83.

15. A special problem, however, would be finding a way to prevent degeneration of the severed nerve endings in the lower brainstem above the break: in higher vertebrates this always occurs. Some technique of artificial nerve regeneration is the major requirement here.

16. G. S. Brindley and W. S. Lewin, "The Sensations Produced by Electrical Stimulation of the Visual Cortex," *Journal of Physiology*, 196 (1968), 479–93.

17. T. Verzar, "Aging of Connective Tissue," *Gerontologia*, 1 (1957), 363–78.

18. N. Seyle and P. Prioreschi, "Stress Theory of Aging," *Aging: Some Social and Biological Aspects*, ed. N. W. Shock (Washington: American Association for the Advancement of Science, 1960), pp. 261–72.

19. A. Carrell and A. H. Ebeling, "Antagonistic Growth Activity and Growth Inhibiting Principles in Serum," *Journal of Experimental Medicine*, 37 (1923), 653–59.

20. R. W. Walford, "Auto-immunity and Aging," *Journal of Gerontology*, 17 (1962), 281–85.

21. T. Hayflick, "The Limited *in vitro* Lifetime of Human Diploid Cell Strains," *Experimental Cellular Research*, 37 (1965), 614–36.

22. P. Alexander, "Is There a Relationship Between Aging, the Shortening of Life Span by Radiation and the Induction of Somatic Mutations?" in *Perspectives in Experimental Gerontology*, ed. N. W. Shock (Springfield: Thomas, 1966), Chap. 20.

23. B. E. Tomlinson, "Morphological Brain Changes in Non-Demented Old People," *Ageing of the Central Nervous System*, edd. H. M. van Praag and A. T. Kalverboer (Haarlem: Bohn, 1972), p. 51.

24. A. D. Dayan, "The Brain and Theories of Ageing," *ibid.*, pp. 64–66.

25. N. M. Sulkin and P. Srevanij, "The Experimental Production of Senile Pigments in the Nerve Cells of Young Rats," *Journal of Gerontology*, 15 (1960), 2–9.

26. K. Nandy and G. H. Bourne, "Effect of Centropheonoxine on the Lipofucin Pigments in the Neurons of Senile Guinea-pigs," *Nature*, 210 (1972), 313ff.

27. Lord Brain and J. N. Walton, *Brain's Diseases of the Nervous System* (7th ed.; London: Oxford University Press, 1969), Chap. 4.

28. M. Ditch et al., "An Ergot Preparation (Hydergine) in the Treatment of Cerebrovascular Disorders in the Geriatric Patient: Double-Blind Study," *Journal of the American Geriatrics Society*, 19 (1971), 208.

29. D. B. Rao and J. R. Norris, "A Double-Blind Investigation of Hydergine in the Treatment of Cerebrovascular Insufficiency in the Elderly," *Johns Hopkins Medical Journal*, 130 No. 5 (1972), 317–24.

30. D. B. Bromley, "Some Effects of Age on the Quality of Intellectual Output," *Journal of Gerontology*, 12 (1957), 318–23; id., "Age Difference in Conceptual Abilities," *Processes of Aging*, edd. R. H. Williams, C. Tibbits, and W. Donahue (New York: Atherton, 1963), Vol. 1.

31. A. T. Welford, *Ageing and Human Skill* (London: Oxford University Press, 1958).

32. D. B. Bromley, "Intellectual Changes in Adult Life and Old Age," *Ageing* (n. 23), pp. 76–100.

33. In his "Death as an Event: A Commentary on Robert Morison," *Science*, 173 (1970), 701–12 n. 10.

34. A. Weismann, *Über die Dauer des Lebens* (Jena, 1882).

35. Comfort, *Ageing*, p. 11.

13

Survival and the Idea of 'Another World'

H. H. PRICE
New College, Oxford

IN THIS PAPER I am concerned only with the conception of survival; with the *meaning* of the Survival Hypothesis, and not with its truth or falsity. When we consider the Survival Hypothesis, whether we believe it or disbelieve it, what is it that we have in mind? Can we form any idea, even a rough and provisional one, of what a disembodied human life might be like? Supposing we cannot, it will follow that what is called the Survival Hypothesis is a mere set of words and not a hypothesis at all. The evidence adduced in favour of it might still be evidence for something, and perhaps for something important, but we should no longer have the right to claim that it is evidence for survival. There cannot be evidence for something which is completely unintelligible to us.

A very great deal of work has been done on the problem of survival, and much of the best work by members of the Society for Psychical Research. Yet there are the widest differences of opinion about the results. A number of intelligent persons would maintain that we now have a very large mass of evidence in favour of survival; that some of it is of very good quality indeed, and cannot be explained away unless we suppose that the supernormal cognitive powers of some embodied human minds are vastly more extensive and more accurate than we can easily believe them to be; in short, that on the evidence available the Survival Hypothesis is more probable than not. Some people—and not all of them are silly or credulous—would even maintain that the Survival Hypothesis is proved, or as near to being so as my empirical hypothesis can be. On the other hand, there are also many intelligent persons who entirely reject these conclusions. Some of them, no doubt, have not taken the trouble to examine the evidence. But others of them have; they may even have given years of study to it. They would agree that the evidence is evidence of *something*, and very likely of something important. But, they would say, it cannot be evidence of survival;

Originally presented as a lecture to mark the seventieth anniversary of the Society for Psychical Research, this paper was first published in the *Proceedings of the Society for Psychical Research*, 50 Part 182 (January 1953), 1–25; reprinted by permission.

there *must* be some alternative explanation of it, however difficult it may be to find out. Why do they take this line? I think it is because they find the very conception of survival unintelligible. The very idea of a "discarnate human personality" seems to them a muddled or absurd one; indeed not an idea at all, but pust a phrase—an emotionally exciting one, no doubt—to which no clear meaning can be given.

Moreover, we cannot just ignore the people who have not examined the evidence. Some of our most intelligent and most highly educated contemporaries are among them. These men are well aware, by this time, that the evidence does exist, even if their predecessors fifty years ago were not. If you asked them why they do not trouble to examine it in detail, they would be able to offer reasons for their attitude. And one of their reasons, and not the least weighty in their eyes, is the contention that the very idea of survival is a muddled or absurd one. To borrow an example from Whately Carington, we know pretty well what we mean by asking whether Jones has survived a shipwreck. We are asking whether he continues to live after the shipwreck has occurred. Similarly it makes sense to ask whether he survived a railway accident, or the bombing of London. But if we substitute "his own death" for "a shipwreck," and ask whether he has survived it, our question (it will be urged) becomes unintelligible. Indeed, it *looks* self-contradictory, as if we were asking whether Jones is still alive at a time when he is no longer alive—whether Jones is both alive and not alive at the same time. We may try to escape from this logical absurdity by using phrases like "discarnate existence," "alive, but disembodied." But such phrases, it will be said, have no clear meaning. No amount of facts, however well established, can have the slightest tendency to support a meaningless hypothesis, or to answer an unintelligible question. It would therefore be a waste of time to examine such facts in detail. There are other and more important things to do.

If I am right so far, questions about the meaning of the word "survival" or of the phrase "life after death" are not quite so arid and academic as they may appear. Anyone who wants to maintain that there is empirical evidence for survival ought to consider these questions, whether he thinks the evidence strong or weak. Indeed, anyone who thinks there is a *problem* of survival at all should ask himself what his conception of survival is.

Now why should it be thought that the very idea of life after death is unintelligible? Surely it is easy enough to conceive (whether or not it is true) that experiences might occur after Jones's death which are linked with experiences which he had before his death, in such a way that his personal identity is preserved? But, it will be said, the idea of after-death *experiences* is just the difficulty. What kind of experiences could they conceivably be? In a disembodied state, the supply of sensory stimuli is perforce cut off, because the supposed experient has no sense organs and no nervous system. There can therefore be no sense-perception. One has no means of being aware of material objects any longer; and if one has not, it is hard to see how one could have any emotions or wishes either. For all the emotions and wishes we have in this present life are concerned directly or indirectly with material objects, including of course our own organisms and other organisms, especially other human ones. In short, one could only be said to have experiences at all, if one is aware of some sort of a *world.* In this way, the idea of survival is bound up with the idea of "another world" or a "next world." Anyone who maintains that the idea of survival is after all intelligible must also be claiming that we can form some conception, however rough and provisional, of what "the next world" or "other world" might be like. The sceptics I have in mind would say that we can form no such conception at all; and this, I think, is one of the main reasons why they hold that the conception of survival itself is unintelligible. I wish to suggest, on the contrary, that we *can* form some conception, in outline at any rate, of what a "next world" or "another" world might be like, and consequently of the kind of experiences which disembodied minds, if indeed there are such, might be supposed to have.

The thoughts which I wish to put before you on this subject are not at all original. Something very like them is to be found in the chapter on survival in Whately Carington's book *Telepathy* (London: Methuen, 1945), and in the concluding chapter of Professor C. J. Ducasse's book *Nature, Mind and Death* (LaSalle: Open Court, 1951). Moreover, if I am not mistaken, the Hindu conception of *Kama Loka* (literally, "the world of desire") is essentially the same as the one I wish to discuss; and something very similar is to be found in Mahayana Buddhism. In these two religions, of course, there is not just one "other world" but several different "other worlds," which we are supposed to experience in succession; not merely the next world, but the next but one, and another after that. But I think it will be quite enough for us to consider just the next world, without troubling ourselves about any additional other worlds which there might be. It is a sufficiently difficult task, for us Western people, to convince ourselves that it makes sense to speak of any sort of after-death world at all. Accordingly, I shall use the expressions "next world" and "other world" interchangeably. If anyone thinks this is an oversimplification, it will be easy for him to make the necessary corrections.

The next world might be conceived as a kind of dream-world. When we are asleep, sensory stimuli are cut off, or at any rate are prevented from having their normal effects upon our brain-centres. But we still manage to have experiences. It is true that sense-perception no longer occurs, but something sufficiently like it does. In sleep, our image-producing powers, which are more or less inhibited in waking life by a continuous bombardment of sensory stimuli, are released from this inhibition. And then we are provided with a multitude of objects of awareness, about which we employ our thoughts and towards which we have desires and emotions. These objects which we are aware of behave in a way which seems very queer to us when we wake up. The laws of their behaviour are not the laws of physics. But however queer their behaviour is, it does not at all disconcert us at the time and our personal identity is not broken.

In other words, my suggestion is that the next world, if there is one, might be a world of mental images. Nor need such a world be so "thin and insubstantial" as you might think. Paradoxical as it may sound, there is nothing imaginary about a mental image. It is an actual entity, as real as anything can be. The seeming paradox arises from the ambiguity of the verb "to imagine." It does sometimes mean "to have mental images." But more usually it means "to entertain propositions without believing them"; and very often they are false propositions, and moreover we *dis*believe them in the act of entertaining them. This is what happens, for example, when we read Shakespeare's play *The Tempest*, and that is why we say that Prospero and Ariel are "imaginary characters." Mental images are not in this sense imaginary at all. We do actually experience them, and they are no more imaginary than sensations. To avoid the paradox, though at the cost of some pedantry, it would be well to distinguish between *imagining* and *imaging*, and to have two different adjectives "imaginary" and "imagy." In this terminology, it is imaging, and not imagining, that I wish to talk about; and the next world, as I am trying to conceive of it, is an *imagy* world, but not on that account an imaginary one.

Indeed, to those who experienced it an image-world would be just as "real" as this present world is; perhaps so like it, that they would have considerable difficulty in realizing that they were dead. We are, of course, sometimes told in mediumistic communication that quite a lot of people do find it difficult to realize that they are dead; and this is just what we should expect if the next world is an image-world. Lord Russell and other philosophers have maintained that a material object in this present physical world is nothing more or less than a complicated system of *appearances*. So far as I can see, there might be a set of visual images related to each other perspectivally, with front views and side views and back views all fitting neatly together in the way that ordinary visual appearances do now. Such a group of images might contain tactual images too. Similarly it might contain auditory images and smell images. Such a family of interrelated images would make a pretty good object. It would be quite a satisfactory substitute for the material objects which we perceive in this present life. And a whole world composed of such families of mental images would make a perfectly good world.

It is possible, however, and indeed likely, that some of those images would be what Francis Galton called *generic* images. An image representing a dog or a tree need not necessarily be an exact replica of some individual dog or tree one has perceived. It might rather be a representation of a *typical* dog or tree. Our memories are more specific on some subjects than on others. How specific they are depends probably on the degree of interest we had in the individual objects or events at the time when we perceived them. An event which moved us deeply is likely to be remembered specifically and in detail; and so is an individual object to which we were much attached (for example, the home of our childhood). But with other objects which interested us less and were less attended to, we retain only a "general impression" of a whole class of objects collectively. Left to our own resources, as we should be in the other world, with nothing but our memories to depend on, we should probably be able to form only generic images of such objects. In this respect, an image-world would not be an exact replica of this one, not even of those parts of this one which we have actually perceived. To some extent it would be, so to speak, a generalized picture, rather than a detailed reproduction.

Let us now put our question in another way, and ask what kind of experience a disembodied human mind might be supposed to have. We can then answer that it might be an experience in which *imaging* replaces sense-perception; "replaces" it, in the sense that imaging would perform much the same function as sense-perception performs now, by providing us with objects about which we could have thoughts, emotions, and wishes. There is no reason why we should not be "as much alive," or at any rate *feel* as much alive, in an image-world as we do now in this present material world, which we perceive by means of our sense-organs and nervous systems. And so the use of the word "survival" ("life after death") would be perfectly justifiable.

It will be objected, perhaps, that one cannot be said to be alive unless one has a body. But what is meant here by "alive"? It is surely conceivable (whether or not it is true) that *experiences* should occur which are not causally connected with a physical organism. If they did, should we or should we not say that "life" was occurring? I do not think it matters much whether we answer Yes or No. It is purely a question of definition. If you define "life" in terms of certain very complicated physico-chemical processes, as some people would, then of course life after death is by definition impossible, because there is no longer anything to be alive. In that case, the problem of survival (*life* after bodily death) is misnamed. Instead, it ought to be called the problem of after-death *experiences*. And this is in fact the problem with which all investigators of the subject have been concerned. After all, what people want to know, when they ask whether we survive death, is simply whether experiences occur after death, or what likelihood, if any, there is that they do; and whether such experiences, if they do occur, are linked with each other and with *ante mortem* ones in such a way that personal identity is preserved. It is not physico-chemical processes which interest us, when we ask such questions. But there is another sense of the words "life" and "alive" which may be called the psychological sense; and in this sense "being alive" just *means* "having experiences of certain sorts." In this psychological sense of the word "life," it is perfectly intelligible to ask whether there is life after death, even though life in the physiological sense does *ex hypothesi* come to an end when someone dies. Or, if you like, the question is whether one could feel alive after bodily death, even though (by hypothesis) one would not *be* alive at the time. It will be just enough to satisfy most of us if the *feeling* of being alive continues after death. It will not make a halfpennyworth of difference that one will not then *be* alive in the physiological or biochemical sense of the word.

It may be said, however, that "feeling alive" (life in the psychological sense) cannot just be equated with having experiences in general. Feeling alive, surely, consists in having experiences of a special sort, namely *organic sensations*— bodily feelings of various sorts. In our present experience, these bodily feelings are not as a rule separately attended to unless they are unusually intense or unusually painful. They are a kind of undifferentiated mass in the background of consciousness. All the same, it would be said, they constitute our feeling of being alive; and if they were absent (as surely they must be when the body is dead) the feeling of being alive could not be there.

I am not at all sure that this argument is as strong as it looks. I think we should still feel alive—or alive enough—provided we experienced emotions and wishes, even if no organic sensations accompanied these experiences, as they do now. But in case I am wrong here, I would suggest that *images* of organic sensations could perfectly well provide what is needed. We can quite well image to ourselves what it feels like to be in a warm bath, even when we are not actually in one; and a person who has been crippled can image what it felt like to climb a mountain. Moreover, I would ask whether we do not feel alive when we are dreaming. It seems to me that we obviously do—or at any rate quite alive enough to go on with.

This is not all. In an image-world, a dream-like world such as I am trying to describe, there is no reason at all why there should not be *visual* images resembling the body which one had in this present world. In this present life (for all who are not blind) visual percepts of one's own body form as it were the constant centre of one's perceptual world. It is perfectly possible that visual images of one's own body might perform the same function in the next. They might form the continuing centre or nucleus of one's image world, remaining more or less constant while other images altered. If this were so, we should have an additional reason for expecting that recently dead people would find it difficult to realize that they were dead, that is, disembodied. To all appearances they *would* have bodies just as they had before, and pretty much the same ones. But, of course, they might discover in time that these image-bodies were subject to rather peculiar causal laws. For example, it might be found that in an image-world our wishes tend *ipso facto* to fulfil themselves in a way they do not now. A wish to go to Oxford might be immediately followed by the occurrence of a vivid and detailed set of Oxfordlike images; even though, at the moment before, one's images had resembled Piccadilly Circus or the palace of the Dalai Lama in Tibet. In that case, one would realize that "going somewhere"—transferring one's body from one place to another—was a rather different process from what it had been in the physical world. Reflecting on such experiences, one might come to the conclusion that one's body was not after all the same as the physical body one had before death. One might conclude perhaps that it must be a "spiritual" or "psychical" body, closely resembling the old body in appearance, but possessed of rather different causal properties. It has been said, of course, that phrases like "spiritual body" or "psychical body" are utterly unintelligible, and that no conceivable empirical meaning could be given to such expressions. But I would rather suggest that they might be a way (rather a misleading way perhaps) of referring to a set of body-like images. If our supposed dead empiricist continued his investigations, he might discover that his whole world—not only his own body, but everything else he was aware of—had different causal properties from the physical world, even though everything in it had shape, size, colour, and other qualities which material objects have now. And so eventually, by the exercise of ordinary inductive good sense, he could draw the conclusion that he was in "the next world" or "the other world" and no longer in this one. If, however, he were a very dogmatic philosopher, who distrusted inductive good sense and preferred a priori reasoning, I do not know what condition he would be in. Probably he would never discover that he was dead at all. Being persuaded, on a priori grounds, that life after death was impossible, he might insist on thinking that he must still be in this world, and refuse to pay attention to the new and strange causal laws which more empirical thinking would notice.

I think, then, that there is no difficulty in conceiving that the experience of feeling alive could occur in the absence of a physical organism; or, if you prefer to put it so, a disembodied personality could *be* alive in the psychological sense, even though by definition it would not be alive in the physiological or biochemical sense.

Moreover, I do not see why disembodiment need involve the destruction of personal identity. It is, of course, sometimes supposed that personal identity depends on the continuance of a background of organic sensation—the "mass of bodily feeling" mentioned before. (This may be called the somato-centric analysis of personal identity.) We must notice, however, that this background of organic sensation is not literally the same from one period of time to another. The very most that can happen is that the organic sensations which form the background of my experience now should be *exactly similar* to those which were the background of my experience a minute ago. And as a matter of fact, the present ones need not *all* be exactly similar to the previous ones. I might have a twinge of toothache now which I did not have then. I may even have an overall feeling of lassitude now which I did not have a minute ago, so that the whole mass of bodily feeling, and not merely part of it, is rather different; and this would not interrupt my personal identity at all. The most that is required is only that the majority (not all) of my organic sensations should be closely (not exactly) similar to those I previously had. And even this is needed only if the two occasions are close together in my private time series; the organic sensations I have now might well be very unlike those I used to have when I was one year old. I say "in my private time series." For when I wake up after eight hours of dreamless sleep my personal identity is not broken, though in the physical or public time series there has been a long interval between the last organic sensations I experienced before falling asleep, and the first ones I experience when I wake up. But if similarity, and not literal sameness, is all that is required of this "continuing organic background," it seems to me that the continuity of it could be perfectly well preserved if there were organic *images* after death very like the organic sensations which occurred before death.

As a matter of fact, this whole "somato-centric" analysis of personal identity appears to me highly disputable. I should have thought that Locke was much nearer the truth when he said that personal identity depends on memory. But I have tried to show that even if the "somato-centric" theory of personal identity is right, there is no reason why personal identity need be broken by bodily death, provided there are images after death which sufficiently resemble the organic sensations one had before; and this is very like what happens when one falls asleep and begins dreaming.

There is, however, another argument against the conceivability of a disembodied person, to which some present-day linguistic philosophers would attach great weight. It is neatly expressed by Mr. A. G. N. Flew when he says, "people are what you meet."[1] By a "person" we are supposed to mean a human organism which behaves in certain ways, and especially one which speaks and can be spoken to. And when we say, "this is the same person whom I saw yesterday," we are supposed to mean just that it is the same human organism which I saw yesterday, and also that it behaves in a recognizably similar way.

"People are what you meet." With all respect to Mr. Flew, I would suggest that he does not in this sense "meet" *himself*. He might indeed have had one of those curious out-of-body experiences which are occasionally mentioned in our records, and he might have seen his body from outside (if he has, I heartily congratulate him); but I do not think we should call this "meeting." And surely the important question is, what constitutes my personal identity *for myself*. It certainly does not consist in the fact that other people can "meet" me. It might be that I was for myself the same person as before, even at a time when it was quite impossible for others to meet me. No one can "meet" me when I am dreaming. They can, of course, come and look at my body lying in bed; but this is not "meeting," because no sort of social relations are possible between them and me. Yet, although temporarily "unmeetable," during my dreams I am still, for myself, the same person that I was. And if I went on dreaming *in perpetuum*, and could never be "met" again, this need not prevent me from continuing to be, for myself, the same person.

As a matter of fact, however, we can quite easily conceive that "meeting" of a kind might still be possible between discarnate experients. And therefore, even if we do make it part of the definition of "a person," that he is capable of being met by others, it will still make sense to speak of "discarnate persons," provided we allow that telepathy is possible between them. It is true that a special sort of telepathy would be needed; the sort which in life produces *telepathic apparitions*. It would not be sufficient that A's thoughts or emotions should be telepathically affected by B's. If such telepathy were sufficiently prolonged and continuous, and especially if it were reciprocal, it would indeed have some of the characteristics of social intercourse; but I do not think we should call it "meeting," at any rate in Mr. Flew's sense of the word. It would be necessary, in addition, that A should be aware of something which could be called "B's body," or should have an experience not too unlike the experience of *seeing* another person in this life. This additional condition would be satisfied if A experienced a telepathic apparition of B. It would be necessary, further, that the telepathic apparition by means of which B "announces himself" (if one may put it so) should be recognizably similar on different occasions. And if it were a case of meeting some person *again* whom one had previously known in this world, the telepathic apparition would have to be recognizably similar to the physical body which that person had when he was still alive.

There is no reason why an image-world should not contain a number of images which are telepathic apparitions; and if it did, one could quite intelligently speak of "meeting other persons" in such a world. All the experiences I have when I meet another person in this present life could still occur, with only this difference, that percepts would be replaced by images. It would also be possible for another person to "meet" me in the same manner, if I, as a telepathic agent, could cause him to experience a suitable telepathic apparition, sufficiently resembling the body I used to have when he formerly "met" me in this life.

I now turn to another problem which may have troubled some of you. If there be a next world, *where* is it? Surely it must be somewhere. But there does not seem to be any room for it. We can hardly suppose that it is up in the sky (i.e., outside the earth's atmosphere) or under the surface of the earth, as Homer and Vergil seemed to think. Such suggestions may have contented our ancestors, and the Ptolemaic astronomy may have made them acceptable, for some ages, even to the learned; but they will hardly content us. Surely the next world, if it exists, must be somewhere; and yet, it seems, there is nowhere for it to be.

The answer to this difficulty is easy if we conceive of the next world in the way I have suggested, as a dream-like world of mental images. Mental images, including dream images, are in a space of their own. They do have spatial properties. Visual images, for instance, have extension and shape, and they have spatial relations to one another. But they have no spatial relation to objects in the physical world. If I dream of a tiger, my tiger-image has extension and shape. The dark stripes have spatial relation to the yellow parts, and to each other; the nose has a spatial relation to the tail. Again, the tiger image as a whole may have spatial relations to another image in my dream, for example to an image resembling a palm tree. But suppose we have to ask how far it is from the foot of my bed, whether it is three inches long, or longer or shorter; is it not obvious that these questions are absurd ones? We cannot answer them, not because we lack the necessary information or find it impracticable to make the necessary measurements, but because the questions themselves have no meaning. In the space of the physical world these images are nowhere at all. But in relation to other images of mine, each of them is somewhere. Each of them is extended, and its parts are in spatial relations to one another. There is no a priori reason why all extended entities must be in physical space.

If we now apply these considerations to the next world, as I am conceiving of it, we see that the question "where is it?" simply does not arise. An image-world would have a space of its own. We could not find it anywhere in the space of the physical world, but this would not in the least prevent it from being a spatial world all the same. If you like, it would be its own "where."[2]

I am tempted to illustrate this point by referring to the fairy-tale of Jack and the Beanstalk. I am not of course suggesting that we should take the story seriously. But if we were asked to try to make sense of it, how should we set about it? Obviously the queer world which Jack found was not at the top of the beanstalk in the literal, spatial sense of the words "at the top of." Perhaps he found some very large pole rather like a beanstalk, and climbed up it. But (we shall say) when he got to the top he suffered an abrupt change of consciousness, and began to have a dream or waking vision of a strange country with a giant in it. To choose another and more respectable illustration: In Book VI of Vergil's *Aeneid*, we are told how Aeneas descended into the Cave of Avernus with the Sibyl and walked from there into the other world. If we wished to make the narrative of the illustrious poet intelligible, how should we set about it? We should suppose that Aeneas did go down into the cave, but that once he was there he suffered a change of consciousness, and all the strange experiences which happened afterwards—seeing the River Styx, the Elysian Fields, and the rest—were part of a dream or vision which he had. The space he passed through in his journey was an image space, and the River Styx was not three Roman miles, or any other number of miles, from the cave in which his body was.

It follows that when we speak of "passing" from this world to the next, this passage is not to be thought of as any sort of movement in space. It should rather be thought of as a change of consciousness, analogous to the change which occurs when we "pass" from waking experience to dreaming. It would be a change from the perceptual type of consciousness to another type of consciousness in which perception ceases and imaging replaces it, but unlike the change from waking consciousness to dreaming in being irreversible. I suppose that nearly everyone nowadays who talks of "passing" from this world to the other does think of the transition in this way, as some kind of irreversible change of consciousness, and not as a literal spatial transition in which one goes from one place to another place.

So much for the question "where the next world is," if there be one. I have tried to show that if the next world is conceived of as a world of mental images, the question simply does not arise. I now turn to another difficulty. It may be felt that an image-world is somehow a deception and a sham, not a real world at all. I have said that it would be a kind of dream-world. Now, when one has a dream in this life, surely the things one is aware of in the dream are not *real* things. No doubt the dreamer really does have various mental images. These images do actually occur. But this is not all that happens. As a result of having these images, the dreamer believes, or takes for granted, that various material objects exist and various physical events occur; and these beliefs are mistaken. For example, he believes that there is a wall in front of him and that by a mere effort of will he succeeds in flying over the top of it. But the wall did not really exist, and he did not really fly over the top of it. He was in a state of delusion. Because of the images which he really did have, there *seemed* to him to be various objects and events which did not really exist at all. Similarly, you may argue, it may *seem* to discarnate minds (if indeed there are such) that there is a world in which they live, and a world not unlike this one. If they have mental images of the appropriate sort, it may even *seem* to them that they have bodies not unlike the ones they had in this life. But surely they will be mistaken. It is all very well to say, with the poet, that "dreams are real while they last"—that dream-objects are only called "unreal" when one wakes up, and normal sense-perceptions begin to occur with which the dream experiences can be contrasted. And it is all very well to conclude from this that if one did *not* wake up, if the change from sense-perception to imaging were irreversible, one would not call one's dream-objects unreal, because there would then be nothing with which to contrast them. But would they not still *be* unreal for all that? Surely discarnate minds, according to my account of them, would be in a state of permanent delusion; whereas a dreamer in this life (fortunately for him) is only in a temporary one. And the fact that a delusion goes on for a long time, even forever and ever, does not make it any less delusive. Delusions do not turn themselves into realities just by going on and on. Nor are they turned into realities by the fact that their victim is deprived of the power of detecting their delusiveness.

Now, of course, if it were true that the next life (supposing there is one) is a condition of permanent delusion, we should just have to put up with it. We might not like it; we might think that a state of permanent delusion is a bad state to be in. But our likes and dislikes are irrelevant to the question. I would suggest, however, that this argument about the "delusiveness" or "unreality" of an image-world is based on confusion.

One may doubt whether there is any clear meaning in using the words "real" and "unreal" *tout court*, in this perfectly general and unspecified way. One may properly say "this is real silver, and that is not," "this is a real pearl and that is not," or again "this is a real pool of water, and that is only a mirage." The point here is that something X is mistakenly believed to be something else Y, because it does resemble Y in some respects. It makes perfectly good sense, then, to say that X is not really Y. This piece of plated brass is not real silver, true enough. It only looks like silver. But for all that, it cannot be called "unreal" in the unqualified sense, in the sense of not existing at all. Even the mirage is something, though it is not the pool of water you took it to be. It is a perfectly good set of visual appearances, though it is not related to other appearances in the way you thought it was; for example, it does not have the relations to tactual appearances, or to visual appearances from other places, which you expected it to have. You may properly say that the mirage is not a real pool of water, or even that it is not a real physical object, and that anyone who thinks it is must be in a state of delusion. But there is no clear meaning in saying that it is just "unreal" *tout court*, without any further specification or explanation. In short, when the word "unreal" is applied to something, one means that it is different from something else, with which it might be mistakenly identified; what that something else is may not be explicitly stated, but it can be gathered from the context.

What, then, could people mean by saying that a next world such as I have described would be "unreal"? If they are saying anything intelligible, they must mean that it is different from something else, something else which it does resemble in some respects, and might therefore be confused with. And what is that something else? It is the present physical world in which we now live. An image-world, then, is only "unreal" in the sense that it is not really physical, though it might be mistakenly thought to be physical by some of those who experience it. But this only amounts to saying that the world I am describing would be an *other* world, other than this present physical world, which is just what it ought to be; other than this present physical world, and yet sufficiently like it to be possibly confused with it, because images do resemble percepts. And what would this otherness consist in? First, in the fact that it is a *space* which is other than physical space; secondly, and still more important, in the fact that the *causal laws* of an image-world would be different from the laws of physics. And this is also our ground for saying that the events we experience in dreams are "unreal," that is, not really physical, though mistakenly believed by the dreamer to be so. They do in some ways closely resemble physical events, and that is why the mistake is possible. But the causal laws of their occurrence are quite different, as we recognize when we wake up; and just occasionally we recognize it even while we are still asleep.

Now let us consider the argument that the inhabitants of the other world, as I have described it, would be in a state of delusion. I admit that some of them might be. That would be the condition of the people described in the mediumistic communications already referred to—the people who "do not realize that they are dead." Because their images are so like the normal percepts they were accustomed to in this life, they believe mistakenly that they are still living in the physical world. But, as I already tried to explain, their state of delusion need not be permanent and irremediable. By attending to the relations between one image and another, and applying the ordinary inductive methods by which we ourselves have discovered the causal laws of this present world in which *we* live, they too could discover in time what the causal laws of *their* world are. These laws, we may suppose, would be more like the laws of Freudian psychology than the laws of physics. And once the discovery was made, they would be cured of their delusion. They would find out, perhaps with surprise, that the world they were experiencing was *other* than the physical world which they experienced before, even though like it in some respects.

Let us now try to explore the conception of a world of mental images a little more fully. Would it not be a *"subjective"* world? And surely there would be many *different* next worlds, not just one; and each of them would be private. Indeed, would there not be as many next worlds as there are discarnate minds, and each of them wholly private to the mind which experiences it? In short, it may seem that each of us, when dead, would have his own dream-world, and there would be no common or public next world at all.

"Subjective," perhaps, is a rather slippery word. Certainly, an image-world would have to be subjective in the sense of being mind-dependent, dependent for its existence upon mental processes of one sort or another; images, after all, are mental entities. But I do not think that such a world need be completely private, if telepathy occurs in the next life. I have already mentioned the part which telepathic apparitions might play in it in connection with Mr. Flew's contention that "people are what you meet." But there is more to be said. It is reasonable to suppose that in a disembodied state telepathy would occur more frequently than it does now. It seems likely that in this present life our telepathic powers are constantly being inhibited by our need to adjust ourselves to our physical environment. It even seems likely that many telepathic "impressions" which we receive at the unconscious level are shut out from consciousness by a kind of biologically motivated censorship. Once the pressure of biological needs is removed, we might expect that telepathy would occur continually, and manifest itself in consciousness by modifying and adding to the images which one experiences. (Even in this life, after all, some dreams are telepathic.)

If this is right, an image-world such as I am describing would not be the product of one single mind only, nor would it be purely private. It would be the joint product of a group of telepathically interacting minds and public to all of them. Nevertheless, one would not expect it to have unrestricted publicity. It is likely that there would still be *many* next worlds, a different one for each group of like-minded personalities. I admit I am not quite sure what might be meant by "like-minded" and "unlike-minded" in this connection. Perhaps we could say that two personalities are like-minded if their memories or their characters are sufficiently similar. It might be that Nero and Marcus Aurelius do not have a world in common, but Socrates and Marcus Aurelius do.

So far, we have a picture of many "semi-public" next worlds, if one may put it so; each of them composed of mental images, and yet not wholly private for all that, but public to a limited group of telepathically interacting minds. Or, if you like, after death everyone does have his own dream, but there is still some overlap between one person's dream and another's because of telepathy.

I have said that such a world would be mind-dependent, even though depend-ent on a group of minds rather than a single mind. In what way would it be mind-dependent? Presumably in the same way as dreams are now. It would be dependent on the *memories* and the *desires* of the persons who experienced it. Their memories and their desires would determine what sort of images they had. If I may put it so, the "stuff" or "material" of such a world would come in the end from one's memories, and the "form" of it from one's desires. To use another analogy, memory would provide the pigments, and desire would paint the picture. One might expect, I think, that desires which had been unsatisfied in one's earthly life would play a specially important part in the process. That may seem an agreeable prospect. But there is another which is less agreeable. Desires which had been *repressed* in one's earthly life, because it was too pain-ful or too disgraceful to admit that one had them, might also play a part, and perhaps an important part, in determining what images one would have in the next. And the same might be true of repressed memories. It may be suggested that what Freud (in one stage of his thought) called "the censor"—the force or barrier or mechanism which keeps some of our desires and memories out of consciousness, or only lets them in when they disguise themselves in symbolic and distorted forms—operates only in this present life and not in the next. How-ever we conceive of "the censor," it does seem to be a device for enabling us to adapt ourselves to our environment. And when we no longer have an environ-ment, one would expect that the barrier would come down.

We can now see that an after-death world of mental images can also be quite reasonably described in the terminology of the Hindu thinkers as "a world of desire" (*Kama Loka*). Indeed, this is just what we should expect if we assume that dreams, in this present life, are the best available clue to what the next life might be like. Such a world could also be described as "a world of memories"; because imaging, in the end, is a function of memory, one of the ways in which our memory-dispositions manifest themselves. But this description would be less apt, even though correct as far as it goes. To use the same rather inadequate language as before: the "materials" out of which an image-world is composed would have to come from the memories of the mind or group of minds whose world it is. But it would be their desires (including those repressed in earthly life) which determined the way in which these memories were used, the precise kind of dream which was built up out of them or on the basis of them.

It will, of course, be objected that memories cannot exist in the absence of a physical brain, nor yet desires, nor images either. But this proposition, however plausible, is after all just an empirical hypothesis, not a necessary truth. Certainly there is empirical evidence in favour of it. But there is also empirical evidence against it. Broadly speaking one might say, perhaps, that the "normal" evidence tends to support this materialistic or epiphenomenalist theory of memories, images, and desires, whereas the "supernormal" evidence on the whole tends to weaken the materialist or epiphenomenalist theory of human personality (of which this hypothesis about the brain-dependent character of memories, images, and desires is a part). Moreover, any evidence which direct-ly supports the Survival Hypothesis (and there is quite a lot of evidence which does, provided we are prepared to admit that the Survival Hypothesis is intelligible at all) is *pro tanto* evidence against the materialistic conception of human personality.

In this paper, I am not trying to argue in favour of the Survival Hypothesis. I am only concerned with the more modest task of trying to make it intelligible. All I want to maintain, then, is that there is nothing self-contradictory or logically absurd in the hypothesis that memories, desires, and images can exist in the absence of a physical brain. The hypothesis may, of course, be false. My point is only that it is not absurd; or if you like, that it is at any rate intelligible, whether true or not. To put the question in another way, when we are trying to work out for ourselves what sort of thing a discarnate life might conceivably be (if there is one), we have to ask what kind of *equipment*, so to speak, a discarnate mind might be supposed to have. It cannot have the power of sense-perception, nor the power of acting on the physical world by means of efferent nerves, muscles, and limbs. What would it have left? What could we take out with us, as it were, when we pass from this life to the next? What we take out with us, I suggest, can only be our memories and desires, and the power of constructing out of them an image-world to suit us. Obviously we cannot take our material possessions out with us; but I do not think this is any great loss, for if we remember them well enough and are sufficiently attached to them, we shall be able to construct image-replicas of them which will be just as good, and perhaps better.

In this connection I should like to mention a point which has been made several times before. Both Whately Carington and Professor Ducasse have referred to it, and no doubt other writers have. But I believe it is of some importance and worth repeating. Ecclesiastically minded critics sometimes speak rather scathingly of the "materialistic" character of mediumistic communications. They are not at all edified by these descriptions of agreeable houses, beautiful landscapes, gardens, and the rest. And then, of course, there is Raymond Lodge's notorious cigar.[3] These critics complain that the next world as described in these communications is no more than a reproduction of this one, slightly improved perhaps. And the argument apparently is that the "materialistic" character of the communications is evidence against their genuineness. On the contrary: as far as it goes, it is evidence *for* their genuineness. Most people in this life do like material objects and are deeply interested in them. This may be deplorable, but there it is. If so, the image-world they would create for themselves in the next life might be expected to have just the "materialistic" character of which these critics complain. If one had been fond of nice houses and pleasant gardens in this life, the image-world one would create for oneself in the next might be expected to contain image-replicas of such objects, and one would make these replicas as like "the real thing" as one's memories permitted; with the help, perhaps, of telepathic influences from other minds whose tastes were similar. This would be all the more likely to happen if one had not been able to enjoy such things in this present life as much as one could wish.

But possibly I have misunderstood the objection which these ecclesiastical critics are making. Perhaps they are saying that if the next world is like this, life after death is not worth having. Well and good. If they would prefer a different sort of next world, and find the one described in these communications insipid and unsatisfying to their aspirations, then they can expect to get a different one

—in fact, just the sort of next world they want. They have overlooked a crucial point which seems almost obvious; that if there is an after-death life at all, there must surely be many next worlds, separate from and as it were impenetrable to one another, corresponding to the *different* desires which different groups of discarnate personalities have.

The belief in life after death is often dismissed as "mere wish-fulfilment." Now, it will be noticed that the next world as I have been trying to conceive of it is precisely a wish-fulfilment world, in much the same sense in which some dreams are described as wish-fulfilments. Should not this make a rational man very suspicious of the ideas I am putting before you? Surely this account of the other world is "too good to be true"? I think not. Here we must distinguish two different questions. The question whether human personality continues to exist after death is a question of fact, and wishes have nothing to do with it one way or the other. But *if* the answer to this factual question were "Yes" (and I emphasise the "if"), wishes might have a very great deal to do with the kind of world which discarnate beings would live in. Perhaps it may be helpful to consider a parallel case. It is a question of fact whether dreams occur in this present life. It has been settled by empirical investigation, and the wishes of the investigators have nothing to do with it. It is just a question of what the empirical facts are, whether one likes them or not. Nevertheless, granting that dreams do occur, a man's wishes might well have a very great deal to do with determining what the content of his dreams is to be; especially unconscious wishes on the one hand, and, on the other, conscious wishes which are not satisfied in waking life. Of course the parallel is not exact. There is one very important difference between the two cases. With dreams, the question of fact is settled. It is quite certain that many people do have dreams. But in the case of survival, the question of fact is not settled, or not at present. It is still true, however, that though wishes have nothing to do with it, they have a very great deal to do with the kind of world we should live in after death, *if* we survive death at all.

But perhaps this does not altogether dispose of the objection that my account of the other world is "too good to be true." Surely a sober-minded and cautious person would be very shy of believing that there is, or even could be, a world in which all our wishes are fulfilled? How very suspicious we are about travellers' tales of Eldorado or descriptions of idyllic South Sea islands! Certainly we are, and on good empirical grounds. For they are tales about this present material world; and we know that matter is very often recalcitrant to human wishes. But in a dream-world Desire is king. This objection would only hold good if the world I am describing were supposed to be some part of the *material* world— another planet perhaps, or the Earthly Paradise of which some poets have written. But the next world as I am trying to conceive of it (or rather next worlds, for we have seen that there would be many different ones) is not of course supposed to be part of the material world at all. It is a dream-like world of mental images. True enough, some of these images might be expected to resemble some of the material objects with which we are familiar now; but only if, and to the extent that, their percipients *wanted* this resemblance to exist. There is every reason, then, for being suspicious about descriptions of this present material world, or alleged parts of it, on the ground that they are "too good to be true";

but when it is a "country of the mind" (if one may say so) which is being described, these suspicions are groundless. A purely mind-dependent world, if such a world there be, would *have* to be a wish-fulfilment world.

Nevertheless, likes and dislikes, however irrelevant they may be, do of course have a powerful psychological influence upon us when we consider the problem of survival; not only when we consider the factual evidence for or against, but also when we are merely considering the theoretical implications of the Survival Hypothesis itself, as I am doing now. It is therefore worthwhile to point out that the next world as I am conceiving of it need not necessarily be an agreeable place at all. If arguments about what is good or what is bad did have any relevance, a case could be made out for saying that this conception of the next world is "too bad to be true," rather than too good. As we have seen, we should have to reckon with many different next worlds, not just with one. The world you experience after death would depend upon the kind of person you are. And if what I have said so far has any sense in it, we can easily conceive that some people's next worlds would be much more like purgatories than paradises —and pretty unpleasant purgatories too.

This is because there are *conflicting* desires within the same person. Few people, if any, are completely integrated personalities, though some people come nearer to it than others. And sometimes when a man's desires appear (even to himself) to be more or less harmonious with one another, the appearance is deceptive. His conscious desires do not conflict with one another, or not much; but this harmony has been achieved only at the cost of repression. He has unconscious desires which conflict with the neatly organized pattern of his conscious life. If I was right in suggesting that repression is a biological phenomenon, if the "threshold" between conscious and unconscious no longer operates in a disembodied state, or operates much less effectively, this seeming harmony will vanish after the man is dead. To use scriptural language, the secrets of his heart will be revealed—at any rate to himself. These formerly repressed desires will manifest themselves by appropriate images, and these images might be exceedingly horrifying—as some dream-images are in this present life, and for the same reason. True enough, they will be "wish-fulfilment" images, like everything else that he experiences in the next world as I am conceiving of it. But the wishes they fulfil will conflict with other wishes which he also has. And the emotional state which results might be worse than the worst nightmare; worse, because the dreamer cannot wake up from it. For example, in his after-death dream-world he finds himself doing appallingly cruel actions. He never did them in his earthly life. Yet the desire to do them was there, even though repressed and unacknowledged. And now the lid is off, and this cruel desire fulfils itself by creating appropriate images. But unfortunately for his comfort, he has benevolent desires as well, perhaps quite strong ones; and so he is distressed and even horrified by these images, even though there is also a sense in which they are just the ones he wanted. Of course his benevolent desires too may be expected to manifest themselves by appropriate wish-fulfilment images. But because there is this conflict in his nature, they will not wholly satisfy him either. There will be something in him which rejects them as tedious and insipid. It is a question of the point of view, if one cares to put it so. Suppose a person has two conflicting desires *A* and *B*. Then from the point of view of desire *A*, the images which fulfil desire *B* will be unsatisfying, or unpleasant, or even horrifying; and vice versa from the point of view of desire *B*. And unfortunately, both points of view belong to the same person. He occupies them both at once.

This is not all. If psychoanalysts are right, there is such a thing as a desire to be punished. Most people, we are told, have guilt-feelings which are more or less repressed; we have desires, unacknowledged or only half-acknowledged, to suffer for the wrongs we have done. These desires too will have their way in the next world, if my picture of it is right, and will manifest themselves by images which fulfil them. It is not a very pleasant prospect, and I need not elaborate it. But it looks as if everyone would experience an image-purgatory which exactly suits him. It is true that his unpleasant experiences would not literally be punishments, any more than terrifying dreams are, in this present life. They would not be inflicted upon him by an external judge; though, of course, if we are theists, we shall hold that the laws of nature, in other worlds as in this one, are in the end dependent on the will of a Divine Creator. Each man's purgatory would be just the automatic consequence of his own desires; if you like, he would punish himself by having just those images which his own good feelings demand. But, if there is any consolation in it, he would have these unpleasant experiences because he *wanted* to have them; exceedingly unpleasant as they might be, there would still be something in him which was satisfied by them.

There is another aspect of the conflict of desires. Every adult person has what we call "a character"; a set of more or less settled and permanent desires, with the corresponding emotional dispositions, expressing themselves in a more or less predictable pattern of thoughts, feelings, and actions. But it is perfectly possible to desire that one's character should be different, perhaps very different, from what it is at present. This is what philosophers call a "second-order" desire, a desire that some of one's own desires should be altered. Such second-order desires are not necessarily ineffective, as New Year resolutions are supposed to be. People can within limits alter their own characters, and sometimes do; and if they succeed in doing so, it is in the end because they *want* to. But these second-order desires—desires to alter one's own character—are seldom effective immediately; and even when they appear to be, as in some cases of religious conversion, there has probably been a long period of subconscious or unconscious preparation first. To be effective, desires of this sort must occur again and again. I must go on wishing to be more generous or less timid, and not just wish it on New Year's day; I must train myself to act habitually—and think too—in the way that I should act and think if I possessed the altered character for which I wish. From the point of view of the present moment, however, one's character is something fixed and given. The wish I have at half-past twelve today will do nothing, or almost nothing, to alter it.

These remarks may seem very remote from the topic I am supposed to be discussing. But they have a direct bearing on a question which has been mentioned before: whether, or in what sense, the next world as I am conceiving of it should be called a "subjective" world. As I have already said, a next world such as I have described *would* be subjective, in the sense of mind-dependent. The minds which experience it would also have created it. It would just be the manifestation of their own memories and desires, even though it might be the joint creation of a number of telepathically interacting minds, and therefore not wholly private. But there is a sense in which it might have a certain objectivity all the same. One thing we mean by calling something "objective" is that it is so whether we like it or not, and even if we dislike it. This is also what we mean by talking about "hard facts" or "stubborn facts."

At first sight it may seem that in an image-world such as I have described there could be no hard facts or stubborn facts, and nothing objective in this sense of the word "objective." How could there be, if the world we experience is itself a wish-fulfilment world? But a man's character *is* in this sense "objective"; objective in the sense that he has it whether he likes it or not. And facts about his character are as "hard" or "stubborn" as any. Whether I like it or not, and even though I dislike it, it is a hard fact about me that I am timid or spiteful, that I am fond of eating oysters or averse from talking French. I may wish sometimes that these habitual desires and aversions of mine were different, but at any particular moment this wish will do little or nothing to alter them. In the short run, a man's permanent and habitual desires are something "given" which he must accept and put up with as best he can, even though in the very long run they are alterable.

Now in the next life, according to my picture of it, it would be these permanent and habitual desires which would determine the nature of the world in which a person has to live. His world would be, so to speak, the outgrowth of his character; it would be his own character represented before him in the form of dream-like images. There is therefore a sense in which he gets exactly the sort of world he wants, whatever internal conflicts there may be between one of these wants and another. Yet he may very well dislike having the sort of character he does have. In the short run, as I have said, his character is something fixed and given, and objective in the sense that he has that character whether he likes it or not. Accordingly his image-world is also objective in the same sense. It is objective in the sense that it insists on presenting itself to him whether he likes it or not.

To look at the same point in another way: the next world as I am picturing it may be a very queer sort of world, but still it would be subject to causal laws. The laws would not, of course, be the laws of physics. As I have suggested already, they might be expected to be more like the laws of Freudian psychology. But they would be laws all the same, and objective in the sense that they hold good whether one liked it or not. And if we do dislike the image-world which our desires and memories create for us—if, when we get what we want, we are horrified to discover what things they were which we wanted—we shall have to set about altering our characters, which might be a very long and painful process.

Some people tell us, of course, that all desires, even the most permanent and habitual ones, will wear themselves out in time by the mere process of being satisfied. It may be so, and perhaps there is comfort in the thought. In that case the dream-like world of which I have been speaking would only be temporary, and we should have to ask whether after the next world there is a next but one. The problem of survival would then arise again in a new form. We should have to ask whether personal identity could still be preserved when we were no longer even dreaming. It could, I think, be preserved through the transition from this present, perceptible world to a dream-like image world of the kind I have been describing. But if even imaging were to cease, would there be anything left of human personality at all? Or would the state of existence—if any—which followed be one to which the notion of personality, at any rate our present notion, no longer had any application? I think that these are questions upon which it is unprofitable and perhaps impossible to speculate. (If anyone wishes to make the attempt, I can only advise him to consult the writings of the mystics, both Western and Oriental.) It is quite enough for us to consider what the *next* world might conceivably be like, and some of you may think that even this is too much.

You have have noticed that the next world, according to my account of it, is not at all unlike what some metaphysicians say *this* world is. In the philosophy of Schopenhauer, this present world itself, in which we now live, is a world of "will and idea." And so it is in Berkeley's philosophy too; material objects are just collections of "ideas," though according to Berkeley the will which presents these ideas to us is the will of God, acting directly upon us in a way which is in effect telepathic. Could it be that these idealist metaphysicians have given us a substantially correct picture of the next world, though a mistaken picture of this one? The study of metaphysical theories is out of question nowadays. But perhaps students of psychical research would do well to pay some attention to them. *If* there are other worlds than this (again I emphasize the "if"), who knows whether with some stratum of our personalities we are not living in them now, as well as in this present one which conscious sense-perception discloses? Such a repressed and unconscious awareness of a world different from this one might be expected to break through into consciousness occasionally in the course of human history, very likely in a distorted form, and this might be the source of those very queer ideas which we read of with so much incredulity and astonishment in the writings of some speculative metaphysicians. Not knowing their source, they mistakenly applied these ideas to this world in which we now live, embellishing them sometimes with an elaborate façade of deductive reasoning. Viewed in cold blood and with a sceptical eye, their attempts may appear extremely unconvincing and their deductive reasoning fallacious. But perhaps, without knowing it, they may have valuable hints to give us if we are trying to form some conception, however tentative, of "another world." And this is something we must try to do if we take the problem of survival seriously.

NOTES

1. *University*, Vol. 2, No. 2, p. 38, in a symposium on "Death" with Professor D. M. Mackinnon. Mr. Flew obviously uses "people" as the plural of "person"; but if we are to be linguistic, I am inclined to think that the nuances of "people" are not quite the same as those of "person." When we use the word "person," in the singular or the plural, the notion of consciousness is more prominently before our minds than it is when we use the word "people."

2. Conceivably its geometrical structure might also be different from the geometrical structure of the physical world. In that case the space of the next world would not only be other than the space of the physical world, but would also be a different *sort* of space.

3. Sir Oliver Lodge, *Raymond Revised* (London: Methuen, 1922), p. 113.

14

Immortality and Resurrection

STEWART R. SUTHERLAND

University of London

IN RECENT YEARS there has been some lively discussion of the questions of immortality and resurrection. Within the Christian tradition there has been debate at theological and exegetical level over the relative merits of belief in the immortality of the soul, and belief in the resurrection of the dead as an account of life after death.[1] Further to this, however, there has been the suggestion that there may be good philosophical reasons for preferring the latter to the former. It is just this contention which I propose to discuss.

I intend in the first section of the paper to outline the problems which have been set against belief in the immortality of the soul. I shall then consider in sections II and III whether or not the belief in the doctrine of the resurrection of the body can deal with these problems any more adequately than can the doctrine of the immortality of the soul. In the final section I shall discuss difficulties which arise within the Christian tradition and to which I do not believe that either doctrine offers a satisfactory solution, and which suggest the inadequacy of this kind of approach as an account of the *religious* belief in life after death.

I

There are at least two kinds of problems which must be faced by any who believe in the immortality of the soul, prior to, or apart from, the question of what *grounds* there might be for holding such a belief. These two groups of questions I shall refer to respectively as (*a*) Identity problems, and (*b*) Conceivability problems.

Two questions which arise under (*a*) can be put as follows: (i) Is spatio-temporal continuity of the body a *necessary* criterion of identity in the case of persons? Bernard Williams, for example, has argued that bodily continuity is a necessary condition of personal identity and that "the omission of the body takes away all content from the idea of personal *identity*."[2] (ii) The second question arising under (*a*) is that, even granted that souls are logically distinct

Reprinted by permission from *Religious Studies*, 3 (1967–68), 377–89.

from bodies, can we identify me with my soul, either embodied or disembodied? As Flew points out: "Unless I *am* my soul, the survival of my soul will not be *my* survival."[3]

Conceivability problems, for example whether it is conceivable that non-corporeal souls could be subjects of experiences, are very closely related to identity problems. For instance, if bodily continuity is a necessary condition of personal identity, then the existence of non-corporeal persons is inconceivable. It might also seem, conversely, that if it is established that the existence of disembodied persons is conceivable, then bodily continuity cannot be at all a *condition* of personal identity. I hope to show, however, that such a statement of the possibilities before us is oversimplified. The second connection between conceivability and identity problems is that, even if we do show that it is at least conceivable that some kind of non-corporeal persons do exist, it may not be clear that these persons could be identified with any body–mind complexes who ever did exist, who do exist, or who ever will exist. That is to say, conditions under which we might specify that this non-corporeal soul is *numerically the same person* as Nero who fiddled while Rome was burning, have to be agreed upon: they cannot be assumed to exist.

Clearly for both groups of problems Williams' claim that bodily continuity is a necessary condition of personal identity is crucial. His position is based upon the consideration of the following problem case. The kind of situation, in which the claim that bodily continuity is not a necessary condition of personal identity is fully tested, is one where, for example, one morning Charles woke up and exhibited character traits, and made memory claims, very different from those which his family and friends were accustomed to expect of him. A little reflection might indicate that all these new personality factors "point unanimously to the life-history of some one person in the past—for instance, Guy Fawkes" (p. 237). Is it conceivable that we might ever have good reasons to decide that in fact Charles *is* Guy Fawkes?

Williams argues that we could not, on the following grounds. If it is conceivable that this situation could arise in the case of Charles, it is also conceivable that it could arise *simultaneously* in the case of Charles' brother Robert. If it did we should then have two people both claiming to have the memories, and both exhibiting the character, of Guy Fawkes. In such a situation, Williams argues, we should not be tempted to identify either Charles or Robert with Guy Fawkes. If that is the case, so long as such a situation is logically possible, why, if only Charles exhibits these personality changes, should we believe ourselves to be on any stronger grounds in claiming that Charles is Guy Fawkes? The point is that where bodily continuity is excluded, there is always the possibility of reduplication. Where there is that possibility, we are dealing with a one–many relation, but, as Williams wants to claim, ". . . identity is a one–one relation, and . . . no principle can be a criterion of identity for things of type T if it relies on what is logically a one–many or many–many relation between things of type T."[4] Only the spatio-temporal continuity of the body can guarantee a one–one relation in this context, and this is the basis of Williams' claims that if the body is completely omitted from our reckoning, then there are no good grounds for saying that Charles and Guy Fawkes are identical, rather than that they might possess exactly similar characters and could in principle have memories of exactly similar reactions to exactly similar events.

I do not propose to go systematically through all the recent literature on this point, and the variety of proposed counter-examples to Williams, which have been constructed.[5] These will be mentioned as they are relevant to the rest of our discussion. What I am concerned with is the *general* statement of Williams' position. He does argue as if the logic of our concept of personal identity is such that, unless there is the possibility in principle of there being bodily continuity, then the concept of identity can have no application. That is to say, it is argued that bodily continuity is at least *part* of what we mean when we say that so and so is in fact the same man as we saw yelling abuse at the referee on Saturday afternoon. If this is not the case then we find that we can no longer distinguish between the concepts of identity and exact similarity. In the case of Charles, for example, what could it mean to say "No, it is not just that he has exactly similar character and memories to Guy Fawkes, he in fact is Guy Fawkes"? What more do we mean to assert if we claim identity rather than exact similarity?[6]

II

There are, it seems to me, at least three different ways in which a person who wants to believe in life after death might wish to take issue with Williams' argument. The first is to argue simply that even in the case of mind–body complex *in this life*, other sufficient conditions can be given under which identity might be asserted, for example, memory and character. I think that put baldly in this fashion such an approach simply will not do. My justification for saying this would simply involve repeating the arguments of Williams and Nerlich, which I do not propose to do, and arguing that moves other than this are required to make this approach worth reviving. What such possible moves are I shall discuss in relation to the second and third possible ways of challenging Williams' position. The second way is that which we find adopted by a full-blooded believer in the bodily resurrection of the dead, and I shall postpone discussion of this till section III of the paper. The third way which I want to examine now, I shall refer to as Price's way.[7]

In his paper, Price tackles the problem of conceivability. Is the possibility of there being after-death experiences for disembodied minds an intelligible one? Price argues that it is, and provides a sophisticated account of what such an existence might be like. His suggestion is to compare "the next world" to a kind of dream-world, in which the basic mode of experience is image-experience rather than sense-experience. In such a world our images provide us with the "objects about which we could have thoughts, emotions, and wishes." Imaging here, of course, is not to be confused with imagining, nor "imagy" with imaginary. The next world is an imagy world but not an imaginary world. Thus, the real/unreal distinction is being detached from any overtones of the material/immaterial distinction, but Price does not detach it completely from the notion of objectivity. Hence he avoids the *prima facie* risk of solipsism by allowing the possibility of "the sort of telepathy . . . which in this life produces telepathic apparitions." The other point which I wish to mention is the strong links which Price sees holding between the images of the next world and the stock memories and (sometimes repressed) desires which we have built up in this world. The kind of image-world which we then have, including its public aspect of images shared by "like-minded" people, will be (causally?) related to the present world of sense-experience.

This latter point particularly suggests to me that what Price says here of disembodied existence is quite compatible with, in the first instance, Strawson's account of "person" as a logically primitive concept: ". . . of a type of entity such that *both* predicates ascribing states of consciousness *and* predicates ascribing corporeal characteristics, a physical situation, etc., are equally applicable to a single individual of that single type."[8] And, of course, in the last section of his chapter on Persons, Strawson does allow a "logically secondary existence" to the concept of a pure individual consciousness, in terms of which we might conceive of our own personal survival, though he gives, compared with Price, a rather truncated account of the possibilities of experience open to such a being. It is clear, however, that, *if* we are to allow such a possibility of existence, then Price's account of a much wider range of possible experience is not logically inferior to Strawson's version of the individual who "must always think of himself as *dis*embodied, as a *former person*" (p. 116). But the important point is that the notion of disembodied survival is, to use a phrase to which we shall return later: ". . . consonant with the conception of man as a . . . psycho-physical unity."[9]

What Price has argued does not on the other hand seem to be compatible with Williams' rather stronger thesis that to talk of personal identity at all is to talk of bodily continuity. On Williams' insistence that bodily continuity is a necessary condition of personal identity there seems to be no possible place for even a "logically secondary existence" of disembodied souls. Consequently, although Price has argued in a way which is *compatible* with the conception of man as a "psycho-physical unity," he is required to challenge the alleged necessary relation holding between the concepts of personal identity and bodily continuity.

From the information available in Price's paper, and in his letter of reply to Flew (pp. 171ff.), the following line of argument between Price's position and Williams' position can be constructed. Problem cases can be posed about our use of the phrase "same man," in relation to living people, for example the documented cases of people who suffer from what seems to be alternation of (at least two) different personalities. There the criterion of bodily continuity is satisfied, but not those of memory and character traits. Do we here say, in spite perhaps of a Jekyll and Hyde type of situation (the only difference is that, as far as we know, the Jekyll personality is not *at all* responsible for the creation of the Hyde personality), that we are dealing with one and the same person? Rather, I suggest, is it the case that we should admit that our rules for the use of the phrase "same person" have broken down.

Of course, this is compatible with Williams' position as expressed in his Aristotelian Society paper, for there he carefully avoids committing himself to the claim that bodily continuity is a necessary *and* sufficient condition for the ascription of personal identity. However, the Jekyll and Hyde type of situation does bring out the importance of both memory and character traits in the attribution of personal identity. Now, the holder of a position similar to that of Price is entitled to ask, What would Williams say were our situation different from what it is? What for example if we woke up one morning to find ourselves no longer to be our old embodied selves, but to be disembodied image-experients?[10] Price has shown to be logically conceivable at least the possibility that we could be conscious of such an existence. In that situation, what would the position be for those who hold Williams' view?

It could be insisted, that is, reaffirmed, that bodily continuity is a necessary condition of personal identity, and that therefore we should simply be wrong to assert the identity of embodied and disembodied subjects of experiences. The point could be made that reduplication is logically possible in this situation, that two disembodied subjects *could* turn up in the next world, for every person whom we meet in this world. But, it must be asked, precisely how much does this establish? It certainly establishes that as things are we seem to have at least one condition of personal identity which confirms the uniqueness of any person. But does it establish that the concept is somehow logically bound to the notion of bodily continuity? To quote an article to which I shall refer later: "The fact that *in the world as it is* we unhesitatingly deny personal identity when bodily continuity is absent does not mean that we must do this in the absence of continuity in any imaginable world. Assertions and denials of personal identity are made against the background of disbelief in the existence of Junonians or anything like them" (J. M. Shorter, p. 84). For the purposes of this argument image-experients are sufficiently like the Junonians (to whom we shall return) to make Shorter's comment apt.

In an earlier article (*Analysis*, 21.1, p. 22) Nerlich argues that the whole point of the reduplication argument is to challenge those who do not accept bodily continuity as a necessary condition to produce a set of sufficient conditions which leaves out bodily continuity and still manages to distinguish between exact similarity and identity. I am arguing that, on the basis of Price's article, a different challenge to the necessity of bodily continuity can be offered. This involves, as above, tracing out the conceivability of disembodied existence and then asking: What in the face of this possibility would be the situation over the ascription of identity? It seems rather arbitrary to insist that we should automatically apply a condition of identity developed in the face of one empirical situation, were a completely new set of facts to come to light. Of course, in this new situation we should not be logically guarded against the possibility of reduplication challenging our use of the concept of identity. But, in the absence of any evidence of reduplication, and such a case is the one under consideration, would that be grounds for objecting that we do not have good reasons for deciding to identify these image experients with those mind–body complexes which existed in *this* world?

The crux of the defence which I am offering against Williams' position involves distinguishing between asserting that (*a*) bodily continuity is necessarily a condition of every attribution of personal identity, and (*b*) bodily continuity is as a matter of fact a condition of most (or even all so far) attributions of personal identity. In the former case, no change in the empirical circumstances could lead to the dropping of the condition of bodily continuity; in the latter, such a possibility as that sketched by Price would, it is suggested, lead to reasonable grounds for extending the present use of the concept of personal identity, though, of course, there is obviously no compulsion in this. There is clearly an element of convention in all this, but to speak of convention is not necessarily to speak of what is arbitrary. There seem in this situation to be very good reasons for extending the use of the concept of identity, although this should not be taken as a denial that we might have to re-alter our conventions should we then come across a number of cases of reduplication. But, should the circumstances be as specified above, and taken with the rest of Price's paper this is a comparatively well-defined account of a possible mode of life after death, then there seem to be adequate grounds for the assertion that we can conceive what it might be like for us to conceive of ourselves as post-mortem image-experients.

Before concluding this section, I must briefly return to a question left unanswered at the end of section I: In *this* context, what more do we mean to assert if we claim identity rather than exact similarity? If we claim that the image-experient Fred is the same person as the pre-mortem mind–body complex Fred, what more are we saying than that the post-mortem Fred has the same character traits as the pre-mortem Fred, and exactly the same memories which we should expect the pre-mortem Fred in post-mortem state to have? What *more* we are doing is to assert a unique relationship between the images experienced by the post-mortem Fred and the life led by the pre-mortem Fred. The uniqueness might be expressed as follows: the images experienced by the post-mortem Fred, in so far as they are grounded in the pre-mortem world, are grounded exclusively in what Fred did and experienced in his pre-mortem existence. Thus, for example, whether the prime minister parted his hair on the right side or the left side this morning will not affect the post-mortem images which I may expect to have—unless, that is, he were sufficiently eccentric to match his political sympathies for the day to a right or left hair-parting as the case may be, in which case, the kinds of experience to which I am later subjected may be related in some sense to how he parted his hair, but only *because* my experiences were affected, and only in relation to *how* they were affected.

Now the grounds for making this assertion of identity in any particular case are weaker or stronger as the evidence builds up for the similarity of post-mortem Fred's character and memories to pre-mortem Fred's character and memories. Thus as it happens, the evidence which we (as distinct from, say, an omniscient deity) could build up would also be an indication of similarity, but this does not imply that the distinction between similarity and identity has no meaning in this context. It has, and this would be part of our justification, in the absence of evidence to the contrary (and reduplication would be a primary example of such evidence), for taking the evidence not just as indication of similarity, but as pointing to *identity*. In any case image-experients would have within their world the distinction between similarity and identity, for example, one could think that the person with whom one is in telepathic communication is very similar to the person with whom one communicated a short time ago, but it is not the *same* person because that other person is in fact at the moment presenting himself as a telepathic apparition in a different area of one's image space.

In sections I and II, I have outlined two of the three central problems which have to be faced by any belief in the immortality of the soul: the problem of conceivability, and the problem of identity. The third problem, that of the possible grounds for such a belief, is not my concern in this article. I have argued that neither of these two problems is insuperable, though a footnote has to be added that the kind of sketch of a conceivable after-life which has been offered has clearly not been drawn with the primary aim of satisfying Christian theologians.

III

I now turn, as indicated earlier, to the concept of the resurrection of the body. The discussion will centre on the question of whether, in the light of the conclusions arrived at in section II, there are any good philosophical reasons for preferring this to a belief in the immortality of the soul.

The leading contemporary proponent of this view is perhaps Dr. Hick, who, in the paper referred to above, implies a twofold advantage which the belief in the resurrection of the body has over the belief in the immortality of the soul:

> Against this philosophical background [*sc.* a rejection of mind–body dualism] the specifically Christian (and also Jewish) belief in the resurrection of the flesh, or body, in contrast to the Hellenic notion of the survival of a disembodied soul, might be expected to have attracted more attention than it has. For it is consonant with the conception of man as an indissoluble psychophysical unity, and yet it also offers the possibility of an empirical meaning for the idea of "life after death" [p. 270].

The advantages of the one belief over the other are, it is suggested, that it is "consonant with the conception of man as an indissoluble psycho-physical unity" and that it offers a meaningful account of the idea of "life after death." Do these proposed advantages constitute good philosophical reasons for holding to the one belief rather than the other?

In the first case it is worth recalling that Price's notion of "image-experients" is compatible with Strawson's account of person as a logically primitive concept to which ascriptions of both states of consciousness and corporeal characteristics can be made. *A fortiori* this notion is "consonant with the conception of man as a . . . psycho-physical unity." The only advantage which belief in the resurrection of the body has, may be thought to reside in the use of the word "indissoluble."

If we take "indissoluble" in the strong sense, then the resurrectionist has already given his case away. In this strong sense, when the body dies, the man dies, and that is that. If the body "remains" dead, then the man remains dead, and there is no life after death. If however we take "indissoluble" in the weaker sense which Hick shows himself to require, such that it allows the body to remain dead but the man to be alive in another body, then either (1) the dead body and the living body are *entirely* unconnected, in which case it seems that we here have a case, not of identity, but of similarity—the condition which I argued would allow identity without bodily continuity is absent. If, however, (2) the dead body and living body are connected in some way, then I suggest that, if the connection is strong enough to give conditions for asserting identity rather than exact similarity, then the connection is strong enough to suggest that the word "indissoluble" has been drained of the sense which in this context gives it its polemic value.

The second supposed advantage of the doctrine of the resurrection of the body over that of the immortality of the soul is that it offers "the possibility of an empirical meaning for the idea of 'life after death.' " I am not sure how much significance to attach to the word "empirical" here, but the obvious reply is that, when problems of meaning were discussed in relation to the survival of disembodied souls, it was found that this latter was in fact meaningful or conceivable. Hence any advantage for the resurrectionist in terms of meaning has been nullified.

The only other possible advantage which could fall to the belief in bodily resurrection would have to be in terms of its ability to cope with problems of identity. Here again, the discussion in sections I and II have nullified any *prima facie* advantage. It might be thought that since a person is embodied after death then the notion of identity is somehow more in place than where we are dealing with disembodied persons. But as we have seen (cf. Williams), the crucial issue over identity seems to be the presence or absence, not just of a body, but of bodily *continuity*. In this instance, belief in resurrection is no better off than belief in immortality of the soul. The strength of the case for the importance of bodies as a condition of identity lay in the fact that bodily continuity could *guarantee* non-reduplication: but for this, bodily continuity is required, but bodily continuity is, in the nature of the case, denied by Hick (pp. 272–73).

Also it should be noted that a further possible advantage in the case of bodily resurrection is ruled out. This suggested advantage could be brought to mind by J. M. Shorter's account of the Junonians (see above). Shorter has certainly produced a story which is a further way of challenging Williams' insistence on bodily continuity as a necessary condition of identity. His ingenious example is more or less a possible account of bodily resurrection, and runs as follows:

> The Junonians came into being in a rather peculiar fashion. In a certain part of the planet bodies of the normal human sort grow to maturity. While they grow they are in a state similar to a person in a coma. Periodically these "come to life" and start to walk about and talk in a normal sort of way. They have not as a rule to learn a language; they are able to talk English and sometimes other languages too as soon as they "come to life." It also seems to them that they remember doing certain deeds, thinking certain thoughts and witnessing certain events, although these events and deeds they seem to remember certainly did not occur on Juno, so that their bodies were not ever in the right sort of situation for the people in question to have done or witnessed

these things. Now it is a fact that the occasion when each of these Junonians "first came to life" corresponds to the time when someone died in Britain . . . [p. 82].

Shorter goes on to intensify the comparison of "the new-born" Junonians and the newly dead inhabitants of Britain, such that there seems to be a one-to-one correspondence between them, including in terms of their memories (correct and mistaken), character traits, physical appearance, etc. The point is, in such an empirical situation, should we not be able validly to say, "The newly-born Mr. Jones on Juno, is the *same person as* the recently died Mr. Jones in Britain"? There is no continuity of body (Mr. Jones of Britain is buried in Cardiff, and his remains could be exhumed), but may we not legitimately be said to use the language of personal identity here?

Thus the resurrectionist account is not inferior to the view of disembodied life after death, in that it too can come to grips with the problems of identity. The only additional advantage which it might be thought to possess is that, although there is not unequivocal [11] bodily continuity between life before death and life after death, there is after death a bodily continuity which would give in that context a *stronger* concept of identity than that which could be expected in a world of disembodied persons. This has to be agreed, but it is much smaller gain than we might be led to expect from the remarks quoted from Dr. Hick. The important point is that there *is* a concept of identity in the post-mortem world of image-experients.

In this section I have considered the ways in which belief in the resurrection of the body might be thought to be philosophically less vulnerable than belief in the immortality of the soul. My conclusion is that apart from a comparatively minor point the advantage is more apparent than real.

IV

In this final section I propose to step outside of the discussion upon which we have been so far engaged, and, in fact, to consider the suitability of the framework adopted therein for the purposes of the philosopher of religion.

What is going on is a discussion of the conceivability of two different accounts of life after death. I have argued that both accounts are conceptually possible. But is this conclusion of any significance for the philosophy of religion? The quick reply to this is, "Of course, for it discounts the claim of the man who argues that the belief in life after death is incoherent." We are being assured that two beliefs, although possibly empirically false, are logically coherent, but what is now in question is whether either of the two beliefs are to be (at least in part) equated with the religious belief in either immortality or resurrection. I do not believe that a decisive, in the sense of "logically compelling," answer can be given to this question, but I wish to make some comments about the nature of the respective beliefs in question, which should at least help make the issues clearer.

An important and common feature of both proposed accounts is their respective presentation of pre-mortem and post-mortem experience belonging to one temporal continuum. This is not, of course, a fortuitous feature of the accounts: it cannot be thought away, as could, for instance any suggestion that the space of this world and the space of the resurrection world are one spatially related whole. Kant has shown that one of the conditions for the application of the word "experiences" (though in many ways a very odd condition: it is unlike, for example, saying that a condition for the application of the term "cockerel" is that the creature in question should not lay eggs) is that experiences should be temporally ordered. I should also argue that one of the conditions for experiences' being the experiences of one man is that they should be locatable on one time-scale.

From this it is clear that, if a man is to be thought of as having both pre-mortem and post-mortem experiences, these experiences must be thought of as belonging to one temporal series. This unity of temporal series cannot be thought away if identity is to be retained between pre-mortem and post-mortem existence. The point now is, within the Christian tradition at least, can discussion of the religious belief in immortality or resurrection afford to be tied down in this way? Certainly a discussion of the notion of *survival* (it is only fair to Professor Price to point out that it is to such a context that his paper belongs) of interest to psychical researchers can accept this limitation, but is the thinker who wishes to work on the basis of the Christian tradition likely to feel comfortable working with this kind of conception of his belief, whether it be in immortality of the soul or resurrection of the body?

Immediately, of course, arise the questions "What is the Christian belief about life after death?" and "What is the nature of such belief? What is it to hold such a belief?" Even if I could give an adequate answer to those questions it would take us far beyond the scope of this paper. But what I do propose to do is to point to two corollaries of the above discussion which make it difficult to see that sort of discussion as a fruitful approach for the philosopher of religion who wants to concern himself with these matters.

The first point is that both attempts to make life after death conceivable have the effect of imaging death as very near what Wittgenstein denied it to be, "an event in this life." Or, alternatively, to use a sentence written by Kierkegaard in a slightly different context (less different than might at first sight seem): "Reason has reduced it [what is unknown] to likeness with that from which it was unlike." [12] To speak of what lies "beyond the grave," of "life after death," these are common idioms, perhaps the only idioms we have if we are to *deny* that death is irreversible annihilation, if we are to *state* or *say* that life in this space–time world is not all that there is. But to this way of thinking must be put two questions.

(a) Is the religious belief in immortality or resurrection to be regarded as an attempt to treat death as less than death, as the anaesthetic from which we shall awake, perhaps with all our bad teeth pulled? Or is the religious belief one held in the face of the realisation of the gravity and, at least apparent, finality of death?—the finality which sees death as unlike that which is known, and whose opaqueness denies any validity to speculation.

(*b*) Even if we do want to deny that death is irreversible annihilation, the philosopher of religion must ask himself what can be unequivocally *said* here. Much is communicated which is not stated, and I think here of the novel and play rather than the nod and wink. Perhaps the denial that death is irreversible annihilation must be communicated otherwise than by unequivocal *statement*. The philosopher of religion who centres his discussion of immortality and resurrection upon a literalising of the idioms of "life after death," of "this world and the next," must ask himself whether or not he is trying to state what should be otherwise communicated.

The second corollary of the temporal continuity which we have noticed is that if we do adopt this way of thinking we are compelled to rest content with a belief in immortality or resurrection which is a belief in a life of endless duration. But again, it must be asked, what has this to do with the Christian belief, with its language of *eternal* life? The distinction is comparable to that which Descartes drew between that which is infinite and that which is indefinite. Eternal life is not to be equated with endless life.

These questions which I raise are not, to be sure, logically compelling in their querying the adequacy of certain frameworks for the discussion of the beliefs in immortality and resurrection. There is no entailment involved, but this does not mean that finding satisfactory answers to the questions which I have raised would not provide us with good reasons for accepting or rejecting the framework. The attempt to find such answers, and the further discussion of what it is to believe in immortality or resurrection, would take us far beyond one paper on the subject, but my contention is that it is that sort of question to which the philosopher of religion should be turning his attention. Then perhaps some justification might be given for the too-readily assumed belief that a discussion of the conceivability of certain accounts of surviving death is a prime or even a relevant interest for the philosopher whose concern is the religious belief in immortality or resurrection.

NOTES

1. See *Immortality and Resurrection*, ed. K. Stendahl (New York: Macmillan), which includes O. Cullmann's "Immortality of the Soul or Resurrection of the Dead?" as well as comment on the issues raised by Cullmann; also, J. Barr, *Old and New in Interpretation*, Ch. 2, esp. pp. 52–54, for a critique of Cullmann's methods and conclusions.

2. B. A. O. Williams, "Personal Identity and Individuation," *Proceedings of the Aristotelian Society* (1956–7), 241.

3. *Body, Mind and Death* (New York: Collier, 1964), p. 5.

4. In a reply to some criticisms by R. C. Coburn (*Analysis*, Vol. 20) in *Analysis* 21.45.

5. See, e.g., in addition to Coburn, G. C. Nerlich, *Analysis* 18.6, 21.1; J. M. Shorter, *Analysis* 22.4; C. B. Martin, *Analysis* 18.4 and *Religious Belief* (Ithaca: Cornell University Press, 1959), Ch. 6.

6. We could mean that we *intend* to treat him as if he were Guy Fawkes, and either give him a share of the annual profits of firework companies or alternatively

ensure that he spends a rather unpleasant November 5th every year, but this is not to do more than indicate an *attitude towards* him. It is to avoid the question of what grounds there may be for the possibility of adopting such an attitude, and it is precisely this which is in question.

7. See Chapter 13.

8. *Individuals* (London: Methuen, 1959), p. 102. It should also be noted here that, although I claim that what he says here is largely compatible with Strawson's account of persons, Price points out that he believes Locke's account of personal identity to be nearer the truth than what he calls the "somato-centric" analysis of personal identity.

9. See the extract from John Hick's paper "Theology and Verification" reprinted in Flew, *Body, Mind and Death*, p. 270.

10. As Price indicates, finding this out may be not instantaneous but the end product of an inductive process, since it may involve learning how to distinguish "organic sensations" from actually having a body, by coming to learn what the causal laws operating in the next world are.

11. The word "unequivocal" is used here because in Shorter's story there is a kind of continuity insofar as the post-mortem body is already, so to speak, in cold storage, awaiting the moment when it comes to life, and *that* body is continuous. But this does not affect my point.

12. *Philosophical Fragments*, trans. Swenson (2nd ed.; Princeton: Princeton University Press, 1962), p. 57.

15

Immortality

PETER GEACH
University of Leeds

EVERYBODY KNOWS THAT MEN DIE, and though most of us have read the advertisement "Millions now living will never die," it is commonly believed that every man born will some day die; yet historically many men have believed that there is a life after death, and indeed that this after-life will never end. That is: there has been a common belief both in *survival* of bodily death and in *immortality*. Now a philosopher might interest himself specially in immortality, as opposed to survival; conceding survival for the sake of argument, he might raise and examine conceptual difficulties about *endless* survival. But the question of immortality cannot even arise unless men do survive bodily death; and, as we shall see, there are formidable difficulties even about survival. It is these difficulties I shall be discussing, not the special ones about endless survival.

There are various views as to the character of the after-life. One view is that man has a subtle, ordinarily invisible, body which survives the death of the ordinary gross body. This view has a long history, and seems to be quite popular in England at the moment. So far as I can see, the view is open to no philosophical objection, but likewise wholly devoid of philosophical interest; the mind–body problem must after all be just the same for an ethereal body as for a gross one. There could clearly be no philosophical reasons for belief in such subtle bodies, but only empirical ones; such reasons are in fact alleged, and we are urged to study the evidence.

Philosophy can at this point say something: about what sort of evidence would be required. The existence of subtle bodies is a matter within the purview of physical science; evidence for it should satisfy such criteria of existence as physicists use, and should refer not only to what people say they have seen, heard, and felt, but also to effects produced by subtle bodies on physicists' apparatus. The believer in "subtle bodies" must, I think, accept the physicist's criteria of existence; there would surely be a conceptual muddle in speaking of "bodies" but saying they might be incapable of affecting any physical apparatus. For what distinguishes real physical objects from hallucinations, even collective hallucinations, is that physical objects act on one another, and do so in just the same way whether they are being observed or not; this is the point, I think, at which a phenomenalist account of physical objects breaks down. If, therefore, "subtle bodies" produce no physical effects, they are not bodies at all.

How is it, then, that "subtle bodies" have never forced themselves upon the attention of physicists, as X-rays did, by spontaneous interference with physical apparatus? There are supposed to be a lot of "subtle bodies" around, and physicists have a lot of delicate apparatus; yet physicists not engaged in psychical research are never bothered by the interference of "subtle bodies." In the circumstances I think it wholly irrational to believe in "subtle bodies." Moreover, when I who am no physicist am invited to study the evidence for "subtle bodies," I find that very fact suspicious. The discoverers of X-rays and electrons did not appeal to the lay public, but to physicists, to study the evidence; and so long as physicists (at least in general) refuse to take "subtle bodies" seriously, a study of evidence for them by a layman like myself would be a waste of time.

When *philosophers* talk of life after death, what they mostly have in mind is a doctrine that may be called Platonic—it is found in its essentials in the *Phaedo*. It may be briefly stated thus: "Each man's make-up includes a wholly immaterial thing, his mind and soul. It is the mind that sees and hears and feels and thinks and chooses—in a word, is conscious. The mind is the person; the body is extrinsic to the person, like a suit of clothes. Though body and mind affect one another, the mind's existence is quite independent of the body's; and there is thus no reason why the mind should not go on being conscious indefinitely after the death of the body, and even if it never again has with any body that sort of connexion which it now has.

This Platonic doctrine has a strong appeal, and there are plausible arguments in its favour. It appears a clearly intelligible supposition that I should go on after death having the same sorts of experience as I now have, even if I then have no body at all. For although these experiences are connected with processes in the body—sight, for example, with processes in the eyes, optic nerves, and brain—nevertheless there is no necessity of thought about the connexion—it is easy to conceive of someone who has no eyes having the experience called sight. He would be having the same experience as I who have eyes do, and I know what sort of experience that is because I have the experience.

Let us now examine these arguments. When a word can be used to stand for a private experience, like the words "seeing" or "pain," it is certainly tempting to suppose that the giving these words a meaning is itself a private experience —indeed that they get their meaning just from the experiences they stand for. But this is really nonsense: if a sentence I hear or utter contains the word "pain," do I help myself to grasp its sense by giving myself a pain? Might not this be, on the contrary, rather distracting? As Wittgenstein said, to think you get the concept of pain by having a pain is like thinking you get the concept of a minus quantity by running up an overdraft. Our concepts of seeing, hearing, pain, anger, etc., apply in the first instance to human beings; we willingly extend them (say) to cats, dogs, and horses, but we rightly feel uncomfortable about extending them to very alien creatures and speaking of a slug's hearing or an angry ant. Do we know at all what it would be to apply such concepts to an immaterial being? I think not.

One may indeed be tempted to evade difficulties by saying: "An immaterial spirit is angry or in pain if it feels *the same way* as I do when I am angry or in pain." But, as Wittgenstein remarked, this is just like saying: "Of course I know what it is for the time on the Sun to be five o'clock: it's five o'clock on the Sun at the very moment when it's five o'clock here!"—which plainly gets us no forrader. If there is a difficulty in passing from "I am in pain" or "Smith is in pain" to "an immaterial spirit is in pain," there is equally a difficulty in passing from "Smith feels the same way as I do" to "an immaterial spirit feels the same way as I do."

In fact, the question is, whether a private experience does suffice, as is here supposed, to give a meaning to a psychological verb like "to see." I am not trying to throw doubt on there being private experiences; of course men have thoughts they do not utter and pains they do not show; of course I may see something without any behaviour to show I see it; nor do I mean to emasculate these propositions with neo-behaviourist dialectics. But it is not a question of whether seeing is (sometimes) a private experience, but whether one can attach meaning to the verb "to see" by a private uncheckable performance; and this is what I maintain one cannot do to any word at all.

One way to show that a word's being given a meaning cannot be a private uncheckable performance is the following: We can take a man's word for it that a linguistic expression has given him some private experience—e.g. has revived a painful memory, evoked a visual image, or given him a thrill in the pit of the stomach. But we cannot take his word for it that he attached a sense to the expression, even if we accept his *bona fides*; for later events may convince us that in fact he attached no sense to the expression. Attaching sense to an expression is thus not to be identified with any private experience that accompanies the expression; and I have argued this, not by attacking the idea of private experiences, but by contrasting the attaching of sense to an expression with some typical private experiences that may be connected with the expression.

We give words a sense—whether they are psychological words like "seeing" and "pain" or other words—by getting into a way of using them; and though a man can invent for himself a way of using a word, it must be a way that other people *could* follow—otherwise we are back to the idea of conferring meaning by a private uncheckable performance. Well, how do we eventually use such words as "see," "hear," "feel," when we have got into the way of using them? We do not exercise these concepts only so as to pick our cases of seeing and the rest in our separate worlds of sense-experience; on the contrary, these concepts are used in association with a host of other concepts relating, e.g., to the physical characteristics of what is seen and the behaviour of those who do see. In saying this I am not putting forward a theory, but just reminding you of very familiar features in the everyday use of the verb "to see" and related expressions; our ordinary talk about seeing would cease to be intelligible if there were cut out of it such expressions as "I can't see, it's too far off," "I caught his eye," "Don't look round," etc. Do not let the bogy of behaviourism scare you off observing these features; I am not asking you to believe that "to see" is itself a word for a kind of behaviour. But the concept of seeing can be maintained only because it has threads of connexion with these other non-psychological concepts; break enough threads, and the concept of seeing collapses.

We can now see the sort of difficulties that arise if we try to apply concepts like *seeing* and *feeling* to disembodied spirits. Let me give an actual case of a psychological concept's collapsing when its connexions were broken. Certain hysterics claimed to have a magnetic sense; it was discovered, however, that their claim to be having magnetic sensations did not go with the actual presence of a magnet in their environment, but only with their belief that a magnet was present. Psychologists did not now take the line: We may take the patients' word for it that they have peculiar sensations—only the term "magnetic sensations" has proved inappropriate, as having been based on a wrong causal hypothesis. On the contrary, patients' reports of magnetic sensations were thenceforward written off as being among the odd things that hysterical patients sometimes say. Now, far fewer of the ordinary connexions of a sensation-concept were broken here than would be broken if we tried to apply a sensation-concept like seeing to a disembodied spirit.

If we conclude that the ascription of sensations and feelings to a disembodied spirit does not make sense, it does not obviously follow, as you might think, that we must deny the possibility of disembodied spirits altogether. Aquinas for example was convinced that there are disembodied spirits but ones that cannot see or hear or feel pain or fear or anger; he allowed them no mental operations except those of thought and will. Damned spirits would suffer from frustration of their evil will, but not from aches and pains or foul odours or the like. It would take me too far to discuss whether his reasons for thinking this were good ; I want to show what follows from this view. In our human life thinking and choosing are intricately bound up with a play of sensations and mental images and emotions; if after a lifetime of thinking and choosing in this human way there is left only a disembodied mind whose thought is wholly non-sensuous and whose rational choices are unaccompanied by any human feelings—can we still say there remains the same person? Surely not: such a soul is not the person who died but a mere remnant of him. And this is just what Aquinas says (in his commentary on 1 Corinthians 15): *anima mea non est ego,* my soul is not I; and if only souls are saved, *I* am not saved, nor is any man. If some time after Peter Geach's death there is again a man identifiable as Peter Geach, then Peter Geach again, or still, lives: otherwise not.

Though a surviving mental remnant of a person, preserving some sort of physical continuity with the man you knew, would not be Peter Geach, this does not show that such a measure of survival is not possible; but its possibility does raise serious difficulties, even if such dehumanized thinking and willing is really conceivable at all. For *whose* thinking would this be? Could we tell whether *one* or *many* disembodied spirits thought the thoughts in question? We touch here on the old problem: what constitutes there being two disembodied minds (at the same time, that is)? Well, what constitutes there being two pennies? It may happen that one penny is bent and corroded while another is in mint condition; but such differences cannot be what make the two pennies to be two—the two pennies could not have these varied fortunes if they were not already distinct.

In the same way, differences of memories or of aims could not constitute the difference between disembodied minds, but could only supervene upon a difference already existing. What does constitute the difference between two disembodied human minds? If we could find no ground of differentiation, then not only would that which survived be a mere remnant of a person—there would not even be a surviving individuality.

Could we say that souls are different because in the first instance they were souls of different bodies, and then remain different on that account when they are no longer embodied? I do not think this solution would do at all if differentiation by reference to different bodies were merely retrospective. It might be otherwise if we held, with Aquinas, that the relation to a body was not merely retrospective—that each disembodied human soul permanently retained a capacity for reunion to such a body as would reconstitute a man identifiable with the man who died. This might satisfactorily account for the individuation of disembodied souls; they would differ by being fitted for reunion to different bodies; but it would entail that the possibility of disembodied human souls stood or fell with the *possibility* of a dead man's living again *as a man*.

Some Scholastics held that, just as two pennies or two cats differ by being different bits of matter, so human souls differ by containing different "spiritual matter." Aquinas regarded this idea as self-contradictory; it is at any rate much too obscure to count as establishing a possibility of distinct disembodied souls. Now this recourse to "spiritual matter" might well strike us merely as the filling of a conceptual lacuna with a nonsensical piece of jargon. But it is not only Scholastic philosophers who assimilate mental processes to physical ones, only thinking of mental processes as taking place in an *immaterial* medium; and many people think it easy to conceive of distinct disembodied souls because they are illegitimately ascribing to souls a sort of differentiation—say, by existing *side by side*—that can be significantly ascribed only to bodies. The same goes for people who talk about souls as being "fused" or "merged" in a Great Soul; they are imagining some such change in the world of souls as occurs to a drop of water falling into a pool or to a small lump of wax that is rubbed into a big one. Now, if only people *talked* about "spiritual matter," instead of just thinking in terms of it unawares, their muddle could be more easily detected and treated.

To sum up what I have said so far: The possibility of life after death for Peter Geach appears to stand or fall with the possibility of there being once again a man identifiable as Peter Geach. The existence of a disembodied soul would not be a survival of the person Peter Geach; and even in such a truncated form, individual existence seems to require at least a persistent possibility of the soul's again entering into the make-up of a man who is identifiably Peter Geach.

This suggests a form of belief in survival that seems to have become quite popular of late in the West—at any rate as a half-belief—namely, the belief in reincarnation. Could it in fact have a clear sense to say that a baby born in Oxford this year is Hitler living again?

How could it be shown that the Oxford baby was Hitler? Presumably by memories and similarities of character. I maintain that no amount of such evidence would make it reasonable to identify the baby as Hitler. Similarities of character are of themselves obviously insufficient. As regards memories: If on growing up the Oxford baby reveals knowledge of what we should ordinarily say only Hitler can have known, does this establish a presumption that the child is Hitler? Not at all. In normal circumstances we know when to say "only he can have known that"; when queer things start happening, we have no right to stick to our ordinary assumptions as to what can be known. And suppose that for some time the child "is" Hitler by our criteria, and later on "is" Goering? or might not several children simultaneously satisfy the criteria for "being" Hitler?

These are not merely captious theoretical objections. Spirit-mediums, we are told, will in trance convincingly enact the part of various people: sometimes of fictitious characters, like Martians, or Red Indians ignorant of Red Indian languages, or the departed "spirits" of Johnny Walker and John Jamieson; there are even stories of mediums' giving convincing "messages" from people who were alive and normally conscious at the time of the "message." Now, a medium giving messages from the dead is not said to be the dead man, but rather to be controlled by his spirit. What then can show whether the Oxford child "is" Hitler or is merely "controlled" by Hitler's spirit? For all these reasons the appearance that there might be good evidence for reincarnation dissolves on a closer view.

Nor do I see, for that matter, how the mental phenomena of mediumship could ever make it reasonable to believe that a human soul survived and communicated. For someone to carry on in a dramatic way quite out of his normal character is a common hysterical symptom; so if a medium does this in a trance, it is no evidence of anything except an abnormal condition of the medium's own mind. As for the medium's telling us things that "only the dead can have known," I repeat that in these queer cases we have no right to stick to our ordinary assumptions about what can be known. Moreover, as I said, there are cases, as well-authenticated as any, in which the medium convincingly enacted the part of X and told things that "Only X could have known" when X was in fact alive and normally conscious, so that his soul was certainly not trying to communicate by way of the medium! Even if we accept all the queer stories of spirit-messages, the result is only to open up a vast field of queer possibilities— not in the least to force us to say that mediums were possessed by such-and-such souls. This was argued by Bradley long ago in his essay "The Evidences of Spiritualism," and he has never been answered.

How could a living man be rightly identifiable with a man who previously died? Let us first consider our normal criteria of personal identity. When we say an old man is the same person as the baby born seventy years before, we believe that the old man has material continuity with the baby. Of course this is not a criterion in the sense of being what we judge identity by; for the old man will not have been watched for seventy years continuously, even by rota! But something we regarded as disproving the material continuity (e.g. absence of a birthmark, different fingerprints) would disprove personal identity. Further, we believe that material continuity establishes a one–one relation: one baby grows up into one old man, and one old man has grown out of one baby. (Otherwise there would have to be at some stage a drastic change, a fusion or fission, which we should regard as destroying personal identity.) Moreover, the baby body never coexists with the aged body, but develops into it.

Now it seems to me that we cannot rightly identify a man living "again" with a man who died unless *material* conditions of identity are fulfilled. There must be some one–one relation of material continuity between the old body and the new. I am not saying that the new body need be even in part materially *identical* with the old; this, unlike material continuity, is not required for personal identity, for the old man need not have kept even a grain of matter from the baby of seventy years ago.

We must here notice an important fallacy. I was indicating just now that I favour Aquinas' doctrine that two coexisting souls differ by being related to two different bodies and that two coexisting human bodies, like two pennies or two cats, differ by being different bits of matter. Well, if it is difference of matter that makes two bodies different, it may seem to follow that a body can maintain its identity only if at least some identifiable matter remains in it all the time; otherwise it is no more the same body than the wine in a cask that is continuously emptied and refilled is the same wine. But just this is the fallacy: it does not follow, if difference in a certain respect at a certain time suffices to show non-identity, that sameness in that respect over a period of time is necessary to identity. Thus Sir John Cutler's famous pair of stockings were the same pair all the time, although they started as silk and by much mending ended as worsted; people have found it hard to see this, because if at a given time there is a silk pair and also a worsted pair then there are two pairs. Again, it is clear that the same man may be in Birmingham at noon and in Oxford at 7 P.M., even though a man in Birmingham and a man in Oxford at a given time must be two different men. Once formulated, the fallacy is obvious, but it might be deceptive if not formulated.

"Why worry even about material continuity? Would not mental continuity be both necessary and sufficient?" Necessary, but not sufficient. Imagine a new "Tichborne" trial. The claimant knows all the things he ought to know, and talks convincingly to the long-lost heir's friends. But medical evidence about scars and old fractures and so on indicates that he cannot be the man; moreover, the long-lost heir's corpse is decisively identified at an exhumation. Such a case would bewilder us, particularly if the claimant's *bona fides* were manifest. (He might, for example, voluntarily take a lie-detecting test.) But we should certainly not allow the evidence of mental connexions with the long-lost heir to settle the matter in the claimant's favour: the claimant cannot be the long-lost heir, whose body we know lies buried in Australia, and if he honestly thinks he is then we must try to cure him of a delusion.

"But if I went on being conscious, why should I worry which body I have?" To use the repeated "I" prejudges the issue; a fairer way of putting the point would be: If there is going to be a consciousness that includes ostensible memories of my life, why should I worry about which body this consciousness goes with? When we put it that way, it is quite easy to imagine circumstances in which one would worry—particularly if the ostensible memories of my life were to be produced by processes that can produce entirely spurious memories.

If, however, memory is not enough for personal identity; if a man's living again does involve some bodily as well as mental continuity with the man who lived formerly; then we might fairly call his new bodily life a resurrection. So the upshot of our whole argument is that, unless a man comes to life again by resurrection, he does not live again after death. At best some mental remnant of him would survive death; and I should hold that the possibility even of such survival involves at least a permanent *capacity* for renewed human life; if reincarnation is excluded, this means: a capacity for resurrection. It may be hard to believe in the resurrection of the body: but Aquinas argued in his commentary on 1 Corinthians 15, which I have already cited, that it is much harder to believe in an immortal but permanently disembodied human soul; for that would mean believing that a soul, whose very identity depends on the capacity for reunion with one human body rather than another, will continue to exist for ever with this capacity unrealized.

Speaking of the resurrection, St. Paul used the simile of a seed that is planted and grows into an ear of corn, to show the relation between the corpse and the body that rises again from the dead. This simile fits in well enough with our discussion. In this life, the bodily aspect of personal identity requires a one–one relationship and material continuity; one baby body grows into one old man's body by a continuous process. Now, similarly there is a one–one relationship between the buried seed and the ear that grows out of it; one seed grows into one ear, one ear comes from one seed; and the ear of corn is materially continuous with the seed but need not have any material identity with it.

There is of course no philosophical reason to expect that from a human corpse there will arise at some future date a new human body, continuous in some way with the corpse; and in some particular cases there appear strong empirical objections. But apart from the *possibility* of resurrection, it seems to me a mere illusion to have any hope for life after death. I am of the mind of Judas Maccabeus: if there is no resurrection, it is superfluous and vain to pray for the dead.

The traditional faith of Christianity, inherited from Judaism, is that at the end of this age Messiah will come and men rise from their graves to die no more. That faith is not going to be shaken by inquiries about bodies burned to ashes or eaten by beasts; those who might well suffer just such death in martyrdom were those who were most confident of a glorious reward in the resurrection. One who shares that hope will hardly wish to take out an occultistic or philosophical insurance policy, to guarantee some sort of survival as an annuity, in case God's promise of resurrection should fail.

16

Mysticism and the
Paradox of Survival

JOHN J. CLARKE

University of Malaya

SOME CURRENT ACCOUNTS
OF PERSONAL SURVIVAL

THE IDEA OF SURVIVAL AFTER DEATH has itself survived, at least as a logical possibility, the death of many other metaphysical notions. It is not difficult to see why, for it is possible to imagine many things in connection with one's survival of death: one can picture oneself watching one's own funeral, reuniting with one's deceased friends and relatives, reflecting, dwelling on memories, and so forth. Such imaginative pictures can be painted in various thicknesses of colour. One of the most richly coloured portraits in recent years has come from John Hick.[1] His resurrection world, though sequestered from our own stretch of space and time, appears to be as richly detailed as our own. Though no longer made of physical matter, resurrected bodies are to all intents and purposes indistinguishable from our present unregenerate ones, and resurrected people therefore have no special difficulty in identifying their own or other people's bodies. The portrait is as easy as can be on our imaginations, so life-like indeed that one might sometimes wonder whether one is in this world or the next. As an example of a more sparsely drawn picture of survival one might take the notion sketched by Strawson in *Individuals*. It is possible to conceive of one's survival of bodily death, he thinks, but it would be a solitary and unenviable existence, for though one could have experiences, thoughts, and memories as at present, there would be no means of communicating with others, embodied or otherwise, and no way of initiating changes in the world.[2]

One of the persistent problems with the notion of survival is that of understanding how an individual *person* can pass through the needle eye of death and yet still sensibly be called the same person or even a person at all. Obviously this problem becomes more acute as the detail of the picture becomes more

Reprinted by permission from *International Philosophical Quarterly*, 11 (1971), 165–79.

sparse. Thus Strawson's account is not merely, as he admits, "unenticing," but borders on incoherence, for it is not intuitively obvious that the survival of my bare capacity to remember and to contemplate constitutes the survival of what could properly be called "me." The shadows he allows to pass are, one would suppose, attenuated beyond recognition. Hick's more fully drawn portrait probably has the advantage of avoiding such lines of criticism as these, but while he is more skillful in conveying persons whole and entire into the netherworld, there is one very serious deficiency in his account which has not to my knowledge been noticed and on which I propose to focus attention in this paper: his survivors remain human, all too human. It is not that we expect them for *a priori* reasons to be radically changed by this traumatic experience—though I think we would so expect—but rather that strictly speaking they do not appear to have survived death at all but merely *a* death.

Certainly from the point of view of theology such a demi-survival can be of little interest. As I understand the matter, people who have wished for and believed in the soul's survival of death have found both justification for and comfort in this belief because of some kind of change that would thereby be wrought in the soul. Whether in the context of popular theology or metaphysics, the doctrine of immortality has featured not simply as an attractive hypothesis in itself but also as providing a necessary apotheosis for a life which would otherwise be without reason or justice. If life ended with bodily death then the pains and injustices of life would render it pointless, but eternal life hereafter not only compensates for present discomforts but also supposedly gives life a rational justification which it would otherwise lack. Hick's heaven offers neither justification nor comfort. To all intents and purposes it is a replica of our present unhappy estate, without even the prospect of eternal sleep to assuage its unending course. He has in effect merely redescribed the situation from which the problem originally sprang.

There might appear to be some unfairness to Hick in this argument. It is true that his resurrection world is remarkably like our own, but he does make note of two distinctive features: firstly it is situated in a different space from our own such that it has no spatial connections with our world, and secondly its occupants are housed in bodies that are exact replicas of their pre-resurrection abodes with the one difference that they are no longer constituted of physical matter. But it is not very clear in what sense his world is really qualitatively different from our own, for the claim that our bodies are identical with our former ones, except in the one respect that they are not made of physical matter, is not an obviously meaningful one. "Being physical" is not a property that can be added to or subtracted from entities like a coat of paint. However, one may suppose that Hick, were he to elaborate his picture a little more, would insist on further important differences, and in particular he would probably want to claim that in his resurrection world pain and death no longer have dominion. This would certainly be an improvement from the point of view of the believer, and appears to be perfectly conceivable.

However, on both points—pain and death—there are difficulties. As far as the elimination of death is concerned, an unending existence is not necessarily an improvement on our present one, and might even, due to its unconscionable length, represent a considerable deterioration. Nor is it any more self-justifying, for the eternal perpetuation of life as we know it is open to as many of the pessimist's objections as our present finite existence. And as far as pain is concerned, "being painful," like "being physical," is not a property that can be added to or subtracted from the world while leaving everything else as it is. There is some sort of case here for physical pain, for while this undoubtedly serves the important biological function of a warning system, we can easily stretch our imaginations to inventing a more congenial arrangement. But on the other hand nonphysical pain—what we could more usefully call "suffering" —cannot be eliminated without incurring disastrous side-effects. What I have in mind is something like this: suffering does not have a function relative to well-being in the way that physical pain does, for the concept of suffering is *logically* tied to various sorts of typically human activities, unlike pain which is contingently tied. Minimally, and roughly, we can say that being human involves the capacity to make rational choices, and these in turn combine the capacity to assess states of affairs and to assess one's attitudes, desires, needs, wants, and so forth in relation to these states of affairs. But to have choices open to one, and to be able to deliberate about these choices in the light of what one wants and what is the case, necessarily implies the following three possibilities: firstly that one's beliefs about what is the case may be mistaken, secondly that one's chosen course of action may fail to achieve its end, and thirdly that having got what one wanted one may find that it is no longer satisfactory or satisfying. In others words at least *some* forms of suffering are necessary for beings who make rational choices in a world more or less like our own.

Hick's model clearly cannot accommodate this difficulty. There is nothing in his account of the resurrection world which allows us to think of it as being free from suffering and hence as being in some way more acceptable than our present life. The mere elimination of pain, happy enough in itself, is inadequate, for when people have sought in an after-life an assuagement of their condition, they have sought a much deeper transformation. Cosmic engineering, tinkering about with details here and there, leaves the fundamental facts of the human condition unchanged, and hence the problem for which immortality is the supposed solution is left untouched. Furthermore, those who have found earthly life a matter of anguish and regret have often discovered the source of their dissatisfaction at an even more fundamental level, namely in the fact that we live in a world in which things are transitory and which therefore cannot give us any grounds for complete and permanent satisfaction. Such satisfaction, it has been thought, can only be gained in a world where time does not cheat us of the goals of our activities and where the very striving for the satisfaction of our needs and wants has been stilled.

Whether this represents even a coherent fantasy cannot be decided here, but at any rate it is a viewpoint which appears to underlie the Christian "heaven" and the Buddhist "nirvana," and it does at any rate point to those features of our earthly existence which have underlain many peoples' dissatisfaction with it, features which remain unredeemed in Hick's resurrection world. To sum up, then: while Hick's model does not, on the face of it, at any rate, strain our notion of personal identity, he achieves this at the expense of merely reiterating the human condition for which presumably the resurrection world is a sketch of an answer.

These deficiencies are to some extent remedied in the more economically drawn portraits of survival. Thus, in Strawson's version, suffering as a factor necessarily involved in the transactions of human persons in a spatio-temporal world has largely been removed. There are no longer any things or persons to block my choices, and indeed very few choices are still open to me to make. But on the other hand, as we have already noted, such an existence is not exactly an enviable one. Being able to dwell on one's memories presumably allows one to regret deeds one has done and also to regret that one can do nothing about the regret except simply to dwell upon it. At any rate, the possibility of suffering remains, as in the case of fully bodied existence, even if confined within narrower limits. In addition to this it is a singularly pointless existence, not one that could be considered in any way an apotheosis of earthly life, and it remains as unregenerate as the embodied life it has succeeded. One can imagine a ghostly Strawson longing for redemption from his memories and his passive experiences. But whether or not Strawson's account offers justification and comfort, there still remains the difficulty which must beset all thinly drawn portraits of survival—whether in terms of a pure ego, memory traces, stream of consciousness, intellect, will, or whatever—namely, that they demand the bending to breaking point of our usual criteria of personal identity. Whether or not it can be shown that a set of disembodied faculties represents an improvement on their previous embodied form, it is not at all clear that we can speak of a human person experiencing, remembering, deciding, choosing, desiring, and perceiving unless he is endowed with a mobile and sensitive organism.

In considering the notion of survival after death we are therefore presented with the following paradox. Either we survive with our full kit of mental and physical characteristics in more or less the same kind of world as our own, or we carry over with us a flexible list of mental characteristics only. In neither case is the problem for which survival has been offered as a solution—the problem of providing a meaningful and happy apotheosis to a supposedly miserable and senseless existence—solved. The first solution merely restates, in a large measure, the problem; the second dissolves, in varying degrees, the being for whom it is supposedly a solution. Is there any *tertium quid*? Can we offer an account of survival which takes care of both prerequisites, which allows for *persons*, not shadows or memories, to survive, and which makes such survival worthwhile? In the next section we shall explore one such possible account.

MYSTICAL EXPERIENCE AS A MODEL

The tentative solution that I shall put forward here is in terms of a certain kind of mystical experience. First it is necessary to explain how this notion is to be employed.

It might be tempting to propound a solution to the paradox of survival on the basis of the obvious flimsiness of the concept of a person, for is it not the case that at the boundaries of the concept we are accustomed to enjoy a certain amount of freedom of manoeuvre? Where foetuses, for example, or idiots, or split personalities are concerned, we do not have a ready-made decision procedure for the application of the concept, and it might be argued that even though disembodied persons are not central cases of persons they are sufficiently close to such central cases to allow us to assimilate them to the class of persons. But clearly this will not do, for by implication it would allow us to extend quite arbitrarily any concept in any direction we wished. In general what is required for the proper extension of an empirical concept beyond its wonted domain is something like what Kant called a *schema*. According to Kant— though we do not need to borrow the notion from him in all its details—a concept remains vacuous and empty until we produce in our imagination a *schematic* representation of it, thereby providing rules for the application of the concept. To mention one analogy: if Freud's only reason for extending the concepts of "motive," "intention," "desire," and so on, was that these concepts had no fixed boundaries, then his theory of the unconscious would rightly have been rejected as arbitrary. Clearly in order to justify his extended use of these terms it was necessary for him to describe, or at any rate to provide imaginary descriptions of, examples of human activity to which these concepts, hitherto not found to be applicable, could now properly be applied, and indeed much of his work is devoted to precisely this task. What is required in our present case is something similar to this. Obviously we cannot point to actual cases of disembodied persons in the way that Freud could (in a sense) point to cases of unconscious desire, but what we can do is to point to cases of an experience, familiar at least to some earthly denizens, which, though itself not that of a disembodied person, can provide a schematic image of it. It is in this role that I have cast mystical experience.

We must next specify what we mean by "mystical experience." Certainly a wide variety of types of experience has been denoted by this term, but as far as the present paper is concerned there is no need to mention any other feature of them than their variety, for we are here interested in only one sort, namely that which is typically described in terms of *oneness and harmony with the universe*. This kind of experience, which is reduplicated in a variety of different contexts, religious and non-religious, Oriental and Western, takes its rise initially perhaps from a sense of alienation and separation of the individual from the world and from the sense of pain and anguish that arises therefrom. The type of mystical experience in question comes as a radical assuagement of this sense of alienation. The rift between the self and the world is sealed, the sense of separation along with its accompanying anguish and regret is attenuated, and the very multiplicity of the physical world itself appears to the mystic to be dissolved into oneness. In particular it is the sense of the separateness of things including oneself that disappears, to be replaced by a feeling of total unity, harmony, and tranquillity. There are of course varying degrees of oneness and serenity. At its lowest level it can be seen in experiences that can hardly be termed "mystical" at all and which are probably enjoyed sometimes by everybody and frequently by some, namely the kind of experience that involves a close unity with other persons either through love or through some form of absorbing group activity. A more specifically mystical experience—though we would not always describe it as such—can arise in the context of aesthetic contemplation, when we may become so absorbed in listening to a piece of music or in contemplating an art work that all sense of time and of involvement in real life is momentarily lost. Most typically, of course, aesthetic mysticism is associated with the contemplation of and absorption in nature. So-called "nature mystics" are not difficult to find, and one could cite the names of Wordsworth, Rimbaud, and Proust as examples of men who, without benefit of religion, have enjoyed and subsequently described states of blissful absorption in nature. In such states it is quite common that the individual ceases to experience himself as a being separate from the world and imagines that in some way he is dissolved into the object of his contemplation. Thus Tennyson describes an experience in which, as he says,

> . . . out of the intensity of the consciousness of individuality, individuality itself seemed to dissolve and fade away into boundless being, and this is not a confused state but the clearest beyond words . . . where death was an almost laughable impossibility—the loss of personality (if so it were) seemed no extinction, but the only true life.[3]

The absorption of the self into nature and the loss of a sense of the multiplicity of things is frequently accompanied by a sense of timelessness, an experience that is sometimes described as the "timeless moment." For example, much of the *Four Quartets* of T. S. Eliot appears to be devoted to the attempt to capture this feeling in words. Thomas Mann in his novel *The Magic Mountain* was similarly preoccupied, and he attempts in the following passage a "description" of the timeless moment:

> We walk, walk. How long, how far? Who knows? Nothing is changed by our pacing, there is the same as here, once on a time the same as now, or then; time is drowned in the measureless monotony of space, motion from point to point is no motion more, where uniformity rules; and where motion is no more motion, time is no longer time.[4]

And in case these examples should appear to be contrived for the sake of art rather than accurate reportage of an experience, here is a quotation in which a nineteenth-century nature mystic, Richard Jeffries, claims to describe one particular such experience: "It is eternity now. I am in the midst of it. It is about me in the sunshine; I am in it, as the butterfly floats in the light-laden air. Nothing is to come: it is now. Now is by this tumulus, on earth, now; I exist in it."[5]

There are several strands that connect together experiences of this type. They involve an experience of oneness and a corresponding loss of a sense of multiplicity in space and time, an attenuation of the sense of dualism of subject and object, the lessening or loss of one's sense of one's own separate existence, a feeling of bliss and harmony that arises from the loss of all desires and regrets, and in particular a sense of detachment which nullifies all fear of pain and death. So far I have related these experiences only to non-religious and non-metaphysical contexts, but this collection of interconnected characteristics aptly describes also the experiences of certain religious mystics and saints. Let us take Buddhism as an obvious example. The so-called Buddhist path of enlightenment, which represents an attempt to nullify craving and desire, is seen as necessarily involving the overcoming of the sense of the multiplicity of things and a loss of the sense of one's separate existence in space and time. As long as the world appears to exist externally to oneself it will inevitably constitute an object of desire and hence of suffering, and only through the obliteration of this sense of mutual externality can desire and suffering be attenuated. Such a state of desirelessness and of oneness is termed by the Buddhists *nirvana*, a condition that is to be understood, not in terms of a cosmological theory, but rather in the light of certain meditative practices along with the mental and physical discipline required to achieve the appropriate contemplative state. It is a state that can be described as one of complete and blissful detachment from a sense both of one's own self and of the external world, achieved in the first place by sustained concentration on a particular object and later by the complete removal from one's mind of all particular thoughts and ideas. The mysticism of the Upanishads moves in a similar direction. Its famous dictum *tat tvam asi* ("thou art that") sums up its denial of the reality of the self and the world and its affirmation of the ultimate oneness of things, knowledge of which is similarly the fruit of ascetic contemplation rather than of discursive thinking. Similar too is the Taoism of Lao-tze and Chuang-tze which developed independently of the Indian mystical tradition. Here too the central feature is the attainment of harmony and unity with the world through withdrawal and contemplation, "an inner experience" as one commentator has described it, "through which man and the universe interfuse as one."[6]

The West too has produced religious mystics who have given accounts of monistic experiences of a similar kind, but in the interests of economy I shall limit myself to two quotations, the first from Plotinus and the second from Meister Eckhart:

> The man is changed, no longer himself nor self-belonging; he is merged with the Supreme, sunken into It; only in separation is there duality . . . no movement now, no passion, no outlooking desire; . . . reason is in abeyance and intellection and even the very self; . . . all the being calmed he turns neither to this side nor to that, nor even inwards towards himself; utterly resting he has become rest itself.

> So long as the soul beholds forms . . . or herself as something formed: so long is there imperfection in her. Only when all that is formed is cast off from the soul, and she sees the Eternal One alone, then the pure essence of the soul feels the naked unformed essence of the divine unity. . . . What a noble endurance is that where the essence of the soul suffers no suggestion or shadow of difference. . . . There she entrusts herself alone to the One, free from all multiplicity and difference, in which all limitation and quality is lost and is one. This One makes us blessed.[7]

Here, then, we have our schematic model. Its advantages are twofold. In the first place it allows us to speak of the unknown in terms of the known. It has always been a problem for metaphysicians to give sense to talk about matters which are in principle beyond direct empirical observation, and the suggestion I have put forward is that mystical experience does provide us with an imaginative schema, a *via analogica*, by which we may come to understand some of this talk. We are therefore not quite at the extreme disadvantage at which St. Paul imagined us to be when he lamented that "The eye hath not seen . . ." etc., for even though we have not seen the real stuff, we have—or some of us have—seen something like it. In this respect, of course, it is no better than the models of Hick and Strawson, for they too have tried to describe the unfamiliar in terms of the familiar, but, as I have suggested, this familiarity turns out in their cases to be a large disadvantage, for they offer us either the same course again or a similar course with the spices removed. The latter point may appear also to work to the disadvantage of our *tertium quid*, for it too, though not standardly a repetition of a previous course, lacks spice. It is certainly not what many of the faithful look forward to in the after-life, and here perhaps J. S. Mill was for once in tune with popular opinion when he admitted that the only reason for hoping for an after-life lay in the possibility of being united with one's loved ones.

But herein lies the second and perhaps most important feature of our model for if, to put it crudely, the after-life looks like a mystical experience, and if therefore it is devoid of all sense of space and of separate existences in space, and of all sense of before and after, and if therefore there can be no sense of hope or regret, no desiring or wanting, then all possibility of regretting or lamenting one's estate ceases. Not only are the conditions eliciting regret no longer present, but the very possibility of regretting anything at all has been removed. However pleasant the prospect of being reunited with Harriet, Mill has no guarantee that their love will last for all eternity, for even though their happiness might persist, the conditions for unhappiness must remain. The comfort of our new model, therefore, lies in the impossibility of discomfort, and its justification in the impossibility of ever requiring one. As Wittgenstein remarked: "The solution of the problem of life is seen in the vanishing of the problem" (*Tractatus*, 6.521).

OBJECTIONS

It is now time to consider some difficulties that the proposed model inevitably runs into. The first concerns the *language* of mystical experience. This can be approached at several levels, but undoubtedly one of the first criticisms to be voiced against the foregoing remarks is that the argument relies on a spurious similarity between a multitude of reported experiences. It is absurd, the critic might continue, to imagine that the reports of so-called mystical experiences are "pure" and objective. In fact, the language of such reports is thoroughly soaked in the doctrinal presuppositions of the reporters. There is something in this criticism that must be taken seriously, for if our *schematism* turned out to be wholly or even largely metaphysical or religious doctrine, then we would simply be begging the very question we set out to answer; it is necessary for our case that these reports should be as objective as such reports can be. But in fact they pass this test adequately enough. In the first place, as far as the Oriental examples cited are concerned, it is quite wrong to separate doctrine from experience, as if the one is learned intellectually first, as it were, and only subsequently confirmed by esoteric experience. In a sense the doctrine *is* the experience, for the experience is a necessary and a sufficient condition for understanding, the understanding itself not being "*of*" anything, but simply a state of tranquil detachment: there is nothing beyond that to know. It is true that cosmological theories have developed alongside the mystical tradition, but again it is probably a mistake to suppose that the mystical experiences came as a result of the cosmological theories. It is at least highly likely that the doctrines themselves were developed to explain the experiences and that the universal similarity of the latter helps to explain in turn the remarkable similarity between cosmological theories in diverse cultures. It should also be noted that we are relying not only on the reports of religious mystics but also on nature mystics who, though they may have no doctrinal baggage to carry along, nevertheless tell us stories which strikingly resemble those of their religious counterparts.

But still it might be urged that the argument goes wrong at a more fundamental level. Since mystical experience is not available to everyone there is no way for the detached observer to check the reports of mystics, and indeed in the last analysis the mystic appears to be going beyond the limits of what can meaningfully be said. This is a large issue and only a few brief remarks must suffice in reply. It is indeed true that the language employed by mystics to describe their experiences is pushed well to the edge of meaningfulness—as Eliot says, echoing the sentiments of many mystics themselves, "Words strain / Crack and sometimes break, under the burden."[8] But it would be incorrect to claim that their remarks were totally meaningless. No doubt we cannot appreciate fully what the mystic is trying to tell us unless we have trodden the same path ourselves, but enough of what he is saying comes through to us to enable us to be tolerably certain that we would recognize the experience if it came our way. Not everything that he says is totally foreign to us, and as has already been pointed out there is no clean break between fairly common experiences of harmony and integration with the world at the one extreme and full-blown mystical experiences at the other.

For this reason the mystic's words contain a core of meaning for us. Of course his descriptions do not function in quite the way that ordinary empirical descriptions do, but what he has to say does enable us at least to *pin-point* the experience, to place it in a certain framework and to relate it to others. This is borne out by the fact that there is a remarkable superficial resemblance between descriptions of esoteric experiences from radically diverse sources, and it would be odd if not contradictory to refuse to allow a corresponding resemblance between the experiences themselves. In other words, it is reasonable to conjecture that we are dealing here with a fairly universal feature of the human mind, namely the desire for peace, harmony, and the identification of oneself with the world, a desire which finds its highest expression in the feeling that all differences are illusory, that there is no time, no multiplicity, but that all things are really one. My claim is the minimal one that something answering to, or pinpointed by, this sort of description has been experienced by a representative collection of people.

Objections along the foregoing lines are not, I believe, particularly strong, and though they have been dealt with briefly we can now pass on to some more powerful ones. It will no doubt have struck the reader that the mystical model is remarkably thin and sketchy by our own standards, and that therefore it ought reasonably to succumb to the same criticisms that were levelled at the Strawson model. For is it not the case that we too are allowing mere shadows— if that—to pass through death's needle eye, rather than anything that could recognizably be called a "person," let alone the "same" person who existed in a previous life? No doubt we have described a condition which represents a considerable improvement on our earthly existence. It is a state which could plausibly be called blissful (mystics have certainly thought of it as such), in which death, suffering, and indeed any vicissitude whatsoever can be of no consequence, and hence provides the comfort and justification lacking in the other models. But at the same time it looks as if we have so described this blissful condition that *persons* can no longer be sensibly described as participating in it, for one of the necessary conditions for the enjoyment of this blissful state is the attenuation of one's sense of separate existence and the feeling of absorption into some larger whole. A somewhat drastic solution to life's problems!

There are several answers that we can sketch to this objection. The first, and perhaps least telling, answer is that, typically, mystics themselves do not look upon suicide as an alternative to *nirvana*, for there would be little point in undergoing a long and difficult process in self-discipline if the same result could be achieved in a moment by means of a bare bodkin. As Schopenhauer once remarked in this connection, "The cool shades of Orcus allure him only with the false appearance of a haven of rest." More telling than this, though, is the fact that in his descriptions and reports a mystic usually ascribes his experiences to *himself*, and is grateful for the favour done to *him*, rather than to the One, or to the World Soul, or to a corpse. And further they are not only described as *his*, but as his *experiences*, and this would make no sense unless we suppose them to be the experiences of someone, and this "someone" must surely be the person describing them. When a man sets himself the task of acquiring a state of indifference and absorption, he looks forward to achieving this state for *himself*, not for someone or something else.

But there are more important considerations that can be brought in defence of our argument. It is true that the vocabulary of mystics sometimes suggests extinction both of the self and of the world, and for this reason *inter alia* mysticism has often been stigmatized as "negative" or "nihilistic." But this attitude rests on a mistake. The Zen Buddhists, for example, who have frequently had the "nihilistic" label attached to them, have considered the attainment of what they call "self-sustaining independence," not as a weary escape from a life of pain and evil, but as an attempt to experience life more abundantly. The Taoist mystics have likewise believed that in our ordinary everyday attachments to ourselves and to the objects surrounding us we become dead to the value and beauty of things, and that this value and beauty only becomes a reality for us when we have achieved tranquil unity with nature. Furthermore, only in such a state, according to the Taoists, when a man is totally emptied of himself and of his sense of the separateness of things, only then can the full powers of artistic creation in a man be released.

These do not of course reflect the views of all mystics by any means, but it is at least one representative view that mysticism is not a negation but rather some kind of affirmation of the self, the development of one's "real" or "true" self rather than its destruction. The whole vocabulary of "release," "enlightenment," and so forth, which is so typical of this form of mysticism, helps to confirm this view. To the outsider, indeed, the mystic may appear to be as good as dead, but from his own point of view the mystic has moved not from life to death but in the reverse direction. As he now sees the world, it is in ordinary experience, with its "enslavement" to the self and to particular objects, that we live a kind of twilight existence, not in the state of mystical transport where, on the contrary, he claims to have found a more fully real life. This is a view that has been maintained, as we might expect, by Christian mystics as well. Meister Eckhart, for example, who explicitly compares the mystical experience with the beatific vision, maintains that such an experience involves at one and the same time a kind of identification with God and also an affirmation of the life of the individual.[9] We can ignore the fact that this is skating over very thin logical and theological ice, for our only concern here is to show that, as far as the quality of the mystical experience itself goes, the sense of oneness of all things does not appear to exclude the sense of one's own personal identity. Rather, on the contrary, in certain forms of mysticism the two appear to be necessary concomitants of one another.

There is one final problem, which has already been mentioned in passing. It has been argued that an immortal existence, conceived in accordance with the model of a certain kind of monistic experience, not only allows us to talk sensibly of personal survival, but also offers a plausible solution to the "problem of life" with which the doctrine of personal survival has traditionally been closely tied. But one might well wonder whether the faithful, on being proffered the hope of an after-life that resembled the athletic and forbidding heights of asceticism, might no longer regard it as worth the effort. John Stuart Mill probably speaks for the average believer when he images the life to come as a continuation of all that is best in the present one. However, what the foregoing argument has tried to show is that such a conception of survival is misconceived on two counts: firstly that it must necessarily contain the suffering which it was designed to expel, and secondly that it does not represent any rational apotheosis of earthly existence. The only model which fulfills these requirements, and at the same time offers some semblance of a solution to the personal identity problem, is the one wrought from the materials of monistic experience. No doubt the believer will believe what he likes, but this model represents the only account which is fully consistent with the requirements of the problem for which it has traditionally been the solution.

Of course, it could still be argued that I am simply offering a solution to a problem of my own making, and since the believer's problem may be a different one—for example he may not be concerned about what I have called a "rational apotheosis"—he need not be concerned with my solution. In addition, the philosopher who has considered this question may also wonder whether he needs to tie down his discussion to problems concocted elsewhere: like the believer, he may surely set his own tasks. As far as the believer's objection is concerned it could be replied that if his notion of survival is to be anything more than blithely mythological then the problem as well as the solution must meet certain requirements. If the problem is posed simply as one of survival, then something like Hick's resurrection world will do; but such survival, which largely reduplicates earthly life and offers no fundamental transformation of the human condition, would represent an amusing fantasy but hardly anything of importance for philosophy or religion. And similarly for the philosopher's objection, obviously he can set his own problem and proceed to solve it, but if he deals with it as simply a question of logical possibility and nothing more—and this often *is* the manner of treatment—then his problem has no more claim on our attention than any of the other infinite number of questions of logical possibility that could be raised. If philosophical questions are in any obvious sense of the term "serious" ones, then the problem of personal survival of death must be treated as part of a more general issue that has been at the heart of religious and metaphysical thinking.

NOTES

1. "Religious Statements as Factually Significant," *The Existence of God*, ed. John Hick (New York, 1964).
2. *Individuals* (London, 1959), pp. 115–16.
3. Quoted from R. C. Zaehner, *Mysticism Sacred and Profane* (Oxford, 1957), pp. 36–37.
4. From the chapter "By the Ocean of Time" (trans. H. T. Lowe-Porter).
5. Zaehner, p. 47. F. C. Happold has collected descriptions of the experience of the "timeless moment" in his *Mysticism* (London, 1963).
6. Chang Chung-yuan, *Creativity and Taoism* (New York, 1963), Chap. 5.
7. Quoted from C. J. Ducasse, *A Philosophical Scrutiny of Religion* (New York, 1953), p. 283, and from Rudolph Otto, *Mysticism East and West* (New York, 1957), p. 59, respectively.
8. From *Burnt Norton*, said about the problem of describing an atemporal state.
9. Otto, pp. 210–11 and Ch. 4.

17

The Makropulos Case:
Reflections on the Tedium
of Immortality

BERNARD WILLIAMS
Cambridge University

THIS ESSAY STARTED LIFE as a lecture in a series "on the immortality of the soul or kindred spiritual subject."[1] My kindred spiritual subject is, one might say, the mortality of the soul. Those among previous lecturers who were philosophers tended, I think, to discuss the question whether we are immortal; that is not my subject, but rather what a good thing it is that we are not. Immortality, or a state without death, would be meaningless, I shall suggest; so, in a sense, death gives the meaning to life. That does not mean that we should not fear death (whatever force that injunction might be taken to have, anyway). Indeed, there are several very different ways in which it could be true at once that death gave the meaning to life and that death was, other things being equal, something to be feared. Some existentialists, for instance, seem to have said that death was what gave meaning to life, if anything did, just because it was the fear of death that gave meaning to life; I shall not follow them. I shall rather pursue the idea that from facts about human desire and happiness and what a human life is, it follows both that immortality would be, where conceivable at all, intolerable, and that (other things being equal) death is reasonably regarded as an evil. Considering whether death can reasonably be regarded as an evil is in fact as near as I shall get to considering whether it should be feared: they are not quite the same question.

My title is that, as it is usually translated into English, of a play by Karel Čapek which was made into an opera by Janáček and which tells of a woman called Elina Makropulos, *alias* Emilia Marty, *alias* Ellian Macgregor, *alias* a number of other women with the initials EM, on whom her father, the court physician to a sixteenth-century emperor, tried out an elixir of life. At the time of the action she is aged 342. Her unending life has come to a state of boredom,

Reprinted by permission from Professor Williams' *Problems of the Self* (Cambridge: Cambridge University Press, 1973), pp. 82–100.

indifference, and coldness. Everything is joyless: "in the end it is the same," she says, "singing and silence." She refuses to take the elixir again; she dies, and the formula is deliberately destroyed by a young woman among the protests of some older men.

EM's state suggests at least this, that death is not necessarily an evil, and not just in the sense in which almost everybody would agree to that, where death provides an end to great suffering, but in the more intimate sense that it can be a good thing not to live too long. It suggests more than that, for it suggests that it was not a peculiarity of EM's that an endless life was meaningless. That is something I shall follow out later. First, though, we should put together the suggestion of EM's case, that death is not necessarily an evil, with the claim of some philosophies and religions that death is necessarily not an evil. Notoriously, there have been found two contrary bases on which that claim can be mounted: death is said by some not to be an evil because it is not the end, and by others, because it is. There is perhaps some profound temperamental difference between those who find consolation for the fact of death in the hope that it is only the start of another life, and those who equally find comfort in the conviction that it is the end of the only life there is. That both such temperaments exist means that those who find a diagnosis of the belief in immortality, and indeed a reproach to it, in the idea that it constitutes a consolation, have at best only a statistical fact to support them. While that may be just about enough for the diagnosis, it is not enough for the reproach.

Most famous, perhaps, among those who have found comfort in the second option, the prospect of annihilation, was Lucretius, who, in the steps of Epicurus, and probably from a personal fear of death which in some of his pages seems almost tangible, addresses himself to proving that death is never an evil. Lucretius has two basic arguments for this conclusion, and it is an important feature of them both that the conclusion they offer has the very strong consequence—and seems clearly intended to have the consequence—that, for oneself at least, it is all the same whenever one dies, that a long life is no better than a short one. That is to say, death is never an evil in the sense not merely that there is no-one for whom dying is an evil, but that there is no time at which dying is an evil—sooner or later, it is all the same.

The first argument (De rerum natura, 3.870ff., 898ff.) seeks to interpret the fear of death as a confusion, based on the idea that we shall be there after death to repine our loss of the praemia vitae, the rewards and delights of life, and to be upset at the spectacle of our bodies burned, and so forth. The fear of death, it is suggested, must necessarily be the fear of some experiences had when one is dead. But if death is annihilation, then there are no such experiences: in the Epicurean phrase, when death is there, we are not, and when we are there, death is not. So, death being annihilation, there is nothing to fear. The second argument (1091) addresses itself directly to the question of whether one dies earlier or later, and says that one will be the same time dead however early or late one dies, and therefore one might as well die earlier as later. And from both arguments we can conclude nil igitur mors est ad nos, neque pertinet hilum —death is nothing to us, and does not matter at all (830).

The second of these arguments seems even on the face of things to contradict the first. For it must imply that if there *were* a finite period of death, such that if you died later you would be dead for less time, then there *would* be some point in wanting to die later rather than earlier. But that implication makes sense, surely, only on the supposition that what is wrong with dying consists in something undesirable about the condition of being dead. And that is what is denied by the first argument.

More important than this, the oddness of the second argument can help to focus a difficulty already implicit in the first. The first argument, in locating the objection to dying in a confused objection to being dead, and exposing that in terms of a confusion with being alive, takes it as genuinely true of life that the satisfaction of desire, and possession of the *praemia vitae*, are good things. It is not irrational to be upset by the loss of home, children, possessions—what is irrational is to think of death as, in the relevant sense, *losing* anything. But now if we consider two lives, one very short and cut off before the *praemia* have been acquired, the other fully provided with the *praemia* and containing their enjoyment to a ripe age, it is very difficult to see why the second life, by these standards alone, is not to be thought better than the first. But if it is, then there must be something wrong with the argument which tries to show that there is nothing worse about a short life than a long one. The argument locates the mistake about dying in a mistake about consciousness, it being assumed that what commonsense thinks about the worth of the *praemia vitae* and the sadness of their (conscious) loss is sound enough. But if the *praemia vitae* are valuable —even if we include as necessary to that value consciousness that one possesses them—then surely getting to the point of possessing them is better than not getting to that point, longer enjoyment of them is better than shorter, and more of them, other things being equal, is better than less of them. But if so, then it just will not be true that to die earlier is all the same as to die later, nor that death is never an evil—and the thought that to die later is better than to die earlier will not be dependent on some muddle about thinking that the dead person will be alive to lament his loss. It will depend only on the idea, apparently sound, that if the *praemia vitae* and consciousness of them are good things, then longer consciousness of more *praemia* is better than shorter consciousness of fewer *praemia*.

Is the idea sound? A decent argument, surely, can be marshalled to support it. If I desire something, then, other things being equal, I prefer a state of affairs in which I get it to one in which I do not get it, and (again, other things being equal) plan for a future in which I get it rather than not. But one future, for sure, in which I would not get it would be one in which I was dead. To want something, we may also say, is to that extent to have reason for resisting what excludes having that thing: and death certainly does that, for a very large range of things that one wants.[2] If that is right, then for any of those things, wanting something itself gives one a reason for avoiding death. Even though, if I do not succeed, I will not know that, nor what I am missing, from the perspective of the wanting agent it is rational to aim for states of affairs in which his want is satisfied, and hence to regard death as something to be avoided; that is, to regard it as an evil.

It is admittedly true that many of the things I want, I want only on the assumption that I am going to be alive; and some people, for instance some of the old, desperately want certain things when nevertheless they would much rather that they and their wants were dead. It might be suggested that not just these special cases, but really all wants, were conditional on being alive; a situation in which one has ceased to exist is not to be compared with others with respect to desire-satisfaction—rather, if one dies, all bets are off. But surely the claim that all desires are in this sense conditional must be wrong. For consider the idea of a rational forward-looking calculation of suicide; there can be such a thing, even if many suicides are not rational, and even though with some that are, it may be unclear to what extent they are forward-looking (the obscurity of this with regard to suicides of honour is an obscurity in the notion of shame). In such a calculation, a man might consider what lay before him, and decide whether he did or did not want to undergo it. If he does decide to undergo it, then some desire propels him on into the future, and *that* desire at least is not one that operates conditionally on his being alive, since it itself resolves the question of whether he is going to be alive. He has an unconditional or (as I shall say) a *categorical* desire.

The man who seriously calculates about suicide and rejects it only just has such a desire, perhaps. But if one is in a state in which the question of suicide does not occur, or occurs only as total fantasy—if, to take just one example, one is happy—one has many such desires, which do not hang from the assumption of one's existence. If they did hang from that assumption, then they would be quite powerless to rule out that assumption's being questioned, or to answer the question if it is raised; but clearly they are not powerless in those directions —on the contrary they are some of the few things, perhaps the only things, that have power in that direction. Some ascetics have supposed that happiness required reducing one's desires to those necessary for one's existence, that is, to those that one has to have, granted that one exists at all; rather, it requires that some of one's desires should be fully categorical, and one's existence itself wanted as something necessary to them.

To suppose that one can in this way categorically want things implies a number of things about the nature of desire. It implies, for one thing, that the reason I have for bringing it about that I get what I want is not merely that of avoiding the unpleasantness of not getting what I want. But that must in any case be right—otherwise we should have to represent every desire as the desire to avoid its own frustration, which is absurd.

About what those categorical desires must be, there is not much of great generality to be said, if one is looking at the happy state of things: except, once more against the ascetic, that there should be not just enough, but more than enough. But the question might be raised, at the impoverished end of things, as to what the minimum categorical desire might be. Could it be *just* the desire to remain alive? The answer is perhaps "no." In saying that, I do not want to deny the existence, the value, or the basic necessity of a sheer reactive drive to self-preservation: humanity would certainly wither if the drive to keep alive were not stronger than any perceived reasons for keeping alive. But if the question is asked, and it is going to be answered calculatively, then the bare categorical desire to stay alive will not sustain the calculation—that desire itself, when things have got that far, has to be sustained or filled out by some desire for something else, even if it is only, at the margin, the desire that future desires of mine will be born and satisfied. But the best insight into the effect of categorical desire is not gained at the impoverished end of things, and hence in situations where the question has actually come up. The question of life being desirable is certainly transcendental in the most modest sense, in that it gets by far its best answer in never being asked at all.

None of this—including the thoughts of the calculative suicide—requires my reflection on a world in which I never occur at all. In the terms of "possible worlds" (which can admittedly be misleading), a man could, on the present account, have a reason from his own point of view to prefer a possible world in which he went on longer to one in which he went on for less long, or—like the suicide—the opposite; but he would have no reason of this kind to prefer a world in which he did not occur at all. Thoughts about his total absence from the world would have to be of a different kind, impersonal reflections on the value *for the world* of his presence or absence: of the same kind, essentially, as he could conduct (or, more probably, not manage to conduct) with regard to anyone else. While he can think egoistically of what it would be for him to live longer or less long, he cannot think egoistically of what it would be for him never to have existed at all. Hence the sombre words of Sophocles "Never to have been born counts highest of all . . ." (*Oedipus at Colonus* 1224ff.) are well met by the old Jewish reply—"how many are so lucky? Not one in ten thousand."

Lucretius' first argument has been interestingly criticised by Thomas Nagel (see Chapter 4), on lines different from those that I have been following. Nagel claims that what is wrong with Lucretius' argument is that it rests on the assumption that nothing can be a misfortune for a man unless he knows about it, and that misfortunes must consist in something nasty *for* him. Against this assumption that nothing can be a misfortune for a man unless he knows about it, which would normally be thought to constitute a misfortune, though those to whom they happen are and remain ignorant of them (as, for instance, certain situations of betrayal). The difference between Nagel's approach and mine does not, of course, lie in the mere point of whether one admits misfortunes which do not consist of or involve nasty experiences: anyone who rejects Lucretius' argument must admit them. The difference is that the reasons which a man would have for avoiding death are, on the present account, grounded in desires —categorical desires—which he has; he, on the basis of these, has reason to regard possible death as a misfortune to be avoided, and we, looking at things from his point of view, would have reason to regard his actual death as his misfortune. Nagel, however, if I understand him, does not see the misfortune that befalls a man who dies as necessarily grounded in the issue of what desires or sorts of desires he had; just as in the betrayal case, it could be a misfortune for a man to be betrayed, even though he did not have any desire not to be betrayed. If this is a correct account, Nagel's reasoning is one step further away from Utilitarianism on this matter than mine,[3] and rests on an independent kind of value which a sufficiently Utilitarian person might just reject; while my argument cannot merely be rejected by a Utilitarian person, it seems to me, since he must if he is to be consistent, and other things being equal, attach dis-utility to any situation which he has good reason to prevent, and he certainly has good reason to prevent a situation which involves the non-satisfaction of his desires. Thus, granted categorical desires, death has a disutility for an agent, although that disutility does not, of course, consist in unsatisfactory experiences involved in its occurrence.

The question would remain, of course, with regard to any given agent, whether he had categorical desires. For the present argument, it will do to leave it as a contingent fact that most people do: for they will have a reason, and a perfectly coherent reason, to regard death as a misfortune, while it was Lucretius' claim that no-one could have a coherent reason for so regarding it. There may well be other reasons as well; thus Nagel's reasoning, though different from the more Utilitarian type of reason I have used against Lucretius, seems compatible with it and there are strong reasons to adopt his kind of consideration as well. In fact, further and deeper thought about this question seems likely to fill up the appar-ent gap between the two sorts of arguments; it is hard to believe, for one thing, that the supposed contingent fact that people have categorical desires can really be as contingent as all that. One last point about the two arguments is that they coincide in not offering—as I mentioned earlier—any considerations about worlds in which one does not occur at all; but there is perhaps an additional reason why this should be so in the Utilitarian-type argument, over and above the one it shares with Nagel's. The reason it shares with Nagel's is that the type of misfortune we are concerned with in thinking about X's death is X's misfor-tune (as opposed to the misfortunes of the state or whatever); and whatever sort of misfortune it may be in a given possible world that X does not occur in it, it is not X's misfortune. They share the feature, then, that for anything to be X's misfortune in a given world, X must occur in that world. But the Utilitarian-type argument further grounds the misfortune, if there is one, in certain features of X, namely his desires; and if there is no X in a given world, then a fortiori there are no such grounds.

But now, if death, other things being equal, is a misfortune; and a longer life is better than a shorter life; and we reject the Lucretian argument that it does not matter when one dies: then it looks as though—other things always being equal—death is at any time an evil, and it is always better to live than to die. Nagel indeed, from his point of view, does seem to permit that conclusion, even though he admits some remarks about the natural term of life and the greater misfortune of dying in one's prime. But wider consequences follow. For if all that is true, then it looks as though it would be not only always better to live, but better to live always: that is, never to die. If Lucretius is wrong, we seem committed to wanting to be immortal. That would be, as has been repeatedly said, with other things equal. No-one need deny that since, for instance, we grow old and our powers decline, much may happen to increase the reasons for thinking death a good thing. But these are contingencies. We might not age; perhaps, one day, it will be possible for some of us not to age. If that were so, would it not follow then that, more life being per se better than less life, we should have reason so far as that went (but not necessarily in terms of other inhabitants) to live for ever? EM indeed bears strong, if fictional, witness against the desirability of that; but perhaps she still laboured under some contingent limitations, social or psychological, which might once more be eliminated to bring it about that really other things were equal. Against this, I am going to suggest that the supposed contingencies are not really contingencies; that an endless life would be a meaningless one; and that we could have no reason for living eternally a human life. There is no desirable or significant property which life would have more of, or have more unqualifiedly, if we lasted for ever. In some part, we can apply to life Aristotle's marvellous remark about Plato's Form of the Good: "nor will it be any the more good for being eternal: that which lasts long is no whiter than that which perishes in a day" (*Ethica Nicomachea* 1096B4). But only in part; for, rejecting Lucretius, we have already admitted that more days may give us more than one day can.

If one pictures living for ever as living as an embodied person in the world rather as it is, it will be a question, and not so trivial as may seem, of what age one eternally is. EM was 342; because for 300 years she had been 42. This choice (if it was a choice) I am personally, and at present, well disposed to salute—if one had to spend eternity at any age, that seems an admirable age to spend it at. Nor would it necessarily be a less good age for a woman: that at least was not EM's problem, that she was too old at the age she continued to be at. Her problem lay in having been at it for too long. Her trouble was, it seems, boredom: a boredom connected with the fact that everything that could happen and make sense to one particular human being of 42 had already happened to her. Or, rather, all the sorts of things that could make sense to one woman of a certain character; for EM has a certain character, and indeed, except for her accumulating memories of earlier times, and no doubt some changes of style to suit the passing centuries, she seems always to have been much the same sort of person.

There are difficult questions, if one presses the issue, about this constancy of character. How is this accumulation of memories related to this character which she eternally has, and to the character of her existence? Are they much the same kind of events repeated? Then it is itself strange that she allows them to be repeated, accepting the same repetitions, the same limitations—indeed, *accepting* is what it later becomes, when earlier it would not, or even could not, have been that. The repeated patterns of personal relations, for instance, must take on a character of being inescapable. Or is the pattern of her experiences not repetitious in this way, but varied? Then the problem shifts, to the relation between these varied experiences, and the fixed character: how can it remain fixed, through an endless series of very various experiences? The experiences must surely happen to her without really affecting her; she must be, as EM is, detached and withdrawn.

EM, of course, is in a world of people who do not share her condition, and that determines certain features of the life she has to lead, as that any personal relationship requires peculiar kinds of concealment. That, at least, is a form of isolation which would disappear if her condition were generalised. But to suppose more generally that boredom and inner death would be eliminated if everyone were similarly becalmed, is an empty hope: it would be a world of Bourbons, learning nothing and forgetting nothing, and it is unclear how much could even happen.

The more one reflects to any realistic degree on the conditions of EM's unending life, the less it seems a mere contingency that it froze up as it did. That it is not a contingency, is suggested also by the fact that the reflections can sustain themselves independently of any question of the particular character that EM had; it is enough, almost, that she has a human character at all. Perhaps not quite. One sort of character for which the difficulties of unending life would have less significance than they proved to have for EM might be one who at the beginning was more like what she is at the end: cold, withdrawn, already frozen. For him, the prospect of unending cold is presumably less bleak in that he is used to it. But with him, the question can shift to a different place, as to why he wants the unending life at all; for, the more he is at the beginning like EM is at the end, the less place there is for categorical desire to keep him going, and to resist the desire for death. In EM's case, her boredom and distance from life both kill desire and consist in the death of it; one who is already enough like that to sustain life in those conditions may well be one who had nothing to make him want to do so. But even if he has, and we conceive of a person who is stonily resolved to sustain for ever an already stony existence, his possibility will be of no comfort to those, one hopes a larger party, who want to live longer because they want to live more.

To meet the basic anti-Lucretian hope for continuing life which is grounded in categorical desire, EM's unending life in this world is inadequate, and necessarily so relative to just those desires and conceptions of character which go into the hope. That is very important, since it is the most direct response, that which should have been adequate if the hope is both coherent and what it initially seemed to be. It also satisfied one of two important conditions which must be satisfied by anything which is to be adequate as a fulfilment of my anti-Lucretian hope, namely that it should clearly be *me* who lives for ever. The second important condition is that the state in which I survive should be one which, to me looking forward, will be adequately related, in the life it presents, to those aims which I now have in wanting to survive at all. That is a vague formula, and necessarily so, for what exactly that relation will be must depend to some extent on what kind of aims and (as one might say) prospects for myself I now have. What we can say is that since I am propelled forward into longer life by categorical desires, what is promised must hold out some hopes for those desires. The limiting case of this might be that the promised life held out some hope just to that desire mentioned before, that future desires of mine will be born and satisfied; but if that were the only categorical desire that carried me forward into it, at least this seems demanded, that any image I have of those future desires should make it comprehensible to me how in terms of my character they could be my desires.

This second condition the EM kind of survival failed, on reflection, to satisfy; but at least it is clear why, before reflection, it looked as though it might satisfy the condition—it consists, after all, in just going on in ways in which we are quite used to going on. If we turn away now from EM to more remote kinds of survival, the problems of those two conditions press more heavily right from the beginning. Since the major problems of the EM situation lay in the indefinite extension of one life, a tempting alternative is survival by means of an indefinite series of lives. Most, perhaps all, versions of this belief which have actually existed have immediately failed the first condition: they get nowhere near providing any consideration to mark the difference between rebirth and new birth. But let us suppose the problem, in some way or another, removed; some conditions of bodily continuity, minimally sufficient for personal identity, may be supposed satisfied. (Anyone who thinks that no such conditions could be sufficient, and requires, for instance, conditions of memory, may well find it correspondingly difficult to find an alternative for survival in this direction which both satisfies the first requirement, of identity, and also adequately avoids the difficulties of the EM alternative.) The problem remains of whether this series of psychologically disjoint lives could be an object of hope to one who did not want to die. That is, in my view, a different question from the question of whether it will be he—which is why I distinguished originally two different requirements to be satisfied. But it is a question; and even if the first requirement be supposed satisfied, it is exceedingly unclear that the second can be. This will be so, even if one were to accept the idea, itself problematical, that one could have reason to fear the future pain of someone who was merely bodily continuous with one as one now is.[4]

There are in the first place certain difficulties about how much a man could consistently be allowed to know about the series of his lives, if we are to preserve the psychological disjointness which is the feature of this model. It might be that each would in fact have to seem to him as though it were his only life, and that he could not have grounds for being sure what, or even that, later lives were to come. If so, then no comfort or hope will be forthcoming in this model to those who want to go on living. More interesting questions, however, concern the man's relation to a future life of which he did get some advance idea. If we could allow the idea that he could fear pain which was going to occur in that life, then we have at least provided him with one kind of reason which might move him to opt out of that life, and destroy himself (being recurrent, under conditions of bodily continuity, would not make one indestructible). But physical pain and its nastiness are to the maximum degree independent of what one's desires and character are, and the degree of identification needed with the later life to reject that aspect of it is absolutely minimal. Beyond that point, however, it is unclear how he is to bring this later character and its desires into a relation to his present ones, so as to be satisfied or the reverse with this marginal promise of continued existence. If he can regard this future life as an object of hope, then equally it must be possible for him to regard it with alarm, or depression, and—as in the simple pain case—opt out of it. If we cannot make sense of his entertaining that choice, then we have not made sense of this future life's being adequately related to his present life, so that it could, alternatively, be something he might want in wanting not to die. But can we clearly make sense of that choice? For if we—or he—merely wipe out his present character and desires, there is nothing left by which he can judge it at all, at least as something *for him*; while if we leave them in, we—and he—apply something irrelevant to that future life, since (to adapt the Epicurean phrase), when they are there, it is not, and when it is there, they are not. We might imagine him considering the future prospects, and agreeing to go on if he found them congenial. But that is a muddled picture. For whether they are congenial to him as he is now must be beside the point, and the idea that it is not beside the point depends on carrying over into the case features that do not belong to it, as (perhaps) that he will remember later what he wanted in the earlier life. And when we admit that it is beside the point whether the prospects are congenial, then the force of the idea that the future life could be something that he *now* wanted to go on to, fades.

There are important and still obscure issues here,[5] but perhaps enough has been said to cast doubt on this option as coherently satisfying the desire to stay alive. While few will be disposed to think that much can be made of it, I must confess that out of the alternatives it is the only one which for me would, if it made sense, have any attraction—no doubt because it is the only one which has the feature that what one is living at any given point is actually *a life*. It is singular that those systems of belief that get closest to actually accepting recurrence of this sort seem, almost without exception, to look forward to the point when one will be released from it. Such systems seem less interested in continuing one's life than in earning one the right to a superior sort of death.

The serial and disjoint lives are at least more attractive than the attempt, which some have made, to combine the best of continuous and of serial existence in a fantasy of very varied lives which are nevertheless cumulatively effective in memory. This might be called the *Teiresias* model. As that case singularly demonstrates, it has the quality of a fantasy, of emotional pressure trying to combine the uncombinable. One thing that the fantasy has to ignore is the connexion, both as cause and as consequence, between having one range of experiences rather than another, wishing to engage in one sort of thing rather than another, and having a character. Teiresias cannot have a character, either continuously through these proceedings, or cumulatively at the end (if there were to be an end) of them: he is not, eventually, a person but a phenomenon.

In discussing the last models, we have moved a little away from the very direct response which EM's case seemed to provide to the hope that one would never die. But perhaps we have moved not nearly far enough. Nothing of this, and nothing much like this, was in the minds of many who have hoped for immortality; for it was not in this world that they hoped to live for ever. As one might say, their hope was not so much that they would never die as that they would live after their death, and while that in its turn can be represented as the hope that one would not really die, or, again, that it was not really oneself that would die, the change of formulation could point to an after-life sufficiently unlike this life, perhaps, to earth the current of doubt that flows from EM's frozen boredom.

But in fact this hope has been and could only be modelled on some image of a more familiar untiring or unresting or unflagging activity or satisfaction; and what is essentially EM's problem, one way or another, remains. In general we can ask what it is about the imagined activities of an eternal life which would stave off the principal hazard to which EM succumbed, boredom. The Don Juan in Hell joke, that heaven's prospects are tedious and the devil has the best tunes, though a tired fancy in itself, at least serves to show up a real and (I sus- pect) a profound difficulty, of providing any model of an unending, supposedly satisfying, state or activity which would not rightly prove boring to anyone who remained conscious of himself and who had acquired a character, interests, tastes, and impatiences in the course of living, already, a finite life. The point is not that for such a man boredom would be a tiresome consequence of the supposed states or activities, and that they would be objectionable just on the utilitarian or hedonistic ground that they had this disagreeable feature. If that were all there was to it, we could imagine the feature away, along no doubt with other disagreeable features of human life in its present imperfection. The point is rather that boredom, as sometimes in more ordinary circumstances, would be not just a tiresome effect, but a reaction almost perceptual in char- acter to the poverty of one's relation to the environment. Nothing less will do for eternity than something that makes boredom *unthinkable*. What could that be? Something that could be guaranteed to be at every moment utterly absorb- ing? But if a man has and retains a character, there is no reason to suppose that there is anything which could be that. If, lacking a conception of the guar- anteedly absorbing activity, one tries merely to think away the reaction of bore- dom, one is no longer supposing an improvement in the circumstances, but merely an impoverishment in his consciousness of them. Just as being bored can be a sign of not noticing, understanding, or appreciating enough, so equally not being bored can be a sign of not noticing, or not reflecting, enough. One might make the immortal man content at every moment, by just stripping off from him consciousness which would have brought discontent by reminding him of other times, other interests, other possibilities. Perhaps, indeed, that is what we have already done, in a more tempting way, by picturing him just now as at every moment totally absorbed—but that is something we shall come back to.

Of course there is in actual life such a thing as justified but necessary bore- dom. Thus—to take a not entirely typical example—someone who was, or who thought himself, devoted to the radical cause might eventually admit to himself that he found a lot of its rhetoric excruciatingly boring. He might think that he ought not to feel that, that the reaction was wrong, and merely represented an unworthiness of his, an unregenerate remnant of intellectual superiority. How- ever, he might rather feel that it would not necessarily be a better world in which no-one was bored by such rhetoric and that boredom was, indeed, a per- fectly worthy reaction to this rhetoric after all this time; but for all that, the rhetoric might be necessary. A man at arms can get cramp from standing too long at his post, but sentry-duty can after all be necessary. But the threat of monotony in eternal activities could not be dealt with in that way, by regarding immortal boredom as an unavoidable ache derived from standing ceaselessly at one's post. (This is one reason why I said that boredom in eternity would have to be *unthinkable*.) For the question would be unavoidable, in what campaign one was supposed to be serving, what one's ceaseless sentry-watch was for.

Some philosophers have pictured an eternal existence as occupied in some- thing like intense intellectual enquiry. Why that might seem to solve the prob- lem, at least for them, is obvious. The activity is engrossing, self-justifying, affords, as it may appear, endless new perspectives, and by being engrossing enables one to lose oneself. It is that last feature that supposedly makes boredom unthinkable, by providing something that is, in that earlier phrase, at every moment totally absorbing. But if one is totally and perpetually absorbed in such an activity, and loses oneself in it, then as those words suggest, we come back to the problem of satisfying the conditions that it should be me who lives for ever, and that the eternal life should be in prospect of some interest. Let us leave aside the question of people whose characteristic and most personal interests are remote from such pursuits, and for whom, correspondingly, an immortality promised in terms of intellectual activity is going to make heavy demands on some theory of a "real self" which will have to emerge at death. More interesting is the content and value of the promise for a person who *is*, in this life, disposed to those activities. For looking at such a person as he now is, it seems quite unreasonable to suppose that those activities would have the fulfilling or liberating character that they do have for him, if they were in fact all he could do or conceive of doing. If they are genuinely fulfilling, and do not operate (as they can) merely as a compulsive diversion, then the ground and shape of the satisfactions that the intellectual enquiry offers him, will relate to *him*, and not just to the enquiry. The *Platonic introjection,* seeing the satisfactions of studying what is timeless and impersonal as being themselves timeless and impersonal, may be a deep illusion, but it is certainly an illusion.

We can see better into that illusion by considering Spinoza's thought, that intellectual activity was the most active and free state that a man could be in, and that a man who had risen to such activity was in some sense most fully individual, most fully himself. This conclusion has been sympathetically expounded by Stuart Hampshire, who finds on this point a similar doctrine in Spinoza and in Freud: in particular, he writes, "[one's] only means of achieving this distinctness as an individual, this freedom in relation to the common order of nature, is the power of the mind freely to follow in its thought an intellectual order."[6] The contrast to this free intellectual activity is "the common condition of men that their conduct and their judgments of value, their desires and aversions, are in each individual determined by unconscious memories"—a process which the same writer has elsewhere associated with our having any character at all as individuals.[7]

Hampshire claims that in pure intellectual activity the mind is most free because it is then least determined by causes outside its immediate states. I take him to mean that rational activity is that in which the occurrence of an earlier thought maximally explains the occurrence of a later thought, because it is the rational relation between their contents which, granted the occurrence of the first, explains the occurrence of the second. But even the maximal explanatory power, in these terms, of the earlier thought does not extend to total explanation: for it will still require explanation why this thinker on this occasion continued on this rational path of thought at all. Thus I am not sure that the Spinozist consideration which Hampshire advances even gives a very satisfactory sense to the *activity* of the mind. It leaves out, as the last point shows, the driving power which is needed to sustain one even in the most narrowly rational thought. It is still further remote from any notion of creativity, since that, even within a theoretical context, and certainly in an artistic one, precisely implies the origination of ideas which are not fully predictable in terms of the content of existing ideas. But even if it could yield one sense for "activity," it would still offer very little, despite Spinoza's heroic defence of the notion, for *freedom*. Or—to put it another way—even if it offered something for freedom of the intellect, it offers nothing for freedom of the individual. For when freedom is initially understood as the absence of "outside" determination, and in particular understood in those terms as an unquestionable *value*, my freedom is reasonably not taken to include freedom from my past, my character, and my desires. To suppose that those are, in the relevant sense, "outside" determinations, is merely to beg the vital question about the boundaries of the self, and not to prove from premises acceptable to any clear-headed man who desires freedom that the boundaries of the self should be drawn round the intellect. On the contrary, the desire for freedom can, and should, be seen as the desire to be free in the exercise and development of character, not as the desire to be free of it. And if Hampshire and others are right in claiming that an individual character springs from and gets its energies from unconscious memories and unclear desires, then the individual must see them too as within the boundaries of the self, and themselves involved in the drive to persist in life and activity.

With this loss, under the Spinozist conception, of the individual's character, there is, contrary to Hampshire's claim, a loss of individuality itself, and certainly that could make an eternity of intellectual activity, so construed, a reasonable object of interest to one concerned with individual immortality. As those who totally wish to lose themselves in the movement can consistently only hope that the movement will go on, so the consistent Spinozist—at least on this account of Spinozism—can only hope that the intellectual activity goes on, something which could be as well realised in the existence of Aristotle's prime mover, perhaps, as in anything to do with Spinoza or any other particular man.

Stepping back now from the extremes of Spinozist abstraction, I shall end by returning to a point from which we set out, the sheer desire to go on living, and shall mention a writer on this subject, Unamuno, whose work *The Tragic Sense of Life*[8] gives perhaps more extreme expression than anyone else has done to that most basic form of the desire to be immortal, the desire not to die.

> I do not want to die—no, I neither want to die nor do I want to want to die; I want to live for ever and ever and ever. I want this "I" to live—this poor "I" that I am and that I feel myself to be here and now, and therefore the problem of the duration of my soul, of my own soul, tortures me [p. 60].

Although Unamuno frequently refers to Spinoza, the spirit of this is certainly far removed from that of the "sorrowful Jew of Amsterdam." Furthermore, in his clear insistence that what he desperately wants is this life, the life of this self, not to end, Unamuno reveals himself at equal removes from Manicheanism and from Utilitarianism; and that is correct, for the one is only the one-legged descendant of the other. That tradition—Manichean, Orphic, Platonic, Augustinian—which contrasts the spirit and the body in such a sense that the spiritual aims at eternity, truth and salvation, while the body is adjusted to pleasure, the temporary, and eventual dissolution, is still represented, as to fifty per cent, by secular Utilitarianism: it is just one of the original pair of boots left by itself and better regarded now that the other has fallen into disrepair. Bodies are all that we have or are: hence for Utilitarianism it *follows* that the only focus of our arrangements can be the efficient organisation of happiness. Immortality, certainly, is out, and so life here should last as long as we determine—or eventually, one may suspect, others will determine—that it is pleasant for us to be around.

Unamuno's outlook is at the opposite pole to this and, whatever else may be wrong with it, it salutes the true idea that the meaning of life does not consist either in the management of satisfactions in a body or in an abstract immortality without one. On the one hand he had no time for Manicheanism, and admired the rather brutal Catholic faith which could express its hopes for a future life in the words which he knew on a tombstone in Bilbao:

> Aunque estamos in polvo convertidos
> en Ti, Señor, nuestra esperanza fía,
> que tornaremos a vivir vestidos
> con la carne y la piel que nos cubria [p. 79].

At the same time, his desire to remain alive extends an almost incomprehensible distance beyond any desire to continue agreeable experiences: "For myself I can say that as a youth and even as a child I remained unmoved when shown the most moving pictures of hell, for even then nothing appeared quite so horrible to me as nothingness itself" (p. 28). The most that I have claimed earlier against Lucretius is not enough to make that preference intelligible to me. The fear of sheer nothingness is certainly part of what Lucretius rightly, if too lightly, hoped to exorcise; and the *mere* desire to stay alive, which is here stretched to its limit, is not enough (I suggested before) to answer the question, once the question has come up and requires an answer in rational terms. Yet Unamuno's affirmation of existence even through limitless suffering[9] brings out something which is implicit in the claim against Lucretius. It is not necessarily the prospect of pleasant times that creates the motive against dying, but the existence of categorical desire, and categorical desire can drive through both the existence and the prospect of unpleasant times.

Suppose, then, that categorical desire does sustain the desire to live. So long as it remains so, I shall want not to die. Yet I also know, if what has gone before is right, that an eternal life would be unliveable. In part, as EM's case originally suggested, that is because categorical desire will go away from it: in those versions, such as hers, in which I am recognisably myself, I would eventually have had altogether too much of myself. There are good reasons, surely, for dying before that happens. But equally, at times earlier than that moment, there is reason for not dying. Necessarily, it tends to be either too early or too late. EM reminds us that it can be too late, and many, as against Lucretius, need no reminding that it can be too early. If that is any sort of dilemma, it can, as things still are and if one is exceptionally lucky, be resolved, not by doing anything, but just by dying shortly before the horrors of not doing so become evident. Technical progress may, in more than one direction, make that piece of luck rarer. But as things are, it is possible to be, in contrast to EM, *felix oppor-*

tunitate mortis—as it can be appropriately mistranslated, lucky in having the chance to die.

NOTES

1. At the University of California, Berkeley, under a benefaction in the names of Agnes and Constantine Foerster. I am grateful to the committee for inviting me to give the 1972 lecture in this series.

2. Obviously the principle is not exceptionless. For one thing, one can want to be dead: the content of that desire may be obscure, but whatever it is, a man presumably cannot be *prevented* from getting it by dying. More generally, the principle does not apply to what I elsewhere call *non-I desire*: for an account, see my "Egoism and Altruism," *Problems of the Self*, pp. 260ff. They do not affect the present discussion, which is within the limits of egoistic rationality.

3. Though my argument does not in any sense imply Utilitarianism; for some further considerations on this, see the final paragraphs of this paper.

4. One possible conclusion from the dilemma discussed in my "The Self and the Future." For the point, mentioned below, of the independence of physical pain from psychological change, see *Problems of the Self*, p. 54.

5. For a detailed discussion of closely related questions, though in a different framework, see Derek Parfitt, "Personal Identity," *Philosophical Review*, 80 (1971), 3–27.

6. "Spinoza and the Idea of Freedom," reprinted in *Freedom of Mind* (Oxford: Clarendon, 1972), pp. 183ff.; the two quotations are from pp. 206–7.

7. "Disposition and Memory," *ibid.*, pp. 160ff.; see esp. pp. 176–77.

8. *Del sentimiento trágico de la vida*, trans. J. E. Crawford Flitch (London, 1921). Page references in the text are to the 1962 Fontana Library edition.

9. An affirmation which takes on a special dignity retrospectively in the light of his own death shortly after his courageous speech against Millán Astray and the obscene slogan "¡Viva la Muerte!" (see Hugh Thomas, *The Spanish Civil War* [Harmondsworth: Pelican, 1961], pp. 442–44).

BIBLIOGRAPHICAL ESSAY

IT IS SOMEWHAT CUSTOMARY for editors of anthologies to include lengthy, if not exhaustive, bibliographies. Unfortunately, such compilations are often too elongated to be practical (except for the most diligent scholars) and much too indiscriminate to aid the interested student.

The items in this bibliography are, I believe, both selective and tractable. All bibliographical suggestions contained herein involve the writings of contemporary philosophers who can *broadly* be classified within the tradition of Anglo-American (analytic) Philosophy—as is in keeping with the tenor of this volume. No claim, quite obviously, is made for completeness; but I believe that a careful reading of the listed sources below would give one an excellent feel for some basic philosophical problems in thanatology.

Some general works which touch on all of the problems discussed in this book are John Hick's *Death and Eternal Life* (New York: Harper and Row, 1977) and Warren Shibles, *Death* (Whitewater: Language Press, 1974).

Recent interesting attempts to demarcate the ceasing to be of a person (to be read in conjunction with Chisholm's opening essay) include Lawrence C. Becker's biological account of a "human has been" in "Human Being: The Boundaries of the Concept," *Philosophy and Public Affairs*, 4 (1975), 234–59; Robert Veatch's *Death, Dying, and the Biological Revolution* (New Haven: Yale University Press, 1976), particularly pp. 21–76 on defining death; and Dallas M. High's "Death: Its Conceptual Elusiveness," *Soundings*, 55 (1972), 438–58.

To follow up Van Evra's essay, the reader might profitably consult Paul Edwards, "My Death," *The Encyclopedia of Philosophy* (New York: Macmillan, 1967), v 416–19, as well as Antony Flew's "Can a Man Witness His Own Funeral?" *Hibbert Journal*, 54 (1956), 242–50.

Paul Edwards also has some poignant although highly critical comments on Heidegger's analyses of death in "Heidegger and Death as 'Possibility'," *Mind*, 84 (1975), 548–66, and in "Heidegger and Death: A Deflationary Critique," *The Monist*, 59 (1976), 161–86. For a critique of Thomas Nagel's views on why death is regarded as an evil, see Mary Mothersill's "Death," in *Moral Problems*, ed. James Rachels (New York: Harper and Row, 1971), pp. 372–83.

An interesting article bearing on human fears over our impending mortality to compare with Slote's is Jeffrie G. Murphy's "Rationality and the Fear of Death," *The Monist*, 59 (1976), 187–203. An extremely helpful discussion of various philosophical arguments pro and con suicide can be found in Eike-Henner W. Kluge, *The Practice of Death* (New Haven: Yale University Press, 1975), pp. 101–30. For some views on suicide in opposition to Donnelly's negative views on the matter, see R. F. Holland, "Suicide" in *Talk of God*, ed. G. N. A. Vesey (New York: St. Martin's, 1969), pp. 72–85, and Richard Brandt, "The Morality and Rationality of Suicide" in *A Handbook for the Study of Suicide*, ed. Seymour Perlin (New York: Oxford University Press, 1975), pp. 61–76.

In contrast to Nagel's piece on "The Absurd," the reader might consult John Hick's "Towards a Theology of Death" in his *God and the Universe of Faiths* (London: Macmillan, 1973), pp. 180–97. Donnelly's essay on Tolstoy's Ivan Ilych might be read alongside Ilham Dilman's "Wittgenstein on the Soul," in *Understanding Wittgenstein*, ed. Godfrey Vesey (New York: St. Martin's, 1974), pp. 162–92.

With regard to the topics of the final nine essays in the volume dealing with the soul and the prospects for immortality, the reader is well advised to study the underlying philosophical issues raised in the respective conceptual frameworks of dualistic interactionism, scientific materialism, and logical behaviorism, an excellent discussion of which is found in Norman Malcolm's Wittgensteinian-inspired *Problems of Mind: Descartes to Wittgenstein* (New York: Harper & Row, 1971). A careful historical study of Platonic, Aristotelian, Thomistic, Cartesian, and Kantian treatments of the soul and survival, with detailed critical comment, can be found in Antony Flew's "Immortality" in *The Encyclopedia of Philosophy*, IV 139–50.

Other works of general interest are Hywel D. Lewis, *The Self and Immortality* (New York: Seabury, 1973); two works by the noted American dualist, C. J. Ducasse—his Carus Lectures *Nature, Mind, and Death* (LaSalle: Open Court, 1951) and *A Critical Examination of the Belief in a Life After Death* (Springfield: Thomas, 1961); Terence Penelhum's *Survival and Disembodied Existence* (London: Routledge & Kegan Paul, 1970); H. H. Price's *Essays in the Philosophy of Religion* (Oxford: Oxford University Press, 1972); and D. Z. Phillips' non-cognitive challenge to the belief that immortality is logically connected with survival after death in *Death and Immortality* (London: Macmillan, 1970).

For a penetrating study of the nature of the person, see Roderick M. Chisholm's Carus Lectures *Person and Object* (LaSalle: Open Court, 1976); and for interesting comments on Chisholm's views on the transcendent, substantive nature of the self see R. Jerold Clack, "Chisholm and Hume on Observing the Self," *Philosophy and Phenomenological Research*, 33 (1973), 338–48, and Richard T. Hull, "Some Reflections Occasioned by Clack and Chisholm," *ibid.*, 35 (1974), 257–60.

Some other articles: Anthony Quinton, "The Soul," *The Journal of Philosophy*, 59 (1962), 393–409; Jerome Shaffer, "Persons and Their Bodies," *The Philosophical Review*, 75 (1966), 59–77; Jerry H. Gill, "God-Talk and I-Talk" in his *The Possibility of Religious Knowledge* (Grand Rapids: Eerdmans, 1971), pp. 210–25; Robert Young, "The Resurrection of the Body," *Sophia*, 9 (1971), 1–15; and George I. Mavrodes, "The Life Everlasting and the Bodily Criterion of Identity," *Noûs*, 11 (1977), 27–39.

CPSIA information can be obtained
at www.ICGtesting.com
Printed in the USA
LVHW031524040221
678388LV00002B/397